# TAXATION OF COMPANIES

# AND

# COMPANY RECONSTRUCTIONS

## SECOND SUPPLEMENT TO
## THE SEVENTH EDITION

*Up to date to October 1, 2000*

**AUSTRALIA**
LBC Information Services Sydney
Sydney

**CANADA** and **USA**
Carswell
Toronto—Ontario

**NEW ZEALAND**
Brookers
Auckland

**SINGAPORE** and **MALAYSIA**
Sweet & Maxwell Asia
Singapore and Kuala Lumpur

# BRITISH TAX LIBRARY

# TAXATION OF COMPANIES

# AND

# COMPANY RECONSTRUCTIONS

Second Supplement to the
Seventh Edition

By

**RICHARD BRAMWELL**, Q.C., LL.M. (Lond.)
*of the Middle Temple*

**MICHAEL HARDWICK**, M.A. (Oxon.), LL.M.
(Cantab.)
*Solicitor, Partner in Linklaters & Alliance*

**JOHN LINDSAY**, B.A. (Lond.), F.C.A., F.T.I.I.
*Consultant, Linklaters & Alliance*

LONDON
SWEET & MAXWELL
2001

First Edition 1973
Second Edition 1979
Third Edition 1985
Fourth Edition 1988
Fifth Edition 1991
Sixth Edition 1994
Seventh Edition 1999
First Supplement to the Seventh Edition 2000
Second Supplement to the Seventh Edition 2001


Published by
Sweet & Maxwell Limited of
100 Avenue Road,
London NW3 3PF
http://www.sweetandmaxwell.co.uk
Typeset by
Wyvern 21 Ltd,
Bristol
Printed in England by
Bookcraft (Bath)

**A catalogue for this book is available from the British Library**

ISBN 0 421 74470 7

No natural forests were destroyed to make this product.
Farmed timber was used and replanted.

# PREFACE

Once again I am deeply indebted to John Lindsay who, as well as undertaking the work on the greater part of the new material for this Supplement, has found the time to write another new chapter, this time on Financial Instruments (Chapter 3B).

The most notable statutory changes have been the amendments to the group provisions to make them compatible with European Union law, the revisions of double-tax relief and the CFC legislation and the re-casting of Gift Aid.

In the Courts, one of the most striking decisions has been that of the Supreme Court of Ireland on the question of whether the costs of appraising a take-over target qualify as "expenses of management": see *Hibernian Insurance* discussed in Chapter 18. Also of great importance is the decision of the Special Commissioners in *Citibank*, allowing the appeal of the taxpayer company against an attempt to recharacterise financial options as a loan. The decision of the High Court affirming that result was published too late for inclusion in the text (but see [2000] S.T.I. 1546).

This Supplement is up to date as of October 1, 2000.

RB

# HOW TO USE THIS SUPPLEMENT

This is the Second Supplement to the Seventh Edition of *Taxation of Companies and Company Reconstructions*, and has been compiled according to the structure of the main volume.

At the beginning of each chapter of this Supplement the mini table of contents from the main volume has been included. Where a heading in this table of contents has been marked with a square pointer, this indicates that there is relevant information in the Supplement to which the reader should refer. Material that is new to the Cumulative Supplement is indicated by the symbol ■. Material that has been included from the previous Supplement is indicated by the symbol □.

Within each chapter, updating information is referenced to the relevant paragraph in the main volume.

# TABLE OF CASES

*(References are to paragraph numbers)*

# TABLE OF STATUTES

*(References are to Paragraph numbers)*

# TABLE OF STATUTORY INSTRUMENTS

*(References are to Paragraph numbers)*

CHAPTER 2

# THE CHARGE TO CORPORATION TAX AND COMPUTATION OF PROFITS

I. THE CHARGE TO CORPORATION TAX

## Limited liability partneships

The Limited Partnerships Act 2000 makes provision for a new form of legal entity **2–02A**
with a legal personality distinct from that of its members. The Act deals with the tax
treatment of LLP's by inserting new provisions in the Taxes Act and the TCGA. From
a day to be appointed, the profits and chargeable gains of an LLP formed under the
LLP Act are taxed as the profits and gains of the members thus disregarding the
separate existence of the LLP.[1] Limited Liability Partnerships formed under foreign
law are not covered by these tax provisions,[2] and reference should be made to para.
15–01 of this Supplement.

II. THE BASIS OF ASSESSMENT

## Coming within the charge to corporation tax

In *Walker v. Centaur Clothes Group Ltd*,[3] the House of Lords held that a company    **2–15**
is within the charge to corporation tax when an event occurs which renders the com-

---

[1] See ICTA 1988 s.118ZA and TCGA 1992 s.59A.
[2] See the definition of an LLP in section 1(2) of the Limited Liability Partnerships Act 2000.
[3] [2000] S.T.C. 324.

1

pany liable to pay corporation tax (including ACT). This view rendered redundant the contentions that had occupied the lower Courts on the true construction of section 832 of the Taxes Act. The view had been taken by both sides that section 832(1) required that a "source" of income was a necessary element in being within the charge to tax. The House recognised that its decision made section 12(6) redundant insofar as it refers to "chargeable gains".[4]

### Changing accounting dates

**2–18**    By notice in the prescribed form, a company may change the accounting reference date of its previous accounting reference period, *i.e.* the period immediately preceding the period in which the notice is given: see CA 1985, s.225(1) as inserted by S.I. 1996 No. 189, reg. 3(1)(2).

### The small companies rate

**2–21**    The rate of tax for the financial year 2000 is 30 per cent and is set in advance at the same rate for the financial year 2001.[5] The small companies rate is not set in advance because small and medium sized companies do not pay tax by instalments. The rate for the financial year 2000 is 20 per cent.[6]

From the financial year 2000, a new rate of tax is introduced: "the Corporation tax starting rate".[7] This rate of 10 per cent[8] applies to any qualifying company (in particular not a CIHC), with "profits" of £10,000 or less.[9] So it is not an actual requirement that the company be a "starting company". A qualifying company[10] may make a claim that its "basic profits" be charged at the starting rate instead of the small companies rate.[11] The scheme of section 13AA follows closely that of section 13 (small companies rate) with many provisions of section 13 applying for the purposes of section 13AA. Thus, "profits" and "basic profits" are defined by reference to section 13,[12]

---

[4] "if a chargeable gain or allowable loss accrues to a company at a time not otherwise within an accounting period of the company, an accounting period of the company shall then begin for the purposes of corporation tax, and the gain or loss shall accrue in that accounting period." *ibid.* p331*a*.

[5] FA 1999, s.24 and FA 2000 s.35.

[6] FA 2000, s.36.

[7] FA 1999, s.28(6)

[8] FA 1999, s.29.

[9] ICTA 1988, s. 13AA inserted by FA 1999, s.28. The amounts specified by the section are reduced proportionately for short accounting periods: subs. (6).

[10] Defined by *ibid.* s.13AA(8) to exclude non-resident companies. CIHCs and investment trusts with "eligible investment income" for the period. Authorised unit trusts are also excluded: *ibid.* s.468(1A).

[11] *ibid.* s.13AA(1).

[12] *ibid.* s.13AA(7).

and there are provisions corresponding to those which apply for the purposes of the small companies rate where the company in question has one or more "associated companies".[13]

There is a form of marginal relief for companies with profits between £10,000 and £50,000, the relief working in the same way as small companies marginal relief except that it is calculated using the small companies rate at the first stage.[14] For accounting periods spanning April 1, 2000, the two parts of the accounting period are treated as separate accounting periods with apportionment of profits[15] and corresponding reduction in the cash amounts that measure the relief.[16]

## Control by irreducible groups

*R. v. I.R.C. ex p. Newfields Developments Ltd*[17] raised an important question on the ambit of section 13(4) of the Taxes Act which provides that for the purposes of the section:   **2–29**

" 'Control' shall be construed in accordance with section 416".

The issue arose out of an attempt to make two companies "associated" through a person who was a participator in neither but who was an "associate" of participators in both. Section 416(6) provides:

> (6) For the purposes of subsection (2) and (3) above, there may also be attributed to any person all the rights and powers of any company of which he has, or he and associates of his have, control or any two or more such companies, or of any associate of his or of any two or more associates of his, including those attributed to a company or associate under subsection (5) above, but not those attributed to an associate under this subsection; *and such attributions shall be made under this subsection as will result in the company being treated as under the control of five or fewer participators if it can be so treated.*

It was assumed by both parties that for the purposes of section 13, the words before the italics created a free-standing provision (the dispute was whether the provision conferred a power or a duty on the Revenue). The Court of Appeal held that the italicised words govern the circumstances in which attributions can be made (even though control by five or fewer participators is irrelevant for the purposes of section 13), and that as the attributions in question made no difference to the "five or fewer"

---

[13] *ibid.* s.13AA(4), (5).
[14] *ibid.* s.13AA(3), (4), "the fraction" being one-fortieth: *ibid.* s.29.
[15] FA 1999, s.28(7).
[16] ICTA 1988, s.13AA(6).
[17] [2000] S.T.C. 52.

participators issue, they were invalid. The Court noted that in section 756(3), section 416 is applied with specific adaptations designed to fit the purposes of the section.

### Charitable donations: revisions to Gift Aid

**2–48**     From April 1, 2000 the rules governing the corporation tax treatment of charitable donations are simplified by bringing covenanted donations within the Gift Aid regime and by the abolition of the some of the Gift Aid requirements. Also, provision is made for the carry back of Gift Aid payments made by companies that are wholly owned by charities (previously the carry back applied only to covenanted donations).[18]

As respects covenanted donations, the obligation to deduct income tax is abolished by an amendment to section 349 which removes from the ambit of sub-section (1) any "qualifying donation to charity".[19]

As a result of the amendments to section 339:[20]

- the donor company need not be resident in the United Kingdom
- there is no requirement to deduct income tax
- the minimum donation figure for close companies is abolished.

"Qualifying donation" is now defined as:[21]

> "a payment of a sum of money made by a company to a charity, other than—
>     (a) a payment which, by reason of any provision of the Taxes Acts except section 209(4), is to be regarded as a distribution; and
>     (b) a payment which is deductible in computing profits or any description of profits for purposes of corporation tax"

In the hands of the charity, the payment is treated as an annual payment[22] and accordingly is exempt from tax under section 505.

The distribution limitation in para. (a) above is not well thought out. It clearly excludes from Gift Aid any payment by way of dividend (section 209(2)(a)) or purchase of own shares (section 209(2)(b)). As to the allowance for section 209(4) distributions, it will be seen from para. 11–15 that it is doubtful whether that sub-section applies to cash payments. The chief practical problem is whether a gift by a company to a charity that owns all the shares in the company could fall within section 209(2)(b) as a "distribution out of assets in respect of shares". This issue was raised in the debates in Standing Committee H on the Finance Bill, and the Minister gave an assur-

---

[18] See para. 2.52 below.
[19] FA 2000, s.41(4).
[20] *ibid.* s.40.
[21] ICTA 1988, s.339(1).
[22] *ibid.* s.339(4).

ance that section 209(2)(b) would not be applied to gifts that in form are not distributions "in respect of shares".[23]

## Close company restrictions

Section 40 of the Finance Act 2000 makes a number of amendments and additions to the provisions mentioned in the text. Section 339(B) now provides that:

**2–50**

> "(3B) A payment made by a close company is not a qualifying donation if—
>   (a) it is made subject to a condition as to repayment, or
>   (b) the company or a connected person receives a benefit in consequence of making it and either the relevant value in relation to the payment exceeds the limit imposed by sub-section(3DA) below or the amount to be taken into account for the purpose of this paragraph in relation to the payments exceeds £250".

The limits imposed by sub-section (3D) are:
  (a) where the amount of the payment does not exceed £100, 25 per cent of the amount of the payment;
  (b) where the amount of the payment exceeds £100 but does not exceed £1,000, £25;
  (c) where the amount of the payment exceeds £1,000, 2.5 per cent of the amount of the payment.

Other provisions measure benefits and payments: see subss. (3DB)–(3DD).

## Carry back of donations

Section 339(7AA) as revised to take account of the new regime provides:

**2–52**

> "Where—
>   (a) a qualifying donation to a charity is made by a company which is wholly owned by a charity, and
>   (b) the company makes a claim for the donation, or any part of it, to be deemed for the purposes of section 338 to be a charge on income paid in an accounting period falling wholly or partly within the period of nine months ending with the date of the making of the donation,
> the donation or part shall be deemed for those purposes to be a charge on income paid in that accounting period, and not in any later period.

---

[23] Report of the debate in Standing Committee H, March 9, 2000 col.374.

A claim under this subsection must be made within the period of two years immediately following the accounting period in which the donation is made, or such longer period as the Board may allow."

The definition of a company wholly owned by a charity remains as in the main text.

### Gifts of shares and securities to charities

**2–53**      From April 1, 2000 a company that is not a charity may claim that certain disposals to charities give rise to charges on income. The disposals in question are those of "qualifying investments" made otherwise than by way of a bargain at arms length.[24] "Qualifying investment" is defined as shares or securities listed or dealt in on a recognised stock exchange, units in an authorised unit trust, shares in an OEIC and an interest in an offshore fund.[25]

The amount of the charge on imcome is equal to the "relevant amount" which, in the case of a gift is equal to the market value of the investment, and in the case of a sale at an undervalue is equal to the difference between market value and the actual consideration.[1]

---

[24] ICTA 1988 s.587B(1)(2)(a)(ii) and ss.338(2)(za) inserted by FA 2000 s.43.
[25] *ibid.* s.587B(9).
[1] *ibid.* s.587B(4). Subs.(5)–(7) make provision for adjustments to the relevant amount.

# CHAPTER 3

# LOAN RELATIONSHIPS AND WITHHOLDING TAX

## II. GENERAL PRINCIPLES

### Lending of money

In *Citibank Investments Ltd v. Griffin*[1], the Revenue sought to contend that a pair of **3–08A** box options created a "loan" in that one party paid a sum to the other and was bound to receive a larger amount at the expiration of the option periods. The contracts were not expressed in the language of loans. As to this argument the Commissioners held:

> "The legal analysis of the transactions reveals that they were options and not loans. It follow that the legal nature of the transaction to which it is sought to attach a tax consequence is still an option and not a loan. To recharacterise the two options as a loan would be to disregard the legal form and nature of the transactions and to go behind them to some supposed underlying substance.
>
> Further, in our view, the legal nature of the two options taken together cannot be recharacterised as a loan because the real conditions of the transactions do not point to the conclusion that they were loans. The options were purchased under an ISDA master agreement which was an agreement to purchase options and not an agreement for a loan; in particular, the netting provisions and the provisions which applied in the event of default were not appropriate for loans"

---

[1] [2000] S.T.C. (S.C.D.) 92.

III. Computation

## Convertible securities

### *More than negligible likelihood*

**3–45** Section 65 of the Finance Act 1999 has introduced measures to block a tax avoidance scheme involving the use of convertible securities. The scheme essentially involved a company issuing a convertible security, which otherwise satisfied the conditions of section 92 of the Finance Act 1996, at a deep gain in such a way that it did not fall to be treated as a relevant discounted security within the meaning of Schedule 13 to the Finance Act 1996.[2]

As originally drafted, the provisions of Schedule 13, paragraph 3(5)(b) to the Finance Act 1996 determined whether a security was issued at a deep gain by reference to the first occasion on which the holder of a security could require it to be redeemed. Under the scheme the investor had an option to require the security to be redeemed at (say) one year after the date of issue for an amount equal to the issue price of the security and an amount of interest. As interest is disregarded in determining whether a security is issued at a deep gain,[3] this meant that the security did not fall to be treated as a relevant discounted security. Since any gain or loss on the principal of the security is included in calculating the company's capital gains on which corporation tax is payable and is excluded from the provisions of the loan relationship legislation where the conditions of section 92 of the Finance Act 1996 are satisfied, the discount would only have been brought into charge to tax when the security was redeemed.[4] The time at which the tax became payable could have been further deferred if the security had been converted into shares instead of being redeemed. As, so far as an issuer is concerned, convertible securities are fully within the corporate debt regime it was able to obtain relief for the discount on an accruals basis over the life of the security even if the security was issued to a connected party.[5]

Section 65 of the Finance Act 1999 has amended the provisions of Schedule 13 to the Finance Act 1996 and the revised wording provides that whether a security is issued at a deep gain is to be determined by reference to any of the occasions on

---

[2] In order for a convertible security to fall within FA 1996, s.92 it must not be a relevant discounted security: s.92(1)(d).

[3] FA 1996, Sched. 13, para. 3(6).

[4] FA 1996, s.92(4) provides that the convertible security is not treated as a loan relationship for the purposes of TCGA 1992. As only a loan relationship can be treated as a qualifying corporate bond in the case of a company (TCGA 1992, s.117(A1)) a convertible security will be treated as a chargeable asset under the provisions of TCGA 1992, s.251(1) where it is a debt on a security or under TCGA 1992, s.251(7) and (8) where it is not a debt on a security, except that in this latter case no relief will be available for any loss.

[5] The provisions of FA 1996, Sched. 9, paras 17 and 18 only apply where the security is a relevant discounted security.

which the security may be redeemed, whether at the option of the holder or otherwise.[6] In determining the occasions on which the security may be redeemed before maturity, the following are disregarded:

(i) any occasion on which there may be a redemption otherwise than at the option of the person who holds the security. This exception does not apply where the security was issued to a person connected[7] with the issuer or where the obtaining of a tax advantage[8] by any person is the main benefit, or one of the main benefits, that might have been expected to accrue from the provision in accordance with which the security may be redeemed on that occasion;[9]

(ii) where a redemption may occur as a result of the exercise of an option that is exercisable only on the occurrence of an event adversely affecting the holder, or only in the case of a default by any person, provided that it is considered unlikely at the time at which the security is issued that such events would occur.[10]

If either of the above exceptions would also coincide with a date on which the security might be redeemed under other provisions, that occasion of redemption is not to be disregarded for the purposes of determining whether the security is a relevant discounted security.[11]

If a security would have been treated as a relevant discounted security, had it been issued to a person connected with the issuer, and the security is subsequently acquired by a person connected with the issuer or the holder subsequently becomes connected with the issuer, from that date the security will be treated as a relevant discounted security.[12] Where a security would only be treated as a relevant discounted security because it was issued to a person connected with the issuer or was subsequently

---

[6] *ibid.* Sched. 13, para. 3(1), as inserted by FA 1999, s.65(1).

[7] This is defined by reference to ICTA, s.839: FA 1996, Sched. 13, para. 3(7) as inserted by FA 1999, s.65(4). A person will not be treated as connected with the issuer where he would only be treated as connected as a result of holding the relevant discounted security or another security which has been issued under the same prospectus as that security: FA 1996, Sched. 13, para. 3(8) as inserted by FA 1999, s.65(4).

[8] This is defined as having the meaning given by ICTA 1988, s.709(1): FA 1996, Sched. 13, para. 3(1D), as inserted by FA 1999, s.65(1).

[9] FA 1996, Sched. 13, para. 3(1A)(a) and (1C) as inserted by FA 1999, s.65(1). The Inland Revenue has confirmed in correspondence with the authors that the provisions would not apply in the case of an issuer tax call, that is an option for the issuer to redeem the notes in the event of a change in their tax treatment which adversely affects the position of the issuer; *e.g.* it ceases to be possible to pay interest gross on the securities and as a result the issuer is required to increase the level of its interest payments to compensate the holder for the withholding tax.

[10] FA 1996, Sched. 13, para. 3(1A)(b) as inserted by FA 1999, s.65(1).

[11] *ibid.* 13, para. 3(1A) as inserted by FA 1999, s.65(1).

[12] *ibid.* 13, para. 3(1E) as inserted by FA 1999, s.65(1).

acquired by a person who is or becomes connected with the issuer, the security will cease to be treated as a relevant discounted security when it is acquired by a person who is not connected with the issuer.[13]

The Finance Act 1999 provisions apply for accounting periods ending on or after February 15, 1999 but do not apply to any disposal that was completed before that date.[14] Where a company held a security which originally qualified as a convertible security within the meaning of section 92 of the Finance Act 1996 it is deemed to have disposed of the security immediately before and to have reacquired the security immediately after the start of its first accounting period ending on or after February 15, 1999 for an amount equal to the opening value of the security under the authorised accounting policy which the company adopts for that security for that accounting period. Any accrued interest is excluded from that valuation. The deemed disposal is treated as a reorganisation falling within the provisions of section 116 of the Taxation of Chargeable Gains Act 1992 and the difference between the acquisition cost of the security (as uplifted by indexation allowance up to the date of the deemed disposal) and the deemed disposal value will thus be treated as a held over capital gain (or loss) which will be brought into account for tax purposes when the security is disposed of.[15] For these purposes an intra group disposal will not trigger the held over gain but the gain will be crystallised if the security is converted into shares or other securities.[16]

These deemed reorganisation provisions also apply where a company which is not connected with the issuer acquires a Finance Act 1996, section 92 convertible security, which would be treated as a relevant discounted security were it held by a connected person, and that company subsequently becomes connected with the issuer. In such cases the company is deemed to dispose of the security immediately before and to have reacquired the security immediately after the date on which it became connected with the issuer.[17]

## Issuers

Where a company had issued a Finance Act 1996, section 92 convertible security at a discount and this became a relevant discounted security following the Finance Act 1999, section 65 amendment, the provisions of Schedule 9, paragraphs 17 and 18

---

[13] *ibid.* 13, para. 3(1F) as inserted by FA 1999, s.65(1).

[14] FA 1999, s.65(9). The provisions of FA 1999, s.66 do not apply to companies. This is because s.66(1)(b)(ii) refers to an asset being treated as a qualifying corporate bond under the provisions of s.65 on "a disposal on or after 15 February 1999". It is only securities which are not within the charge to corporation tax which are so treated: see s.65(11). Where the holder is within the charge to corporation tax the provisions of s.65 apply from the start of its first accounting period which ends on or after February 15, 1999 unless the disposal of the security had been completed before that date: see s.65(9).

[15] FA 1996, s.92(7)–(11) as inserted by FA 1999, s.65(7).

[16] TCGA 1992, s.116(10), (11).

[17] FA 1999, s.92(7) and Sched. 13, para. 3(1E)(b).

to the Finance Act 1996 apply from the start of the company's first accounting period ending on or after February 15, 1999, if the issuer is connected with the holder within the meaning of those provisions. If the liability had been discharged before that date the provisions of paragraphs 17 and 18 will not apply to the security.[18]

If a company issues a security in a case which would be treated as a relevant discounted security were the holder connected with the issuer within the meaning of Schedule 13, paragraph 3(7) to the Finance Act 1996 and either the holder subsequently becomes connected with the issuer or the security is subsequently acquired by a person who is or becomes connected with the issuer, the provisions of Schedule 9, paragraphs 17 or 18 to the Finance Act 1996 will apply from the start of the accounting period in which the issuer becomes connected with the holder, assuming that the issuer would be connected with the holder within the meaning of those provisions.[19] The connection test in Finance Act 1996, Schedule 9, paragraph 17 is broadly similar to that of Finance Act 1996, Schedule 13, paragraph 3(7); both ultimately look to the Taxes Act 1988, section 416(2)–(6) control test.[20] In the case of a close company, a relevant discounted security issued to or acquired by a participator would fall within the provisions of the 1996 Act, Schedule 9, paragraph 18 whether or not the participator controls the issuer. The Schedule 13 provisions only apply, however (where the security would not otherwise be treated as a relevant discounted security), if the investor controls the issuer in its own right or together with one or more persons with whom it is connected within the meaning of the Taxes Act 1988, section 839.

### Groups

The provision dealing with related transactions between companies in the same group has been amended as a result of the changes to the definition of a CGT group. The provision now applies where, as a result of:

**3–56**

1. a related transaction between two companies that are members of the same CGT group and are within the charge to corporation tax in respect of that transaction; or
2. a series of transactions having the same effect as a related transaction between two companies each of which has been a member of the same CGT group at any time in the course of that series of transactions and is within the charge to corporation tax in respect of that related transaction,

one of the companies (the *transferee company*) directly or indirectly replaces the other (the *transferor company*) as a party to a loan relationship.[21]

---

[18] *ibid.* s.65(10).
[19] FA 1996, Sched. 9, paras 17(1), 18(1).
[20] Sched. 9, para. 17(9) directly refers to ICTA 1988, s.416 control and Sched. 13, para. 3(7) refers to ICTA 1988, s.839 which in turn refers to s.416 control (s.839(8)).
[21] FA 1996, Sched. 9 para. 12(1)(a), (b), as amended by FA 2000 Sched. 29 para. 44(4).

This amendment applies in relation to transactions entered into, or a series of transactions begun, on or after 1 April 2000.[22]

### Partnerships involving companies

**3–56A**    The Inland Revenue has issued a revised Statement of Practice (SP4/98) to cover cases where the partners in a partnership include one or more companies which are within the charge to the loan relationships, foreign exchange and financial instruments legislation. This section considers the application of the statement for the purposes of the loan relationships legislation. The implications of the statement for the purposes of the foreign exchange legislation are considered in Chapter 3A.

The Inland Revenue's view is that the effect of section 114 of the Taxes Act 1988 is to treat a partnership as being a party to loan relationships in its own right, whatever the position under general law. This view differs from the line which the Inland Revenue is taking in certain other cases, for example it treats venture capital partnerships as transparent for tax purposes.

Where the members of a partnership include one or more companies which are within the charge to the loan relationships legislation, in order to determine the profit or loss which should be allocated to such partners, the statement requires that profits or losses of the partnership should be computed on the basis that the loan relationships legislation applies to the partnership in the same way in which it applies to companies.[23] In particular the following should be noted.

1. Where the partnership follows an authorised accounting policy for a loan relationship that policy should be followed for tax purposes. If the accounting policy does not conform to either authorised policy, an authorised accruals accounting policy should be followed for tax purposes.
2. A claim under section 91 of the Finance Act 1996 may be made to set off income tax in the accounting period in which the interest is received rather than the period in which the interest accrued.[24]
3. The provisions of sections 92 (convertible securities) and 93 (securities linked to chargeable assets) apply where the necessary conditions are satisfied (see paragraphs 3–41 to 3–53 of the main work).
4. Bad debt relief is available where the provisions of section 85(3)(c) of and Schedule 9, paragraph 5 to the Finance Act 1996 are satisfied (see paragraphs 3–35 to 3–36 of the main work).

---

[22] FA 2000, Sched. 29 para. 44(5).

[23] SP4/98 paragraphs 6, 10.

[24] FA 1996, s.91 applies where interest is received more than two years after the end of the accounting period in which it was brought into account for tax purposes (see para. 3–06 of the main work).

5. Exchange differences are ignored under the provisions of Schedule 9, paragraph 4 (see paragraph 3–37 of the main work).
6. The following anti-avoidance provisions apply:
   (i) imported losses, Finance Act 1996, Schedule 9, paragraph 10 (see paragraphs 3–85 to 3–86 of the main work);
   (ii) transactions not at arm's length, Finance Act 1996, Schedule 9, paragraph 11 (see paragraphs 3–59 to 3–60 of the main work);
   (iii) loans for unallowable purposes, Finance Act 1996, Schedule 9, paragraph 13 (see paragraphs 3–78 to 3–84 of the main work).
7. The provisions of Finance Act 1996, Schedule 9, paragraph 12, which covers the transfer of loan relationships between members of a group of companies (see paragraphs 3–56 to 3–58 of the main work), do not apply where a loan relationship is transferred to or by a partnership).
8. A change in partnership profit sharing ratios, including a case where a company joins or leaves a partnership, will not in itself give rise to a related transaction[25] as regards a loan relationship to which the partnership is a party.[1]
9. Whether loan relationship debits or credits are treated as trading or as non-trading will depend on the purpose for which the partnership is a party to each loan relationship.[2]

The resulting Schedule D, Case I profit or loss, or Schedule D, Case III non-trading deficit or credit, of the partnership for the accounting period is then apportioned to companies which are within the charge to the loan relationships legislation in the profit sharing ratio for that accounting period. If the members of the partnership include trustees of an authorised unit trust or an open-ended investment company, a separate computation will be required to determine the loan relationship profits or losses which are to be allocated to such entities. This is because the creditor loan relationships of such bodies are excluded from the loan relationships legislation and instead may be liable to income tax under the provisions of the Finance Act 1996, Schedule 13 if such loan relationships are relevant discounted securities.[3] Separate computations may also be required when the Treasury approves the use of a special accounting method for authorised investment trusts and venture capital trusts.[4]

A company is required to include its share of the partnership's loan relationship profit or loss in its own tax computation. Where a company is allocated a non-trading credit or deficit this should be incorporated within the company's own Schedule D,

---

[25] See para. 3–09 of the main text.
[1] Points 1 to 8 are referred to in SP4/98, para. 13.
[2] This follows from the assumption in SP4/98, para. 10 that the loan relationships legislation should be applied to a partnership in the same way in which it applies to a company.
[3] SP4/98, para. 11. The creditor loan relationships of authorised unit trusts and open-ended investment companies are excluded from the loan relationships legislation by the provisions of Finance Act 1996, Sched. 10, para. 2, and S.I. 1997 No. 1154, regs 3, 19(2) respectively.
[4] See FA 1996, Sched. 10, para. 1.

Case III non-trading loan relationship "pool".[5] If the accounting period of the partnership is different from a company's own accounting period the partnership's profits or losses from its loan relationships should be allocated as appropriate (usually on a time basis) between the company's accounting periods.[6]

### Transactions not at arm's length

**3–60**    The exception for a related transaction between two companies that are members of the same group has been amended following the change to the definition of a CGT group. For transaction entered into on or after 1 April 2000, or in the case of a series of transactions, that began on or after this date,[7] the provisions of paragraph 11 will not apply:

1. in the case of any related transaction between companies that are members of the same CGT group (as defined in section 170 of the Taxation of Chargeable Gains Act 1992) and are within the charge to corporation tax in respect of that transaction; or
2. in relation to a member of a group of companies, in the case of any transaction which is a part of a series of transactions having the same effect as a related transaction between two members of the same group that are within the charge to corporation tax in respect of that related transaction.[8]

### Close companies issuing deep discount securities

**3–62**    Add to footnote 11: As noted in paragraph 3–45 above the test to determine whether a security is a relevant discounted security has been amended. This amendment applied from the start of a company's first accounting period which ended on or after February 15, 1999, except where the security was disposed of before that date.

IV. CONNECTED PERSONS

### Meaning of connected persons

**3–64**    The Inland Revenue's view is that a partnership is not a company for the purposes of section 87(3) of the Finance Act 1996 and nor is it a participator or an associate

---

[5] SP4/98, paras 16–19. This non-trading profit or deficit will be calculated taking into account the partnership's debits and credits from its non-trading foreign exchange and financial instrument transactions.

[6] SP4/98, para. 20.

[7] FA 2000, Sched. 29 para. 44(5).

[8] FA 1996, Sched. 9 para. 11(3),(5), as amended by FA 2000 Sched. 29 para. 44(2),(3).

of a participator. As a result the partnership will not be connected with any of its members which provide loans to the partnership. The result is that corporate partners which are fully within the loan relationship legislation will be able to obtain bad debt relief for any losses they suffer on loans made to the partnership. At the same time, however, if a loan from the company to the partnership is forgiven the resulting credit will have to be included in calculating the loan relationship profits or losses of the partnership.[9]

EXAMPLE

> A PLC and B PLC are in partnership and divide profits and losses equally. A PLC makes an interest-free loan of £500,000 to the partnership. The partnership suffers losses and A PLC forgives the loan.
> A PLC is able to claim bad debt relief of £500,000[10] and at the same time is allocated its share of the partnership's loan relationship profits or losses. Assuming that the partnership has no other loan relationship debits or credits for the accounting period in question, A PLC would be allocated a Schedule D, Case III profit of £250,000 (being one-half of £500,000).

As a partnership is not regarded as a participator or as an associate of a participator for the purposes of section 87(3) of the Finance Act 1996 this should mean that venture capital partnerships are not connected with the companies in which they invest, and in particular that close companies should still be able to obtain tax relief for interest payable to the partnership on an accruals basis whether or not the interest is paid within 12 months of the end of its accounting period even if some of the partners are not within the charge to corporation tax.[11]

## Deep discounts

As noted in paragraph 3–45 above the test to determine whether a security is a relevant discounted security has been amended and now, *inter alia*, the legislation

**3–73**

---

[9] *ibid.* paras 22–26.

[10] FA 1996, Sched. 9, para. 11 (*Transactions not at arm's length*) does not apply to the creation of a loan relationship. Thus it would not apply merely because the loan was advanced interest-free. It could, however, apply to restrict relief for a loss if the loan was not forgiven on an arm's length basis. In such cases, however, there would be a corresponding restriction in the amount of the release which was treated as taxable in the partnership's computation.

[11] See FA 1996, Sched. 9, para. 2 which would apply to the interest payable to such partners were the company connected with the partnership.

looks to any occasion on which the holder of the security can require it to be redeemed before maturity. At the same time certain issuer redemptions are no longer disregarded. See paragraph 3–45 above for further information.

VI. WITHHOLDING TAX

### Withholding tax—partnerships with corporate partners

**3–90A**    Where the partners in a partnership include one or more companies, the partnership will be required to deduct income tax from payments of yearly interest which have a United Kingdom source.[12] No income tax will have to be deducted where the loan was advanced by a United Kingdom bank and the recipient is within the charge to corporation tax on the interest payable by the partnership.[13] If the lender is not resident in the United Kingdom and is not within the charge to corporation tax on the interest payable on the loan, the rate of withholding tax can be reduced by a claim under the Interest Article of the double tax treaty between the United Kingdom and the territory in which the lender is resident.[14] The quoted eurobond exemption will not be available, as one of the conditions of section 124 of the Taxes Act 1988 is that the eurobond must be issued by a company.[15] Under the provisions of section 832 of the Taxes Act 1988 a partnership is not treated as a company for tax purposes.

### Quoted eurobond exemption

**3–94**    The provisions of section 124 of the Taxes Act 1988 that are discussed in 3–94 of the main text have been repealed by the Finance Act 2000 in respect of payments of interest that are made on or after 1 April 2001.[16]

Section 124 has been replaced by an amendment to section 349 of the Taxes Act to permit interest to be paid gross on a quoted eurobond.[17] This amendment takes effect for payments of interest that are made on or after 1 April 2001.[18]

The definition of a quoted eurobond has been amended and this revised definition applies to payments of interest made on or after 1 April 2001.[19] Under the revised definition a quoted eurobond is any security that:

---

[12] ICTA 1988, s.349(2)(b).
[13] ICTA 1988, s.349(3)(a); see para. 3–92 of the Main Text.
[14] See para. 3–95 of the Main Text.
[15] ICTA 1988, s.124(6)(a).
[16] FA 2000, s.111(2),(6)(b).
[17] ICTA 1988 s.349(3)(c),(3B), as amended by FA 2000, s.111(2).
[18] FA 2000, s.111(6)(b).
[19] *ibid.* s.111(2),(6)(b).

1. is issued by a company; and
2. is listed on a recognised stock exchange; and
3. carries a right to interest.[20]

The effect of this amendment is that interest falling due for payment on or after 1 April 2001 on *registered* securities may now be paid gross, *irrespective* of the date on which the security itself was issued.

Further, under the revised provisions of section 349, interest may be paid gross to both non-residents and UK residents whether the securities are held in a recognised clearing system and whether payment is made by or through a UK paying agent.

The paying and collecting agent rules which are referred to in the final paragraph of 3–94 of the main text have been abolished with effect for payments of interest made on or after 1 April 2001.[21] It is intended that this regime should be replaced by a reporting requirement that will take effect for payments of interest made or collected on or after 1 April 2001. This requirement is to be introduced by regulation.[22]

## Provisional treaty relief—introduction

The Inland Revenue Financial Intermediaries and Claims Office (FICO) has **3–95A** recognised the difficulties which borrowers face in obtaining authority to apply the treaty rate of withholding tax. Accordingly from September 1, 1999 it introduced a Provisional Treaty Relief (PTR) Scheme. This scheme applies to "one to one" company loans where there is no shareholding relationship or common ownership between the parties and to syndicated loans where there is a syndicate manager. For these purposes a syndicate manager does not have to be an agent bank, as would normally be the case, and the Inland Revenue may be prepared to accept the borrower as a syndicate manager where its tax or accounts department is performing all the functions of an agent bank in the management of a syndicated loan.[23]

*One to one company loans*

So long as there is no shareholding or common ownership between the parties, the borrower can approach FICO for provisional authority to pay interest at the treaty rate of withholding tax as soon as the loan is advanced, or immediately after the loan is assigned from one lender to another. Where FICO has approved a treaty claim or a repayment claim for the lender in respect of another loan in the previous three years it will be prepared to grant the United Kingdom borrower provisional approval to

---

[20] ICTA 1988 s.349(4), as amended by FA 2000, s.111(2).
[21] FA 2000, s.111(1),(6)(a).
[22] TMA 1970, s.18(1)(3A),(3B) as amended by FA 2000, s.145 with respect to amounts paid, credited or received on or after 6 April 2001.
[23] FICO PTR Scheme booklet, section 6.

deduct tax at the treaty rate of withholding tax. This authority is conditional on the Inland Revenue receiving a formal double taxation treaty application from the lender within three months of the date on which it grants provisional treaty approval. If an application is not received within this period, or relief is not found to be due, or is only found to be due in some restricted manner, the provisional relief will be withdrawn and FICO will seek to recover from the borrower the tax which should have been deducted from interest payments, together with interest thereon if appropriate.[24]

*Syndicated loans*

In the case of syndicated loans, where the overseas members are straightforward corporations and are not, for example, see through entities such as US limited liability companies or partnerships, the Inland Revenue will focus on the loan itself and will accept a single composite claim for treaty relief submitted by the syndicate manager on behalf of all the members of the syndicate who are eligible to claim such relief.[25] For these purposes, as mentioned above, the Inland Revenue may be prepared to accept the borrower as a syndicate manager where its tax or finance department is performing all the functions which would normally be performed by an agent bank.[1]

A provisional authority to apply the treaty rate of withholding tax (a PTR notice) will be granted once the composite claim has been submitted by the syndicate manager. For these purposes the Inland Revenue will not require confirmation from the appropriate overseas fiscal authorities that the lender is resident in the relevant territory. The Inland Revenue will look to the syndicate manager to provide it with such information as is necessary for it to consider the composite treaty claim but in so doing the Inland Revenue will recognise that the information provided by the syndicate manager will be no more than that which is represented to it by the syndicate members.[2] The Inland Revenue is prepared to allow a loan to be brought within the PTR Scheme before the syndicate's membership has been extended beyond the loan's original arrangers and co-arrangers, provided that the syndicate manager undertakes to provide details about the syndicate members once the initial syndication has been completed.[3]

If the application is successful, the Inland Revenue will issue a formal notice under the provisions of S.I. 1970 No. 488 to apply the withholding relevant treaty rate(s) of withholding tax. If an application fails for any reason, for example where the special relationship provisions of a double tax treaty apply to interest payable to one of the lenders, the provisional treaty clearance will be withdrawn with retrospective effect and the Inland Revenue will seek to recover from the borrower the tax which should

---

[24] *ibid.* sections 4 and 5.
[25] There is no requirement that all the members of the syndicate have to be eligible to claim treaty relief.
[1] FICO PTR Scheme booklet, section 6.
[2] *ibid.* sections 6 and 9.
[3] *ibid.* section 11.

have been withheld from interest payments, together with interest thereon if appropriate.[4]

The borrower is not obliged to deduct tax at the treaty rate of withholding tax from interest payments upon receipt of a PTR notice and can continue to withhold tax at the normal rate until the issue of a formal notice.[5] As most loans will contain a gross up provision where the rate of withholding tax exceeds the appropriate treaty rate, the majority of borrowers are likely to claim the benefit of the provisional clearance.

*Blocks of Countries* Where the members of the syndicate who are eligible to claim treaty relief are resident in more than one country, the Inland Revenue will normally require the members of a syndicate to be listed on a country by country basis on the application submitted by the syndicate manager.

If the rate of withholding tax is the same for two or more countries, such countries will be grouped together in blocks in the formal clearance issued by the Inland Revenue; for example, Italy and Japan where the treaty rate is 10 per cent. The syndicate manager will only be required to provide the Inland Revenue with changes to the membership of the syndicate if the new lender is resident in a territory where the treaty rate of withholding tax is different from that in which the retiring member is resident.[6]

*Existing Syndicates* It is possible for an existing syndicated loan to be brought within the PTR scheme where treaty relief has already been granted in respect of payments of interest to existing members of the syndicate on a change to the existing members of the syndicate, provided that the syndicate would itself qualify for relief under the scheme.[7]

*Inland Revenue Reviews* The Inland Revenue will periodically seek confirmation of the members of a particular syndicate every 12 to 18 months.[8] It will also want to review the procedures syndicate managers have in place to meet their PTR undertakings and such reviews will generally take place every two to three years.[9]

### Double tax treaty—redenomination of loans

In an article in *Tax Bulletin*, February 1999, the Inland Revenue stated that it considers the redenomination of a loan from one currency to another (including redenomination from Sterling to the Euro, or from the Euro to Sterling) to be a material change **3–95B**

---

[4] *ibid.* sections 6 and 9.
[5] *ibid.* section 9.
[6] FICO PTR Scheme booklet, sections 8 and 11.
[7] *ibid.* section 10.
[8] *ibid.* section 12.
[9] *ibid.* section 13.

in the terms of the loan. In all such cases the borrower is required to notify FICO of the new terms of the loan, being the currency in which the loan is redenominated, the amount of the loan outstanding, the duration of the redenominated loan and the yield or interest on it.

Where the lender is not connected with the borrower[10] and the redenomination takes place on an arm's length basis, any existing treaty clearance will continue to apply. If the lender is connected with the borrower, the Inland Revenue is prepared to treat an existing treaty clearance as continuing in force so long as the redenomination takes place for commercial purposes and the redenominated loan carries an interest rate or yield appropriate to that which would be payable on an arm's length basis on a new loan of the same amount, in the same currency and for the same term. If such conditions are not satisfied the overseas lender will have to submit a fresh application under the Interest Article of the relevant double tax treaty.

---

[10] The article does not define what is meant by connected. It is assumed that whether a lender is connected with a borrower will be determined by reference to the provisions of ICTA 1988, s.209(2)(da) and the Special Relationship Provisions of the relevant double tax treaty.

# FOREIGN EXCHANGE LEGISLATION

## I. OVERVIEW

### Introduction

The Finance Act 1993 introduced a new regime for the taxation of foreign exchange **3A–01** gains and losses. It applies to translation exchange gains and losses on *qualifying assets*, *qualifying liabilities* and *currency contracts* of *qualifying companies*. Each of the terms in italics is considered in Part II below. The legislation took effect from the start of a company's first accounting period which began on or after March 23, 1995 (commencement day). Transitional provisions apply in certain cases where a company was already within the charge to corporation tax before its commencement day and these transitional provisions are considered, in outline, in Part IX. Whilst the foreign exchange legislation is prescriptive in its approach, the underlying intention is that, in most cases, a company's accounting treatment should be followed for tax purposes.

### Recognition of exchange gains and losses

Broadly, exchange gains and losses on qualifying assets, qualifying liabilities and **3A–02** currency contracts are recognised from the date the company acquires the asset, becomes subject to the liability or becomes a party to the currency contract up until the date immediately before the company ceases to own the asset, to be subject to the liability or to be a party to the currency contract. Exchange gains and losses are brought into account for every accounting period which falls between these two dates and also for the accounting period in which the disposal takes place, and have to be calculated by reference to the company's local currency (see below). To the extent that a company is a party to the qualifying asset, qualifying liability or currency contract for the purposes of its trade, any exchange gains will be included in computing its Schedule D, Case I trading profits. In other cases any exchange gains or losses will be included in computing the company's profit or deficit arising on its non-trading loan relationships. The calculation of a company's exchange gains and losses is considered in Part III below.

### Local currency

3A–03    Before the amendments introduced by Finance Act 2000 that are considered in Part VI below, the normal rule was that a company's local currency was taken as sterling regardless of the currency in which it prepared its accounts. It was possible for trading companies to elect to treat the currency in which the accounts of a trade or part of a trade were prepared as the local currency of the trade or of that part of the trade. Following the Finance Act 2000 reforms, a company's local currency is generally taken as the currency in which it accounts for the results of its business, or in the case of part of a business, that part of its business.[1] These provisions are considered in more detail at Part VI below and take effect for accounting periods beginning on or after 1 January 2000 and ending on or after 21 March 2000.[2]

### Anti-avoidance provisions

3A–04    The foreign exchange legislation contains a number of anti-avoidance provisions which are designed to prevent companies from seeking to abuse the legislation. These provisions are considered in Part IV.

### Matching

3A–05    In certain cases a company may use a foreign currency borrowing or a currency contract to hedge an investment in a foreign currency non-monetary asset. As such assets are outside the foreign exchange legislation the normal result would be that any exchange gain or loss on the loan or currency contract would be brought into account

---

[1] FA 1993, ss.92–94, as amended by FA 2000, s.105(1).
[2] FA 2000, s.105(4).

for tax purposes over the life of the loan or currency contract whereas any exchange loss or gain on the matched asset would normally only be brought into account as part of the overall gain or loss when the company disposes of the asset. In order to avoid this mismatch the foreign exchange legislation contains provisions to enable a company to elect to match exchange gains on foreign currency borrowings or currency contracts against an investment in certain assets. In such cases, provided the necessary conditions are satisfied, any exchange gains or losses are deferred over the life of the borrowing or currency contract and are normally brought into account for tax purposes when the company disposes of the asset in question. The scope of matching election provisions are discussed in Part V below.

### Deferral

In certain cases a company is permitted to defer net exchange gains on long-term **3A–06** capital assets and liabilities. The exchange gains are deferred until the next accounting period and are treated as accruing in that next period but can be included in calculating the net exchange gains on long-term capital assets and liabilities which are eligible for deferral relief in that period. Deferral relief is considered in Part VII below.

### Bad debts and unremittable income

The foreign exchange legislation contains provisions to provide relief where a com- **3A–07** pany suffers a bad debt or makes a bad debt provision, or where income which has been received becomes unremittable. These are considered in Part VIII below.

### Excess gains and losses

There are regulations which deal with cases where a company is taxed on a net **3A–08** exchange gain or is able to obtain relief for a net exchange loss on an asset or liability, and it suffers a non-exchange loss or realises a non-exchange profit on the asset or liability which, in either case, falls outside the scope of tax. In such cases an adjustment can be made to reduce the foreign exchange gain or loss on the asset or liability up to the amount of the non-taxable gain or loss on the asset or liability. Following the introduction of the financial instruments and loan relationships legislation, these provisions are likely to be of limited application. They are considered further in Part VIII.

## II. Certain Definitions

### Qualifying company

**3A–09**     Under the provision of section 152 of the Finance Act 1993, any company is treated as a qualifying company with the following exceptions:

(i) trustees of an authorised unit trust, who are deemed to be a company for certain purposes by section 468(1) of the Taxes Act 1988[3];

(ii) a company which is approved as an investment trust for the accounting period in question under section 842 of the Taxes Act 1988[4]; and

(iii) an open-ended investment company.[5]

Whilst it is not explicitly stated, it is clear from the context of the legislation and from statements made by the Inland Revenue that the foreign exchange legislation only applies to companies which are within the charge to corporation tax. In the case of non-resident companies, the foreign exchange legislation applies insofar as qualifying assets, qualifying liabilities or currency contracts of such companies are within the charge to corporation tax (*i.e.* they relate to a United Kingdom branch or agency of that company).

### Qualifying asset

**3A–10**     The following are treated as qualifying assets:

(i) a right to settlement under a qualifying debt (whether or not the debt is a debt on a security)[6];

(ii) a unit of currency[7]; and

(iii) a share held in qualifying circumstances.[8]

*A right to settlement under a qualifying debt*

**3A–11**     A qualifying debt is defined as a debt which falls to be settled by the payment of money or which falls to be settled by the transfer of a right to settlement under another

---

[3] FA 1993, s.152(3).

[4] *ibid.* s.152(4).

[5] S.I. 1997 No. 1554, reg. 17 which inserted a new subsection (2A) to s.152.

[6] FA 1993, s.153(1)(a). The foreign exchange legislation applies the TCGA 1992, s.132 definition of a debt on a security: FA 1993, s.164(11).

[7] *ibid.* s.153(1)(b).

[8] *ibid.* s.153(1)(c).

debt, which itself falls to be settled by the payment of money.[9] The first definition is self-explanatory. The second definition would cover cases, *inter alia*, where the debt could be settled by the transfer of a security, for example, Treasury Stock. In both cases, unlike the loan relationships legislation there is no requirement that the debt has to arise as a result of a transaction for the lending of money and thus, for example, amounts owed for goods and services will fall within this definition.

Certain debts are expressly excluded from the definition of qualifying debts and these include:

(i) a right under a currency contract[10];

(ii) an asset to which section 92 of the Finance Act 1996 applies (convertible securities)[11]; or

(iii) an asset representing a loan relationship to which section 93 of the Finance Act 1996 applies (relationships linked to the value of chargeable assets).[12]

Any interest accruing in respect of a qualifying debt is not treated as part of the debt.[13]

*Shares held in qualifying circumstances*

Shares are held in qualifying circumstances where any profit or loss arising on the **3A–12** share is included in computing the company's Schedule D, Case I trading profits and provided that the value of the asset, as shown in the company's accounts at the end of each accounting period (assuming that the asset is still held at the end of the period) would be found by taking the local currency equivalent at that time of the valuation put on the asset by the company in the nominal currency of the asset.[14] In effect, the company has to value the asset by reference to the currency in which the shares are denominated and then translate this figure into sterling (or its local currency where it has made a local currency election). There is no requirement that the company has to adopt a mark-to-market accounting policy and it would thus be acceptable for a company to follow a lower of cost and market value or a realisation basis for the shares.

## Qualifying liabilities

Each of the following is a qualifying liability:                                                    **3A–13**

(i) a duty to settle under a qualifying debt (whether or not the debt is a debt on a security)[15];

---

[9] *ibid.* s.153(10). For these purposes an ecu is to be treated as money.
[10] FA 1993, s.153(3).
[11] *ibid.* s.153(4)(a).
[12] *ibid.* s.153(4)(b).
[13] *ibid.* s.153(12).
[14] *ibid.* s.153(11).
[15] *ibid.* s.153(2)(a).

(ii) a provision which is deductible in computing the company's Schedule D, Case I trading profits so long as, were the liability to crystallise, the company would be subject to a duty to settle under a qualifying debt[16];

(iii) "short" sales of qualifying debts on securities (*i.e.* where a company contracts to sell a debt on a security and it does not own that security at the date it enters into the contract)[17];

(iv) "short" sales of shares where the shares in question would have been qualifying assets if the company had held the shares.[18]

The definition of a qualifying debt is the same as that used in the case of a qualifying asset[19] and again a liability to settle under a currency contract is not treated as a qualifying debt.[20] Further any interest which has accrued in respect of a qualifying debt is not treated as part of the debt.[21] In the case of a qualifying liability, however, the exclusions for convertible debt and assets linked to chargeable assets **do not** apply.[22]

### Currency contracts

**3A–14** The Finance Act 1993 legislation deals with exchange gains and losses on currency contracts. Any payments made under the terms of a currency contract (other than the exchange of currencies) are dealt with under the Finance Act 1994 financial instruments legislation.[23]

The currency contract provisions of the Finance Act 1993 foreign exchange legislation apply where a qualifying company enters into a currency contract under which:

(i) it becomes entitled to a right and subject to a duty to receive payment at a specified time of a specified amount of one currency (the first currency); and

(ii) it becomes entitled to a right and subject to a duty to pay in exchange and at the same time a specified amount of another currency (the second currency).[24]

It does not matter if the currency contract contains provisions for the contract to be

---

[16] *ibid.* s.153(2)(b).
[17] *ibid.* s.153(2)(c).
[18] FA 1993, s.153(2)(d), (9).
[19] *ibid.* s.153(10).
[20] *ibid.* s.153(5).
[21] *ibid.* s.153(12).
[22] *ibid.* s.153(4).
[23] See FA 1994, ss.150–153 and ss.155–164.
[24] FA 1993, s.126(1).

settled by a net payment representing the difference between the two currencies at the specified time, as opposed to an actual exchange of currencies taking place.[25]

This definition will cover both forward purchases and forward sales of foreign currency (*i.e.* a case where a company contracts to buy or sell a given amount of a foreign currency at a future date) and a currency swap (*e.g.* where two parties agree to an initial exchange of currency and to a re-exchange at the end of the swap period). The definition applies whenever the foreign exchange legislation refers to currency contracts.[1]

## III. CALCULATION OF EXCHANGE GAINS AND LOSSES

This Part considers the provisions within the foreign exchange legislation which **3A–15** determine the date on which a company:

    (i) acquires and disposes of a qualifying asset;
    (ii) becomes subject and ceases to be subject to a qualifying liability; and
    (iii) becomes a party and ceases to be a party to a currency contract.

It also considers the provisions which determine the exchange rate which can be used at a translation time. Finally it considers the ways in which exchange gains and losses are taxed and relieved.

In the majority of cases a company's accounting treatment will be followed for the purposes of the foreign exchange legislation and it should only be necessary to refer to the detail of the following paragraphs where a transaction contains unusual features.

### Date of acquisition of qualifying assets

The general rule is that a company becomes entitled to an asset when it becomes **3A–16** unconditionally entitled to it.[2] In determining whether or not a company is unconditionally entitled to an asset, any transfer by way of security of the asset, or of any interest in, or right over, the asset is ignored.[3] This general rule is modified in a number of cases. These are as follows.

---

[25] *ibid.* s.126(1A). If the contract is settled by a net payment, the payment will be taxed or relieved under the Finance Act 1994 financial instruments legislation, normally in the accounting period in which the company receives or makes the payment, and any net foreign exchange gain or loss which has been recognised under the foreign exchange legislation will normally be reversed in that accounting period under the provisions of FA 1993, s.146.

[1] FA 1993, s.164(2).

[2] *ibid.* s.154(1).

[3] *ibid.* s.154(2).

(i) Where a company agrees to acquire an asset by contract (other than in the case of a currency contract), it is deemed to become entitled to the asset at the date at which the contract is made and not the date at which settlement takes place.[4] If the contract is conditional, it is deemed to acquire the asset when the condition is satisfied.[5]

(ii) If, in preparing its accounts, a company regards itself as having become entitled to a qualifying debt at a date earlier than the date at which it would be deemed to have become entitled to the asset under the normal provisions of the foreign exchange legislation, as long as such treatment is in accordance with normal accountancy practice, the company's accounting treatment will be respected. For these purposes, until the company becomes entitled to the qualifying debt, the nominal amount of the debt will be taken as the amount of the debt as reflected in the company's accounts, so long as such treatment accords with normal accountancy practice. Where the nominal amount shown in the company's accounts differs from the amount which would be shown in accordance with normal accountancy practice, the amount found using normal accountancy practice has to be substituted.[6]

(iii) Where the asset is a debt on a security,[7] or is a share, and under the foreign exchange legislation a company would normally be treated as becoming entitled to an asset at an earlier time, if in its accounts the company treats itself as becoming entitled to the asset at a later time and the accounts are drawn up in accordance with normal accountancy practice, the later time will be treated as the date of acquisition for the purposes of the foreign exchange legislation.[8]

(iv) Where the asset is a right to receive interest, and that interest falls to brought into account for the purposes of the Finance Act 1996 loan relationships legislation, the company is regarded as becoming entitled to the interest when the interest is deemed to have accrued (where the company is following an authorised accruals accounting policy) or when the interest is taken to have become due and payable (where the company is following an authorised market accounting policy).[9]

(v) Where the asset is a right to receive income other than interest, any exchange gains or losses are ignored until the income is received.[10]

(vi) Where a company in drawing up its accounts treats itself as entitled to a qualifying debt, at the time those accounts are drawn up it could reasonably be expected that the company would become entitled to the asset and in a

---

[4] *ibid.* s.154(3).
[5] *ibid.* s.154(5).
[6] FA 1993, s.154(12), (13).
[7] This is defined by reference to the definition in TCGA 1992, s.132: FA 1993, s.164(11).
[8] FA 1993, s.154(13A).
[9] *ibid.* s.154(12A).
[10] *ibid.* s.129(7).

subsequent accounting period it regards itself as ceasing to be entitled to the qualifying debt before the asset comes into existence, the company will be treated as becoming entitled to the asset and as ceasing to be entitled to the asset in accordance with its accounting treatment, provided the company's accounts are drawn up in accordance with normal accountancy practice. In such cases the nominal amount of debt will be the amount reflected in the company's accounts. Where this amount differs from the amount which would be reflected in accordance with normal accountancy practice, the latter amount is taken.[11]

## Date of disposal of qualifying assets

A company is regarded as disposing of an asset when it ceases to be entitled to it.[12]  **3A–17** If it agrees to dispose of the asset by contract, the contract date will be taken as the date of disposal except where the contract is conditional. In this latter case, the date of disposal is taken as the date on which the contract becomes unconditional.[13] This general rule is disapplied if the asset is a debt on security, or is a share, if a company treats itself as ceasing to be entitled to the asset at a later date and the company's accounts are drawn up in accordance with normal accountancy practice.[14]

In the case of both debts on securities and shares, a "first in, first out" basis is used for identification purposes. This rule is disapplied where a company uses some other basis when preparing its accounts and its accounts are prepared in accordance with normal accountancy practice. In such cases the treatment adopted in the company's accounts will be followed for tax purposes.[15]

The legislation also deals with disposals followed by re-acquisition of the same asset. It provides that in such cases the new asset is to be treated as a different asset from the old asset.[16]

## Date at which a company becomes subject or ceases to be subject to a qualifying liability

### Qualifying debts

The general rule is that a company becomes subject to a qualifying liability which  **3A–18** is a qualifying debt when it becomes unconditionally subject to that liability.[17] This general rule is modified in a number of cases:

---

[11] *ibid.* s.156(2)–(4).
[12] FA 1993, s.154(14).
[13] *ibid.* s.154(4), (5).
[14] *ibid.* s.154(13B).
[15] *ibid.* s.154(9), (10), (11).
[16] *ibid.* s.154(6).
[17] *ibid.* s.155(1).

(i) where a company agrees to acquire a liability which is a qualifying debt by transfer, it is regarded as becoming subject to the liability when the contract is made and not at a later transfer date. This rule is modified where the contract is conditional and in such cases the company is regarded as becoming a party to the liability when the condition is satisfied[18];

(ii) if in preparing its accounts a company treats itself as having become subject to a qualifying debt at an earlier time than under the normal rules, providing the company's accounts are prepared in accordance with normal accountancy practice, such treatment will be respected for tax purposes. In this case, until the company is regarded as becoming subject to the liability under the normal rules of the foreign exchange legislation, the nominal amount of the debt is taken as the amount which the company treats as the nominal amount in its accounts or, if different, the amount which it would include were it following normal accountancy practice.[19]

A company is regarded as ceasing to be subject to a qualifying liability which is a qualifying debt when it ceases to be subject to that liability.[20] If it disposes of a liability by way of contract, the contract date is taken as the date of disposal for tax purposes and not the settlement date. If the contract is conditional, then the date on which the condition is satisfied is taken as the date of disposal.[21]

**3A–19** Where a company ceases to be subject to a liability in respect of a qualifying debt and becomes subject to the same liability at a later time, when it becomes subject to that liability for the second time, the liability is treated as if it were a different liability.[22]

The company's accounting treatment will be followed for tax purposes if, in drawing up its accounts, it:

(i) treats itself as subject to a liability which is a qualifying debt in an accounting period (earlier period);

(ii) in a later accounting period, and before the qualifying debt has come into existence, it treats itself as ceasing to be subject to the qualifying debt;

(iii) the company's accounts are prepared in accordance with normal accountancy practice; and

(iv) at the time at which the accounts for the earlier period are prepared it could reasonably be expected that the company would become subject to the liability.

In this case the nominal amount of the qualifying debt will be taken as the amount

---

[18] *ibid.* s.155(2), (4).
[19] FA 1993, s.155(11) and (12).
[20] *ibid.* s.155(13).
[21] *ibid.* s.155(3), (4).
[22] *ibid.* s.155(5).

shown in the company's accounts. Where this amount differs from the nominal value which would be reflected in accordance with normal accountancy practice, the latter amount will be taken.[23]

*Provisions*

In the case of a provision, a company is regarded as becoming subject to the liability when it makes the provision.[24] It is regarded as ceasing to be subject to the liability at the time in which it removes the provision from its accounts, or, where different, the time at which it would remove the provision under normal accountancy practice.[25] If the amount of a provision is varied, the company is treated as having disposed of the original amount of the provision and is regarded as making a new provision on the date on which the variation takes place.[1]    **3A–20**

*Short sales*

In the case of short sales of securities and shares, a company is regarded as becoming subject to the liability on the date at which it enters into the contract and is regarded as ceasing to be subject to the liability when it contracts to acquire securities or shares to settle the short position, unless it ceases to be subject to the liability before that time.[2]    **3A–21**

## Currency contracts

The time at which a company becomes entitled to rights and subject to duties under a currency contract is the date on which it enters into the contract and it will be treated as ceasing to be a party to the contract immediately before its rights and obligations under the contract are settled.[3]    **3A–22**

## Calculation of foreign exchange gains and losses

*Translation times and accrual periods*

The foreign exchange legislation requires that the sterling (or other local currency, see below) equivalent of the basic valuation of each qualifying asset, qualifying liability and currency contract is determined at each translation time. The first translation time is the time at which the company becomes entitled to the qualifying asset,    **3A–23**

---

[23] *ibid.* s.156(2)–(4).
[24] *ibid.* s.155(6).
[25] *ibid.* s.155(7).
[1] *ibid.* s.155(8).
[2] *ibid.* s.155(9), (10), (11).
[3] *ibid.* ss.157 and 158(3).

becomes subject to the qualifying liability or becomes a party to the currency contract, and the final translation time is the time immediately before the company ceases to own the qualifying asset, ceases to be subject to the qualifying liability or ceases to be a party to the currency contract. Additional translation times arise at the end of each accounting period which falls between these two dates. The period between each translation time is termed an accrual period.[4]

EXAMPLE

A PLC has a calendar year end. It entered into a three-year U.S. $1m loan on June 30, 1999 and continues to be a party to the loan until June 30, 2002 when the loan is repaid.
The accrual periods are:
June 30, 1999—December 31, 1999
January 1, 2000—December 31, 2000
January 1, 2001—December 31, 2001
January 1, 2002—June 30, 2002

Effectively the legislation compares the local currency equivalent of the basic valuation of the foreign currency asset, liability or currency contract at the start of an accrual period to the local currency equivalent at the end of the accrual period[54] and any difference is brought into account as an exchange gain or loss. There are provisions to ensure that where the foreign currency amount of a qualifying debt (whether an asset or a liability) varies during an accounting period, any distortions caused by the increase or reduction are eliminated. These provisions essentially follow the accounting treatment that a company would adopt in such cases.[6]

*Basic valuation*

3A–24    Exchange gains and losses have to be determined by reference to the basic valuation of an asset or liability. The basic valuation of an asset or a liability is normally the value which the company puts on it when it acquires the asset or becomes subject to liability. If this valuation is different from the value which would be found under normal accountancy practice, the latter value will be taken as the basic valuation of the asset or liability in question.[7] Where the company values the asset or liability in a currency other than the nominal currency of the asset or liability (see below) it is

---

[4] *ibid.* s.158.
[5] *ibid.* ss.125, 126.
[6] *ibid.* s.127.
[7] *ibid.* s.159(1).

required to translate that valuation into the nominal currency of the asset or liability using the London closing exchange rate for those two currencies for the day on which it acquires the asset or becomes subject to the liability.[8] The foreign exchange legislation does not define London closing exchange rate. In its Explanatory Statement[9] at 2.4 the Inland Revenue states that this term covers London rates published by reputable independent bodies such as Reuters, the Bank of England or the Financial Times.

If a company enters into a "short" sale of shares or debts on a security, the basic valuation of this liability is the consideration the company receives for entering into the contract in question. If any of the consideration is not in monetary form that element is required to be brought into account at its open market value expressed in the currency in which any monetary consideration was received.[10] Where the monetary consideration is in a different currency from that in which the underlying shares are denominated, or in which the securities are to be settled, the company is required to translate that amount into the nominal currency of the underlying shares or securities using the London closing exchange rate for the two currencies for the day on which the company becomes subject to the liability.[11]

If a company acquires an asset loan relationship which is a debt on a security, any accrued interest is ignored in arriving at the basic valuation of that asset.[12]

Where a company acquires or becomes subject to a qualifying debt and the amount of that debt varies during an accrual period, an appropriate adjustment is made to the opening value of the qualifying debt at the start of the next accrual period.[13]

*Nominal currency*

*Qualifying debts, provisions and short sales of debts on a security* The nominal **3A–25** currency of the above is the settlement currency of the debt in question. This is the currency in which the ultimate settlement of the debt falls to be made, or in the case of a provision, would fall to be made.[14] Where a debt is repayable in one currency but the amount repayable is calculated by reference to the value of another currency, or of an asset denominated in another currency, that other currency is taken as the settlement currency of the debt.[15]

If the settlement currency of the debt is not certain, for example, there is an option for the debt to be repaid in a different currency, the settlement currency of the debt is determined by reference to what is considered to be the likely settlement currency of

[8] *ibid.* s.159(2).
[9] Inland Revenue Explanatory Statement: Exchange Gains and Losses and Financial Instruments. This statement was originally published in 1995 and is now included as an Appendix to Vol. VI of the Inland Revenue Company Taxation Manual.
[10] FA 1993. s.159(3).
[11] *ibid.* s.159(3), (4) and s.160(1), (4).
[12] *ibid.* s.159(5).
[13] *ibid.* s.159(10)–(12).
[14] *ibid.* s.160(1) and s.161(1), (3).
[15] *ibid.* s.161(2).

the debt at the time at which the company acquires, or becomes subject to, the qualifying debt, enters into the short sale or makes the provision.[16]

For the above purposes the ecu is regarded as a currency.[17]

**3A–26**    *Currency* The nominal currency of a unit of currency is the currency in question.[18]

**3A–27**    *Shares and short sales of shares* The nominal currency of a share and of a short sale of sales is the currency in which the share is (or shares are) denominated.[19]

### Exchange rate at translation times

**3A–28**    The foreign exchange legislation prescribes the exchange rates which can be used at a translation time. Where the translation time arises solely as a result of an accounting period coming to an end, an exchange rate for the two currencies is used in the accounts of the company for the last day of that accounting period and that rate is an arm's length rate, that exchange rate is used. There is no requirement that the exchange rate used has to be the exchange rate for the last day of that accounting period.[20] Where an arm's length rate is not used the London closing exchange rate for the last day of the accounting period has to be used.[21]

Where a translation time arises as a result of a company becoming entitled to an asset or becoming subject to a liability, or ceasing to become entitled to an asset or to be subject to a liability, the exchange rates which can be used are the following.

    (i) Where an average rate is used in the company's accounts and that rate represents an average of arm's length rates for all days falling within a period, provided that the arm's length rate for any day (other than the first) falling within the period is not significantly different from the arm's length rate for the immediately preceding day, that average exchange rate can be used.[22]

    (ii) Where an average rate is not used but an exchange rate is used in the company's accounts, and that exchange rate is an arm's length rate, it is the exchange rate to be used.[23]

    (iii) Where the conditions in (i) or (ii) above do not apply, and it is the company's normal practice to use an average rate, it is required to use the average of London closing exchange rates for the two currencies for all days falling

---

[16] *ibid.* s.161(4).
[17] *ibid.* s.161(5).
[18] *ibid.* s.160(2).
[19] *ibid.* s.160(3), (4).
[20] *ibid.* s.150(5).
[21] *ibid.* s.150(7).
[22] *ibid.* s.150(9).
[23] *ibid.* s.150(10).

within the relevant period (provided that the London closing exchange rate for any given day (other than the first) is not significantly different from the London closing exchange rate for the two currencies for the preceding day).[24]

(iv) If a company does not use an average rate in its accounts, or where there have been significant exchange rate movements during the period, it is required to use the London closing exchange rate for the day in which the translation time falls.[25]

*Currency contracts*

Exchange gains and losses have to be calculated by reference to a company's local **3A–29** currency. The same rules as above apply to determine the exchange rate to be used to translate the currency contract at each translation time. In the case of currency contracts, however, where one of the currencies covered by the contract is the company's local currency it is permissible to use the rate implied by the contract to determine any exchange gains or losses on the contract, whether the translation time is the end of an accounting period or otherwise provided that the rate is an arms length rate.[1] In effect, this means that no exchange gains or losses would be recognised over the life of the contract. This treatment would typically be used where the currency contract is being used as a hedge and the contract rate is also used to translate the asset or liability which is being hedged.

Where neither of the currencies covered by the contract is the company's local currency, for example a US$/Euro currency swap, in a case where a company has a sterling local currency, exchange gains and losses on *both* legs of the currency contract will have to be computed by reference to its local currency.

If a currency contract is closed out by a compensation payment, rather than by an exchange of currency, an adjustment will be made in the accounting period in which the termination takes place to eliminate any net exchange gains or losses which have been recognised over the life of the contract.[2] The reason for this adjustment is that the compensation payment will be taxed or relieved under the Finance Act 1994 financial instruments legislation.

Special provisions also apply where a company closes out a currency contract by entering into a second contract with rights and duties which are reciprocal (*i.e.* identical but opposite) to the first contract. In such cases, the company is treated as ceasing to be a party to the first contract at the date it enters into the second contract and the second contract is ignored for all other purposes of the foreign exchange legislation.[3]

---

[24] *ibid.* s.150(12). Relevant period is defined as the time from the start of the relevant accounting period up to and including the day in which the translation time falls: *ibid.* s.150(14).

[25] *ibid.* s.150(13).

[1] *ibid.* s.150(1)(c), (2)(b), (6), (11).

[2] *ibid.* s.146.

[3] *ibid.* s.147.

### Treatment of exchange gains and losses

3A–30    To the extent that a company is a party to a qualifying asset, qualifying liability or currency contract for the purposes of its trade, any exchange gains and losses are included in computing its Schedule D, Case I trading profits.[4] In all other cases exchange gains and losses are treated as non-trading and are brought into account for tax purposes for the accounting period in question as if they were non-trading credits and debits arising from loan relationships.[5] Such exchange gains and losses will thus be aggregated in determining whether the company has a non-trading credit or a non-trading deficit on its loan relationships for that accounting period for the purposes of the Finance Act 1996 loan relationship legislation. The ways in which a non-trading deficit can be relieved are considered in paragraphs 3–16 to 3–21 of the main work.

### Partnerships

3A–31    Where the partners of a partnership include one or more qualifying companies, the foreign exchange gains and losses of the partnership should be computed as if the partnership were a company in order to determine the share of such exchange gains or losses which are allocable to such partners. The basic valuation of assets and liabilities should be determined using the accounting method used by the partnership.[6]

The anti-avoidance provisions of sections 135 (main benefit), 136 and 136A (loans on non-arm's length terms), 137 (currency contracts on non-arm's length terms) and 138 (arm's length test, non-sterling trades) of the Finance Act 1993 will apply by reference to the circumstances of the partnership.[7] See Part IV below for a discussion of these provisions.

The trading versus non-trading split is determined in the same way as for qualifying companies. Where the partnership has any non-trading exchange gains and losses these should be included with its profits and losses arising from its non-trading loan relationship and financial instrument transactions in order to determine whether it has a net Schedule D, Case III profit or deficit. The corporate partners are then allocated with their share of the resulting profit or deficit and they are required to include this in determining their net profit or deficit from non-trading foreign exchange, loan relationship or financial instrument transactions.[8]

Where the accounting period of the partnership is different from that of a corporate partner the profit or loss of the partnership should be allocated between the relevant accounting periods of the corporate partner, normally on a time basis.[9]

---

[4] *ibid.* s.128.
[5] *ibid.* ss.129 and 130.
[6] SP4/98, paras 9, 14.
[7] *ibid.* para. 14.
[8] *ibid.* paras 16–18.
[9] *ibid.* para. 20.

A partnership may make a matching election,[10] claim deferral relief[11] and elect to compute its trading profits for tax purposes in a currency other than sterling.[12] This is considered further in the sections dealing with these reliefs.

## IV. ANTI-AVOIDANCE MEASURES

The foreign exchange legislation contains a number of anti-avoidance measures. These are as follows.　**3A–32**

### (1) Interest not allowed as a deduction

A company can be denied tax relief for interest paid on a qualifying debt where the　**3A–33** interest payable exceeds a commercial return on the loan principal, expressing that amount in the settlement currency of the debt.[13] The definition of settlement currency is the same as used for other provisions of the foreign legislation (see above).

This provision was introduced to deal with cases where the loan is expressed to be in one currency but is repayable in another and where the interest payable would be reasonable by reference to the first currency, but not the second currency. Presumably the Inland Revenue was concerned that the provisions of section 209(2)(d) of the Taxes Act 1998 might not be wide enough to catch interest payable on such loans.

### (2) Main benefit test

Section 135 contains provisions to deny a company tax relief for an exchange loss　**3A–34** suffered on a qualifying debt (whether that debt is an asset or a liability) if the nominal currency of the debt is such that the main benefit or one of the main benefits that might be expected to arise from the company's holding the asset or owing the liability is the accrual of an exchange loss. In practice, this section is likely to be of limited application and it is difficult to see that the section could apply where the company is a party to the qualifying debt for underlying commercial purposes.

---

[10] *ibid.* paras 33–40.
[11] *ibid.* paras 30–32.
[12] *ibid.* para. 29.
[13] *ibid.* s.60.

IV. ANTI-AVOIDANCE

## (2A)  Main benefit test – non-sterling local currency

3A–34A   A new section 135A of the Finance Act 1993 has been introduced by the Finance Act 2000.[14] This section applies where as regards qualifying assets and liabilities of a company:

1.  a currency other than sterling would be taken as the local currency of the company's business or of part of its business for the purposes of sections 125 to 129 of the Finance Act 1993; and
2.  the main benefit that might be expected to accrue from that currency being the local currency is that no net exchange gain would accrue to the company for those purposes.[15]

Where this condition is satisfied, exchange gains and losses on the company's qualifying assets and liabilities are required to be computed as if the local currency of the business or relevant part were sterling.[16]

   The original wording of this provision, as set out in the 27 March 2000 version of the Finance Bill, could have caught any company that prepared its accounts in a non-sterling currency. The current wording was introduced as a Committee Stage amendment and it is understood that, *inter alia*, one of the intentions behind the revised wording was to make it clear that commercial (and not purely tax) considerations could be taken into account for the purposes of determining whether the main benefit test was satisfied. The Paymaster General, Dawn Primarolo, made a statement about the intended scope of this provision at the Report Stage of the Finance Bill 2000 in response to concerns expressed by the Chartered Institute of Taxation and the Law Society and raised in the House on their behalf by Howard Flight MP. This exchange is reproduced in full at Appendix 1 to this Chapter. It is understood that the Inland Revenue also plans to issue further guidance on the scope of this provision in due course.

## (3)  Arm's length test

3A–35     Section 136 of the Finance Act 1993 contains provisions aimed at non-arm's length transactions. The provisions of section 136 are modified in certain cases by section 136A where the amount of the debt varies during the accounting period in question.

---

[14] *ibid.* s.106(7). The provisions of FA 1993, s.135A have effect for accounting periods beginning on on after Janaury 1, 2000 and ending on or after March 21, 2000: FA 2000, s. 106(17).
[15] *ibid.* s.135A(1).
[16] *ibid.* s.135A(2).

The scope of both sections is limited to qualifying debts, both assets and liabilities. They apply where the transaction, as a result of which the company becomes entitled or subject to the asset or liability, would not have been entered into at all if the parties to the transaction had been dealing at arm's length, or the loan would have been entered into on different terms.[17] In determining whether a transaction falls within the provision all factors are to be taken into account including any interest or other sums that would have been payable, any currency that would have been involved, and the amount that any loan would have been.[18]

EXAMPLE

A PLC borrows from its Dutch subsidiary company in U.S.$ at US prime. A PLC suffers an exchange loss on the loan. Had A PLC borrowed from the market it would have been able to borrow sub-U.S. prime.

On these facts, the non-arm's length provisions could apply to deny A PLC tax relief for the exchange loss in the accounting period in which it accrues, even though it was paying a market rate of interest on the loan. In section 3.7 of its Explanatory Statement the Inland Revenue states, however, that a direction would not normally be made where the transaction's terms do not materially differ from those which would have been agreed at arm's length. Although the requirement for an Inland Revenue direction disappeared with the advent of corporation tax self-assessment it is presumed that companies can still rely on this statement when preparing their tax computations.

Where section 136 or 136A applies to a qualifying debt, relief for an exchange loss arising in an accounting period is denied and instead the exchange loss is treated as "ring-fenced" and it can only be relieved against future exchange gains arising on that loan.[19] There are no provisions for an exchange loss to be carried back to an earlier period if an exchange gain arose on that loan in that earlier period. In its Explanatory Statement, however, the Inland Revenue states that it would not normally apply the provisions of section 136 of the Finance Act 1993 in a case where there was a net exchange gain which had been taxed in earlier years which was greater than or equal to the exchange loss arising on the loan in the current period.[20] This statement was made at the time when a Board direction was necessary in order for the provisions of section 136 to be applied. As noted above, the requirement for a Board direction disappeared with the advent of corporation tax self assessment, although an inspector

---

[17] *ibid.* s.136(1) and s.163A(1).
[18] *ibid.* s.136(15) and s.136A(11).
[19] *ibid.* s.136(2), (3) and s.136A(3), (4).
[20] See section 3.10 of the Explanatory Statement and also Company Taxation Manual at 13899.

is still required to obtain the approval of the Board before imposing a section 136 or 136A adjustment on a company.[21] It is assumed, however, that a company can still apply the Inland Revenue's stated practice when submitting its tax computations under the self assessment regime.

**3A–36**    There are certain exceptions from sections 136 and 136A.

(i) Where the borrower and lender are both members of a capital gains group[22] and an exchange loss arising in one company (first company) for an accrual period would be matched by an equal but opposite exchange gain accruing in the other company (second company) for an accrual period which is coterminous with that of the first company. In order for the exception to apply the two companies must be members of the same group at the time at which the transaction is entered into and throughout the whole of the accounting period which constitutes the accrual period, or in which the accrual period falls.[23] The exception still applies even if one of the companies claims deferral relief on the exchange gain,[24] or if the borrower has made a matching election.[25]

(ii) Where the loan would still have been made if the parties had been dealing at arm's length but the amount of the loan would have been less, the company will be permitted to claim relief for the exchange loss on that lower part of the loan. The balance of the exchange loss will be treated as described above.[1]

(iii) The provisions will not apply to deny a lender tax relief for an exchange loss arising on a loan to the extent that interest is imputed on the loan under the transfer pricing provisions contained within Schedule 28AA of the Taxes Act 1988.[2] Where interest is only imputed on part of the loan (with the balance being treated as quasi-capital funding) then the provisions of sections 136 and 136A are only disapplied in relation to that part of the loan

---

[21] FA 1998, s.110(4)(b).

[22] For accrual periods beginning on or after April 1, 2000, the revised CGT group definition applies (*i.e.*, a company does not have to be resident in the United Kingdom in order to be included as a member of a CGT group; see 23–05 below): FA 1993 s.136(12)(d), and s.136A(10)(d), as amended by FA 2000, Sch. 29 paras 41 and 42 respectively.

[23] FA 1993, s.136(11)–(12) and s.136A(9)–(10). The effect of the last mentioned requirement is that this relief may not be available if each company was not a member of the capital gains group throughout the whole of the other's accounting period. This could cause problems where a company joins an existing group of companies during an accounting period and shortly afterwards a loan is advanced to that company on non-arm's length terms. In such cases the relief under s.136(11)–(12) and s.136A(9)–(10) would not be available for that accounting period. The relief, however, would be available in subsequent periods.

[24] *ibid*. s.136(12)(c) and s.136A(10)(c).

[25] S.I. 1994 No. 3227, reg. 12.

[1] FA 1993, s.136(4), (5), (6) and s.136A(2), (3), (4).

[2] *ibid*. ss.136(7) and 136A(5).

on which interest is imputed and exchange losses on that part of the loan which represents capital funding will still be "ring-fenced".[3]

*Arm's length test—currency contracts*

Section 137 of the Finance Act 1996 contains provisions to ring-fence exchange losses suffered on currency contracts which are entered into on non-arm's length terms. The section applies where the contract would not have been entered into at all if the parties had been dealing at arm's length, or the contract's terms would have been different if they had been so dealing. In determining whether this condition is satisfied, all factors are to be taken into account including any currency that would have been involved and any amount that would have been involved.[4]   **3A–37**

Unlike the provisions of sections 136 and 136A of the Finance Act 1993, the currency contract test is an all or nothing test. Thus, in theory, if the terms of a contract were off market (and there was no compensatory adjustment in the pricing of the contract) then relief for the entire exchange loss on the contract could be ring-fenced. Equally, if a company within the charge to United Kingdom corporation tax entered into a currency contract with an overseas, or even United Kingdom connected party, and the terms of the contract were different from the terms which either company would have entered into had it been dealing with an independent third party, the whole of the exchange loss on the contract arising in an accounting period could be ring-fenced. Under the self-assessment regime this section no longer requires a direction from the Board of Inland Revenue but, before an inspector can impose an adjustment on a company under the provisions of this section, Board approval is required.[5]

In its Explanatory Statement the Inland Revenue states that it would not normally impose an adjustment where the transaction's terms do not materially differ from those which would be agreed at arm's length. Nor would it normally make a direction where an exchange loss arises in an accounting period and the company has been taxed on net exchange gains which arose in earlier accounting periods which are equal to or greater than the exchange loss on the contract in the current accounting period. It also stated that it would not normally make a direction where the contract was between two companies in a United Kingdom capital gains group which have coterminous accounting periods and an exchange loss in one company would be matched by an exchange gain in the other.[6] Whilst such guidance predates the abolition of the requirement for a Board direction, it is assumed that it still remains valid in the self assessment era.

*Arm's length test—non sterling trade*

Section 138 contains provisions which explain how a loss which has been ring-fenced under the provisions of section 136(3), (6) and (10) or 137(3) is to be set off   **3A–38**

---

[3] *ibid.* s.136(8), (9), (10) and s.136A(6), (7), (8).
[4] *ibid.* s.137(4).
[5] FA 1998, s.110(4).
[6] Explanatory Statement, sections 3.7, 3.8 and 3.16.

against future exchange gains where a company has a non-sterling local currency. Where the loss is in a currency different from that in which the gain is expressed, the ring-fenced loss is required to be translated into that other currency using the London closing exchange rate for the two currencies for the first day of the accounting period in which the exchange gain arises. Interestingly this section does not cover a case where an exchange loss on a variable loan has been ring-fenced under the provisions of section 136A. The reason for this is thought to be oversight on the part of the draftsman as section 136A was introduced at a later date by statutory instrument. Nor has the scope of this section been extended to non-trading transactions.

### Change of accounting period

**3A–39**     There are provisions within section 166 of the Finance Act 1993 which apply where a company changes its accounting period in order to increase an exchange loss or to reduce an exchange gain. This section applies where the exchange gain would have been greater or the exchange loss would have been lower, but for the change of accounting period. There is no override for a change for commercial purposes. The section permits the inspector, or on appeal the commissioners, to disregard the change of accounting period and to make such adjustment to the company's corporation tax liability as is just and reasonable.

### V. MATCHING

**3A–40**     The matching regulations[7] permit a company to use either a foreign currency loan[8] or the liability leg of a currency contract[9] (*i.e.* the currency which the company is

---

[7] S.I. 1994 No. 3227 introduced under the provisions of FA 1993, s.134 and Sched. 15, paras 4 and 4A.

[8] *ibid.* reg 5(4). The liability must not be a debt due for goods or services supplied to the company in the ordinary course of its trade and nor must it represent accrued interest.

[9] *ibid.* reg. 5(5). Care will be need to be taken where a currency contract is used for matching to ensure that the contract is settled by an exchange of currencies. If the contract is settled by a compensation payment equal to the difference between the two currencies at the date the contract is settled, the compensation payment will be taxed or relieved under the FA 1994 financial instruments legislation, while any exchange gains or losses which have been recognised over the life of the contract will continue to be treated as matched. This is because the provisions of FA 1993, s.146, which would normally apply to reverse the net foreign exchange gain or loss which had been recognised over the life of the contract, do not apply where exchange gains or losses have been treated as matched as, in such cases, no initial gain or loss is deemed to arise for an accrual period: *ibid.* reg. 5(2). At the time of writing the Inland Revenue was proposing to address this anomaly by an amendment to the provisions of the matching regulations to provide that where a contract is net settled the provisions of FA 1993, s.146 should apply as if the amount of the initial gain or loss on the contract had not been eliminated by the matching regulations.

required to deliver when the contract matures) to match an investment in certain non-monetary assets. If the election is not made any exchange gains or losses on the hedge will remain taxable whereas any exchange gain or loss on the underlying asset will only fall within the charge to tax when that asset is disposed of.

The assets for which a matching election can be made (eligible assets) are:

(i) shares in an overseas resident company in which the United Kingdom company holds at least 20 per cent of the voting power at the time at which the election is made. If the United Kingdom company's share of the voting power subsequently falls below 20 per cent, the matching election will still continue in force[10]. At the time of writing the Inland Revenue was proposing to amend the scope of this provision so that it applies where the non-resident company prepares its accounts in a different currency to that used by the company that is making the matching election;

(ii) shares in a 90 per cent United Kingdom resident subsidiary company where the subsidiary has made a local currency election to compute its trading profits in a currency other than sterling.[11] In this case the shares will cease to be eligible for matching if the company ceases to be a 90 per cent subsidiary[12]. At the time of writing the Inland Revenue was proposing to amend this provision so that it applies where a 90 per cent United Kingdom resident company prepares its accounts in a different currency to that of its parent company (including cases where the subsidiary prepares its accounts in sterling). Assuming that the amendment is made, it will no longer necessary for the 90 per cent United Kingdom resident subsidiary to be carrying on a trade;

(iii) a debt on a security which is not a qualifying asset and which under the terms of issue can be converted into or exchanged for shares of companies falling within (i) or (ii) above[13];

(iv) a net investment in a branch outside the United Kingdom where the company has made a local currency election to compute the trading profits of the branch for United Kingdom corporation tax purposes in a currency other than sterling[14]. At the time of writing the Inland Revenue was proposing to amend this provision so that it applies where the branch accounts are not prepared in the company's local currency;

(v) the chargeable assets of an overseas branch of a United Kingdom company where no election has been made to compute the trading profits of the branch

---

[10] *ibid.* reg. 5(6)(a) and 5(9).

[11] *ibid.* reg. 5(6)(b).

[12] The ICTA 1988, s.838 definition of a 90% subsidiary is used except that it is extended to cover indirect ownership: *ibid.* reg. 5(7)(b).

[13] *ibid.* reg. 5(6)(c).

[14] *ibid.* reg. 5(6)(d).

in a currency other than sterling[15]. At the time of writing the Inland Revenue was proposing to amend this provision so that it applies only where the accounts of the branch are prepared in the same currency in which the company as a whole prepares its accounts;

   (vi)  ships[16];

   (vii)  aircraft.[17]

For the purposes of a matching election all shares in a company are treated as a single asset.[18]

**3A–41**    The qualifying debt or the liability leg of the currency contract (matching liability) does not have to be in the same currency in which the eligible asset is carried in the company's accounts. The requirement instead is that the company is able to reduce substantially any exchange risk which would otherwise arise from it holding the particular asset.[19]

A matching election normally only takes effect from the date on which it is made and once made it is irrevocable.[20] It is possible, however, to backdate a matching election to the date the eligible asset was acquired, provided that the matching election is made within 92 days of that date.[21] A company does not have to elect to match the whole of an asset and instead it can elect to match a part of the asset. If a company makes a partial matching election it can elect to match:

   (i)  a fixed percentage of the asset;

   (ii)  a specified portion of the asset at the time at which the election is made; or

   (iii)  a proportion of the asset on a formula basis.[22]

The company can subsequently vary the amount of the asset which is to be treated as matched under (i) or (ii) above. This subsequent election can be backdated by up to 92 days.[23] Where a company is already a party to the loan or currency contract at the date it acquires the eligible asset, or where it does not elect for matching to be backdated to the date on which it acquired the asset, the exchange gain or loss on the matching liability for the accounting period in which the matching election is made will normally be apportioned on a time basis between the period up until the election is made and the period for which the matching election has effect. This treatment is modified if there is a significant fluctuation in exchange rates during the relevant accounting period, in which case the exchange gain or loss for the part of the period

---

[15] *ibid.* reg. 5(8).

[16] *ibid.* reg. 5(6)(e). A ship is not defined within the regulations.

[17] *ibid.* reg. 5(6)(e). An aircraft is not defined within the regulations.

[18] *ibid.* reg. 5(7)(aa).

[19] *ibid.* reg. 5(4)(b), (5).

[20] *ibid.* reg. 10(1)(b), (c).

[21] *ibid.* reg. 11(2).

[22] *ibid.* reg. 10(2)(c).

[23] *ibid.* regs 10(3) and 11(3).

before the matching election took effect and for that part of the period for which it had effect is calculated on an actual basis.[24]

A matching election must contain details of the following:          **3A–42**

(a) the asset to be matched;

(b) if a partial matching election is made, the basis on which the asset is to be treated as matched (*i.e.* which of the three options described above the company wishes to adopt); and

(c) The relevant provisions of regulation 5 of S.I. 1994 No. 3227 under which the asset qualifies for matching treatment.[25]

Once a matching election has been made, it will remain in force so long as the company continues to own the eligible asset in question. If a company ceases to be subject to all or part of the matching liability which was used for the initial matching, there are provisions to ensure that other loans or currency contracts to which the company is a party at that date will be treated as matched if any of those liabilities would be a suitable hedge against the eligible asset in question.[1]

There are anti-avoidance provisions to prevent a company from artificially terminating a matching election by disposing of the asset and reacquiring the asset at a later date. These provisions apply where the asset is reacquired under a contract made in a 60-day period starting 30 days before the disposal of the asset. Where these provisions apply, for the purposes of the matching regulations the disposal and reacquisition are ignored.[2]

In order for matching treatment to apply, the company has to adopt the required accounting treatment. In the case of eligible assets, other than ships and aircraft, matching treatment will only apply where exchange gains and losses on both the eligible asset and the matching liability are taken to reserves. This particular provision is designed to track the accounting treatment which would normally be applied under Statement of Standard Accounting Practice 20 (SSAP 20). Where this condition is not satisfied, any exchange loss on the matching liability will continue to be treated as matched but any exchange gain on the matching liability will be treated as taxable in the accounting period in which it accrues.[3]

**Partial matching—anti-avoidance provisions**

An anti-avoidance provision applies where a company elects to treat an asset as     **3A–43**
partially matched and subsequently increases the extent to which the asset is to be

---

[24] *ibid.* reg. 5(2), (3).
[25] *ibid.* reg. 10(2).
[1] *ibid.* reg. 10(5).
[2] *ibid.* reg. 7(2).
[3] *ibid.* reg. 10(4).

treated as matched. This provision applies where only part of a liability is treated as matched or where a company was a party to another liability which was eligible for matching at the date at which the matching election was made and, in each case, where exchange gains or losses on all or part of the liability are taken to reserves in excess of the exchange gains and losses which are treated as matched by virtue of the matching election. In such cases, to the extent that exchange gains and losses which are taken to reserves exceed the matched gains and losses, any exchange loss will effectively be treated as matched whereas any exchange gain will be treated as taxable in the accounting period in which it accrues.[4] This particular measure is aimed at cases where a company initially elected only to treat a small proportion of an asset as matched and then, if an exchange gain arose on the matching liability, it subsequently elected to increase the amount of the asset which was treated as matched.

### Reorganisations

**3A–44**    Where an eligible asset is transferred under certain "no gain no loss" provisions, including *inter alia*, sections 139, 140A and 171 of the Taxation of Chargeable Gains Act 1992, any matched gain or loss on the matching liability is not brought into charge to tax. Instead, the matched gain or loss is deemed to be transferred to the transferee company and is brought into account for tax purposes when the matched asset is disposed of by that company (otherwise than as a result of a "no gain no loss" disposal). The matching election, however, does not transfer with the asset and if the transferee company wishes to treat the asset as matched it will need to make a new matching election.[5]

Where a company has elected to match shares or securities in another company, if those shares are subsequently disposed of as a result of a share for share exchange which satisfies the requirements of section 135 of the Taxation of Chargeable Gains Act 1992, or in the case of securities, the securities are converted into or are exchanged for shares of the issuer and the reorganisation satisfies the requirements of section 132 of the 1992 Act, the disposal and acquisition will be ignored for the purposes of the matching election and the matching election will continue to apply to the replacement asset.[6]

Where shares or securities are exchanged for qualifying corporate bonds in a case where section 132 or 135 would apply, but for the provisions of section 116 of the 1992 Act, the net exchange gain or loss which has accrued up to the date of the reorganisation is held over and is brought into charge to tax when the replacement qualifying corporate bonds are disposed of.[7]

---

[4] *ibid.* reg. 5(3A). See also the article in the Inland Revenue *Tax Bulletin*, August 1996 and Company Taxation Manual, section 13700.

[5] *ibid.* reg. 8.

[6] *ibid.* reg. 9.

[7] *ibid.* reg. 9.

### Hedging an investment in indirect subsidiaries

A matching election can only be made in respect of a direct investment, that is a **3A–45** company cannot elect to match shares that are held by an overseas sub-holding company. This problem can be overcome, in practice, by adopting an appropriate accounting treatment for the overseas sub-holding company. For example, if a United Kingdom company is holding shares in a U.S. company and a Danish company via a Dutch BV, it would be possible for the United Kingdom company effectively to match the underlying investments of the BV if, instead of carrying its investment in the BV in Dutch guilders, it reflected its investment in the BV as a multi-currency investment. In this case the investment in the BV would be recorded as the sum of the carrying value in dollars and Danish kroner of the BV's underlying investments. If this accounting treatment is adopted, the company could treat dollar and kroner borrowings as matched against its investment in the BV for both tax and accounting purposes. Section 2.23 of the Explanatory Statement makes it clear that such treatment will be acceptable for tax purposes. It is also acceptable for United Kingdom GAAP purposes.

### Interest-free loans

In its Explanatory Statement, the Inland Revenue has stated that it would not normal- **3A–46** ally seek to challenge an interest-free foreign currency loan under transfer pricing legislation where the loan is made in order to enable a subsidiary company to make a matching election.[8] The Revenue also states that the anti-avoidance provisions of sections 135 to 137 would not normally be applied in such cases.[9]

If a loan is advanced interest-free, care will need to be taken, however, to ensure that the provisions of the Finance Act 1996, Schedule 9, paragraph 13 do not apply, so far as the lender is concerned. For example, if the lender funds the loan by entering into a specific foreign currency borrowing at interest it would need to demonstrate that it was within its business or other commercial purposes to use the funds to make an interest-free loan to another group company. It is considered that this should be possible where the lender is the direct or indirect parent of the borrower. In other cases, the position is less clear.

### Disposal of matched assets

Except where a company has elected to match its net investment in an overseas **3A–47** branch, the net exchange gain or loss which has been treated as matched under the

---

[8] Section 2.24. This statement was made before ICTA 1988, Sched. 28AA was enacted. Under Sched. 28AA no interest would normally be imputed on an interest-free loan made between two U.K. resident companies.

[9] Sections 2.24 and 3.15.

matching regulations is brought into charge to tax on the disposal of the eligible asset unless the asset is reacquired in a 60-day period starting 30 days before the disposal takes place.[10] Where a company makes a part disposal a proportionate part of the matched exchange gain or loss is brought into charge to tax.[11] If the eligible assets are shares, securities or chargeable assets of an overseas branch, the matched exchange gain or loss is treated as a capital gain or loss and is brought into account for tax purposes in the accounting period in which the disposal of the eligible asset takes place.[12] If the eligible asset is a ship or an aircraft, the matched gain or loss is treated as a foreign exchange gain or loss which accrues in the accounting period in which the disposal of the asset takes place.[13]

### Corporate partnerships and matching elections

**3A–48**    Originally the Inland Revenue had taken the view in SP 9/94 (which has now been withdrawn) that a matching election could only be made by a partnership of which a company was a member where the eligible asset was a ship or an aircraft, or was a chargeable asset of an overseas branch for which no local currency election had been made. In November 1998 the Inland Revenue issued a revised statement of practice, SP 4/98. In the revised statement, the Inland Revenue now accepts that a matching election can be made in respect of any eligible asset.

Under the Inland Revenue's revised practice, a matching can only be made in the case of corporate partnership where it is signed by all the corporate partners who are within the charge to corporation tax. The election applies for the purpose of calculating the exchange gains or losses of the partnership which are attributable to the corporate partners. Where the eligible asset is disposed of, the matched gain or loss is allocated to each of the corporate partners and is dealt with in the same way for tax purposes as if the corporate partners had held the asset in their own right.[14]

The Inland Revenue's view is that in order for matching treatment to be applied, the matching liability must be owed by the partnership and that it is not possible for a corporate partner to elect to match one of its own liabilities against an eligible asset held by the partnership. The partnership also has to comply with the accounting treatment described above, *i.e.* exchange gains and losses on both eligible assets and matching liabilities must be taken to reserves, (except in the case of ships and aircraft).

Where there is a change in the composition of the partnership and/or in its profit

---

[10] S.I. 1994 No. 3227, reg. 7(1), (2). The matched exchange gain or loss continues to be treated as matched where the asset is reacquired in the 60-day period. If the asset is the company's net investment in an overseas branch the matched exchange gain or loss is never brought into charge to tax.

[11] *ibid.* reg. 7(8).

[12] *ibid.* reg. 7(6).

[13] *ibid.* reg. 7(7).

[14] SP4/98, paras 33–40.

sharing ratio, the net held over matched exchange gain or loss is calculated at that date and the retiring corporate partner, or the corporate partner whose profit share has reduced, is allocated with the appropriate proportion of the matched gain or loss on the eligible liability. This is then brought into account for tax purposes in the accounting period of that corporate partner in which the partnership reorganisation takes place. The reason for this is that in such cases the corporate partner would be treated as having made a disposal, or a part disposal, of the underlying asset under the provisions of paragraph 4 of Statement of Practice D12.[15]

### Controlled foreign companies (CFC)

The matching regulations permit a United Kingdom company which holds, or the   **3A–49** United Kingdom companies which together hold, the majority interest in a CFC, to make a matching election on behalf of a CFC for the purpose of calculating its chargeable profits under the provisions of Schedule 24 to the Taxes Act 1988.[16] The same time-limits will normally apply in the case of this election, *i.e.* the matching election will take effect from the date it is made unless it is made within 92 days of the date the eligible asset was acquired, in which case it can be backdated to that date. An election, however, can be backdated to the start of an accounting period if a direction is given for that accounting period, the election is made within 92 days of the date of the direction and no direction has been made for an earlier period and nor has a direction been avoided for such a period as a result of the CFC pursuing an acceptable distribution policy. It is not clear how this provision will be applied under the self-assessment regime as it is no longer necessary for a direction to be made in order for an apportionment to be made under the CFC legislation.[17]

## VI. LOCAL CURRENCY

### Position for accountancy periods that ended on or before December 31, 1999

As discussed above, normally, a company's local currency is deemed to be sterling,   **3A–50** irrespective of the currency in which it prepares its accounts.[18] A company can, however, elect to compute the profits of the whole or part of its trade in a currency other than sterling.[19] In the case of a United Kingdom resident company, an election to compute part of the profits of a trade in a foreign currency can only be made for an

---

[15] *ibid.* para. 39.
[16] S.I. 1994 No. 3227, reg. 6.
[17] *ibid.* reg. 11(5).
[18] FA 1993, s.149.
[19] *ibid.* ss.93, 94 and 149 and S.I. 1994 No. 3230.

overseas branch or in respect of a United Kingdom ring-fenced oil and gas trade. A company can specify a different currency for different branches.[20] A United Kingdom resident company can, however, elect to compute all of the profits of its trade in a foreign currency and an overseas company can make a local currency election for its United Kingdom branch.[21]

A company can only elect to use a local currency other than sterling where:

(i) it is the currency of the primary economic environment in which the trade or the relevant part of the trade is carried on; and

(ii) one of the conditions set out in (a) to (c) below is satisfied.[22]

    (a) A currency may be specified in an election as a local currency if the accounts[23] are prepared in that currency in accordance with normal accountancy practice.[24]

    (b) A currency may be specified by a company resident in the United Kingdom as a local currency if the accounts, so far as they relate to the trade or part in question, are prepared from the financial statements relating to the trade, or part, using the closing rate/net investment method (as prescribed under the heading Foreign Currency Translation in SSAP 20), and those statements are prepared in that currency. This provision will apply in the case of overseas branches of United Kingdom resident companies.[25]

    (c) A currency may be specified in an election made by a company not resident in the United Kingdom as a local currency if it is the currency in which the financial statements relating to that trade, or part, are prepared in accordance with normal accountancy practice.[1]

In addition to the above it was also possible for certain companies which had prepared accounts for the trade, or part, in foreign currency before their commencement day, and which were within the charge to corporation tax before that date, to elect to use that currency as the local currency for the trade in question.[2]

---

[20] S.I. 1994 No. 3230, regs 3, 4.

[21] *ibid*. reg. 3(1).

[22] *ibid*. reg. 5(2).

[23] For the purposes of the local currency regulations, accounts are defined as:
    (i) the annual accounts of the company prepared in accordance with Part VII of the Companies Act 1985, or
    (ii) if the company is not required to prepare such accounts, the accounts which it is required to keep under the law of its home State or, if it is not required to keep accounts, such of its accounts as most closely correspond to accounts which it would have been required to prepare if the provisions of that Part applied to the company: *ibid*. reg. 2.

[24] *ibid*. reg. 5(3).

[25] *ibid*. reg. 5(4).

[1] *ibid*. reg. 5(5).

[2] *ibid*. reg. 5(6), (7).

The factors which will be taken into account by the Inland Revenue in assessing **3A–51**
whether the currency is the currency of the primary economic environment in which
the trade or part of the trade is carried on, are whether it is:

(a) the currency in which the net cash flows of the trade, or part, are generated
or expressed in the relevant accounting records;
(b) the currency in which the company manages the profitability of the trade, or
part, so far as it is affected by currency exposure;
(c) the currency in which the company's share capital and its reserves are denominated, in the case of a company which is resident in the United Kingdom;
(d) the currency to which the company, or where the trade or part is carried on
through a branch, that branch, is exposed in its long-term capital borrowings
(although long term is not defined the Inland Revenue regard borrowings of
more than one year as long term)[3];
(e) the currency which is the generally recognised currency in which trading in
the principal market of the trade or part is carried on.[4]

The Regulations do not require a majority or any particular number of factors to be
present and the relevance of each factor will depend on the type of trade in question
and the way in which the company operates.[5]
A local currency election will take effect from the start of the next accounting **3A–52**
period following that in which it is made. An election must contain the following:

(i) a statement of the reasons why the company believes that the above requirements are met in respect of the trade, or part, for the first accounting period
in which the election is to have effect;
(ii) particulars of the nature of the trade, or part, and the place where it is carried
on; and
(iii) whether the company wishes to use an average rate or a closing rate to
translate its trading profits found in foreign currency into sterling.[6] If the
election is silent, the closing rate will apply.[7] If a company initially elects
to use an average rate it is possible for it to vary the election at a later date
to use the closing rate for future periods. It is not possible, however, for a
company to elect to use an average rate at a later date if it did not specify
that it wished to use an average rate in its original election.[8]

---

[3] Explanatory Statement, s. 4.8.
[4] S.I. 1994 No. 3230, reg. 6.
[5] See s. 4 of the Explanatory Statement for a discussion of the weight the Inland Revenue
places on the above factors.
[6] S.I. 1994 No. 3230, regs 8(1), 10(1).
[7] FA 1993, ss.93(6)(b).
[8] S.I. 1994 No. 3230, reg. 8(3), (4).

A local currency election will remain in force so long as the conditions for the election continue to be satisfied. These include, *inter alia*, that the company continues to prepare its accounting records for the trade, or part, in the appropriate foreign currency.[9]

Where the election applies, the profits of the trade or part are calculated for Schedule D, Case I purposes in foreign currency, except that capital allowances are disregarded. The resulting profit or loss is then translated into sterling using the exchange rate specified in the election and an adjustment is then made for capital allowances to arrive at the Schedule D, Case I profit or loss for the trade, or part.[10]

**3A–53**     It should be noted that a local currency election only applies for the purpose of computing a company's Schedule D, Case I profits. If a company is party to foreign currency qualifying assets or liabilities or currency contracts for non-trading purposes, the exchange gain or loss on such assets or liabilities will have to be computed as if the company's local currency was sterling. Where a company is a party to a qualifying asset or liability or to a currency contract partly for trading purposes and partly for non-trading purposes, the exchange gain or losses on such assets or liabilities will first be calculated by reference to sterling in order to find the proportion which is attributable to non-trading purposes and then any trading exchange gains or losses will be determined by reference to the local currency in question.[11]

Where a company made a local currency election in respect of the ecu, or a currency which is participating in the euro, that election was extended also to the euro with effect from January 1, 1999. There are special provisions which apply where a company had made elections to compute part of its trade in currencies which are participating in the euro. The reader is referred to the Regulations for further information on this point.[12]

### Local currency election—partnerships

**3A–54**     Where at least one of the partners in a partnership is a qualifying company, the partnership may make an election to compute its trading profits in a currency other than sterling for the purpose of determining the trading profits or losses of the partnership which are allocable to partners which are qualifying companies. Any election must satisfy the conditions of S.I. 1994 No. 3230 which will be applied to the partnership as if it were a company and must be signed by all the partners who, at the time the election is made, are companies within the charge to corporation tax. Any election will be treated as irrevocable and will not cease to be valid as a result of subsequent partnership changes.[13]

---

[9] *ibid.* reg. 10(3), (4).
[10] FA 1993, ss.93(2)–(5) and 94(4)–(10).
[11] *ibid.* s.149.
[12] S.I. 1998 No. 3177, European Single Currency (Taxes) Regulations 1998, regs. 44–47.
[13] SP4/98, para. 29. This represents a change in practice as in SP9/94, which was superseded by SP4/98, the IR's view was that a local currency election could only be made by a partnership where all the members were qualifying companies.

### Accounting periods beginning on or after January 1, 2000 and ending after March 21, 2000

Finance Act 2000 introduced changes to the foreign exchange local currency provisions. These changes took effect for accounting periods which began on or after 1 January 2000 and which ended on or after 21 March 2000. The broad effect of these changes is that a company's local currency for all or part of its business will be the currency in which it prepares the accounts of the business, or the relevant part of the business. A new anti-avoidance provision, section 135A of the Finance Act 1993, was introduced by the Finance Act 2000 to cover cases where a company has a non-sterling local currency. The scope of this provision is considered at 3A–33A above. The reforms introduced by the Finance Act 2000 do not apply for the purposes of determining the local currency of a CFC and in such cases the local currency has to be determined as described at 16–21 of this supplement.

**3A–54A**

Where a company was eligible to elect to use a non-sterling local currency under the pre-Finance Act 2000 regime (see above), it was able to elect that the revised local currency provisions should not apply to it until the start of its first accounting period beginning on or after 1 July 2000. Such an election had to be made on or before 31 August 2000.[14]

Under section 92[15] of the Finance Act 1993, the basic rule is that a company's profits[16] and losses[17] for corporation tax purposes should be computed in sterling. In such cases, where a company incurs a receipt or expense in a currency other than sterling and it translates such items into sterling in its accounts, this treatment will be followed for tax purposes provided that:

(a) the company uses an arm's length exchange rate for the date on which it becomes entitled to the receipt, or incurs (or is treated as incurring) the expenditure[18]; or

(b) it uses an average arm's length rate[19] for a period ending with that day or for a period of up to three months which includes that day provided that the arm's length exchange rate for any day in that period (except the first) is not significantly different from that for the preceding day. [20]

---

[14] FA 2000, s.105(5).

[15] As amended by FA 2000, s.105(1).

[16] Profits are defined as including gains, income and any charges falling to be made under CAA 1990, s.28 or s.61(1): FA 1993, s.92(2), as inserted by FA 2000, s.105(1).

[17] "Losses" are defined as including management expenses and any allowances falling to be made under CAA 1990, s.28 or s.61(1): FA 1993, s.92(2), as inserted by FA 2000, s.105(1).

[18] FA 1993, s.94(1)(a), (2)(a), as inserted by FA 2000, s.105(1).

[19] An "arm's length exchange rate" is defined as such exchange rate as might reasonably be expected to be agreed between persons dealing at arms length. An "average arms length exchange rate" in relation to a period is defined as the rate which represents an appropriate average of arms length exchange rates for period: FA 1993, s.94(8), as inserted by FA 2000, s.105(1).

[20] FA 1993, s.94(1), (2)(b), as inserted by FA 2000, s.105(1).

Where neither of these conditions is satisfied, that company is required to use the London closing rate for the relevant day.[21]

**3A–54B** The basic rule is varied in a number of cases:

1. Where a United Kingdom resident company prepares its accounts in a currency other than sterling in accordance with normal accounting practice, that currency is taken to be the company's local currency.[22]

2. Where a non-resident prepares the accounts of its United Kingdom branch[23] for tax purposes in a currency other than sterling in accordance with normal accounting practice, that currency is taken as the branch's local currency.[24]

3. Where a company's accounts as a whole are prepared in sterling but, so far as relating to the business, they are prepared, using the closing rate/net investment method[25], from financial statements prepared in a currency other than sterling, that currency is taken as the local currency of the business. *Inter alia*, this provision would apply where a United Kingdom resident company accounts for the results of an overseas branch in a currency other than sterling or where part of its domestic activities are accounted for in a different currency. The scope of the provision, however, is not restricted to United Kingdom resident companies. A company is permitted to use different currencies for different businesses.[1]

4. Where a non-resident company submits a return of accounts to the Inland Revenue in sterling and at the same time accounts for part of its activities in a currency other than sterling (non-sterling business). In such cases the treatment adopted in the branch's return of accounts will be followed for tax

---

[21] *ibid.* s.94(1)(b), as inserted by FA 2000, s.105(1).

[22] *ibid.* s.93(2)(a), as inserted by FA 2000, s.105(1). A company's accounts are defined as:
1. the annual accounts of the company prepared in accordance with Part VII of the Companies Act 1985 or Part VIII of the Companies (Northern Ireland) Order 1986; or
2. in the case of a company that is not incorporated in the United Kingdom, the accounts which it is required to keep under the of its home State. A company's home State is the country or territory under whose laws the company is incorporated; or
3. if the company's is not required to prepare statutory accounts under the law of its home State, this test is judged by reference to such of the company's accounts as most closely corresponds to accounts which it would have been required to prepare had it been subject to the provision of the Companies Act 1985: FA 1993, s.93(7), as inserted by FA 2000, s.105(1).

[23] "Branch" is defined as including any collection of assets and liabilites: FA 1993, s.93(7), as inserted by FA 2000, s. 106(1).

[24] FA 1993, s.93(2)(b), as inserted by FA 2000, s.105(1). The same definition of accounts applies as discussed in footnote 22.

[25] This is defined by reference to the definition used in Statement of Standard Accounting Practice 20. "Foreign Currency Translation" that was issued in April 1983 by the Institute of Chartered Accountants in England and Wales.

[1] FA 1993, s.93(3)(a), as inserted by FA 2000 s.105(1).

purposes so long as the results of the non-sterling business are incorporated in the branch's return of accounts using the closing rate/net investment method.[2]

*Computation of profits and losses for tax purposes*

Where a company uses a currency other than sterling as the local currency for all **3A–54C** or part of its business in accordance with any of the cases that are specified in 1. to 4. above, the profits and losses of the business (or part) for tax purposes are computed by first deducting the local currency amount of brought forward management expenses, brought forward Schedule D Case I trading losses and any non-trading deficits on loan relationships that are being set off against the profits of that period by an election under the provisions of section 83(2)(d) of the Finance Act 1996 (see 3 – 16 of the main text). The definition of profits, however, excludes chargeable gains.[3] The resulting profit is then translated into sterling.[4]

The authors understand from the Inland Revenue that a Schedule D Case I trading loss, management expense or a non-trading deficit only needs to be translated into sterling to the extent that:

(i) it is offset against other taxable profits for the accounting period in question;
(ii) it is surrendered as group relief; or
(iii) in the case of a Schedule D Case I loss or a non-trading deficit, to the extent that the company has elected to carry back the loss or deficit to the previous accounting period.

To the extent that a Schedule D Case I trading loss, management expense or non-trading deficit is not so relieved it may be carried forward in the company's local currency.

*Exchange rates to be used for translation purposes*

Section 94 prescribes the exchange rates that are to be used: **3A–54D**

(a) where any receipt or expense that is included in computing the company's taxable profits is incurred in a currency other than the company's local currency[5];
(b) to determine the local currency equivalent of the sterling amount expressed

---

[2] *ibid.* s.93(3)(b), as inserted by FA 2000, s.105(1).
[3] *ibid.* s.93(7), as inserted by FA 2000, s.105(1). Chargeable gains still have to be determined by following the rule in *Bentley v. Pike* [1981] S.T.C. 360; that is by comparing the sterling equivalent of the acquisition cost of the asset, determined using the exchange rate for the date of acquisition and the sterling acquisition and the sterling equivalent of the disposal proceeds, determined using the exchange rate for the date of disposal.
[4] *ibid.* s.93(4), as inserted by FA 2000, s.105(1).
[5] *ibid.* s.94(4)(a), as inserted by FA 2000, s.105(1).

in the provisions of sections 22B (first-year allowances), 34 (writing-down allowances), 35 (contributions to expenditure, and hiring of cars), 38C (long life assets-individuals and partnerships), 38D (long life assets - de minimus limits) or 79A (reduction in qualifying use) of the Capital Allowances Act 1990[6]; and

(c) to translate the company's profits and losses of the company's business (or part) for an accounting period from its local currency into sterling.[7]

In a case falling within (a) above, the company is required to translate the receipt or expense into its local currency using the London closing exchange rate for the day on which the company becomes entitled to the receipt or incurs (or is treated as incurring) the expense.[8]

In a case falling within (b) above, the sterling amount is determined by reference to the London closing rate for the date on which the company incurs the capital expenditure.[9]

In a case falling within (c) above, the normal rule is that the profits and losses for the period should be translated into sterling using the London closing rate for the last day of the accounting period in question.[10] There are two exceptions to this rule:

(i) in a case falling within 1. or 2. in the list above, a company may elect to use an average arm's length rate for the period to translate the profits of its business (or relevant part) into sterling. Such an election may be made by notice in writing at any time in the first accounting period for which the company wishes it to have effect. Once made, an election can only be withdrawn with effect from the start of the next accounting period following that in which the company withdraws the election. If a company withdraws an election, it may not again elect to use an average rate before the third anniversary of the date on which the withdrawal took effect.[11]

(ii) in a case falling within 3. or 4. above, where a company uses an average arm's length rate when preparing the accounts of the business (or part), that exchange rate is to be used.[12]

*Change of reporting currency*

**3A–54E**   The legislation does not address what happens where a company changes the currency in which it accounts for the results of all or part of a business and the company moves from one non-sterling currency to another. (The position where a company

---

[6] *ibid.* s.94(4)(b) as inserted by FA 2000, s.105(1).
[7] *ibid.* s.94(3), as inserted by FA 2000, s.105(1).
[8] *ibid.* s.94(4)(a), (8), as inserted by FA 2000, s.105(1).
[9] *ibid.* s.94(4)(b), (8), as inserted by FA 2000, s.105(1).
[10] *ibid.* s.94(3), (8), as inserted by FA 2000, s.105(1).
[11] *ibid.* s.94(5), (6), as inserted by FA 2000, s.105(1).
[12] *ibid.* s.94(7), (8), as inserted by FA 2000, s.105(1).

moves from a sterling local currency to a non-sterling local currency is covered by the legislation and is considered below). Although section 94(4)(a) of the Finance Act 1993 refers to brought forward amounts that are dealt with under section 93(4)(b) of the Finance Act 1993, the definition of "relevant day"[13] does not deal with the exchange rate that should be used where trading losses, management expenses or a non-trading deficit is brought forward to the current period in a currency other than the company's local currency. This is because the definition of "relevant day" in this context is the day on which the company incurs or is treated as incurring the expense. There is nothing within the foreign exchange legislation, or indeed within the Corporation Tax Acts that determines the date on which a brought forward amount should be treated as arising in a future accounting period. The authors understand that where a company changes its reporting currency from one non-sterling currency to another, the Inland Revenue will be prepared to allow any brought forward amounts to be translated into the new local currency using the same procedures that apply where a company moves from a sterling local currency to a non-sterling local currency. These are considered under Transitional rules below.

*Transitional rules*

Where a company, which had previously prepared its tax computations in sterling, **3A–54F** uses a non-sterling local currency for the first time for all or part of its business, brought forward losses under 392B or 393 of the Taxes Act 1988, brought forward management expenses, or brought forward non-trading deficits that relate to that business (or part), are translated into the local currency of the business (or part) using the London closing rate for the last day of the immediately preceding accounting period.[14] Brought forward balances on capital allowance pools are also translated into the company's local currency at that exchange rate.[15]

## VII. DEFERRAL RELIEF

It is possible for a company to elect to defer exchange gains on long-term qualifying **3A–55** debts (both assets and liabilities) which are capital in nature. For these purposes, long term means that the asset or liability had a life of at least one year at the time at which the company acquired the asset or became subject to the liability.[16] Whether the qualifying debt is capital in nature will be determined by reference to tax case law. The fact that a debt is held to be capital in nature will not prevent any exchange gains or losses from being included in computing the company's Schedule D, Case I

---

[13] *ibid.* s.94(8), as inserted by FA 2000, s.105(1).
[14] FA 2000, s.105(2).
[15] *ibid.* s.105(3).
[16] FA 1993, s.143(4).

trading profits as the revenue versus capital distinction has no relevance for the foreign exchange legislation, other than for the purpose of determining a company's entitlement to deferral relief.

In the case of a company which is not a member of a group and which does not have any other associated companies, the maximum amount in respect of which deferral relief can be claimed is the lower of:

(i) the company's net unrealised exchange gains on qualifying capital debts; and

(ii) the company's net exchange gains on all qualifying debts and currency contracts.

The resulting figure is then reduced by an amount equal to 10 per cent of the company's taxable profits for that accounting period, before taking account of group relief and ignoring the deferral claim.[17] A claim for deferral relief must normally be made within two years of the end of the relevant accounting period.[18] Where such a claim is made, the gain is deferred until the following account period when it will be brought into account as an exchange gain accruing in that accounting period. The carried forward gain will be eligible for deferral relief in that next accounting period, subject to the restrictions discussed above.[19]

**3A–56** Where a qualifying debt on which deferral relief has been claimed is replaced, the exchange gain which has been deferred can continue to be eligible for deferral where:

(i) the replacement debt is fixed in amount;

(ii) any amount of the principal, once repaid, cannot be redrawn;

(iii) any interest which is not paid when due is added to the principal amount of the loan on the due date and is repayable on the same terms as the loan principal; and

(iv) the company acquires or becomes subject to the replacement debt in a 60-day period beginning 30 days before it ceases to be a party to the original debt.[20]

If the replacement debt is less than the amount of the original debt, the exchange gain which has been deferred will be pro-rated and the gain which is attributable to the part of the debt which is not replaced will cease to be eligible for deferral relief.[21] It is possible for a debt to be replaced by one or more debts and in this case it will be assumed that an earlier debt takes precedence over a later debt unless a company

---

[17] *ibid.* s.141.
[18] *ibid.* s.139(6).
[19] FA 1993, s.140(3)–(11).
[20] S.I. 1994 No. 3228, reg. 2(2), (3), (10).
[21] *ibid.* reg. 2(4).

elects otherwise.[22] The replacement debt does not have to be in the same currency as the original debt.

The calculation of the amount eligible for deferral is varied where the company has income or chargeable gains which are eligible for double tax credit relief and also where the company is a member of a group. An examination of these provisions is beyond the scope of this book and the reader is referred to the provisions of S.I. 1994 No. 3228, regulations 3 and 4 respectively.

The deferral relief provisions are also varied where a company uses a non-sterling local currency to compute the results of all or part of its business for tax purposes.[23] In such cases deferral relief is calculated by reference to the sterling equivalent of exchange gains and losses for the period, as determined by reference to the company's local currency. These exchange gains and losses are translated into sterling at the exchange rate used to translate the company's results for the period into sterling. When the deferral reverses in the following period the sterling equivalent is found using the exchange rate used for that period to translate the company's results in local currency into sterling. In each case the use of this exchange rate effectively tracks the way in which the sterling equivalent of the company's results is determined.[24]

### Deferral relief—partnerships

Where the partners in a partnership include one or more qualifying companies, the **3A–57** partnership can claim deferral relief for the purposes of determining the foreign exchange gains and losses of the partnership which are allocable to such partners. The amount of any exchange gain which can be deferred will be restricted to that part which is attributable to qualifying companies. When the deferred gain reverses in the following accounting period, the gain will be allocated to the qualifying corporate partners. The effect, therefore, is that each of the partners which is a qualifying company can, in effect, make a deferral claim in respect of that part of the partnership's net exchange gains on long-term capital assets and liabilities which are allocated to it. The Inland Revenue is of the view, however, that a corporate partner cannot make a deferral claim in respect of a gain allocated to it if the partnership has not made a claim. For the purpose of determining the exchange gains of the partnership which are eligible for deferral relief, the rules which apply to groups of companies will not be regarded as applying to the partnership.[25]

Any exchange gains or losses of the partnership which are allocated to a qualifying

---

[22] *ibid.* reg. 2(7), (8).
[23] FA 1993 s.142, as amended by FA 2000, s.106(9), (10), (11). Whilst the side note to s.142 confusingly is still worded "Deferral: non sterling trades", the effect of the FA 2000 amendments is to extend the scope of this section to non-trading activities.
[24] FA 1993, s.142.
[25] SP4/98, paras 30–32.

corporate partner will be ignored for the purpose of determining the exchange gains of that company which are eligible for deferral relief.[1]

## VIII. Irrecoverable Debts, Unremittable Income and Excess Gains and Losses

### Irrecoverable debts

**3A–58**    Where a company is a party to a qualifying debt, whether as a lender or a borrower and all of the outstanding debt could reasonably have been regarded as irrecoverable immediately before the end of an accounting period, the company is treated as if it had ceased to be entitled to the asset or subject to the liability immediately before the end of that accounting period.[2] This means that the exchange gain or loss on the asset or liability will be brought into account for that accounting period but thereafter exchange gains and losses will be ignored. If in a later accounting period all or part of the amount outstanding could reasonably be regarded as becoming recoverable, the company is treated as if it had become entitled to an asset or subject to a liability of an amount equal to that part of the debt.[3] Where only part of the debt is reinstated the amount to be reinstated will be determined by reference to the settlement currency of the debt. If only part of the debt is reinstated and later more of the debt becomes recoverable, the company will be treated as if the nominal amount of the debt outstanding had increased.[4]

If part of a qualifying debt, whether an asset or liability, could be regarded as being irrecoverable immediately before the end of an accounting period (first accounting period) the outstanding debt is reduced by that amount (calculated by reference to the settlement currency of the debt) at the start of the next accounting period. If all or part of that amount outstanding could reasonably be regarded as recoverable at any time after the end of the first accounting period, the nominal amount of the debt outstanding is deemed to have increased at that time. The amount of the increase is again determined by reference to the settlement currency of the debt. If only part of the debt is reinstated and a further part of the outstanding debt becomes recoverable at a later date the nominal amount of the debt is deemed to have increased by a like amount at that time.[5]

[1] *ibid.* para. 31.
[2] FA 1993, s.144(1). S.144 does not define what is meant by irrecoverable but s. 13383 of the Company Taxation Manual states that inspectors will use the same approach as used for the purposes of ICTA 1988, s.74(j).
[3] *ibid.* s.145(1), (2).
[4] FA 1993, s.145(4), (5).
[5] *ibid.* ss. 144(1)–(3) and 145(3)–(5).

### Unremittable income

The calculation of exchange gains and losses is varied where the company has **3A–59** received income which has become unremittable in whole or in part and the company has made a claim for relief from tax on that income under the provisions of section 584 of the Taxes Act 1988. In such cases the exchange gain or loss is calculated on the underlying debt or foreign currency for the accrual period and is deemed to accrue evenly on a daily basis. No exchange gain or loss is regarded as accruing for any day in the period for which the income was unremittable. Where only part of the income is unremittable, exchange gains and losses are reduced in the same way on that part of the underlying debt or foreign currency.[6] If income which was unremittable during an accounting period becomes remittable at any time in that period, that time will be treated as a deemed translation time and exchange gains or losses will be recognised on the underlying debt or foreign currency from that time until the end of the accounting period.[7]

### Excess gains and losses

These provisions apply where:                                        **3A–60**

  (i) a net exchange gain has been recognised on an asset or a liability;
 (ii) the company acquired the asset, or became subject to the liability as a result of an arm's length transaction; and
(iii) when the company ceases to be entitled to the asset or subject to the liability, as a result of an arm's length transaction, it incurs a loss (non-exchange loss) for which no relief is available under the Taxes Acts.[8]

In such cases if the company makes a claim, an exchange loss equal to the lower of the non-exchange loss (as reduced by any non-taxable compensation that the company receives for the loss) and the net exchange gain will be deemed to accrue in the accounting period in which the company ceases to be entitled to the asset or to be subject to the liability.[9] If the company, or another company in its capital gains group, subsequently makes a recovery in respect of the non-exchange loss there will be a claw-back of the relief which has been claimed up to the lower of the recovery or the relief which has been obtained.[10]

The provisions also apply where a company makes a gain (non-exchange gain) on the disposal of an asset or a liability which is not liable to tax under the provisions of

---

[6] *ibid.* Sched. 15, para. 3(4) and S.I. 1994 No. 3227, reg. 3.
[7] S.I. 1994 No. 3227, reg. 3(4).
[8] FA 1993, s.148 and S.I. 1994 No. 3229, reg. 2(1), (2).
[9] S.I. 1994 No. 3229, reg. 2(1), (3).
[10] *ibid.* reg. 3.

the Taxes Acts and it has obtained relief for a net exchange loss on the asset or liability. In this case an exchange gain is deemed to accrue in the accounting period in which the disposal takes place up to the lower of the non-exchange gain or net exchange loss.[11]

Following the introduction of the financial instruments and loan relationships legislation, the above provisions are likely to be of limited application. They may apply to the extent that a non-trading loss on a loan accrued before April 1, 1996, when the loan relationship legislation took effect, and relief for that loss is not available under the provisions of section 253 or 254 of the Taxation of Chargeable Gains Act 1992, or possibly where relief for a loss on a loan is denied under the loan relationship connected party rules (see paragraph 3–63 *et seq.*).[12] It is also possible that the provisions may be in point where a borrower is released from a loan relationship and no tax charge arises on the release under the connected party rules.[13]

## IX. Transitional Rules

**3A–61**     A detailed study of the transitional rules is beyond the scope of this book. As, however, the transitional rules can apply for up to six years (and in some cases for a longer period) from a company's commencement day, the transitional rules cannot be ignored. This section aims to provide an overview of the transitional rules which still have ongoing relevance. These provisions deal with:

— fixed debts where exchange gains and losses fell outside the scope of tax before a company's commencement day;
— fluctuating debts where exchange gains and losses fell outside the scope of tax before a company's commencement day;
— pre-commencement chargeable assets;
— exchange gains and losses on realisation basis assets and liabilities of financial traders and general insurance companies; and
— certain pre-commencement capital losses which a company was able to relieve against certain post commencement foreign exchange gains.

---

[11] *ibid.* reg. 2(4).

[12] The Inland Revenue considers that relief is not available under these provisions where relief for a loss is denied under the loan relationship connected party rules on the grounds that FA 1996, s.80(5) prevents relief from being given for the loss under other provisions of the Taxes Act. In the instant case it is considered that it is arguable that the effect of the regulations is to reduce the amount of a foreign exchange gain which has previously been treated as taxable rather than to give relief for the loan relationship loss *per se* in which case s.80(5) ought not to restrict the relief which is available under the foreign exchange legislation.

[13] This assumes that the regulations would apply in such cases: see the reasoning in the above footnote.

### Fixed debt

The transitional rules apply to fixed debt (both assets and liabilities) to which a  **3A–62**
company was a party at its commencement day where exchange gains and losses on
the debt in question were outside the scope of tax under the old regime. A fixed loan
is defined as a loan which is fixed in both term and amount.[14] Such loans are subject
to what is termed the "kink test" until the loan is repaid.

The intention behind the "kink" test is to ensure that the net exchange gain or loss
on the debt which is brought into charge to tax post commencement under the foreign
exchange regime does not exceed the overall exchange gain or loss on the debt (both
pre and post commencement day). It can, however, give rise to accounting and tax
mismatches. For example, if there is a pre-commencement gain on the loan, relief for
a post commencement loss on the loan would be denied up to the amount of the
pre-commencement gain, to the extent that the loss exceeds the net gain on the loan
which has been taxed under the foreign exchange regime in earlier periods.

The "kink" test continues to apply to a replacement loan where the original loan is
repaid early and the borrower enters into a replacement loan in a foreign currency
within a 60-day period starting 30 days before the original loan was repaid. If the
"kink" test applies to a replacement loan it will only apply for the period of the
original loan and, where the new loan is greater than the old, to an amount of the new
loan which is equal to the original loan.[15] The "kink" test does not apply on a group
basis and thus the "kink" test is brought to an end if the debt in question is assigned
or novated to another group company.

### Fluctuating debt

Transitional rules apply to fluctuating debt which was outside the scope of tax under  **3A–63**
the old regime. Fluctuating debt is any debt which does not satisfy the requirements
of the fixed debt test.[16] Under the transitional rules, fluctuating debt remains outside
the foreign exchange regime for up to six years from a company's commencement
day (unless an election was made to bring such debt within the new regime from the
company's commencement day: the time-limit for this election was the later of 92
days after the company's commencement day or September 21, 1995).

If, however, the amount of the debt increases during this six-year period, including
an increase following an earlier repayment of part of the debt (even if, following the
increase, the amount of the debt is still lower than or equal to the amount of the debt
at the company's commencement day), the whole of the debt is brought within the

---

[14] See S.I. 1994 No. 3226, reg. 3(6)–(9) for the detailed conditions which have to be satisfied.
Certain discounted debt is treated as fixed debt for the purpose of this regulation: see *ibid.*
reg. 3(9).

[15] S.I. 1994 No. 3226, reg. 22.

[16] *ibid.* reg. 3(1).

foreign exchange regime from the date on which the amount of the debt is increased.[17]

Where fluctuating debt comes within the foreign exchange regime before the end of the six-year transitional period, during the remainder of this six-year period the company is permitted to deduct from the exchange gains or losses on the debt the exchange movement on the lowest amount of the debt during the accounting period in question, or if lower, the lowest amount of the debt since the company's commencement day. If a loan is repaid during an accounting period, the lowest amount of the debt will be the lower of the outstanding balance immediately before the loan was repaid, or the lowest amount of the loan since the company's commencement day, and not zero.[18]

EXAMPLE

A Ltd has a calendar year end and had a U.S. $10,000 borrowing at its commencement day on January 1, 1996. The balance outstanding remained unchanged until March 31, 1998 when the loan reduced to U.S. $8,000. It subsequently increased back to U.S. $10,000 on June 30, 1998. The outstanding balance then remained unchanged until June 30, 1999 when it reduced to U.S. $9,000. The loan was repaid on September 30, 1999.

In this case the loan would have come within the FOREX regime on June 30, 1998. Exchange gains and losses on the loan would be reduced by the exchange movement on the lowest amount of the loan during the accounting period, *i.e.* U.S. $8,000 for the year ended December 31, 1998.

In the year to December 31, 1999 the exchange movement on the loan until the loan was repaid on September 30 would be reduced by exchange movements on U.S. $8,000 (as this amount was lower than the lowest amount of the loan during the accounting period).

### Pre-commencement chargeable assets

**3A–64**      These transitional rules apply where an asset was within the charge to corporation tax on capital gains before a company's commencement day. Normally this provision will apply to a debt on a security or an assigned debt. Where foreign currency was a chargeable asset before a company's commencement day this would also come within the scope of these provisions. Under the transitional rules a calculation is done of the capital gain or loss which would have arisen if the asset had been disposed of at market value immediately before the company's commencement day and this amount

---

[17] *ibid.* reg. 3(2), (5).
[18] *ibid.* reg. 3(3), 4.

is treated as a held-over capital gain or loss. A modified "kink" test is applied to the debt over its remaining life, the effect of which is to set off any held-over capital gain or loss against post commencement exchange losses or gains.[19]

Any held-over capital gain or loss which is not dealt with under the "kink" test is taxed as a capital gain or is treated as a capital loss in the accounting period in which the disposal of the asset takes place. Where a held-over capital loss is crystallised, a company can elect to treat the capital loss as a foreign exchange loss. This loss is only available for relief against foreign exchange gains within the company (it is not treated as a non-trading debit) and it cannot be carried back to earlier periods.[20] (This treatment can be contrasted with the transitional rules for chargeable debt under the corporate debt regime. In this case a company can elect to treat held-over capital losses as forming part of its non-trading debits in the accounting period in which the loss is crystallised.)[21]

### Realisation basis trading assets and liabilities

In certain cases a financial trading company or a general insurance company may **3A–65** only have been liable to tax on exchange gains or losses on qualifying assets or liabilities on a realisation basis before the introduction of the foreign exchange legislation. In such cases the normal rule is that a calculation is done of the gain or loss which would have arisen had the asset or liability been disposed of at the value at which it was recorded in the company's accounts immediately before its commencement day and this amount is then held-over. Again, a modified "kink" test is applied to the asset or liability over its remaining life, the effect of which is to set off any held-over gain or loss against any post commencement exchange losses or gains. Any amount which has not been dealt with under the modified "kink" test is brought into account for tax purposes in the accounting period in which the company disposes of the asset or ceases to be subject to the liability.[22] As an alternative a company had the option of spreading any net gain or loss on all its realisation basis assets and liabilities in equal instalments over a six-year period starting with its commencement day. Following the introduction of the corporate debt legislation the time-limit for making this election was extended to September 30, 1996.[23]

### Election to set off certain pre-commencement capital losses against certain post commencement foreign exchange gains

Under the foreign exchange transitional rules it was possible for a company to elect **3A–66** within 92 days of its commencement day (or, if later, by September 21, 1995) to set

---

[19] S.I. 1994 No. 3226, regs 6(3) and 9–14.
[20] *ibid.* reg. 14(5).
[21] FA 1996, Sched. 15, para. 9.
[22] S.I. 1994 No. 3226, regs 7–8 and 10–13.
[23] *ibid.* reg. 15.

off capital losses realised on foreign currency, currency contracts and foreign currency denominated debts against certain post commencement exchange gains. The exchange gains in question are exchange gains on foreign currency assets and currency contracts on which the company would have been liable to tax under the capital gains legislation had the foreign exchange regime not been introduced.[24]

## X. Appendix 1

**3A–67** This Appendix reproduces the debate on Clause 106 of the Finance Bill (now section 106 of the Finance Act 2000) at the Report Stage of the Finance Bill 2000.

### Clause 106

### FOREIGN EXCHANGE GAINS AND LOSSES: USE OF LOCAL CURRENCY

**Mr Flight:** I beg to move amendment No. 155, in page 77, line 11, leave out clause 106.

This is a probing amendment. We have been approached by the Chartered Institute of Taxation and the Law Society, which are still concerned about the wide scope of the wording of proposed new section 135A of the Finance Act 1993. In their opinion, the new provision is still capable of catching many companies that prepare their accounts in foreign currency for perfectly normal, commercial reasons rather than because of tax factors.

Both organisations expressed the concern that the test remains an expected main benefit test as opposed to a purpose test. The question posed is what is the main benefit that might be expected to accrue from exchange gains having to be computed for tax purposes by reference to a particular currency, rather than the relevant question as to what is the main benefit that might be expected to accrue from drawing up commercial accounts in a particular currency. The expected benefits of a transaction is the expected result, whereas a purpose test is a motive test.

A company's motive in choosing to use a particular reporting currency might have been to avoid exchange fluctuations where the majority of its assets or liabilities are denominated in that currency, but, applying the proposed new section 135A, it may be possible to conclude that the expected main benefit of using the currency was that the company would avoid realising an exchange gain under the foreign exchange legislation.

The key concerns about this anti-avoidance provision are whether wider commercial factors can be taken into account and at which time the expected main benefit test is to be applied. Those issues exercised the institute and the Law Society; both expressed

---

[24] *ibid.* reg. 16.

concern that the new test could catch a large number of investment companies that the reforms in clauses 106 and 107 are introduced to assist.

Will the Minister offer assurances that commercial factors can be taken into account, and that the expected benefit is to be judged at the time when a company first prepares its accounts in foreign currency? Will she also confirm that the provisions of the section will not apply when a company is preparing its accounts in foreign currency, in accordance with normal accounting practice, in order to avoid its results being distorted by exchange rate fluctuations? The current provisions are widely drawn, and it would be most welcome and helpful if the Minister would give us a clear statement on the cases to which the anti-avoidance provision might be applied.

**Dawn Primarolo:** The amendment would remove clause 106. That clause contains several provisions to support changes introduced by clause 105 to improve the tax system for international companies. Those changes have been widely welcomed because they will make the United Kingdom a more attractive base for international companies.

As those supporting measures are necessary to enable the new system to fit in with the existing law, I realise that the Opposition's attempt to drop the whole clause is not serious. Indeed, the hon. Member for Arundel and South Downs (Mr. Flight) admitted that the amendment is a probing one, and that the real concern is about the part of clause 106 that deals with the new anti-avoidance measures in the clause: the new section 135A of the Finance Act 1993, designed to stop the new rules established under clause 105 being exploited to avoid tax.

As the hon. Gentleman knows, the effect of section 135A is to undo the application of the new rules where the main benefit that might be expected to accrue to a company from using a particular currency in its accounts is that a taxable currency gain would not be recognised. In Committee, the Government made it clear that the rule will apply only where net exchange gains would be cancelled out. That demonstrates that we are interested in the overall position of the company and not in the effect of individual transactions considered in isolation.

The hon. Gentleman continues to express concerns about the scope of the rule, however, so I shall try to reassure him with some comments that I prepared earlier— as they say on "Blue Peter". These comments will also cover points of interest to others who read our proceedings.

Let me emphasise first that the new rule is intended to catch avoidance. It is not aimed at any particular type of company or business, but seeks to ensure that the new system of calculating tax, based on a company's accounts, cannot be abused to avoid tax. So trading companies and investment companies conducting their business in a normal, commercial way will not be affected. The point of the test is to establish whether the main benefit that might be expected to accrue to a company from the structuring and accounting of assets and liabilities in a particular currency is that a net exchange gain would be avoided.

The wording of the test allows for commercial considerations to be taken into account. For example, even if the currency adopted in the company's accounts was particularly weak or strong, if it made commercial sense to use that particular currency and the company's assets and liabilities in that currency were broadly matched, no net exchange gains would have been expected to have been avoided, and the section would not apply.

Where a net gain has been avoided, the test would still be whether the main benefit from using the currency was the furtherance of the commercial purposes of the company or the avoidance of that exchange gain. The Government believe that a company will normally be able to judge whether it would pass or fail this test. In particular, a company will know whether the decision to account in a particular currency makes commercial sense or whether the structuring and accounting of the company's affairs has been skewed to avoid generating taxable exchange gains.

To conclude, let me reiterate that the new rule is intended to tackle avoidance. It will not affect legitimate business undertaken by any company, whether that company is a trading company or an investment company. However, it will affect companies that aim to exploit the new rules for a tax benefit.

I hope that those remarks clarify the scope of the provision and give the hon. Gentleman some of the reassurances that he and others seek on the implementation of the clause. The Inland Revenue will also be providing some written guidance on how the provision will be applied. Given this clarification, perhaps the hon. Gentleman will now feel able to withdraw his amendment. It is only regrettable that we did not have an opportunity to cover these points more fully in Committee.

**Mr. Flight:** I thank the Paymaster General for her helpful comments. I beg to ask leave to withdraw the amendment.

*Amendment, by leave, withdrawn.*[25]

---

[25] Hansard 19 July 2000, columns 478, 479, 480.

CHAPTER 3B

# TAXATION OF FINANCIAL INSTRUMENTS

This chapter considers the taxation treatment of financial instrument derivative con- **3B–01** tracts. Parts I to VI consider the tax treatment of those derivative contracts which fall within the Finance Act 1994 financial instruments legislation and Part VII addresses the taxation treatment of those financial instrument contracts which, for whatever reason, fall outside this legislation. An explanation of the more common types of derivative contracts is given in an Appendix to this Chapter and contracts that are discussed in the Appendix appear in italics in the text.

## I. Finance Act 1994 Financial Instruments Legislation: An Overview

The financial instruments legislation was introduced by the Finance Act 1994 and **3B–02** took effect from the start of a company's first accounting period beginning on or after March 23, 1995.[1] The date that a company came within the charge to the financial instruments legislation is termed its 'commencement day'.[2] Transitional rules apply in certain cases where a company was a party to an interest rate contract or interest rate

---

[1] FA 1994, s.147(4)(b) and S.I.1994 No. 3225 which appointed March 23 as the appointed day for the purposes of s.147.
[2] FA 1994, s.147(4)(a).

option at its Commencement Day. The scope of these transitional rules is considered in Part V below.

**3B–03**     The financial instruments legislation applies to **interest rate contracts, interest rate options, currency contracts, currency options, debt contracts and debt options to which a qualifying company** is a party. Each of the terms in bold is considered in Part II below, as are the conditions which have to be satisfied in order for a contract or option to fall within the financial instruments legislation. Where a contract or option falls within the financial instruments legislation, it is referred to as a **qualifying contract**. The broad intention of the financial instruments legislation is that profits and losses on qualifying contracts should be recognised for tax purposes on the basis on which these are reflected in a company's accounts. Two accounting policies are permitted: an acceptable accruals and an acceptable mark to market accounting policy. In order for a company's accounting treatment to be followed for tax purposes, first, the accounting policy used for the contract must be in accordance with the normal accounting practice by reference to which the company's accounts are prepared and secondly, the accounting policy must meet certain conditions specified by the financial instruments legislation. These conditions are considered further in Part III below.

### Intra-group transfers

**3B–04**     Unlike the loan relationships legislation there are no provisions that treat a qualifying contract as continuing where the benefit of a contract is transferred between companies within a United Kingdom group. Thus the transfer of the contract will be treated as a disposal by the transferor and as an acquisition by the transferee.

### Trading v. non-trading split

**3B–05**     If a company is a party to a qualifying contract wholly for the purposes of its trade, any profits or losses on the qualifying contract will be included as part of the company's Schedule D Case I trading profits.[3] If a company is a party to a qualifying contract wholly for non-trading purposes, any profits or losses on arising on that contract will be included as part of the company's profits or losses arising on its non-trading loan relationships.[4] Where a company is a party to a qualifying contract partly for trading purposes, and partly for non-trading purposes, any profits or losses

---

[3] *ibid.* s.159. s.159 takes precedence over ICTA 1988, s.74: FA 1994, s.159(4).

[4] *ibid.* s.160. The ways in which such profits and losses are respectively taxed and relieved is considered in paragraphs 3—15 to 3—21 of the main work.

on the qualifying contract are apportioned between trading and non-trading use on a just and reasonable basis.[5]

### Special provisions

There are provisions within the financial instruments legislation to modify the tax treatment for insurance companies which are carrying on life assurance business and also to determine how the taxable profits of partnerships, which include one or more qualifying companies, are to be calculated. These provisions are considered in Part VI below.

**3B–06**

### Anti-avoidance provisions

The financial instruments legislation contains a number of anti-avoidance provisions to counter transfers of value between associated companies, non-arm's length transactions and, in certain cases, to counter contracts being entered into with counterparties resident in tax havens. These provisions are considered in Part IV below.

**3B–07**

### II. QUALIFYING COMPANIES AND QUALIFYING CONTRACTS

### Qualifying companies

The financial instruments legislation applies to all United Kingdom resident companies and United Kingdom branches of non-resident companies[6] except open ended investment companies and authorised unit trusts (see Part VI below). The provisions within the financial instruments legislation dealing with currency contracts and options do not apply to approved investment trusts (see Part VI below).

**3B–08**

---

[5] *ibid.* s.159(3) and s.160(1).

[6] Qualifying company is defined in FA 1994, s.154. The definition of a qualifying company within s.154 is not limited to U.K. resident companies. In order for the financial instruments legislation to apply, however, a company is required to have an accounting period, see ss.155 to 173. An accounting period is not defined in FA 1994 and thus the definition within ICTA 1988, s.12 applies (since this definition applies for corporation tax purposes) which in turn means that the company must be within the charge to corporation tax. The result is thus that the scope of the legislation is limited to United Kingdom resident companies and United Kingdom branches of non-resident companies. The same view is expressed in section 5.1 of the Inland Revenue's Explanatory Statement on the Foreign Exchange and Financial Instruments Legislation (Explanatory Statement).

### Qualifying contracts

**3B–09**    The financial instruments legislation applies to interest rate contracts, interest rate options, currency contracts, currency options, debt contracts, and debt options. In each case specific requirements have to be satisfied in order for a particular contract or option to fall within the financial instruments legislation. The requirements that have to be satisfied in each case are considered below.

### Interest rate contracts

**3B–10**    In order for an interest rate contract to be treated as a qualifying contract for the purposes of the financial instruments legislation, the key requirement is that under the terms of the contract, whether unconditionally or subject to certain conditions being fulfilled, the company is entitled to receive, or is obliged to make, at a time specified in the contract, a variable rate payment.[7] This is defined as a payment, the amount of which falls to be determined wholly or mainly by applying a variable interest rate to the notional contract principal amount for a period specified in the contract.[8] This definition would thus cover, for example, the floating rate payments due under the terms of a fixed/floating *interest rate swap*. The financial instruments legislation does not define "variable interest rate" but in its Explanatory Statement the Inland Revenue states that this means a rate of interest which may vary over time, *e.g.* LIBOR.[9] The notional principal amount does not have to be constant over the life of the contract and can be increased or reduced.[10]

At the same time, all other payments which a company may make or receive under the terms of the contract must fall within one of the following:

1. another variable rate payment.[11] This would be appropriate in the case of a *basis swap* where payments on one floating rate basis are exchanged for payments on another floating rate basis; or

---

[7] FA 1994, s.149(1)(a), (2).

[8] *ibid.* s.149(6). In section 6.12 of its Explanatory Statement the Inland Revenue states that under the provisions of the Interpretation Act 1978, the singular is to be taken as including the plural and thus the reference to a specified time and a specified period includes a number of specified times and specified periods. The Inland Revenue also states that the reference to 'wholly or mainly' has been included to ensure that, for example, contracts are not excluded simply because payments due under the terms of the contract need to be grossed up to take account of withholding tax.

[9] Inland Revenue Explanatory Statement section 6.12.

[10] This is because the provisions of FA 1994, s.149(2) require the payment to be calculated by applying a specified variable interest rate to a notional principal amount for a time specified in the contract. There is nothing to prevent a different principal amount being used for a different period. Section 6.12 of the Explanatory Statement confirms that the definition in FA 1994, s.149(2) is intended to cover amortising swaps.

[11] FA 1994, s.149(1)(b), (2).

2. a fixed rate payment.[12] This is defined as a payment, the amount of which falls to be determined (wholly or mainly) by applying a fixed rate of interest to the notional contract principal amount for a specified period [13]; or

3. a fixed payment. This is defined as a payment of a fixed amount which is specified in the contract;[14] or

4. certain other payments made in connection with the acquisition or disposal of the contract.[15]

Examples of contracts that fall within the definition of interest rate contracts are *interest rate swaps; caps, floors* and *collars; forward rate agreements;* and *interest rate futures.* Each of these contracts is explained in the Appendix to this Chapter.

### Interest rate options

The definition of an interest rate option includes an option to enter into an interest **3B–11** rate contract (*e.g.* a *swaption*) and an option over an interest rate option. In order for an interest rate option to be a qualifying contract for the purposes of the financial instruments legislation, the only permitted payments which may be made under the terms of the option are those set out in section 151 of the Finance Act 1994.[16]

The financial instruments legislation does not define an 'option' and thus this term must take its normal meaning. The Inland Revenue considers that where a contract is automatically exercised it will not fall to be treated as an option for the purposes of the financial instruments legislation.[17]

### Currency contract

Currency contracts are the only financial instruments that are also dealt with under **3B–12** the foreign exchange legislation. In order for a contract to fall within the definition of

---

[12] *ibid.* s149(1)(b), (3).

[13] *ibid.* s.149(6). In section 6.12 of its Explanatory Statement the Inland Revenue states that under the Interpretation Act 1978 references to the singular include the plural. Thus this definition would cover a number specified periods. In the same section the Inland Revenue also states that the reference to wholly or mainly is intended to ensure that contracts are not excluded simply because, for example, payments need to be grossed up to take account of withholding tax. The Revenue also states in section 6.12 that a fixed rate interest would include a specified rate, *e.g.* 8%, or the fixed yield on a specified Treasury bond (this does not have to be expressed in the contract has a percentage amount).

[14] FA 1994, s.149(1)(b), (3), (6).

[15] *ibid.* s.149(1)(b) and s.151. These payments are common to all qualifying contracts and are considered at 3B–24 below.

[16] *ibid.* s.149(5). These payments are common to all qualifying contracts and are considered under the heading 'other payments' at 3B–24 below.

[17] See section 6.5 of its Explanatory Statement.

a currency contract under the financial instruments legislation it is necessary that, under the terms of the contract, the qualifying company:

1. becomes entitled to a right to receive and subject to a duty to receive payment at a specified time of a specified amount of one currency (the first currency); and
2. becomes entitled to a right and subject to a duty to pay in exchange and at the same time a specified amount of another currency (the second currency).[18]

This wording effectively tracks the provisions of section 126(1) of the Finance Act 1993 (see 3A–14 of this Supplement).

The above the definition would thus cover a *forward currency contract,* a *currency future,* as well as the exchange of currency that takes place where a *currency swap* is unwound.

In its Explanatory Statement the Inland Revenue states that 'specified time' would cover a number of specified times (on the basis that, under the Interpretation Act 1978, the singular includes the plural). The definition would thus also cover an *amortising currency swap* so long as the amortisation profile was set out in the terms of the swap. The Revenue also states that it does not matter if the payments which each of the parties is due to make under the terms of the contract are in fact made on different dates; all that is required in its view is that the entitlement to receive and the obligation to make a payment must arise at the same time.[19]

For the purposes of the financial instruments legislation, as well as the foreign exchange legislation, it does not matter if a currency contract is settled by a payment equal to the difference between the two currency payments covered by the contract.[20] A contract will also still be a qualifying contract even if it does not provide for an exchange of currencies to take place but, instead, provides that the contract is to be settled by a compensation payment equal to the difference between the two currency payments by reference to which the contract is written, as calculated at the settlement date.[21]

Example

X PLC has entered into a forward purchase of US $1,000,000 in return for a sterling payment. The contract is to be settled by a payment equal to the differ-

---

[18] FA 1994, s.150(2).
[19] See sections 6.12 and 6.13 of the Explanatory Statement.
[20] FA 1993, s.126(1A) and FA 1994, s.150(9). Where a currency contract is settled by a payment equal to the difference at the settlement date between the two currency payments due under the terms of the contract, any exchange gains and losses that have been recognised over the life of the contract under the foreign exchange legislation are reversed in the accounting period in which the contract is terminated: FA 1993, s.146.
[21] FA 1994, s.150(11), (12).

ence between the contract price and the spot price at the date of settlement. The contract price is £1 = US $1.55. The actual exchange rate on the date that the contract matures is £1 = US $1.60. As the price of the US $ has moved against X PLC, it makes a payment to the counterparty of £20,161 which is the difference between the contract price and the current spot price.

The foreign exchange legislation only deals with exchange gains and losses on the currency payments due under the contract and it is not prescriptive as to what other payments may be included under the terms of the contract. The financial instruments legislation, however, specifies what other payments may be included under the terms of a currency contract. These are:

(i) an initial exchange of currencies at the date at which the contract takes effect.[22] This would cover currency swaps where, typically, there would be an initial exchange of currencies at the start of the contract and a re-exchange of currencies when the swap terminates;

(ii) payments and receipts determined wholly or mainly by applying a specified interest rate for a specified time to a specified amount of the first and second currencies.[23] This provision would thus cover swap differential payments over the life of a currency swap. There is no requirement in this case that either of the specified rates of interest must be a variable rate of interest; and

(iii) certain payments made or received in connection with the acquisition or disposal of a currency contract.[24].

## Currency option

The definition of a currency option includes:

3B–13

(i) an option to enter into a currency contract (*e.g.* an option to enter into a forward currency contract)[25];

(ii) an option to enter into an option over a currency contract.[1]

(iii) an option to acquire a specified amount of one currency in return for a payment of a specified amount in another currency (e.g. where a company has an option to buy or sell a specified amount of a foreign currency)[2]; and

---

[22] *ibid.* s.150(4), (5).

[23] *ibid.* s.150(3). A specified rate of interest is defined as a rate of the value which at any time is that of a specified rate interest: s.150(5).

[24] *ibid.* s.150(1)(b) and s.151. These payments are common to all qualifying contracts and are discussed under the heading "other payments" at 3B–24 below.

[25] *ibid.* s.150(6).

[1] *ibid.* s.150(6).

[2] *ibid.* s.150(7).

(iv) a conditional currency contract; that is a currency contract which will come into effect where a specified condition (or specified conditions) are satisfied.[3]

In order for a currency option to be treated as a qualifying contract for the purposes of the financial instruments legislation, the payments which are due under the terms of the option must fall within those permitted by section 151 of the Finance Act 1994.[4]

## Debt contracts

**3B–14**    In the marketplace, debt contracts are written both by reference to 'actual' loan relationships and also to 'notional' loan relationships.[5] To deal with this there are two definitions of debt contracts set out in the financial instruments legislation to cover each of these two types of debt contract.

*Debt contracts written by reference to "actual" loan relationships*

**3B–15**    For these purposes a contract is a debt contract if, not being an interest rate contract or option or a currency contract or option;

1. it is a contract under which, whether unconditionally or subject to conditions being fulfilled, a qualifying company has any entitlement, or is subject to any duty, to become a party to a loan relationship; and
2. the only transfers of money or money's worth for which the contract provides (apart from those that will be made under the loan relationship) fall within the following categories[6]:

(i) a payment of an amount representing the price for becoming a party to the relationship. This provision would apply where the contract covers the purchase or sale of a loan relationship and the contract is settled by the delivery of that loan relationship[7];

(ii) a payment of an amount determined by reference to the value at any time of the money debt by reference to which the relationship subsists. This provision is intended to cover cases where the seller has an option to make a cash

---

[3] *ibid.* s.150(8).

[4] *ibid.* s.150(6), (7). The payments falling within s.151 are common to all qualifying contracts and are considered under the heading 'other payments' at 3B–24 below.

[5] For example, LIFFE gilts and bond futures are written by reference to notional gilts and bonds and are required to be settled by the delivery respectively of gilts or bonds that are listed on a list maintained by the Exchange.

[6] *ibid.* s.150A(1).

[7] *ibid.* s.150A(5)(a).

payment equal to the market value of the debt securities, as opposed to the delivery of the debt securities in question[8];

(iii) a settlement payment of an amount determined by reference to the difference at specified times between:

(a) the price for becoming a party to the relationship; and

(b) the value of the money debt by reference to which the relationship subsists, or (if the relationship were in existence) would subsist.[9]

This provision would cover a case where a debt contract is net settled (i.e., a payment is made by one party that is equal to the difference between the contract price and the then value of the underlying loan relationship

(iv) certain payments made or received in connection with the acquisition or disposal of the debt contract.[10]

The definition of a debt contract is extended to cover an entitlement to become a party or a duty to become a party to an equivalent loan relationship and an entitlement to receive or a duty to make one or more payments falling within (i) to (iii) above.[11]

*Contracts written by reference to "notional" loan relationships*

In this case a contract will be a debt contract if it is does not fall within the definition discussed at 3B–15 above, it is not an interest rate contract or option or a currency contract or option and: **3B–16**

1. it is a contract under which, whether unconditionally or subject to conditions being fulfilled, a qualifying company has any entitlement, or is subject to any duty, to become treated as a person with rights and liabilities corresponding to those of a party to a loan relationship[12]; and

2. the only transfers of money or money's worth for which the contract provides are:

(i) a settlement payment of an amount determined by reference to the difference at specified times between —

(a) the price for becoming a treated as a person with rights and liabilities corresponding to those of a party to a loan relationship; and

(b) the value of the money debt by reference to which the relationship subsists or (if the relationship existed) would subsist. [13]

---

[8] *ibid.* s.150A(5)(b).

[9] *ibid.* s.150A(5)(c).

[10] *ibid.* s.150A(1), (5) and s.151. The permitted payments under s.151 are common to all qualifying contracts and are considered under the heading 'other payments' at 3B–24 below.

[11] *ibid.* s.150(3).

[12] *ibid.* s.150A(2)(a).

[13] *ibid.* s.150A(2)(b), (6).

This provision would cover the case where a contract that is written by reference to a notional loan relationship is settled by a payment equal to the difference between the market value of the notional loan relationship and the 'purchase price' of that notional relationship under the terms of the debt contract, as well as variation margin payments over the life of a debt futures contract; and

(ii) certain payments or receipts made in connection with the acquisition or disposal of the debt contract.[14]

The definition of this type of debt contract is also extended to cover an entitlement or a duty to become a party to an equivalent 'notional' loan relationship under the provisions of section 150A(4) of the Finance Act 1994. This states that the provisions of section 150A(3) will apply for the purposes of contracts written by reference to notional loan relationships in the same way as they apply to contracts written by reference to actual loan relationships. Section 150A(3)(b) in turn provides for certain cash payments to be made under the terms of a debt contract which is written by reference to an actual loan relationship and these payments are set out in section 150A(5). These payments are discussed at 3B–15 at 2.(i) to (iii) above. It is considered that such payments are not permissible in the case of a contract that is written by reference to a notional loan relationship. This is because section 150A(2)(b) provides that the only payments that are permitted under the terms of such a contract are those set out in subsection (6) (see 3B–2 above) and section 151. Section 150A(6) does not cross refer to subsection (4) and thus it would appear that the effect of the wording within subsection (4) is merely to apply the provisions of subsection (3), in so far as they relate to a contract written by reference to an entitlement or a duty to become treated as a party to an equivalent notional loan relationship. Further support for this conclusion can be drawn from the fact that the provisions of subsection (5)(c)(ii) in effect reproduce the provisions of subsection (6). By contrast the provisions of section 150A(1)(b), which deal with contracts written by reference to actual loan relationships, specifically include payments made under subsection (5) within the definition of permitted payments.

### Other provisions in a debt contract

**3B–17**  Where a contract contains provisions relating to a debt contract and provisions which have effect for other purposes, any provisions within the contract that relate to a debt contract are treated as a separate contract for all purposes of the financial instruments legislation. Any payments due under the contract that cannot be attributed either to the debt contract element or to the other provisions contained within the contract are to be apportioned between these two elements of the contract on a just

---

[14] *ibid.* s.151. These are common to all qualifying contracts and are considered under the heading "other payments" at 3B–24 below.

and reasonable basis.[15] In section 13482 of the Company Tax Manual, the Inland Revenue states that, *inter alia*, this subsection would apply where loan relationships are issued with warrants which give the holder rights to subscribe for additional loan relationships, so that any profit or loss arising on such warrants is taxed under the financial instruments legislation.

The effect of the provisions of section 150A(8) of the Finance Act 1994 is that a debt contract will not be prevented from being treated as a debt contract where it contains other provisions, even if those other provisions would not fall within the definition of qualifying payments for the purposes of the financial instruments legislation (so long as the non-qualifying payments in question do not relate to the debt contract element of the contract). Further, where a contract contains provisions relating to a debt contract and provisions relating to another contract which falls within the financial instruments legislation, as the debt contract element of the contract is treated as a separate contract for all purposes of the financial instruments legislation, this in turn will mean that the other part of the contract will also fall within the financial instruments legislation, assuming that it satisfies the necessary conditions for the appropriate qualifying contract.

*Exception for debt contracts over certain convertible and indexed securities*

The definition of a loan relationship for the purposes of the debt contract provisions **3B–18** contained within the financial instruments legislation is the same as that used for the purposes of the loan relationships legislation (see paragraph 3–07 of the main text), except that the following are not treated as loan relationships:

1. any loan relationship represented by an asset to which section 92 of the Finance Act 1996 applies (convertible securities: see 3–41 to 3–46 of the main text)[16]; or
2. any loan relationship to which section 93 of the Finance Act 1996 applies (securities indexed to chargeable assets: see 3–47 to 3–53 of the main text).[17]

In order for a debt contract over a convertible security, or a security indexed to chargeable assets, to fall outside the financial instruments legislation, it would appear that the conditions of sections 92 or 93 of the Finance Act 1996, as appropriate, must be satisfied as regards the company which has agreed to sell the loan relationship under the terms of the debt contract. One of the conditions of each of these sections is that any gain realised on the sale of the loan relationship in question must not be included as part of the holder's Schedule D Case I trading profits. This effectively means that, in order for a debt contract over such loan relationships to fall outside the

---

[15] *ibid.* s.150A(8), (9).
[16] *ibid.* s.150A(10)(a).
[17] *ibid.* s.150A(10)(b).

financial instruments legislation from the standpoint of the company that has contracted to buy the loan relationship (the purchaser):

1. the counterparty to the contract must not be a company which is carrying on a financial trade or a general insurance company; and
2. any gain or loss on the underlying loan relationship, were it to be acquired by the purchaser, would not be taken into account in computing the purchaser's Schedule D Case I trading profits.

If a debt contract that is written by reference to a convertible security, or a security that is linked to the value of a chargeable asset, falls outside the financial instruments legislation, in the authors' view the contract falls to be treated as a contract over a qualifying corporate bond for the purposes of section 115 of the Taxation of Chargeable Capital Gains Act 1992, so long as the contract is a contract to acquire the securities in question. This is because a section 92 or section 93 of the Finance Act 1996 security is still treated as a loan relationship and is only subject to corporation tax on chargeable gains by virtue of the provisions of section 92(4) and section 93(4) respectively. The provisions of these subsections only apply to the *actual* loan relationship and do not govern the treatment of a contract written by reference to that loan relationship. As such assets are otherwise treated as loan relationships it is considered that they will be treated for all purposes of the Taxation of Chargeable Gains Act 1992 as qualifying corporate bonds by virtue of the provisions of section 117(A1) of the Taxation of Chargeable Gains Act 1992 where the provisions of section 92(4) and 93(4) do not apply. The contract in turn will be exempt from corporation tax on capital gains by virtue of the provisions of section 115 of the Taxation of Chargeable Gains Act 1992 provided that it is a contract to acquire the convertible or indexed security in question.

*Settlement in money's worth*

**3B–19**     Where all or part of a payment due under the terms of a debt contract is settled by the transfer of money's worth having a value equal to the payment, or part, in question this is treated as a payment of that amount.[18]

*Interaction with the loan relationships legislation*

**3B–20**     This is considered in Part III below at 3B–55.

## Debt options

**3B–21**     A debt option is defined as an option to enter into a contract which would be a debt contract, or an option to enter into such an option. In order for a debt

---

[18] *ibid.* s.150A(11).

option to be treated as a qualifying option for the purposes of the financial instruments legislation, the only payments which are permitted under the terms of the option are payments falling within section 151 of the Finance Act 1994 (see 3B–24 below).[19] It is permissible for these payments to be settled in whole or in part in money's worth.[20]

*Debt options over certain convertible and indexed securities*

As in the case of debt contracts, a loan relationship over an asset which falls within **3B–22** section 92 or section 93 of the Finance Act 1996 is not treated as a loan relationship for the purposes of section 150A of the Finance Act 1994.[21] The conditions that have to be satisfied in order for the exclusion to apply are discussed at 3B–18 above. For the same reasons as are set out at 3B–18 above, it is considered that options that are written by reference to section 92 or section 93 of the Finance Act 1996 assets will be treated as options over qualifying corporate bonds and thus any gain or loss on such options will fall outside the charge to corporation tax on chargeable gains by virtue of the provisions of section 115 of the Taxation of Chargeable Gains Act 1992.

*Interaction with the loan relationships legislation*

This is considered in Part III below at 3B–55. **3B–23**

## Other payments

An interest rate contract or option, a currency contract or option or a debt contract **3B–24** or option may include the following provisions:

1. a payment of a premium to enter into the contract or option[22];
2. a payment of a reasonable fee for arranging the contract or option[23];
3. a payment of reasonable costs incurred in respect of the contract or option.[24] The Inland Revenue has stated in section 6.1 of its Explanatory Statement that this wording, *inter alia*, would cover a reasonable fee paid by a qualifying company for a guarantee. In the same section the Inland Revenue states that where a guarantor takes over obligations under a contract under the terms of a guarantee, the payments made by the guarantor will fall within

---

[19] *ibid.* s.150A(7) and s.151.
[20] *ibid.* s.150A(11).
[21] *ibid.* s150A(10).
[22] *ibid.* s.151(1).
[23] *ibid.* s.151(2)(a).
[24] *ibid.* s.151(2)(b).

the provisions of the financial instruments legislation where the guarantor completely takes over the contract;

4. a payment for securing, or made in consequence of, the variation or termination of the contract or option[25]; and

5. a compensation payment for, or made in consequence of, a failure to comply with the contract or option.[1]

### Effect of non-qualifying payments

**3B–25**   If amounts are due or payable under the terms of a contract or option and such amounts do not fall within the scope of the permitted payments for the type of contract or option in question, the contract or option will still fall within the financial instruments legislation, provided that the present value of such payments is small when compared to the present value of all permitted payments.[2] This calculation is carried out at the date the contract is entered into or, if later, the date that the terms of the option or contract are varied to include the non-qualifying payment or payments.[3] For the purposes of this calculation any payments due under the contract are treated as positive and are aggregated with any receipts due under the terms of the contract. Where the contract provides for a net payment to be made of the difference between two amounts, for the purposes of this provision the payment is taken as a payment equal to the aggregate of those two amounts.[4] The legislation does not address how such calculations are to be performed where the details of the payments that might be due under the terms of the contract are not known, for example in the case of an interest rate cap or a cash settled debt contract.

The financial instruments legislation does not define "small". In the Committee Stage Debate on the 1994 Finance Bill the Economic Secretary to the Treasury stated that:

> ". . . I would normally expect a value to be small if it was less than 5% of the aggregate value of the qualifying payments. That does not rule out the possibility of a company successfully arguing that a value of greater than 5% is small on the facts of a particular case." [5]

In its Explanatory Statement the Inland Revenue has said that, where both parties to the contract are qualifying companies, and this point is in dispute, they may exercise

---

[25] *ibid.* s.151(2)(c).
[1] *ibid.* s.151(2)(d).
[2] *ibid.* s.152(1).
[3] *ibid.* s152(3).
[4] *ibid.* s.152(2).
[5] Hansard February 3, 1994 col.51.

a right of joint appeal to the Commissioners to ensure that the same decision is binding on both companies.[6]

If a non-qualifying payment is regarded as being "small", such that the contract or option still falls within the financial instruments legislation, the non-qualifying payment itself will be disregarded for all purposes of the financial instruments legislation.[7] As the non-qualifying payment is ignored for all purposes of the financial instruments legislation, this means that the anti-double counting provisions of section 173 of the Finance Act 1994 will not apply and thus the taxpayer will not be prevented from being able to obtain relief for the payment under other provisions of the Tax Acts. At the same time, the party to which the payment is made could still be liable to tax on that payment under other provisions of the Tax Acts. A payment or receipt that is ignored under the provisions of section 152 is more likely to be relievable or taxable under other provisions of the Tax Acts where the company entered into the contract for trading purposes.

If, however, the non-qualifying payment is not small, the entire contract or option will fall outside the financial instruments legislation. In this case, if the company entered into the contract or option for trading purposes, any profit or loss on the contract would be generally be included in computing its Schedule D Case I trading profits under general principles. In other cases, any gain or loss may be included in computing the company's capital gains on which corporation tax is payable or, possibly, may be dealt with under the provisions of Schedule D Case VI. The treatment of derivative contracts that fall outside the financial instruments legislation are considered in more detail in Part VII below.

## Netting of payments

Section 13473 of the Company Tax Manual states that the netting of payments due **3B–26** under the terms of a qualifying contract, so that only a single payment is made either to or by the qualifying company, will not prevent the contract from being treated as a qualifying contract.

Where a company enters into a number of derivative contracts with the same **3B–27** counterparty, each transaction would normally be governed by the terms of the same International Swaps and Derivatives Association (ISDA) Master Agreement between the two parties. On one view, each derivative could be regarded as forming part of the same contract. At 6.7 to 6.10 of its Explanatory Statement the Inland Revenue states:

---

[6] See section 6.16 of the Explanatory Statement.
[7] FA 1994, s.152(1).

### Q. What Is The Treatment If Payments Between The Same Counterparties Over A Number Of Contracts Are Netted Under The Terms Of A Master Agreement?

6.7 The Revenue have considered the question of netting of payments in the context of the Master Agreement of the International Swaps and Derivatives Association. Although the Master Agreement and all Confirmations which govern the transactions are to form a single agreement between the parties, the Revenue's view is that prior to default, each transaction may fairly be regarded as being a separate agreement giving rise to a separate profit or loss.

6.8 This analysis is capable of applying equally where there is an election for netting under the terms of the Master Agreement on the basis that, in such a case, the transactions may be regarded as involving constructive payments of the gross amounts.

6.9 The analysis does not, however, run counter to the view that in certain events, a single payment flows in respect of all agreements between the same counterparties under the netting provisions contained in the ISDA Master Agreement.

6.10 The position under other Master Agreements may be less certain, particularly if, every time a fresh transaction is entered into, that agreement seeks to subsume that transaction into previous transactions between the same parties and under the same Master Agreement so as to produce a single resulting agreement. However, provided it is possible to compute separately the components of net cash flows and rights and obligations under such a Master Agreement and allocate them to the individual transactions, the legislation will be applied to individual qualifying contracts in the same way that it would have applied had the individual transaction been wholly free-standing.

### III. RECOGNITION OF PROFITS AND LOSSES

**3B–28**     The financial instruments legislation recognises profits and losses arising on qualifying contracts as a result of qualifying payments, and in the case of qualifying contracts that are accounted for on a mark to market basis, as a result of a change in the market value of the contract. Profits and losses on qualifying contracts are normally recognised for tax purposes on the same basis as they are recognised in a company's accounts, assuming that the company adopts an acceptable accruals or an acceptable mark to market accounting policy for the qualifying contract in question. This Part considers the meaning of qualifying payments, the conditions which have to be satisfied in order for an accruals or mark to market accounting policy to satisfy the requirements of the financial instruments legislation and finally the interaction of the financial instruments legislation with respectively the foreign exchange and loan relationships legislation.

## Qualifying payments

These are the payments made or received under the terms of a qualifying contract **3B–29** which are taken into account in computing profits and losses on a qualifying contract for the purposes of the financial instruments legislation.[8]

### *Interest rate contracts and interest rate options*

In both cases, the definition of qualifying payments is the same as the payments **3B–30** that are permitted under the terms of respectively, an interest rate contract[9] or an interest rate option.[10]

### *Currency contracts*

The definition of qualifying payments under a currency contract covers the pay- **3B–31** ments that are permitted under the terms of a currency contract, except that an exchange of currency is not treated as a qualifying payment for the purposes of the financial instruments legislation.[11] If, however, the contract is settled by a payment equal to the difference between the two currency payments due under the terms of the contract, the settlement payment is treated as a qualifying payment.[12] The reason for this difference in treatment is because exchange gains and losses on currency contracts are dealt with under the foreign exchange legislation. If a currency contract is settled by a payment equal to the difference between the two currency payments due under the terms of the contract, any net exchange gains or losses that have been recognised over the life of the contract under the foreign exchange legislation are reversed in the accounting period in which the contract is terminated as the termination payment is dealt with under the financial instruments legislation.[13] The interaction of the financial instruments and foreign exchange legislation is considered at 3B–48 below.

In addition, where a company recognises a forward premium or forward discount on a currency contract in its accounts, this forward premium or discount is treated as a qualifying payment that is payable or receivable when the exchange of currency takes place.[14] Typically, a forward premium or discount will be recognised where a

---

[8] *ibid.* s.153.

[9] *ibid.* s.153(1)(a), (d).

[10] *ibid.* s.153(1)(d).

[11] *ibid.* s.153(1)(b), (d).

[12] *ibid.* s.153(1)(b).

[13] See FA 1993, s.146 and FA 1994, ss. 155 and 161. The termination of a qualifying contract is considered further in 3B–42 to 3B–44 below.

[14] FA 1994, s.153(4), (5).

company revalues a currency contract in its accounts and accounts for that contract using an acceptable accruals accounting policy. This treatment is considered further in 3B–50 below.

*Currency options*

**3B–32**    The definition of qualifying payments in the case of currency options includes all permitted payments, except where an option is settled by an exchange of currencies and in this latter case such currency payments are ignored for all purposes of the financial instruments legislation. If, however, an option is settled by a payment equal to the difference between the two currency payments that are due under the terms of the currency option, the settlement payment is brought into account as a qualifying payment for the purposes of the financial instruments legislation.[15]

*Debt contract and debt options*

**3B–33**    The definition of qualifying payments in the case of debt contracts and debt options is the same as the payments that are permitted under the terms of such qualifying contracts. There is one exception; this is where a debt contract is settled by the delivery of a loan relationship. In such cases, the transfer of the loan relationship is not treated as a qualifying payment made or received by either party to the qualifying contract in question.[16] The interaction of the financial instruments and loan relationships legislation is considered further at 3B–55 below.

*All qualifying contracts*

**3B–34**    In addition to the payments that have been referred to above which are specific to a particular type of qualifying contract, the financial instruments legislation also recognises payments which, if they were made under the terms of the contract, would fall within section 151 of the Finance Act 1994 (see "other payments" above), as well as a payment for securing the acquisition or disposal of the contract.

Further, where a company closes out its rights or obligations under an interest rate or a currency contract by entering into a reciprocal contract, a payment received or made by the company to enter into the reciprocal contract is treated as a qualifying payment but, thereafter, any further payments which are made or received under the terms of both the original qualifying contract and the reciprocal contract are ignored for the purposes of the financial instruments legislation.[16a]

**Accounting policies**

**3B–35**    The intention of the financial instruments legislation is, broadly, that profits and losses on qualifying contracts and options should be recognised for tax purposes on

---

[15] *ibid.* s.153(1)(c), (d).
[16] *ibid.* s.153(1)(ca), (d).
[16a] *ibid.* s.153(3).

the basis in which they are recognised in a company's accounts. This is subject to the company adopting either a mark to market or accruals accounting policy for the contract which satisfies that the requirements of section 156 of the Finance Act 1994.[17] For the purposes of the following discussion, where an accounting policy satisfies the requirements of this section it will be referred to as an "acceptable" accruals or an "acceptable" mark to market accounting policy, as appropriate. If, for whatever reason, a company's accounting treatment for a particular contract does not satisfy the requirements of section 156 of the Finance Act 1994, the company will be required to follow either an acceptable accruals or an acceptable mark to market accounting policy for the contract in question. The decision as to which accounting treatment should be applied is to be made by the company in conjunction with its Inspector of Taxes. However, if it is not possible for the two parties to reach an agreement the company's inspector can specify what accounting treatment the company must follow for the contract in question.[18]

*Mark to market accounting policy*

A mark to market accounting policy satisfies the requirements of section 156 of the Finance Act 1994 provided that[19]:  **3B–36**

1. computing the profits or losses on the contract on that basis is in accordance with normal accountancy practice (see 3B–38 below)[20];
2. all relevant payments[21] under the contract are allocated to the accounting periods in which they become due and payable[22]; and
3. the method of valuation adopted is such as to secure the contract is brought into account at a fair value.[23] "Fair value" is defined as being the amount which, if the qualifying company disposed of the contract to a knowledgeable and willing party dealing at arms length, it would be able to obtain or as the case may be, would have to pay.[24] In section 13504 of the Company Taxation Manual, the Inland Revenue states that it is acceptable for a company to determine the fair value of the contract using:
   (i) the bid price of the contract (the price that a dealer would pay for contract);
   (ii) the offer price of the contract (the price at which a dealer would sell the contract); or

---

[17] *ibid.* s.156(1).
[18] *ibid.* s.156(2).
[19] *ibid.* s.156(3).
[20] *ibid.* s.156(3)(a).
[21] A relevant payment is defined as a qualifying payment made or received or falling to be made or received by the qualifying company: *ibid.* s.156(7).
[22] *ibid.* s.156(3)(b).
[23] *ibid.* s.156(3)(c).
[24] *ibid.* s.156(7).

(iii) the mid-market price of the contract. This is the mid point between the bid and offer prices. Where a mid-market price is used, it is acceptable for a company to allow for such items as credit or liquidity risk, so long as these take reasonable account of the circumstances of the counter-parties and are not in the nature of general reserves.

This is subject to the proviso that the method adopted accords with generally accepted market practice and is followed consistently in the company's accounts.

*Accruals accounting policy*

**3B–37**   An accruals accounting policy satisfies the requirements of section 156 Finance Act 1994 for a qualifying contract provided that[25]:

1. computing the profits or losses on the contract on that basis is in accordance with normal accountancy practice (see 3B–38 below)[1];
2. all relevant payments[2] under the contract are allocated to the accounting periods to which they relate, without regard to the accounting periods in which they are made or received, or become due and payable[3]; and
3. where such payments relate to two or more such periods, they are apportioned between those periods on a just and reasonable basis.[4] In determining whether a relevant payment has been correctly apportioned between two or more accounting periods, regard will be had to any reciprocal (but not other) payments. A reciprocal payment is another payment (including a conditional payment) that represents consideration or part consideration for the payment in question.[5]

In section 13262 of the Company Taxation Manual, the Inland Revenue states that either a straight-line or economic apportionment basis may be used to apportion payments and receipts between different accounting periods so long as the method chosen is followed consistently for payments and receipts.

*Normal accountancy practice*

**3B–38**   Whether accounting for a particular contract using an acceptable accruals or an acceptable mark to market accounting policy is in accordance with normal accounting practice is to be determined by reference to the normal accountancy practice by refer-

---

[25] *ibid.* s.156(4).

[1] *ibid.* s.156(4)(a).

[2] The definition of a relevant payment is the same as that set out above in the case of an acceptable mark to market accounting policy.

[3] FA 1994, s.156(4)(b).

[4] *ibid.* s.156(4)(c).

[5] *ibid.* s.156(7), (8).

ence to which the company's statutory accounts (in the case of United Kingdom incorporated companies), or the accounts which an overseas incorporated company is required to keep in its home State[6], are prepared. Where an overseas incorporated company is not required to keep accounts in its home State, the accounts which will be used for these purposes are its accounts which correspond most closely with United Kingdom statutory accounts.[7]

### Prescriptive accounting treatment

In certain cases the financial instruments legislation specifies how the profit or loss **3B–39** for an accounting period is to be determined. These cases are where:

1. a qualifying company has entered into linked currency options;
2. a qualifying company changes its accounting treatment for a qualifying contract;
3. a qualifying contract is terminated;
4. a qualifying company closes out a qualifying contract by entering into a reciprocal contract;
5. payments due under a qualifying contract are considered to be irrecoverable;
6. a qualifying company is released from its obligations to make a payment or payments due under the terms of a qualifying contract; and
7. certain anti-avoidance provisions apply. These provisions are considered further in Part IV below.

Each of 1 to 6 is considered further below and the anti-avoidance provisions referred to in 7 are discussed in Part IV.

### Linked currency options

There is only one case in which is the financial instruments legislation is prescript- **3B–40** ive as to the accounting treatment which has be followed for a qualifying contract. This is in the case of linked currency options and in such cases, a company is required to follow a mark to market accounting policy for such qualifying contracts. Currency options are regarded as linked for the purposes of the financial instruments legislation where each of the following conditions is satisfied:

(i) each party to the currency option contracts is able to exercise a currency option against the other party to those contracts. This condition is also

---

[6] Home State is defined as the country or territory under whose laws the company is incorporated: FA 1994, s.156(6).
[7] FA 1994, s.156(6).

regarded as satisfied where an option is exercisable by either party against an associated company[8] of the other party to the currency option contracts; and

(ii) the options must be exercised (if at all) at the same, or substantially same time and the rights and duties which would arise if either option contract were exercised are substantially the same as if the other option contract were exercised.[9]

Effectively this definition means that the exercise price of each option is essentially the same and thus, whichever way exchange rates move, one of the parties will exercise its option. The economic effect of such linked currency options is the same as if the qualifying company had entered into a currency contract. The same treatment is applied to linked conditional currency contracts. As mentioned at 3B–13 above conditional currency contracts are treated as currency options for the purposes of the financial instruments legislation.[10]

### Change of accounting policy

**3B–41**     Where a company adopts a different accounting treatment for a qualifying contract from that which it used in the immediately preceding accounting period, an adjustment will be made in the year of change to ensure that there is no double counting. The relevant provisions are set out in sections 155 and 158 of the Finance Act 1994. Effectively these provisions compare the profits and losses that have been recognised on the qualifying contract under the former accounting policy to the profits and losses which would have been recognised in previous accounting periods, had the company always followed its new accounting treatment. Any difference is taxed or relieved into the accounting period in which the change of accounting policy takes place.

Unlike the loan relationships legislation, the financial instruments legislation does not contain any measures to deal with a case where a company changes its accounting treatment for a contract during an accounting period. This is because under the provisions of section 156 of the Finance Act 1994 a company is required to follow an accounting treatment for a contract for an accounting period. Thus if a company changes its accounting treatment for a contract during an accounting period it will have to agree with its Inspector of Taxes which accounting treatment it is to follow for tax purposes for that accounting period.

---

[8] This is defined within the meaning of ICTA 1988, s.416(1), *i.e.*, one company controls the other or both companies are under the control of the same third person. The two companies will also be treated as associated if either of these tests have been satisfied in the previous 12 months.

[9] FA 1994, s.157.

[10] *ibid.* s.157(7).

### Termination of a qualifying contract

Section 161 of the Finance Act 1994 applies where a qualifying contract is termin-  **3B–42**
ated. The treatment that is applied in such cases depends on whether the contract is
accounted for using an acceptable accruals or an acceptable mark to market basis.

*Contract is accounted for using an acceptable accruals basis*

Section 161 of the Finance Act 1994 contains provisions for specific adjustments  **3B–43**
where a contract is accounted for using an acceptable accruals basis. In such cases,
the company is required to make adjustments for any amounts receivable or payable
under the terms of the contract which have been taken into account in the current and
any previous accounting periods and which are no longer payable or receivable as a
result of the termination of the contract.[11] The company will, however, be taxed on,
or will be able to obtain relief for, any payment made or received to terminate the
contract.[12]

*Contract is accounted for on a mark to market basis*

Section 161 of the Finance Act 1994, however, is silent as regards the adjustments  **3B–44**
that should be made where a contract that is accounted for using an acceptable mark
to market accounting policy is terminated. This is because there are provisions within
subsection 155(4) and (7) of the Finance Act 1994 to deal with this. Section 155(3)
provides that the provisions of section 155 apply, *inter alia*, where section 161 applies.
Although section 161, itself, contains no specific provisions to deal with the termination of qualifying contracts that are accounted for using a mark to market basis,
equally there is nothing within the wording of the section which limits its scope to
cases where a qualifying contract is accounted for using an acceptable accruals basis.

Where a qualifying contract which is accounted for on a mark to market basis is
terminated wholly or partly by a qualifying payment, section 155(7) provides that the
value of the contract is deemed to be nil for the purposes of the financial instruments
legislation immediately before the company ceases to be a party to the contract.[13] At
the same time, the adjustment provided for by section 155(4) will ensure that any
payment made or received as a result of the contract being terminated is brought into
account for purposes of the financial instruments legislation.

---

[11] *ibid.* s.161(2).

[12] This is because the payment made to terminate the contract is treated as a qualifying payment
under the provisions of s.153(2)(b) and it is taken into account in computing the profit or
loss on the contract under the provisions of s.155(5). s.155 applies, *inter alia* where s.161
applies.

[13] The provisions of s.155(7) do not apply, however, where none of the payments that a company makes to discharge the qualifying contract are qualifying payments: *ibid.* s.155(8).

Example

> Alpha PLC is a financial trader and has sold an interest rate cap. It accounted for this interest rate contract using a mark to market accounting policy and during the year ended December 31, 2000 it decided to terminate the contract early and it made a payment to the counterparty in full and final settlement of all future payments which might be due under the terms of the contract. The contract was terminated on September 30, 2000 in return for a payment of £500,000. The contract was carried in Alpha PLC's accounts at that date as a liability of £495,000. Under the provisions of section 155(7) this liability would be reversed immediately before Alpha PLC ceased to be a party to the contract and at the same time Alpha PLC would be able to obtain a deduction for the payment it made to terminate the contract. The effect of these two adjustments is that Alpha PLC would be able to obtain relief for the additional payment of £5,000 (£500,000–£495,000) it made to cancel its obligations.

Where, however, none of the payments that are made to terminate a qualifying contract are qualifying payments, the value of the contract immediately before the contract is terminated is not deemed to be nil for the purposes of the financial instruments legislation.[14] This means that any movement in the market value of the contract is recognised for tax purposes up to and including the date on which the contract is terminated. An example of such a contract would be a currency contract that is accounted for on a mark to market basis and which is settled by an exchange of currency payments that are due under the terms of contract (as discussed in 3B–31 above, where a currency contract is settled by an exchange of currencies, the exchange is not treated as a qualifying payment).

**Reciprocal contract**

3B–45    Where a qualifying company closes out an interest rate or currency contract (first contract) by entering into another contract with obligations that are reciprocal to the first contract, any payment made or received by the company in order to enter into the reciprocal contract is treated as a qualifying payment in relation to the first contract and thereafter all further payments made under the terms of both the qualifying contract and the reciprocal contract are ignored for the purposes of the financial instruments legislation.[15]

---

[14] As discussed above, s.155(8) disapplies s.155(7) in such cases.
[15] FA 1994, s.153(3).

### Irrecoverable payments

There are provisions in section 163 of the Finance Act 1994 to cover a case where:   **3B–46**

1. a company is entitled to receive a qualifying payment;
2. it has included the whole or any part of this payment in computing its taxable profits for the current or any previous accounting period; and
3. the whole or any part of the payment that was outstanding immediately before the end of an accounting period payment can reasonably be regarded as having become irrecoverable in that period.

In such cases, on a claim in being a made by the company within two years of the end of that period, it is entitled to a deduction for such amount of the payment as has already been taken into account for tax purposes in computing its profits and losses on the contract and which can reasonably be regarded as having becoming irrecoverable in that period.[16]

If a company makes a such a claim and some or all of the payment becomes recoverable in a later accounting period, the company is required to include the amount which becomes recoverable in computing its profits or losses on that contract in that accounting period.[17]

The Inland Revenue has stated in its Explanatory Statement that where a company accounts for a qualifying contract on a mark to market basis and the credit risk of the counterparty is included in arriving at the market value of the qualifying contract, there is no need for the company to make a claim under section 163 of the Finance Act 1994.[18]

### Released payments

If at any time during an accounting period a company is released from any payment   **3B–47**
(released payment) that it is due to make under the terms of a qualifying contract by the other party to the contract then, to the extent that the company has claimed relief for the payment in the current or any previous accounting period, it is required to include the amount that is released in computing its profits or losses on that contract for that accounting period.[19] It is also prevented from claiming relief for any part of the released payment in any subsequent accounting period.[20]

---

[16] *ibid.* s.163(1) to (3).

[17] *ibid.* s.163(4).

[18] See section 6.23.

[19] FA 1994, ss. 155, 164.

[20] This is because, as the payment is no longer payable, it will not be a relevant payment for the purposes of s.156 and thus cannot be included in computing the company's profits and losses on that contract for tax purposes in future accounting periods. A relevant payment is defined as a qualifying payment made or received or falling to be made or received by a qualifying company: *ibid.* s.156(7).

### Currency contracts—interaction with the foreign exchange legislation

3B–48    Currency contracts are the only qualifying contracts which are also specifically dealt with under the provisions of the foreign exchange legislation. The intention of the two regimes is that exchange gains and losses on a currency contract should be taxed under the foreign exchange legislation, to the extent that they are recognised in a company's accounts[21] whilst all payments made in connection with the contract, other that an exchange of currencies, will be dealt with under the financial instruments legislation. To avoid double counting, therefore, any exchange of currencies that takes place under the terms of a currency contract is not treated as a qualifying payment for the purposes of the financial instruments legislation.

*Avoidance of double counting where a currency contract is accounted for on a mark to market basis*

3B–49    Where a company accounts for a currency contract using a mark to market basis, exchange gains and losses will be included in arriving at the closing value of the contract at the end of an accounting period. In order to avoid double counting, section 162 of the Finance Act 1994 provides that any exchange gain or loss on the contract is to be ignored in arriving at the value of the contract for the purposes of the financial instruments legislation. There is no stated requirement that, in order for such an adjustment to be made, the exchange gains or losses on the contract must be brought into account for the purposes of the Finance Act 1993 foreign exchange legislation.[22] In practice it is unlikely to be necessary for a qualifying company to separate the profit or loss on a contract for an accounting period between the amount that falls to be dealt with under the foreign exchange legislation and the amount that is dealt with under the financial instruments legislation since the profit and loss on the contract will be treated in the same way under both regimes.

*Recognition of forward premium or discount where a currency contract is accounted for using an acceptable accruals basis*

3B–50    Where a company adopts an accruals basis of accounting for a currency contract it can adopt one of two accounting treatments: it can account for the contract using implied rate accounting or it can re-value the contract in its accounts. Where a company adopts implied rate accounting, the contract is translated into the company's reporting currency using the exchange rate implied in the contract such that no exchange gain or loss is recognised over the life of the contract. Typically, this treat-

---

[21] See 3A—29 of this supplement for a description of the ways in which exchange gains and losses on currency contracts are recognised for the purposes of the foreign exchange legislation.

[22] FA 1994, s.162 refers to exchange gains whereas the exchange gains that are taken into account for the purposes of the foreign exchange legislation are referred to as initial exchange gains or losses: see ss125–126 FA 1993.

ment would be adopted where the contract is being used to hedge a foreign currency asset or liability. The use of implied rate accounting is acceptable for the purposes of the foreign exchange legislation provided that:

1. one of the currencies covered by the contract is the company's local currency,
2. the exchange rate implied in the contract is an arm's length rate; and
3. using implied rate accounting for the contract in question is in accordance with normal accountancy practice.[23]

Where a company revalues a currency contract in its accounts, it will also recognise the forward premium or discount on that contract and will accrue it over the life of the contract. The forward premium or discount is the difference between the spot price of the currency which the company is buying or selling under the terms of the currency contract and the price it is paying receiving under the terms of the contract (forward price). The forward price is calculated by adjusting the spot price of the currency in question at the date the company enters into the contract by the interest differential between the two currencies for the period covered by the contract. Section 153(4) and (5) of the Finance Act 1994 provides that where a company accounts for a contract on this basis, the forward premium or discount is taken into account as a qualifying payment for the purposes of the financial instruments legislation. A forward premium arises where the forward price is higher than the spot price and a forward discount arises where the forward price is lower than the spot price.

Example

X PLC has a September 30 year end and enters into a forward purchase of US $1,000,000 on April 1, 2001 for settlement on December 31, 2001. The contract price is £1 = US $1.55 and the spot price on April 1, 2001 is £1 = US $1.60. Had the US $ been purchased at the spot price on April 1, 2001, the cost would have been £625,000 as compared to the contract price of £645,161. As it costs more to buy the US$ forward, the difference between the contact price and the spot price of £20,161 is termed a forward premium.

X PLC accounts for the contract on an accrual basis and revalues the contract in its accounts, it would initially record the contract at the spot price in its accounts and would then retranslate the contract at the then spot rate at September 30, 2001. Any exchange rate movement would be dealt with under the foreign exchange legislation. It would again retranslate the contract on December 31, immediately before it is settled and again any exchange movement between (in

---

[23] FA 1993, s.150(6), (11).

this case) the opening value of the contract at October 1, 2001 and the value of the US $ at December 31, 2001 would be dealt with under the foreign exchange legislation.

Where a contract is accounted for on an accruals basis and is revalued in a company's accounts, the (in this case) forward premium is amortised over the life of the contract. Assuming that the premium is amortised on a straight line basis, X PLC would reflect £13,440 of the premium in its accounts for the year to September 30, 2001 and the balance of £6,721 in its accounts to September 30, 2002.

*Currency contract settled by a compensation payment*

**3B–51**  Where a currency contract is settled by a payment equal to the difference between the two currency payments that are due under the terms of the contract at the settlement date, as opposed to an actual exchange of currency payments taking place, an adjustment is made under the foreign exchange legislation to eliminate any exchange gain or loss on the contract that has been recognised over the life of the contract under the foreign exchange legislation.[24] The intention in such cases is that the termination payment is brought into account for the purposes of the financial instruments legislation under the provisions of section 161 of the Finance Act 1994 (see above).

**Currency options**

**3B–52**  Currency options are not dealt with under the foreign exchange legislation. Where a currency option is settled by an exchange of currencies taking place, the exchange of currencies itself, will not be treated as a qualifying payment for the purposes of the financial instruments legislation.

*Accruals accounting policy*

**3B–53**  Where a currency option is accounted for on an accruals basis and the option is exercised a company would generally treat itself as having acquired the currency in question at the option price. Any subsequent gain or loss on the currency would be dealt with under the foreign exchange legislation.

*Mark to market accounting policy*

**3B–54**  Where a currency option is accounted for using a mark to market accounting policy, any exchange gain or loss on the contract will be recognised up to the date on which the exchange of currencies takes place and any exchange movements will not be ignored in determining the market value of the option.[25]

---

[24] FA 1993, s.146. See 3A—29 of the Supplement.
[25] FA 1994, s.155(4) and s.156(3). The exclusion within FA 1994, s.162 only applies to exchange gains on currency contracts.

If a currency option is settled by an exchange of currency, the provisions of section 155(7) of the Finance Act 1994 will not apply to treat the value of the currency options as nil immediately before the company ceases to be a party to that qualifying contract. This is because an exchange currency is not treated as a qualifying payment for the purposes of the financial instruments legislation.[1] The result is that any gain or loss on a currency option will be recognised under the financial instruments legislation up to the date that the option is exercised, or the option expires unexercised.

**Interaction with the loan relationships legislation**

Where a loan relationship is acquired or is disposed of under the terms of a debt contract or option, it is possible that both the loan relationships and the financial instruments legislation could apply to any payments made under the terms of the debt contract or option. To deal with this interaction, section 101 of the Finance Act 1996 provides that, to the extent that a profit or loss is taken into account for an accounting period under the loan relationships legislation, it will not be taken into account for the purposes of the financial instruments legislation. The effect of this wording is that profits and losses on debt contracts or options will be dealt with under the financial instruments legislation in an accounting period if the company was not a party to a loan relationship by virtue of that qualifying contract in that accounting period. If, in a later accounting period, the company becomes a party to a loan relationship by virtue of the contract, any profits or losses on the contract which are recognised in the company's accounts in that later will normally be taxed or relieved under the loan relationships legislation and will be ignored for the purposes of the financial instruments legislation.

**3B–55**

Concerns have been expressed that the provisions within section 150A(11) of the Finance Act 1994[2] could result in double counting where a debt contract or option is accounted for using an authorised accruals basis and is settled by the delivery of a loan relationship. Such concerns are largely ill founded. This is because where a contract or option is settled by the delivery of a loan relationship, the transfer of the loan relationship is not treated as a qualifying payment and is thus ignored for the purposes of the financial instruments legislation.[3] This thus means that where there is an inherent gain on the debt contract or option, such a gain will not be dealt with under the financial instruments legislation where the contract or option is settled by the transfer of a loan relationship. In such cases the purchaser would normally account for the loan relationship at the price payable under the terms of the option and the inherent gain would be recognised under the loan relationship legislation when the company disposes of the loan relationship in question. The only way in which the

---

[1] *ibid.* ss. 153(1)(c), 155(7), (8) and s.161.
[2] This provides that the transfer of money's worth having a value of any amount shall be treated as payment of that amount for the purposes of FA 1994, s.150A.
[3] See 3B–33 above.

authors can conceive that double counting could arise would be if there is no provision within the terms of a contract or option for it to be settled by the delivery of a loan relationship, but the holder accepts a loan relationship in settlement of the payment to which it is entitled under the terms of that qualifying contract. In such cases no double counting would arise, so long as the company in question treats the loan relationship in its accounts as having been acquired for a value equal to the payment which it would otherwise have been entitled to receive under the terms of the debt contract or option.

## Intra-group transfers

**3B–56**    Unlike the loan relationships legislation there are no provisions within the financial instruments legislation dealing with the transfer of the benefits and obligations of a qualifying contract from one group company to another. It may be possible to assign the benefit of an option contract where the holder has purchased the option contract in question. In other cases it will be necessary to transfer the benefits and obligations of the contract by novation; that is a tripartite agreement between the two group companies and the third party counterparty whereby the parties all agree that one group company should be substituted for the other as a party to the contract with the third party. It is considered that the non-arm's length and value shifting anti-avoidance provisions might apply to such intra-group transactions, unless the successor company pays or receives an arm's length premium for taking over the benefits and obligations of the contract in question. It is further considered that any payment paid or received by the transferor would be treated as a termination payment while any payment made or received by the transferee would fall to be taken into account as a qualifying payment (albeit that it is not made under the terms of the contract) under the provisions of section 153(2)(b) of the Finance Act 1994 as a payment for securing the acquisition of the contract.

## Exclusivity of the financial instruments legislation

**3B–57**    Anti-double counting provisions are contained within section 173 of the Finance Act 1994. Where a qualifying company receives a payment under the terms of a contract or option and the payment is chargeable to corporation tax as part of the company's taxable profits, or is otherwise taken into account as a receipt in computing the company's taxable profits for the purposes of the financial instruments legislation, section 173 provides that:

    (i) the amount shall not be taken into account for corporation tax purposes otherwise than under the provisions of the financial instruments legislation;

    (ii) the amount shall not be taxable under any other provisions of the Tax Acts; and

(iii) shall be excluded from being taken into account as the consideration for a disposal of an asset under the provisions of the Taxation of Chargeable Gains Act 1992.[4]

This thus means that where, for example, the value shifting provisions of sections 165 and 166, or the non-arm's length provisions of section 167 of the Finance Act 1994 apply (see Part IV below), and a receipt is not treated as taxable in a taxpayer's hands, the receipt could be treated as taxable under other provisions of the Corporation Tax Acts.

Where a qualifying company is liable to make a payment under the terms of a contract or option any amount which is taken into account as a deduction in computing the company's profits or losses for the purposes of the financial instruments legislation:

(a) is not allowable as a deduction in computing the profits or losses of the company for other purposes of the Tax Acts;

(b) is not allowable, otherwise than under the financial instruments legislation, as a deduction in computing any other income or profits or gains or losses of the company for the purposes of the Taxes Acts;

(c) may not be treated as a charge on income for the purposes of corporation tax, and

(d) is excluded from being taken into account under section 38 of the Taxation of Chargeable Gains Act 1992 as a deduction in the computation of chargeable gains.[5]

It is considered that the wording of section 173(3) would not prevent a taxpayer from being able to obtain relief under other provisions of the Tax Acts for an amount for which relief is denied under the financial instruments legislation, whether under the provisions of section 152 (non-qualifying payments), or under the value shifting, non-arm's length or transactions with non-residents anti-avoidance provisions that are considered below. Where a taxpayer is a party to the contract for the purposes of its trade, any such payment would be deductible in computing the company's Schedule D Case I trading profits. In other cases it is possible, although far from certain, that the payment might be eligible to be taken into account in computing the company's chargeable gains for the accounting period in question. The capital gains treatment of contracts that fall outside the financial instruments legislation is considered at Part VII below.

---

[4] FA 1994, s.173(1), (2).
[5] *ibid.* s.173(3), (4).

## IV. ANTI-AVOIDANCE PROVISIONS

### Value shifting

**3B–58**     Sections 165 of the Finance Act 1994 contains provisions which are aimed at blocking value shifting transactions between associated companies. The definition of associated companies in section 416 of the Taxes Act 1988 applies for the purposes of this section.[6] Section 165 of the Finance Act 1994 counters transfers of value between associated companies, whether these take place directly, or indirectly via an unconnected third party company. A transfer of value is deemed to have taken place if, immediately after a qualifying contract is entered into, or an option is allowed to lapse, the value of the qualifying company's net assets is less as a direct result of the transfer and the value of the associated company's net assets is more than it otherwise would have been. In determining whether this condition is satisfied, any reasonable arrangement fees or other reasonable expenses which either associated company may have paid to enter into the transaction are ignored.[7] Whilst section 165 refers to an option being allowed to lapse, the provisions of the section will only apply where an "in the money" option (*i.e.* where it would be to the advantage of the holder to exercise the option) is allowed to lapse. This is because any premium that the holder paid to enter into the option contract is disregarded for purposes of section 165.[8]

The provisions of section 165 of the Finance Act 1994 also apply to transactions indirectly between associated companies using a third party company as an intermediary. In order for section 165 to apply in such cases two conditions have to be satisfied:

1. the transaction in question is entered into, or the option is allowed to lapse, in pursuance of an arrangement entered into within the third party; and
2. as a result of those arrangements, a transfer value is or will be made directly or indirectly to an associated company by the third party or a company that is associated with the third party.[9]

Where it appears to an Inspector of Taxes that there is a transfer of value by a

---

[6] *ibid.* s.165(11). Under ICTA 1988, s.416(1), two companies are associated if one company controls the other or both companies are under the control of the same third person. The two companies are also treated as associated if either of these conditions was satisfied at any time in the previous 12 months. Control is defined by reference to ICTA 1988, s.416.

[7] *ibid.* s.165(5).

[8] The Inland Revenue has confirmed in section 6.27 of its Explanatory Statement that this is how it will interpret this provision in the case of options.

[9] *ibid.* s165(6) to (8).

qualifying company to the third party he may, by notice in writing, require the company within such time (not less than 30 days) as may be specified in the notice, to furnish him with such information as is in its power, and as he reasonably requires for purpose of determining whether the third party is an associated third party for the purposes of section 165 of the Finance Act 1994.[10]

Where section 165 applies to a qualifying contract, the transfer of value is ignored in computing the transferor's profits or losses (or the connected party transferor, in the case of an indirect transfer) arising on that qualifying contract.[11]

If the counterparty to the qualifying contract is a qualifying company, a corresponding adjustment is made to eliminate the transfer of value from being taken into account for the purposes of computing the profits or losses arising to that company on the qualifying contract.[12] Where a transfer of value takes place to a qualifying company, and the transferor is not a qualifying company, the transfer of value will not be ignored in computing the transferee's profit or loss on that qualifying contract. In the case of an indirect transfer of value the above adjustments only apply to an associated company and not any non-associated third party intermediary.

**Transactions not an arm's length**

Section 167 Finance Act 1994 contains provisions which are aimed at preventing a **3B–59** qualifying company from claiming relief for losses arising on any qualifying contract which is entered into on non-arm's length terms. This section applies where, if the parties to the transaction had been dealing at arm's length, the transaction would not have been entered into at all, or its terms would have been different. These provisions only apply to transactions, to the extent that they are not dealt with under the transfer of value provisions that are discussed above.[13]

In determining whether the contract or option was entered into on arm's length terms, all factors can be taken into account. These include:

1. in the case of an interest rate option or contract, any notional principal amounts and rates of interest that would have been involved[14];
2. in the case of a currency contract or option, any currencies and amounts that would have been involved[15];

---

[10] *ibid.* s.165(9).
[11] *ibid.* s.165(2).
[12] *ibid.* s.166(2).
[13] *ibid.* s.167(8).
[14] *ibid.* s.167(9)(a).
[15] *ibid.* s.167(9)(b).

3. in the case of a debt contract or option, the amount of the debt by reference to which any loan relationship that would have been involved would have subsisted, and any terms as to repayment, redemption or interest that, in the case of that debt or any asset representing it, would have been involved[16]; and

4. in all cases, any transactions in which are related to the transaction in question.[17] The definition of other transactions is not restricted to other financial instruments transactions. Thus, for example, where a company enters into a financial instruments contract on off-market terms because the contract is linked to some other transaction, so long as the overall transaction is arm's length, the provisions of section 167 of the Finance Act 1994 will not apply.

Where section 167 of the Finance Act 1994 applies to a contract, an adjustment is made to the profits and losses arising on the contract. If the other party to the contract is a qualifying company any profit or loss on the contract is ignored for the purposes of the financial instruments legislation.[18]

If the other party is not a qualifying company, for each accounting period for which the qualifying company is a party to the contract, any amounts payable by the qualifying company that are allocated to that period are ignored. Any amounts that are receivable under the terms of the contract that are allocated to that accounting period are reduced by the lower of the payments which have been disallowed for that period, and the gross income arising on the contract for that period.[19] For each accounting period, other than the first, a check is made to ensure that the cumulative profit on the contract which has been recognised for the purposes of the financial instruments legislation does not exceed the overall net profit on the contract.[20] The effect of these provisions is that a company is denied relief for any cumulative net loss on the contract but is taxed on any cumulative net profit.

Where a contract would still have been entered into had the parties been dealing at arms length, but its terms would have been different, the adjustments which have been described above will apply only to the non-arm's length provisions included within the contract.[21]

---

[16] *ibid.* s.167(9)(ba).

[17] *ibid.* s.167(9)(c).

[18] *ibid.*, s.167(3). This is the effect of the provisions of this subsection once account has been taken of the interaction with s.155.

[19] *ibid.* s.167(4).

[20] *ibid.* s.167(5), (6).

[21] *ibid.* s.167(7).

### Transactions with non-residents

These provisions apply, with certain exceptions (see below), where:  **3B–60**

1. a qualifying company enters into a qualifying contract with a non-UK resident counterparty;
2. a qualifying company becomes a party to a qualifying contract to which a non-UK resident is a party; and
3. a non-UK resident becomes a party to a contract to which a qualifying company is a party.

In such cases, subject to certain exceptions that are considered below, the provisions of section 167(4) and (5) apply to the contract and the same adjustments are applied as discussed above.[22] This means that the qualifying company is unable to claim tax relief for any loss arising on the contract and that it will be liable to tax on any net profit arising on the contract.

The exceptions to this provision apply where:  **3B–61**

(i) the non-resident is resident in a territory that has an Interest Article in its Double Tax Treaty with the United Kingdom (regardless of the rate of withholding tax specified in the Interest Article) and it is a party to the contract as a principal and not as an agent or a nominee for another person. Where the non-resident is acting in an agency or representative capacity, this test has to be considered by reference to the territory in which the principal is resident[23];

(ii) the contract is entered into by a United Kingdom branch or agency of the non-resident entity solely for the purposes of a trade or part of a trade carried on through that branch or agency and the non-resident is a party to the contract otherwise than as an agent or nominee of another person[24]; or

(iii) the qualifying company is a bank[25], building society[1] or financial

---

[22] *ibid.* s.168(1), (2).
[23] *ibid.* s.168(5), (6).
[24] *ibid.* s.168(4).
[25] A bank is defined as including: the Bank of England; any institution authorised under the Banking Act 1987; and a European authorised institution (as defined in the Banking Coordination (Second Council Directive) Regulations 1992) which has lawfully established a branch in the United Kingdom for the purposes of accepting deposits: *ibid.* s.177(1).
[1] This term is not defined in the financial instruments legislation and thus it must take its normal meaning.

trader[2] and it holds the qualifying contract solely for purposes of a trade, or part of a trade, carried on by it in the United Kingdom, and it is a party to the contract otherwise than as an agent or nominee of another person.[3]

## V. Transitional Provisions

**3B–62**     Currency contracts and currency options to which a company was a party at its commencement day came within the financial instruments regime from that date. There were provisions for a catch up adjustment, to the extent that payments and receipts under the terms of such contracts and options had not been taken into account in computing a taxpayer's taxable profits (whether such payments had been included as part of its Schedule D Case I trading profits or whether these had previously been included in computing its capital gains on which corporation tax is payable).

**3B–63**     Interest rate contracts and options to which a qualifying company was a party at its commencement day remain outside the financial instruments legislation until the sixth anniversary of that date. Any contracts or options to which a taxpayer is still a party at the sixth anniversary of its commencement day are brought within the financial instruments legislation from that date, but with no catch up adjustment. As an alternative, a taxpayer was able to elect to bring existing interest rate contracts and options within the financial instruments legislation from its commencement day. This election

---

[2] A financial trader is defined as: an authorised person under Chapter III of Part I of the Financial Services Act 1986; an exempted person under section 43 of that Act; a European authorised institution (see footnote 25 above for a definition of this term) which has lawfully established a branch in the United Kingdom for the purpose of carrying on investment business; and any person not falling within the foregoing who is approved by the Board: *ibid.* s.177(1).

The Inland Revenue has issued a statement of practice (SP 3/95) in which it states that in considering whether to approve a person who does not fall within the first three of the above tests, the company would have to satisfy the Inland Revenue that: it is carrying on a trade, the profits or losses which fall to be dealt with under Schedule D Case I; this trade includes the provision of qualifying contracts to counterparties in the normal course of that trade; and the relevant part of the trade, on its own, satisfies the test in *C.I.R. v. Livingston* (11 T.C. 542). In the Inland Revenue's view the effect of this last requirement is that the operations involved must be of the same type and carried on in the same way as those which are characteristic of ordinary trading in the line of business in which the venture is made. If the company enters into contracts with associated companies, the Inland Revenue considers that it will be easier to for the company to demonstrate that this condition is satisfied if it enters into contracts with the third parties to a significant extent on the same terms. Failing this, the company will need to demonstrate that it is conducting its operations with its associated customers the same way as if the parties had been unconnected.

[3] FA 1994, s.168(3).

had to be made within three months of company's commencement day and, in the case of a group of companies, the election had to be made by the principal company of the group on behalf of all group companies.[4]

Debt contracts and options were brought within the financial instruments legislation as a result of changes introduced in the Finance Act 1996. Where such contracts were previously not within the charge to tax, they came within the charge to tax from April 1, 1996.[5] There was no provision for a catch up adjustment where such contracts or options were accounted for on an acceptable accruals basis and profits and losses on the contract or option had previously been outside the scope of tax (*e.g.* a contract or option over a QCB which is exempt from corporation tax on capital gains by virtue of the provisions of section 115 of the Taxation of Chargeable Gains Act 1992). Where profits and losses on such contracts and options were previously included as part of a qualifying company's Schedule D Case I trading profits or as part of its chargeable gains, there was provision for a catch up adjustment to the extent that amount had not been taken into account for tax purposes under the old basis but would have been taken into account in earlier accounting periods, had the financial instruments legislation always applied.[6]  **3B–64**

## VI. Special Types of Company

### Insurance and mutual trading companies

Life insurance business  **3B–65**

Special provisions apply in the case of life insurance business and the reader is referred to the provisions of Schedule 18 of the Finance Act 1994 for further information on this point.

Mutual trading companies

To the extent that a financial instruments contract is held by a mutual trading company for the purposes of non-life business, any profit or loss on the contract is  **3B–66**

---

[4] *ibid.* s.148(2) to (8). The TCGA 1992, s.170 definition of group applied for these purposes: FA 1994, s.148(9).
[5] *ibid.* s.147A.
[6] FA 1996, Sched. 15 para. 25. FA 1994, s.147A is expressed to be subject to these provisions.

treated as a non-trading profit or loss for the purposes of the financial instruments legislation.[7]

## Authorised Unit Trusts and Open Ended Investment Companies

**3B–67**    Authorised unit trusts (AUTs) which are treated as companies for some purposes of the Tax Acts and open ended investment companies (OEICs), do not fall to be treated as qualifying companies for the purposes of the financial instruments legislation.[8] AUTs and OEICs have an exemption from tax on profits arising from trading in derivatives[9] and are also exempt from corporation tax on capital gains.[10] This thus means that any profits or losses on derivative transactions will generally be ignored in computing the taxable profits of such bodies (unless the transaction falls within the scope of the income into capital anti-avoidance provisions of Schedule 5AA of the Taxes Act 1988—these are considered at 3B–79 below).

## Approved Investment Trusts

**3B–68**    In the case of approved investment trusts (as defined in section 842 of the Taxes Act 1988), the financial instruments legislation does not apply to currency contracts or currency options[11] and gains and losses such contracts will normally be dealt with under the capital gains regime. As approved investment trusts are exempt from corporation tax on capital gains[12] this means that profits and losses on such contracts will fall outside the charge to tax so long as they are not entered into for trading purposes or speculative purposes and so long as they are not caught by the income into capital anti-avoidance provisions of Schedule 5AA of the Taxes Act 1988 (see 3B–79 below).

## Partnerships involving qualifying companies

**3B–69**    Section 172 of the Finance Act 1994 provides that where the partners of a partnership include one or more qualifying companies, and the partnership is a party to a

---

[7] FA 1994, Sched. 18 para. 3
[8] *ibid.* s.154(2). In the case of open ended investment companies the provisions of s.154 are applied by S.I. 1997 No. 1154, regs 3, 5 and 18.
[9] ICTA 1988, s.468AA, as extended to OEICs by S.I. 1997 No. 1154 Regs 9, 11.
[10] TCGA 1992, s.100, as extended to OEICs by S.I. No. 1154 Reg. 5(1), (3).
[11] FA 1994, s.154(3).
[12] TCGA 1992, s.100.

financial instruments contract, two computations of the partnership's profit or loss for the period are required: one on the basis that the partnership is a qualifying company, to determine the profits which are allocable to the partners that are qualifying companies; and one to determine the profits which are allocable to the remaining partners. Further guidance is given in SP4/98 which also applies for the purposes of the loan relationships and foreign exchange legislation (see 3–56A and 3A–31 of this supplement). This statement provides that, for the purposes of determining the profits which are allocable to qualifying companies, the partnership will be treated as if it were a qualifying company and the anti-avoidance provisions in sections 165 to 168 will apply to the partnership in the same way in which they apply to a qualifying company.

SP4/98 provides that the profits or losses arising from qualifying contracts should be determined at the partnership level and each of the partners that is a qualifying company should then be allocated with its share of the partnership profits. Whether the profits or losses on qualifying contracts are regarded as being of a trading or non-trading nature will be determined by reference to the purpose or purposes for which the partnership is a party to each contract.[13]

Where a partnership is a party to a qualifying contract for non-trading purposes, any profits or losses arising on that contract will be included in the non-trading loan relationship 'pool' of the partnership and the corporate partners will be allocated with their share of the net profit or deficit on that pool. Each corporate partner will then be required to include its share of that net profit or deficit in arriving at the net profit or deficit on its own non-trading loan relationship "pool" for the accounting period in question.[14]

The statement of practice also provides that where one of the partners is an authorised investment trust, a further computation is required to determine the profits of the partnership which are allocable to that company. This is because, as noted at 3B–68 above, any gains and losses realised by investment trusts on currency contracts and options are not taxable under the financial instruments legislation.

## VII. OTHER CONTRACTS

This part considers the tax treatment of financial instrument derivative contracts which fall outside the financial instruments legislation for whatever reason. **3B–70**

---

[13] SP4/98 paras 10, 15.
[14] SP4/98 para. 16.

### Schedule D Case I

**3B–71**    Where a financial trader or general insurance company is a party to a derivatives contract for trading purposes, any profits or losses on the contract will be included as part of the company's Schedule D Case I trading profits. Other companies are unlikely to enter into such contracts as trading transactions in their own right. Where, however, such a company enters into a derivative contract in order to hedge a transaction undertaken for trading purposes the Inland Revenue is prepared to treat any profit or loss on the hedge as forming part of the company's Schedule D Case I trading profits (which the authors consider reflects the correct tax treatment).[15] Where a non-financial sector company enters into a speculative transaction that is not ancillary to an underlying trading transaction, depending on the facts, this transaction might be held to be a trading transaction in its own right.[16]

### Capital gains or Schedule D Case VI

**3B–72**    Where profits or losses on a contract are not included in computing a company's Schedule D Case I trading profits, the question is how should any profit or loss on the contract be treated for tax purposes. Until 1985, it was the Inland Revenue's normal practice to assess gains and losses on commodity and financial derivatives under Schedule D Case VI following the Court of Appeal's decision in *Cooper v. Stubbs*[17] and the subsequent decision of the High Court in *Townsend v. Grundy*[18], though it accepted that a "one off" transaction might fall to be dealt with under the capital gains legislation.[19] In 1985 the capital gains legislation was amended to bring exchange traded commodity and financial derivatives contracts and options within the capital gains regime and these measures were further extended by section 81 of the Finance (No 2) Act 1987 to over-the-counter contracts and options where the counterparty to the contract is an authorised person or listed institution within the meaning of the Financial Services Act 1986. The following sections consider whether such contracts might be taxed under the capital gains rules or under the provisions of Schedule D Case VI.

---

[15] SP14/91 para 7.
[16] SP14/91 para 8.
[17] 10 T.C. 29.
[18] 18 T.C. 140
[19] Inland Revenue Capital Gains Manual section 56042.

## Capital gains treatment

In order to determine how a derivatives contract is dealt with under the capital gains **3B–73**
regime it is necessary to determine whether the derivatives contract is a financial
future or an option. This is because financial futures and options are taxed on a slightly
different basis. The capital gains legislation does not define the meaning of an option.
However, it is clear from the provisions dealing with options that the holder is required
to *exercise* the option.[20] It is the Inland Revenue's view that, where an option contract
settles automatically where it is in the holder's favour, the contract does not fall to be
treated as an option for capital gains tax purposes and instead should be treated as a
financial future.

*Financial futures*

Financial futures are taxed under the provisions of section 143 of the Taxation of **3B–74**
Chargeable Gains Act 1992. This section applies where any gains arising to a person
the course of dealing in commodity or financial futures would be taxable under Schedule D otherwise than as a trading transaction. The meaning of financial futures is not
defined in the section but in SP 14/91 the Inland Revenue states that the term is a
wide term and covers:

1. contracts for future delivery of shares, securities, foreign currency or other
   financial instruments;
2. contracts that are settled by payment of cash differences determined by
   movements in the price of such instruments (including contracts where
   settlement is based on the application of an interest rate or a financial
   index to a notional principal amount), as well as contracts settled by
   delivery; and
3. both exchange traded and over the counter contracts.[21]

In order for a financial futures contract to fall within section 143 of the Taxation
of Chargeable Gains Act 1992, the contract either needs to be traded on a recognised
futures exchange[22] or the other party to the contract needs to be an authorised person

---

[20] TCGA 1992, ss. 144(2), 144A(1)(a).
[21] SP14/91 para. 2.
[22] TCGA 1992, s.143(2).

or listed institution within the meaning of the Financial Services Act 1986.[23] Where section 143 applies, the financial future is not treated as a wasting asset and thus the company will be able to set-off the full amount of any premium that it paid to enter into the contract against any amounts it receives from the counterparty and more importantly any payments made by the taxpayer that are not so relieved are allowable as capital losses. This section also covers contracts where amounts are received or are required to be paid over the life of the contract.[24] Each receipt is treated as a part disposal and (and thus the gain or loss on the contract has to computed using the provisions of section 42 of the Taxation of Chargeable Gains Act 1992). Where a company closes out a contract (first contract) by entering into a reciprocal contract, that transaction is treated as the disposal of an asset (being its outstanding obligations under the first contract) and any payment received by or made by the company is treated respectively as consideration for the disposal or as an incidental cost of making of the disposal.[25]

Where an interest rate or currency contract falls outside the financial instruments

---

[23] *ibid.* s.143(3). An authorised person is a member of a self regulatory body such as PIA, IMRO or the SFA. A listed institution is a listed money market institution within the meaning of section 43 of the Financial Services Act 1986 whose name appears on a list published by the Financial Services Authority. It is considered that the tentative view expressed by the Special Commissioners in *Griffin v. Citibank Investments NA* that a contract has to be dealt in on an exchange in or in order to fall within this subsection of s.143 represents misunderstanding of the legislative provision. This subsection was introduced by F(No 2)A 1987, s.81(3) specifically to bring OTC contracts within the capital gains regime; this intention is evidenced by the 1987 Budget Day Inland Revenue press release dated March 17, 1987. This stated that the intention of the amendment was to extend the capital gains tax treatment in FA 1885, s.72 (the provisions within this section dealing with the tax treatment of financial futures are now contained in TCGA 1992, s.143) to certain over-the-counter financial futures and options. The notes to this press release stated:

The "over-the-counter" market is a fast developing market in financial futures and options written mainly by major banks and other institutions. It can offer instruments which are tailor-made to fit the precise needs of particular customers, instead of the standardised product offered by the exchanges. The Financial Services Act 1986 introduces a system of authorisation and a regulatory framework within which those concerned will have to operate. Against this background the Government have decided to extend section 72 to certain over the counter options and futures.

It is proposed therefore that section 72 [FA 1985] be extended to:-
1. gains on commodity and financial futures (including forwards) where one of the parties to the transaction is either an "Authorised person" or a "Listed Institution" within the meaning of Financial Services Act 1986,
2. gains on financial options granted by or, in certain circumstances, to an authorised person or listed institution,
3. gains on options which relate to quoted shares and securities and are arranged through a Stock Exchange member."

[24] *ibid.* s.143(6). While this subsection covers payments that are made over the life of a contract, it is primarily aimed at cases where a contract is partially closed out.

[25] *ibid.* s.143(5).

legislation for whatever reason, the contract would normally fall within section 143, assuming that the counterparty to the contract is an authorised person or listed institution. The position is uncertain, however, in the case of *interest rate swaps* or of swap differential payments that are payable under the terms of a *currency swap*. The Inland Revenue considers that interest rate and equity or total return swaps fall outside the provisions of this section.[1] The basis for the Inland Revenue's view is not clear. Whilst swaps are not similar to contracts that are traded on a recognised futures exchange, and thus could not be termed a "financial future" in the strictest sense of the word, the provisions of section 143, in so far as they relate to off-market contracts are not limited to contracts that are similar to exchange traded contracts. Swaps are a widely used OTC financial derivative contract and it is difficult to see why a swap should be excluded from the provisions of section 143 when, for example, an interest rate cap or collar was considered to fall within the provisions of this section before the financial instruments legislation came into force. Further, the wording of subsection (6) would appear to permit payments made over the life of a swap to be taken into account as a receipt or payment for the purposes of the Taxation of Chargeable Gains Act 1992.[2]

If a financial futures contract falls outside section 143, the question that then arises is whether any gain or loss on that contract should be dealt with under the provisions of Schedule D Case VI or whether the contract still falls within the capital gains tax legislation, but outside the provisions of section 143. Schedule D Case VI applies to any annual profits or gains not falling under any other Case of Schedule D and which are not chargeable to tax under Schedule A or E.[3] It is an established principle that profits and gains in the context of Schedule D Case VI must mean profits and gains *ejusdem generis* with the profits and gains specified in the preceding Cases of Schedule D.[4] In *Cooper v. Stubbs*[5], the Court of Appeal held by a majority decision that a series of transactions in cotton futures by two cotton brokers in their private capacity were assessable to tax under Schedule D Case VI, the Commissioners having decided that the individuals were not carrying on a trade. It is questionable whether the Court of Appeal's decision in *Cooper v. Stubbs* is still good authority for assessing any profit on a derivatives contract to tax under the provisions of Schedule D Case VI. First, the decision was a majority decision. Secondly, and more importantly, the decision was made at a time when higher courts felt themselves to be bound by a decision on a

---

[1] Section 11.2.5.3 of the Inland Revenue Banking Manual states that in the context of TCGA 1992, s.143 "the expression financial future should not be taken as extending to instruments such as interest rate swaps or any other swap, for example, of interest type payments against the yield derived from a Stock Index or similar types of arrangement."

[2] Payments made under the terms of an *interest rate cap or collar* were so treated before the financial instruments legislation came into force.

[3] ICTA 1988, s.18(3).

[4] See the judgment of Viscount Dunedin in *Jones v. Leeming* (1930) 15 T.C. 333 at 359 where he cites the judgment of Lord Blackburn in the *Attorney-General v. Black* (1871) 1 T.C. 54.

[5] (1925) 10 T.C. 29.

question of fact by the Commissioners.[6] The facts of this case pointed strongly to a conclusion that the taxpayer was trading in derivatives and, indeed, two of the Lord Justices of Appeal expressed this view in their speeches whilst the third held that the taxpayer was trading.[7]

On the strength of the decision in *Cooper v. Stubbs*, the Inland Revenue sought to argue in *Leeming v. Jones*[8] that a profit realised from an option over two Malay rubber estates in a case where the Commissioners had held that the taxpayer was not trading should be assessed to tax under Schedule D Case VI. The Inland Revenue lost at all levels. In the Court of Appeal, Lawrence L.J. opined:

> "I have the greatest difficulty in seeing how an isolated transaction of this kind, if it be not an adventure in the nature of trade, can be a transaction *ejusdem generis* with such a transaction and thus fall within Case VI. All the elements that would go to make such a transaction an adventure in the nature of trade in my opinion would be required to make it a transaction *ejusdem generis* with such an adventure. It seems to me that in the case of an isolated transaction of purchase and resale of property there is no middle course open. It is either an adventure in the nature of trade or else it is simply a case of sale and repurchase of property."[9]

Lawrence L.J.'s ratio was referred to in the judgments of four of the five Law Lords (one of whom included Lord Warrington of Clyffe, who as Warrington LJ had been a member of the Court of Appeal that had decided *Cooper v. Stubbs*). *Cooper v. Stubbs* was distinguished by the House of Lords as in that case there had been a regular pattern of activity which was akin to trading which had been entered into in order to generate revenue, whereas in instant case the transactions were of an isolated nature.

On the basis of the above, it is considered that in order for any profit or loss on a

---

[6] The House of Lords subsequently decided in *Edwards v. Bairstow and Harrison* 36 T.C. 207 that a higher court could overturn a decision of the commissioners on a question of fact where it was satisfied that the facts found are such that no person acting judicially and properly instructed as to the relevant law could have come to the determination under appeal.

[7] The decision by the Court of Appeal in Cooper v. Stubbs that it was not in a position to overturn the Commissioners' decision became a principle that applied to future decisions. This principle was reversed by the House of Lords in *Edwards v.Bairstow and Harrison* op cit. On the basis of this later decision it is considered that, were *Cooper v. Stubbs* to be decided today, the courts would conclude that the taxpayer was carrying on a trade. The decision in *Cooper v. Stubbs* was followed in a subsequent High Court decision, *Townsend v. Grundy* 18 T.C. 140, in a case where the Commissioners found that dealing in futures by a taxpayer did not amount to a trading activity. This decision again pre-dated the House of Lords' judgment in *Edwards v. Bairstow and Harrison*. It should be noted that at the time at which both *Cooper v. Stubbs* and *Townsend v. Grundy* were decided, capital gains tax had not been introduced and thus had the contracts fallen outside Schedule D Case VI the gains would have been tax free in the taxpayers' hands.

[8] (1930) 15 T.C. 333.

[9] *ibid.* at 357.

derivatives contract to fall within Schedule D Case VI, the profit must be capable of being assessed under the preceding Cases of Schedule D. There are thus two possible ways in which a profit or loss on a derivatives contract could fall within Schedule D Case VI:

1. where a non-trading currency contract or option, debt contract or option or interest rate contract or option falls outside the Finance Act 1994 Financial Instruments legislation (in this case as the income on contracts that fall within the financial instruments legislation is assessable to tax under Schedule D Case III); and
2. where there is a regular pattern of activity, or where there is a speculative transaction which in each case has all the hallmarks of a trading transaction, but in each case is not treated as a trading transaction. Given the decision in *Edwards v. Bairstow and Harrison*, it is unlikely that such an instance would arise today as a decision of the Commissioners that a taxpayer was not trading, where the evidence pointed clearly to the contrary, would generally be overturned by a higher court.

Where, however, a one-off transaction is not speculative and is not included in computing a company's Schedule D Case I trading profits, it is difficult to see how any profit or loss arising on the transaction could fall to be taxed under Schedule D Case VI. In such cases it is considered that any profit or loss on the contract may be assessable to corporation tax on capital gains if either the contract itself can be held to constitute an asset or if the contract could be considered to relate to the disposal of an asset. This might not be as helpful to the taxpayer as it may seem since if a contract falls outside section 143 there is nothing to prevent the contract from being treated as a wasting asset and thus to prevent any premium that a company paid to enter into the contract from being deemed to waste over the life of the contract. This could mean that where payment is only received at the maturity the contract, the taxpayer would be taxed on the full amount of the payment and would be unable to obtain relief for any premium it paid to enter into the contract.

### Options

The capital gains treatment of options varies depending on whether the taxpayer **3B–75** has bought or sold an option. For purposes of the following a discussion, where a company has granted an option it will be referred to as the grantor and if a company has purchased an option it will be referred to as the holder.

### Grantor

Under section 144 of the Taxation of Chargeable Gains Act 1992, the grant of an **3B–76** option is treated as the disposal of an asset by the taxpayer, even if the taxpayer has agreed to grant an option which binds it to sell an asset which it does not own, should the holder exercise the option. If the holder subsequently exercises the option, the grant of the option and the transaction entered into as result of the option being exercised are treated as being a single transaction. If the option binds the grantor to sell an asset, the option premium is treated as being part of the consideration for the disposal of the asset and if the grantor is required to purchase an asset, the consideration for the option is deducted from the acquisition cost of the asset.[10]

### Holder

**3B–77**    Under section 144 of the Taxation of Chargeable Gains Act 1992, the exercise of the option by the holder is not treated as the disposal of an asset but, instead, the acquisition of the option and the transaction entered into by the holder are treated as a single transaction and if the option binds the grantor to sell the option premium is treated as being part of the consideration paid by the holder for the asset. Where the option binds the grantor to purchase an asset the option premium paid by the holder is treated as being an incidental cost of disposing of the asset.[11]

### Cash settled options

The above rules apply in the same way for the grantor and the holder where the contract is to be settled by a cash payment, should the holder exercise his rights under the option.[12]

### Wasting assets

**3B–78**    An option is treated as a wasting asset unless it is a quoted option to subscribe for shares in a company, a traded option, or a financial option, or an option to acquire assets exercisable by a person intending to use then, if acquired, for the purpose of a trade carried on by him.[13] Where a holder is not carrying on a financial trade it would need to ensure that the option fell within the definition of a traded option or a financial option. A traded option is defined as an option which, at the time of abandonment or other disposal, is listed on a recognised stock exchange or a recognised futures exchange.[14]

A financial option is defined as an option which is not a traded option but which:

1. relates to currency, shares, securities or an interest rate and is granted (otherwise than as an agent) by a member of a recognised stock exchange, by an authorised person within the meaning of the Financial Services Act 1986 or by a listed institution within the meaning of section 43 of that Act; or
2. relates to shares or securities which are dealt in on a recognised stock

---

[10] *ibid.* s.144(2).
[11] *ibid.* s.144(3).
[12] *ibid.* s.144A.
[13] *ibid.* s.146(1).
[14] *ibid.* s.144(8)(b), as applied by *ibid.*, s.146(4).

exchange and is granted by a member of such an exchange, acting as an agent; or

3. relates to currency, shares, securities or an interest rate and is granted to an authorised person or listed institution within the meaning of 1 above concurrently and in association with an option which is granted by that authorised person or listed institution to the grantor of the option; or

4. relates to shares or securities which are dealt in on a recognised exchange and is granted to a member of such an exchange, including such a member acting as an agent.[15]

*Transactions in futures and options designed to produce a guaranteed return*

Before 1997 it was possible for a taxpayer to enter into derivative transactions that **3B–79** were designed to produce a 'guaranteed' return which was broadly equivalent to investing the net premium paid to enter into the transaction at interest. Such transactions were attractive where the gain would have been taxable under the capital gains provisions and where the taxpayer had unrelieved capital losses. Anti-avoidance provisions were introduced in the Finance Act 1997 and are now contained in Schedule 5AA ICTA 1988. These apply where the gain realised from such transactions would otherwise be assessable under the capital gains provisions. A transaction falls within these provisions if a guaranteed return is produced from one or more disposals of futures or options. A guaranteed return is deemed to arise whenever the risks from fluctuations in the underlying subject matter are so eliminated or reduced as to produce a return from the disposal or disposals of futures or options, the amount of which is not to any significant extent attributable (otherwise than incidentally) to any such fluctuations and which equates, in substance, to the return on an investment of money at interest.[16] These provisions also apply where the future or option is settled not by cash but by the delivery of another asset. Where the provisions apply, the resulting gain is assessed to tax under Schedule D Case VI. The reader is referred to Schedule 5AA ICTA 1988 for further information on these provisions.

VIII. APPENDIX 1—SOME COMMON DERIVATIVES CONTRACTS

**Caps Floors and Collars**

*Cap*

A cap is an interest rate contract between two parties, A and B. In a return for a **3B–80** premium paid by A, B agrees to make payments to A if interest rates exceed a limit specified in the contract at any time during the period covered by the contract. Such

---

[15] *ibid.* s144(8)(c), as applied by *ibid.*, s.146(4).
[16] ICTA 1988, Sched 5AA, para. 3.

payments will be determined by reference to the amount that the actual interest rate exceeds the limit specified in the cap, as applied to the specified principal amount.

Example

A PLC enters into an interest rate cap with B PLC for five years in order to hedge a floating rate loan that it has entered into for the purposes of its trade. Under the terms of the contract, B PLC undertakes, in return for an initial payment from A PLC, to make payments to A PLC if interest rates exceed 7% during the five-year period. The contract principal amount is set at £10 m. In the six months to June 30, 2002, interest rates move to 7.5%. B PLC makes a payment to A PLC of £25,000 (£10 m × 0.5% × 6/12).

Under an authorised accruals accounting policy, the cap premium would be amortised over the life of the loan and any receipts under the cap would be set against A's interest expense on the loan.

*Floor*

**3B–81** A floor is the opposite of an interest rate cap. Under the terms of an interest rate floor A PLC would undertake, in return for an initial premium, to make payments to B PLC if interest rates fall below a specified limit. Again such payments are determined by reference to a notional contract principal amount.

Example

A PLC enters into an interest rate floor with B PLC for five years. The floor limit is set at 6% and the notional contract principal amount is £10 m. In the six months to June 30, 2003, interest rates fall to 5.5%. A PLC therefore makes a payment to B PLC of £25,000 (£10 m × 0.5% × 6/12).

Typically, a company would enter into a floor in order to reduce the cost of an interest rate cap (*i.e.* the premium that it receives for entering into the floor can be set against the cost of the premium that it has to pay to enter into an interest rate cap).

*Collar or cylinder*

A collar or a cylinder is the term given to a combination of an interest rate cap and an interest rate floor, the collar or cylinder being the difference between the limit set under the terms of the interest rate floor and the ceiling set under the interest rate cap.

## Currency forward contract

This is a contract between two parties for the forward purchase or sale of foreign currency. It is typically used where a company wishes to hedge its currency exposure. For example, A PLC has contracted to purchase plant and machinery for US $1.6 m and this price is payable in three months time. It wishes to hedge its exchange rate exposure and therefore enters into a contract to buy US $1.6 m in three months time. This way it will be able to "fix" the cost of the plant and machinery in sterling terms.

Where a company enters into a contract to buy or sell foreign currency at a future date, the contract price is determined by adjusting the spot rate at the date that the contract is concluded by the interest differential between the two currencies covered by the contract. If the company is buying a weaker currency the forward price will be cheaper than the current spot price. Conversely, if a company is buying a stronger currency, the forward price will be higher than the current spot price. The difference between the spot price and the forward price is termed a forward premium (where the forward price is higher) or forward discount (where the forward price is cheaper). This forward premium or forward discount would be amortised over the life of a currency contract where the contract is accounted for on an accruals basis and the contract is revalued in a company's accounts (see example at 3B–50 for further explanation).

## Currency future

A currency future is an exchange traded contract. It is similar to a currency contract **3B–82** in that the purchaser of the future agrees to buy or sell a particular currency on the specified settlement day. During the period of the contract each of the parties is entitled to receive variation margin payments from the other if the contract is "in the money" and is obliged to make payments to the other if the contract is "out of the money".[17] Typically, most exchange traded currency futures contracts are closed out by a reciprocal contract rather than being settled by an exchange of currencies.

---

[17] These payments will be made via the clearing house for the exchange.

### Currency option

**3B–83**    A currency option can take a number of forms. It can include an option to exchange a specified amount of one currency for a specified amount of another currency. It can also cover an option to enter into a forward currency contract or a currency swap. For the purposes of the financial instruments legislation, a conditional currency contract is also treated as a currency option.

### Currency swap

**3B–84**    A currency swap is, in effect, a combination of an initial or spot exchange of currencies and a forward currency contract. At the outset of the swap there will be an exchange of currency (the exchange rate between the two currencies is usually the spot rate on the day on which the exchange takes place) and a re-exchange of currency will take place when the contract is terminated, again usually at the same exchange rate. The interest differential between the two currencies is usually dealt with by a series of swap differential payments over the life of the swap, as opposed to by an initial premium.

As in the case of an interest rate swap, it is possible to write a currency swap as an amortising swap, with exchanges of a proportional amount of the two currencies taking place over the life of the swap.

Example

A PLC would like US $1.6m funding for five years and it can borrow more cheaply in sterling than it can in US $. Another company, B PLC, would like five-year sterling funding. It can borrow more cheaply in US $ than it can in sterling. By entering into a currency swap each company can obtain funding in its desired currency, but at a lower cost. For the purposes of this example it is assumed that the US $ : sterling exchange rate on the day on that the initial exchange of currency takes place is 1.6 : 1.

A PLC would borrow £1m and B PLC would borrow US $1.6m. The two companies would then enter into a currency swap. Under the terms of the currency swap A PLC would pay £1m to B PLC in exchange for US $1.6m at the start of the swap and at the end of the five-year period A PLC would pay B PLC US $1.6m in exchange for £1m. During the period of the swap, A PLC would be liable to make swap differential payments to B PLC equal to a specified US $ interest rate, as applied to US $1.6m and it would be entitled to receive swap differential payments from B PLC that are determined by applying a specified interest rate to £1m.

Initial exchange

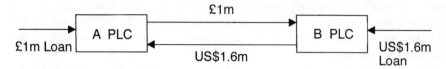

Swap differential payments

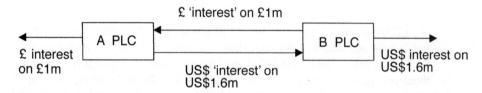

Re-exchange

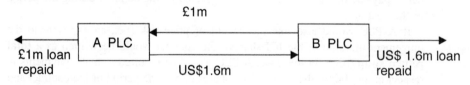

## Debt contracts and futures

Debt contracts and futures are written by reference to actual or notional bonds and **3B–85** gilts. They can either be settled by physical delivery (*i.e.*, the delivery of the bonds or gilts in question) or by a cash payment equal to the difference between the market value of the bonds or gilts at the date of settlement and the contract price. Typically, a company might enter into a bond or gilt contract as a means of hedging its long term interest rate exposure.

Exchange traded bond and gilts contracts are termed futures. In the case of LIFFE, for example, gilt and bond futures are written over notional gilts and bonds respectively and the contract (if not closed out before maturity by the company entering into an equal and opposite contract) is required to be settled by the delivery of gilts or bonds (as appropriate) that are listed on a list maintained by the exchange.

### Equity or equity index swap

**3B–86**    This is a transaction in which one party pays periodic amounts of a given currency based on a fixed price or a fixed rate and the other pays periodic amounts of the same currency or a different currency based on the performance of a share of an issuer, a basket of shares of several issuers or an equity index such as the Standard and Poor's 500 Index. Such contracts do **not** fall within the provisions of the financial instruments legislation and nor does the Inland Revenue consider that such contracts fall within the provisions of section 143 of the Taxation of Chargeable Gains Act 1992. As discussed at 3B–74 above, the authors disagree with this view.

Example

A PLC would like to have the benefit of investing in ICI shares for three years but it does not want to hold such shares. In order to be in the same economic position as being "long" the ICI shares, it could enter into an equity swap for a three year period. It wishes to invest £500,000 and therefore the equity swap is written by reference to such number of ICI shares as a market value of £500,000 at the date the contract takes effect. Under the terms of the equity swap A PLC is required to make floating rate payments determined by applying (say) LIBOR + 0.2% to £500,000 and would be entitled to receive amounts equal to the dividends payable on the number of shares covered by the contract during the period of the contract.

If A PLC would also like the benefit of price risk (*i.e.*, an exposure to the movement in value of the ICI shares), the contract would be written as a **total return swap** (q.v.). In this case, A PLC would be required to make payments in respect of any fall in the value of the shares during the period of the contract and would be entitled to receive payments equal to any growth in value of the equities during the period of the contract as is illustrated in the diagram below. Typically, each party to the contract would be required to provide collateral to the other if the price of the shares moved against it over the life of the contract.

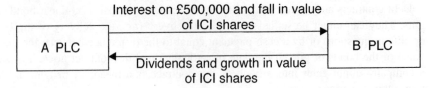

### Forward rate agreement (FRA)

**3B–87**    This is an interest rate contract that has largely been developed in the interbank market. It is an arrangement that enables a purchaser to "fix" its interest rate in advance for a specified future period. It is, in effect, an agreement to pay or receive, on an agreed future date, the difference between the interest rate specified in the contract and the actual interest rate for the specified future period, as applied to a notional principal amount. Typically, such contracts are settled at the start of the period initially covered by the contract and the settlement payment is discounted to reflect this.

Example

A PLC is a bank and it wishes to hedge its floating rate exposure for six months. On July 1, 2001 it enters into a FRA covering the period from January 1, 2002 to June 30 to 2002. The rate specified in the FRA is 6% and the notional contract principal amount is £10m. If the six month LIBOR interest rate at January 1, 2002 is (say) 6.5%, A PLC would receive a payment and if the six month LIBOR interest rate was less than 6%, A PLC would be obliged to make a payment under the terms of the FRA. The effect of an FRA contract is that A PLC would have 'fixed' its cost of funds for the six month period at 6%.

**Interest rate option**

This term can cover a number of contracts.

*Exchange traded contracts*

This is a contract that it is traded on a recognised futures exchange. In some respects it is similar to an **FRA** (q.v.) but it operates in "reverse". If a company wishes to hedge itself against a rise in interest rates, it would buy an FRA whereas it would need to sell an interest rate future. Typically, such futures are traded by reference to a set notional contract principal amount and therefore a company may have to enter into a number of futures contracts in order to achieve the desired level of hedging. Under the terms of the future, if interest rates exceed the limit specified in the contract, the seller will be entitled to receive a payment from the counterparty. If, however, interest rates fall, the seller is required to make a payment to the counterparty. An interest rate future is valued on a mark to market basis on a daily basis by the clearing house for the exchange and each party to the contract is required to make a variation margin payment to the clearing house if the market value of the contract moves against that party. This payment is then passed on to the other party to the contract. The effect of this is that if the contract runs to maturity, no amount would normally be payable since all interest rate movements would have been dealt with by the variation margin payments. Unlike an FRA settlement payment made in connection with an interest rate future are not discounted.

*OTC option contracts*

**3B–88**   An interest rate option can also cover an option to enter into an interest rate contract. For example, it could cover an option to enter into an **interest rate swap** (q.v.), termed a **'swaption'**.

## Interest rate swap

An interest rate swap is an agreement between two parties, under the terms of which, typically, each of the parties undertakes to pay the other an amount equal to a specified rate of interest applied to the notional principal amount of the contract. Such payments are termed 'swap differential payments'. A typical swap would be a floating rate for fixed rate interest swap. That it is where one of the parties agrees to make payments to the other by applying a fixed rate of interest to the notional contract principal amount whilst the other agrees to make payments determined by applying a specified floating rate of interest to the same principal amount.

Sometimes, in the case of a fixed for floating swap, a fixed payment may be substituted for a payment by reference to a fixed rate of interest.

It is also possible to swap payments on one floating rate basis for another. Such swaps are termed **basis swaps**.

Typically, an interest rate swap would be used by a company to cut of the cost of its borrowing. An example would be where a company wants floating rate funding but such funding is relatively more expensive for that company than fixed rate funding. What the company might do in such circumstances is to borrow on fixed rate terms and then to enter into a floating rate for fixed rate interest swap. The company would make floating rate payments under the terms of the swap and would receive fixed rate payments which it could then use to satisfy its interest liability. As a result of entering into the interest rate swap, the company is now, effectively, borrowing at a floating rate of interest and this is how its interest expense would generally be reflected in its accounts.

The notional principal of an interest rate swap does not have to remain constant over the life of the swap and, for example, it could reduce over the life of a swap (amortising swap) where a swap is used as a hedge against a loan that is being repaid in instalments.

Example

A PLC wants five-year floating rate funding. It can obtain floating rate funding at LIBOR + 0.2% and also has access to fixed rate borrowing at 7%. At the same time another company, B PLC, has access to floating rate borrowing at LIBOR

+ 0.9% and also has access to fixed rate borrowing at 8.5%. B PLC would prefer fixed rate borrowing. A PLC enters into a fixed rate loan and B PLC enters into a floating rate loan. Both companies then enter into an interest rate swap.

By entering into an interest rate swap both A PLC and B PLC can obtain their desired funding at a lower cost. Under the terms of the interest rate swap, A PLC makes floating rate payments to B PLC determined by applying LIBOR to the notional contract principal whilst B PLC makes fixed rate payments to A PLC at 7.2%.

The effect of the interest rate swap is that each of the companies will have reduced the cost of borrowing on the desired basis by 0.4%.

A PLC could have obtained floating rate funding at LIBOR + 0.2%. By entering into the interest rate swap, it has obtained floating rate funding at LIBOR – 0.2% (7% – 7.2% + LIBOR) = LIBOR – 0.2%, an overall saving of 0.4%.

B PLC could have obtained fixed rate funding at 8.5%. By entering into the interest rate swap it is net cost of funds becomes (LIBOR + 0.9% + 7.2% – LIBOR) = 8.1%, again an overall saving of 0.4%.

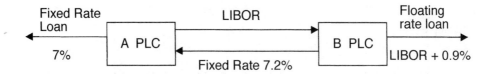

| | A PLC | B PLC |
| --- | --- | --- |
| With swap | LIBOR – 0.2% | 8.1% |
| Without swap | LIBOR + 0.2% | 8.5% |
| Saving | 0.4% | 0.4% |

**Options**

Options may be divided into two broad categories: **call options** and **put options**.    **3B–89**

A **call option** gives the holder the right (but not an obligation) to buy a specified quantity of a commodity or a financial instrument at a fixed price at a future date.

A **put option** gives the holder the right (but not an obligation) to sell an underlying commodity or financial instrument at a fixed price at a future date.

Where an option is capable of being exercised only on a specified future date it is referred to as a **European style** option and if it is capable of being exercised at any time in a specified future period it is referred to as an **American style** option.

## Total Return Swap

**3B–90**    A total return swap is a transaction in which:

1. one party pays either a single amount or periodic amounts based on the total return on one or more loans, debt securities or other financial instruments ( each a "reference obligation") that are issued, guaranteed or otherwise entered into by a third party. Such payments are calculated by reference to interest, dividend and fee payments as well as any appreciation in the market value of the reference obligation; and
2. the other party pays either a single amount or periodic amounts determined by reference to a specified notional amount and any depreciation in value of each reference obligation.

As mentioned at 3B–74 the Inland Revenue do not consider that swaps fall within section 143 of the Taxation of Chargeable Gains Act 1992. The authors disagree with this view.


Example


A PLC would like the economic benefit of holding specified debt securities without actually owning such securities. Accordingly, it enters into a total return swap. Under the terms of the swap it will pay 'interest' on a specified amount (typically, the market value of the securities at the start of the contract and will be liable to make a payment in respect of any fall in value of the securities during the period covered by the contract. The counterparty, B PLC, would be obliged to make payments to A PLC equal to any dividends payable on the reference securities over the period of the contract and would also be required to make a payment to A PLC in respect of any growth in value of the securities during the period covered by the contract.

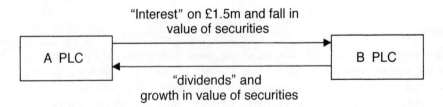

CHAPTER 4

# COMPLIANCE

## I. INTRODUCTION

### Assessment of persons other than a company

9. on a company which has claimed group relief for an accounting period from another company (surrendering company) where another company (chargeable company) has also claimed group relief from the surrendering company for that period and the amount of group relief available to the chargeable company from the surrendering company subsequently reduces and as a result the chargeable company's corporation tax liability for that accounting period increases. In such cases if the chargeable company fails to pay such additional tax within six months of the last date for which it could make or withdraw a group relief claim for that accounting period the additional tax may be recovered form any other company that has claimed group relief from the surrendering company for that period.[1]

10. on other group companies where corporation tax due by a non-resident group member is not paid within six months of the time that it becomes payable. Where the non-resident company is a consortium company, any corporation tax which is not paid by that company within six months of the time that is

**4–06**

---

[1] FA 1988, Sched. 18 para. 75A, as inserted by FA 1999, s.92(3),(7) for accounting periods ending after June 30, 1999.

becomes payable may be assessed on a member of the consortium or, where the member of the consortium is itself a member of a group of companies, on any other company which is a member of that group of companies.[2] This is considered further at 4–10A below.

### Recovery of tax payable by a non-resident company

**4–10A**    As mentioned later in this supplement (see paras 22–04 and 23–05) following amendments introduced by the Finance Act 2000, it is now possible for a United Kingdom branch of a non-resident company to be included within a group relief and a capital gains group. The Inland Revenue has been given powers to collect corporation tax that has been assessed on a non-resident company (taxpayer company) for an accounting period from certain other companies where such tax remains unpaid after the end of six months from the time at which it becomes payable.[3] For the purposes of these provisions a company is defined as any body corporate.[4] The companies from which such tax can be recovered are:

1. any company which was at any time in the relevant period a member of the same group of companies as the taxpayer company. Two companies will be regarded as members of the same group whenever one is the 51% subsidiary of the other or both are 51% subsidiaries of a third company[5];
2. where the taxpayer company is a consortium company, any company that was at any time in the relevant period a member of the consortium that owned the taxpayer company. A company is treated as a member of the consortium for these purposes where it would be treated as a consortium member for the purposes of the group relief legislation[6];
3. any company which was at any time in the relevant period a member of the same group of companies as a company which at that time was a member of a consortium that owned the taxpayer company. For these purposes a company will be treated as a member of the same group of companies where it would be so treated for the purposes of group relief.[7]

For the above purposes the relevant period is the period ending with the date that the tax first became payable and starting on the later of:

---

[2] FA 2000, Sched.28.
[3] FA 2000, Sched. 28 para. 1.
[4] *ibid*. Sched. 28 para. 6(1).
[5] *ibid*. Sched. 28 para. 2(1)(a), (3)(a).
[6] *ibid*. Sched. 28 para. 2(1)(b), (4).
[7] *ibid*. Sched. 28 para. 2(1)(c), (3)(b), (4).

(a) twelve months before the start of the accounting period for which the tax is payable; or

(b) April 1, 2000.[8]

*Assessment procedures*

In order to be able to collect tax owed by non-resident company from one of the above companies, the Inland Revenue is required to serve a notice on the company requiring it within thirty days of the date that the notice is served to pay the amount of unpaid tax, or in the case of a consortium member, the appropriate proportion of that tax.[9]

In the case of a consortium member the appropriate amount of the tax is a proportion of the unpaid tax determined as follows:

(a) where the company on which the notice is served is a member of the consortium, the share that it had in the consortium for the relevant period[10];

(b) in the case of a company that is a member of the same group as the consortium member(s), the share which companies in that group had in the consortium for the relevant period[11]; or

(c) where the company is both a member of the consortium in its own right and also a member of a group where one or more other companies in that group hold shares in the consortium, the higher of that company share in the consortium and the groups' share in the consortium at any time during the relevant period.[12]

A member's share in a consortium for the relevant period is the lowest of the following percentages:

(i) the percentage of the ordinary share capital of the taxpayer company which is beneficially owned by that member;

(ii) the percentage to which that member is beneficially entitled of any profits available for distribution to equity holders of the taxpayer company; and

(iii) the percentage to which that member would be beneficially entitled of any assets of the taxpayer company available for distribution to equity holders on a winding-up.

---

[8] *ibid.* Sched. 28 para. 2(2).

[9] *ibid.* Sched. 28 para. 3. The notice must state the amount of corporation tax assessed on the non-resident company for the accounting period in question, the date when it first became payable and the amount that is required to be paid by the company on which the notice is served.

[10] *ibid.* Sched. 28 para. 5(1)(a).

[11] *ibid.* Sched. 28 para. 5(1)(b).

[12] *ibid.* Sched. 28 para. 5(1)(c).

If any of these percentages have fluctuated in the relevant period an average percentage over the period is taken.[13]

A notice must be served within three years beginning with the date on which the liability of the taxpayer company for the accounting period in question is finally determined.[14]

Where an assessment is made on a company to collect unpaid corporation tax due by a non-resident company, that company will also be responsible for discharging any interest payable on the outstanding tax for the period from the date at which the tax became due by the non-resident company up until the date that the company discharges this liability.[15]

## The right of recovery

**4–10B**    Where corporation tax due by a non-resident company is assessed on another company, that other company has a right to recover that tax from the non-resident company.[16] Where a company discharges a tax liability of a non-resident company as a result of a notice being served on it under the provisions of Schedule 28 to the Finance Act 2000, that company is not permitted to claim a deduction for the tax that is so assessed in computing its income or profits for any tax purposes.[17]

## III. Payments, Repayments and Tax Refunds

## Large companies—payment by instalments

**4–21**    The Corporation Tax (Instalment Payments) Regulations took effect from the start of a company's first accounting period which ended on or after July 1, 1999[18] and, broadly, require a large company to pay its annual corporation tax liability in, normally, four instalments, two of which fall during the accounting period and two of which fall after the end of the accounting period.

---

[13] *ibid.* Sched. 28 para. 5(3).

[14] *ibid.* Sched. 28 para. 4. There are provisions in this paragraph to determine the date on which the tax liability becomes finally determined where unpaid tax is charged in consequence of a determination under FA 1998 Sched. 18 para. 36 or para. 37; where the unpaid tax is charged in a self-assessment; and where the unpaid tax is charged in a discovery assessment.

[15] TMA 1970 s.87A(3), as amended by FA 2000, Sched. 28 para. 3(4).

[16] *ibid.* Sched. 28 para. 6(2).

[17] *ibid.* Sched. 28 para. 6(3).

[18] S.I. 1998 No. 3175, reg.1(2).

A large company is a company whose profits[19] for the accounting period exceed the upper relevant maximum amount for small companies' relief purposes.[20] This limit is currently £1.5 million for the financial year to March 31, 2000. The limit is proportionally reduced where an accounting period is less than 12 months in length. If the company has associated companies, the limit for the accounting period in question is divided by 1 plus the number of associated companies in order to determine the quarterly payment threshold for each of the companies.[21]

A company will not, however, be treated as a large company for an accounting period if:

(i) its total liability for that period does not exceed £5,000 in the case of an accounting period ending before July 1, 2000, or £10,000 in the case of an accounting period ending on or after July 1, 2000[22]; or.

(ii) its profits for that period do not exceed £10 million and it was not a large company in the 12 months preceding that accounting period. If the company has associated companies[23] this limit is divided by 1 plus the number of such companies and if the accounting period in question is less than 12 months in length the limit is proportionately reduced. For these purposes a company will not be treated as a large company in the preceding period of 12 months if:

(a) during any part of that preceding period it either did not exist or did not have an accounting period; or

(b) the company was not a large company for the purposes of the Regulations for an accounting period which fell within or ended in that preceding period. For these purposes a company will be regarded as a large company for that accounting period if the only reason why it was not treated as a large company for that period was because it fell within this exemption.[24]

---

[19] Profits are defined as the amount of the company's profits chargeable to corporation tax and franked investment income, other than franked investment income which the company receives from companies within the group. Group is defined as within the meaning of ICTA 1988, s.247, *i.e.* a U.K. resident company and all its direct and indirect U.K. resident 51% subsidiary companies: *ibid.* reg.2.

[20] As defined in ICTA 1988, s.13 except that the exclusions within ICTA 1988, s.434(3A), (3B) (Life Assurance Companies policy holders' share of franked investment income and foreign dividends respectively) and FA 1989, s.88(4) (Life Assurance Companies—exclusion for policy holders' share of a company's relevant profits) are disregarded: *ibid.* reg. 3(1), (4), (5).

[21] *ibid.* reg. 3(5).

[22] *ibid.* reg. 3(2).

[23] For these purposes where the company's preceding accounting period ended immediately before the start of its current accounting period the number of associated companies is the number at the end of the previous period. In other cases the number to be used is the number of such companies at the start of the current accounting period: *ibid.* reg. 3(5).

[24] *ibid.* reg. 3(3), (6), (7).

*Due dates*

The first quarterly payment is normally due six months and 13 days after the start of the accounting period and the final payment is due three months and 14 days after the end of the accounting period. Depending on the length of the accounting period, additional quarterly payments (subject to there being a maximum of four) are payable three months after the end of the immediately preceding instalment payment.[25] This means that where a company's accounting period is 12 months in length its quarterly instalment payments will be due as follows:

6 months and 13 days after the start of the accounting period;
9 months and 13 days after the start of the accounting period;
13 days after the end of the accounting period; and
3 months and 14 days after the end of the accounting period.

If the length of the accounting period is such that the date which is three months and 14 days from the end of the accounting period falls earlier than the date which is six months and 13 days from the start of the accounting period, the full amount of the company's tax liability is treated as becoming due and payable on the date which is three months and 14 days from the end of the accounting period.[1] This provision will thus apply where a company has an accounting period which is less than three months in length.

The amount of each quarterly payment is determined by reference to the formula:

$$3 \times \frac{CTI}{n}$$

CTI is the company's total liability[2] for the accounting period and $n$ is the number of complete months and fractional months in the accounting period. The percentage for a fractional month is determined by dividing the number of days in that incomplete month by 30 and then expressing the resulting percentage to two decimal places.[3]

The amount which is treated as payable on the first instalment date is the lower of the amount given by the above formula and the company's tax liability for that accounting period. The amount which is treated as payable for each subsequent instal-

---

[25] *ibid.* reg. 5(2), (3).

[1] *ibid.* reg. 5(4).

[2] This is the amount of tax payable for that period by the company as calculated in accordance with FA 1998, Sched. 18, para. 8(1) (*i.e.* the company's corporation tax payable for the period as reduced by all available set offs and reliefs, including income tax deducted from payments received by the company), less the amount (if any) of deductions from payments made to the company under the subcontractor provisions of ICTA 1988, s. 559: *ibid.* reg. 2(3).

[3] *ibid.* reg. 5(5), (9).

ment payment, other than the last, is the amount given by the above formula and the balance of the company's total liability for that accounting period. That which is treated as becoming due and payable on the final instalment date is the balance of the company's total liability for that accounting period.[4]

*Refunds*

If a company considers at any time that it has paid too much tax under the quarterly instalment regime as a result of a change in its circumstances after the payment was made, for example if the company's taxable profits are significantly less than anticipated, it can apply for a repayment of the tax which it considers it has overpaid.[5] The request for a repayment must set out the amount which the company considers should be repaid and the grounds on which it considers that its tax liability for the period is less than it originally estimated. A company can also apply for a refund where it has appealed against an amendment of an assessment or an assessment and the appeal has not been determined. In such cases it can apply to the commissioners to whom its appeal has been referred for a determination of the amount which should be repaid to the company pending the outcome of its appeal.[6]

*Interest*

Any tax which is underpaid or overpaid at each instalment date will attract interest from that date. Special rates of interest apply up until nine months and one day after the end of the accounting period when the normal interest on overdue tax regime comes into force.[7] One company in a group can surrender an overpayment of tax to another and in such cases the claimant company will be treated as if it had paid the tax on the same day as the surrendering company.[8]

*Records*

The Inland Revenue has the power to demand the production of records from the company in support of its quarterly payments. These powers may be exercised at any time after the filing date for the accounting period in question, subject to a minimum period of notice of 30 days. The Revenue has the power both to inspect the company's calculations in support of its quarterly payments, or in support of the reason why no

---

[4] *ibid.* reg. 5(6)–(8).
[5] The Inland Revenue confirmed that a repayment could be claimed at any time in an article in its February 2000 Tax Bulletin.
[6] S.I. 1998 No. 3175, reg. 6.
[7] The rates of interest on underpaid and overpaid tax under the instalment provisions are base rate plus 1% and base rate minus 0.25 respectively—S.I. 1989 No. 1297 regs 3ZA and 3BA, as amended by S.I. 2000 No. 893.
[8] FA 1989, s.102(4) and (5A)–(5F) as inserted by S.I. 1998 No. 3175, reg. 9 (as revised by S.I. 1999 No. 1929).

payments were made or of a repayment claim, as well as its underlying books and records.[9]

In a press release issued on June 8, 1999, the Revenue stated that it may seek to make use of its information powers where there are indications that a company may have deliberately or recklessly failed to comply with its payment obligations under the Regulations, or fraudulently or negligently made a claim for a repayment. Where the Revenue believes this to be the case, it will request all the necessary evidence in order to form a judgement as to whether the company, or persons acting on its behalf, acted deliberately or recklessly in failing to make its payments as they fell due or, in later failing to correct the position as newer and more accurate information became available.

*Penalties*

A penalty of twice the amount of interest due on tax underpaid under the Regulations will be payable if the company, or person acting on its behalf, deliberately or recklessly fails to pay instalment payments or if the company, or person acting on its behalf, fraudulently or negligently makes a claim for a repayment of tax.[10] In its June 8 press release, the Inland Revenue stated that it would only seek to impose such a penalty where it was clear that the failure was not merely due to negligence and that it was deliberate or reckless. The press release also states that the Inland Revenue will only seek a penalty in the most serious cases involving "flagrant abuse of the Regulations" and that before an inspector can impose such a penalty he will be required to seek Head Office approval.

*Transitional provisions*

For an initial period the Instalment Payment Regulations will apply on a limited basis for accounting periods ending before July 1, 2002. The amount of a company's tax liability which has to be paid on an instalment basis for such periods is:

| | |
|---|---|
| —an accounting period ending on or after July 1, 1999 but before July 1, 2000; | 60 per cent |
| —an accounting period ending on or after July 1 2000 but before July 1, 2001; and | 72 per cent |
| —an accounting period ending on or after July 1, 2001 but before July 1, 2002. | 88 per cent |

In each of the above cases, the balance of the company's tax liability for the accounting period in question is due nine months and one day from the end of that accounting period.

---

[9] S.I. 1998 No. 3175, regs 10–12.
[10] *ibid.* reg. 13 and TMA 1970, s.59E(4).

*Transitional rules—anti-avoidance provisions*

There are provisions to prevent a company from deferring payment of its tax under the transitional rules. These apply, with certain limited exceptions, where after November 25, 1997 and before June 30, 2002 the company either changes the date on which its accounting period begins or ends or transfers its taxable profits to another company in the same group and in each case the effect is that corporation tax is payable later than it otherwise would have been. In such cases the company is required to account to the Inland Revenue for an amount equal to interest on the corporation tax which has been deferred from the date the tax would otherwise have been payable, but for action taken by the company, until the date the tax is paid.[11]

The exceptions for a change to the start or end date of an accounting period are:

(i) where the change of accounting data derives from a decision made before or as a result of facts in existence at November 25, 1997;

(ii) an accounting period coming to an end as a result of the company beginning or ceasing to carry on a trade, or the company becoming or ceasing to be United Kingdom resident or the company ceasing to be within the charge to corporation tax. This exception does not apply where the accounting period comes to an end as a result of the transfer of the company's activities to another group company;

(iii) an accounting period coming to an end as a result of the transfer of the whole or part of the long-term business of an insurance company to another company in accordance with a scheme sanctioned by a court under Part I of Schedule 2C to the Insurance Companies Act;

(iv) the change arises as a result of:

  (a) a change in the ultimate control of the company giving rise to the alignment of the company's accounting period with that of its new parent company, where the change is effected before the end of the accounting period of the new ultimate parent company in which the change occurs; or

  (b) a notice by the company under section 224(2) of the Companies Act 1985 (specification of accounting reference date not later than nine months after the date of incorporation) in order to align the company's accounting period with that of its ultimate parent company.[12]

The exceptions for a transfer of part of the company's profits to another group company are:

(i) the accounting period of the transferee company begins and ends on the same dates as the transferor and the transferor has not changed the date or dates of any of its accounting periods;

---

[11] *ibid.* reg. 14. For these purposes a group is defined as a parent company and its 51% subsidiaries: *ibid.* reg. 14(11)(b).

[12] *ibid.* reg. 14(6).

(ii) as a result of the transfer of profits, the profits of the transferor company for the accounting period in which the transfer is effected, or for any subsequent accounting period, are reduced by an amount not exceeding £5 million, or as proportionately reduced where the accounting period is less than 12 months in length; or

(iii) the transferee company is resident outside the United Kingdom and is not trading in the United Kingdom through a branch or agency, or if it is so trading the transferred profits are not included in computing the profits of that branch or agency.[13]

### Groups—payment of tax by representative company

**4–24**    Under section 36 of the Finance Act 1998, the Inland Revenue can enter into arrangements with some or all of the members of a group of companies for one representative member, the Nominated Member, to pay quarterly payments of tax on behalf of other members of that group. The Inland Revenue has now produced a non-negotiable contract into which the Nominated Member can enter in order for it to pay the tax payments due by participating group companies. The references to clauses which follow are references to the clauses of that contract.

For the purpose of the group payment arrangements, a group consists of a company and all its 51 per cent subsidiaries, the 51 per cent subsidiaries of those subsidiaries, and 51 per cent subsidiaries of those subsidiaries and so on.[14]

EXAMPLE

A
| 51%
B
| 51%
C
| 51%
D
| 51%
E

---

[13] *ibid.* reg. 14(7), (8).
[14] FA 1998, s.36(4).

In the above example, A, B, C, D and E could be included within a group payment arrangement. There is no requirement that all companies within a group have to be included within the group payment arrangement, or, indeed, that the ultimate United Kingdom resident holding company has to be included within the arrangement. Thus, for example, it would be possible for (say) D and E to be within one payment group and for A, B and C to be in another. Further, while the Nominated Member has to be United Kingdom resident there is no requirement that all the other companies (Participating Companies) within the group payment arrangement have to be United Kingdom resident. Thus, it would be possible to include a United Kingdom branch of an overseas company within the arrangement.[15] In order for a company to be included within a group payment arrangement, its accounting period:

(i) must be co-extensive with that of the Nominated Member; or
(ii) whilst not co-extensive with the period of account of the Nominated Member, must fall wholly within and be coterminous with the accounting period of the Nominated Member; or
(iii) must fall wholly within but end before the end of the Nominated Member's accounting period and its subsequent accounting period must end on the same date as that of the Nominated Member.[61]

An accounting period which satisfies the above criteria is defined as a Relevant Accounting Period.[17] The provision in (iii) above is designed to cover, *inter alia*, a case where a company within the group payment arrangement ceases to trade thus bringing an accounting period to an end, but its accounting reference date remains unchanged. A company can only be included within a group payment arrangement if it has filed a tax return and paid the tax due for its last but one accounting period.[18]

Unlike a VAT Group, the companies which are included within a group payment arrangement do not have joint and several liability for the tax of all other group members and each company continues to be responsible for discharging its own tax liability.[19] A group payment arrangement applies for an accounting period of the Nominated Member. Under the terms of the group payment arrangements, the Inland Revenue will undertake that it will not seek to pursue any of the Participating Companies for settlement of their tax liabilities until the closing date.[20] This is defined as the later of:

---

[15] See definitions in clause 1 of the Group Payment Arrangement contract and also an article on Group Payment Arrangements in the Inland Revenue *Tax Bulletin*, April 1999 pp. 647–650.
[16] Clauses 1 and 2.
[17] Clause 1.
[18] See Inland Revenue *Tax Bulletin*, April 1998 at p. 648.
[19] FA 1998, s.36(3).
[20] Clause 5, Group Payment Arrangement Contract. Closing date is defined in clause 1.

(i) the latest filing date[21] of any of the Participating Companies for a company tax return for a Relevant Accounting Period; and

(ii) the earliest date on which all of the Participating Companies have either submitted company tax returns for every Relevant Accounting Period or in the absence of such a return, have had their tax determined by the Board of Inland Revenue for that accounting period under the provisions of Schedule 18, paragraphs 36–39 to the Finance Act 1998.[22]

Until the closing date, there is no requirement that the Nominated Member must specify how the payments it makes on behalf of group companies are to be allocated within the group. This is subject to an exception in a case where a company leaves the group during the accounting period (see below). If a Nominated Member considers that it has paid too much tax at any stage before the closing date it is able to request the repayment of the excess from the Inland Revenue. Where a repayment is made, any interest due on the sum refunded will not be paid until after the closing date for that accounting period.[23]

In order to be effective, a group must send a signed arrangement document to an Inland Revenue Group Payment Team normally no later than two months before the first payment of tax is due under the quarterly instalment regime. The group payment arrangement will take effect from the start of the accounting period of the Nominated Member for which it is made and will normally continue to apply for subsequent accounting periods unless it is terminated by either party. An agreement can only be terminated for an accounting period if notice is given before the date on which the first quarterly instalment is due for payment.[24] Once a group payment arrangement has been concluded, it is possible to include or exclude a company from the arrangement for an accounting period if notification is given to the Inland Revenue before the date the first quarterly instalment period is due for that accounting period.[25] It should be noted, however, that it will only be possible to include a company which has joined the group within the group payment arrangement for an accounting period if the Relevant Accounting Period conditions set out above are satisfied. Where a company leaves the group during an accounting period, it will be excluded from the

---

[21] This is defined in clause 1 as having the meaning given by FA 1998, Sched. 18, para. 14. This defines filing date as the last day of whichever of the following periods is the last to end:

(a) 12 months from the end of the period for which the return is made;

(b) if the company's statutory accounting period is not longer than 18 months, 12 months from the end of that period; or

(c) if the company's statutory accounting period is longer than 18 months, 30 months from the beginning of that period; or

(d) three months from the date on which the notice requiring the return was served.

[22] Clauses 1 and 5.

[23] Clause 4.

[24] Clause 18.

[25] Clauses 15 and 16.

group payment arrangements from the date on which it leaves the group and the Inland Revenue will have the right to pursue the company for any unpaid tax for that period.[1] The Nominated Member can determine whether any of the tax paid by the group, up to the date that the departing company leaves the group, is to be allocated to that company. An apportionment may be made at the date on which the Nominated Member apportions payments made for that accounting period to all Participating Companies or, at an earlier date, for example the date the company leaves the group.[2]

Where the Nominated Member itself leaves the group, the payments made by the Nominated Member will continue to be available to the group and the group can elect for another company to act as the nominated member on behalf of the group.[3]

The Nominated Member is required to remove a company from the group payment arrangement if the company leaves the group or if the company fails to meet the accounting period criteria.[4] If the Nominated Member fails to remove such a company, the Inland Revenue has the power to remove that company. The Inland Revenue also has the power to remove a company if the Board has reason to believe that the company was not a member of the group at the time it was included within the group payment arrangement. The Inland Revenue can exercise its powers to remove a company from the group payment arrangement up to six months before the closing date for that accounting period. If a company is excluded from the group payment arrangements the same consequences ensue as in the case where a company leaves the group.[5]

The Inland Revenue can terminate the group payment arrangement if:

(i) any of the Participating Companies fails to meet its obligations to pay corporation tax or to file its company tax return for any accounting period whilst a group payment arrangement is in force; or

(ii) the Nominated Member is in breach of any of its obligations under the arrangement; or

(iii) the Inland Revenue has reason to believe that any member of the group of companies (whether or not such member has been included within the group payment arrangements) may become liable to tax under section 767A or 767AA of the Taxes Act 1988.[6]

Whilst this provision gives the Inland Revenue the right to terminate the arrangement in a wide range of circumstances, the Inland Revenue has stated that it will only terminate an arrangement under this provision in cases where there has been a serious failure or breach or a pattern of non-compliance, and not for minor matters.[7] If a group

---

[1] Clauses 13 and 14.
[2] Clause 14(c).
[3] Clause 22.
[4] Clause 13.1.
[5] Clauses 13.2 and 14.
[6] Clause 19.
[7] See Guidance Notes on clause 19. These Guidance Notes were issued in conjunction with the Group Payment Arrangement Contract.

payment arrangement is terminated by the Inland Revenue, the group will not be entitled to register for a new arrangement for the next accounting period.[8]

After the closing date, the Board will give notice to the Nominated Member of the additional payments of tax which are required, or alternatively details of any overpayment. On receipt of this notice, the Nominated Member can irrevocably specify how payments made under the arrangement should be apportioned amongst the Participating Companies.[9] If the Nominated Member fails to make the apportionment, the Inland Revenue can make an apportionment instead. This apportionment will be made on the basis of the liabilities of the Participating Companies as disclosed on their returns and the Nominated Member has 30 days from the date the Board gives notice of its apportionment to vary the apportionment.[10]

The Inland Revenue also has the power to reapportion payments among the Participating Companies if the liabilities of one or more of them remains outstanding after an apportionment by the Nominated Member and the Nominated Member cannot amend such an apportionment.[11] The Inland Revenue has, however, indicated that it will only exercise such powers if the Nominated Member's apportionment leaves an underpayment for a Participating Company and the Inland Revenue cannot recover the shortfall from that company.[12] Where payments are allocated to a Participating Company, whether by the Nominated Member or by the Inland Revenue, such payments will be treated as if they had been paid by the Participating Company on the dates on which they were paid by the Nominated Member.[13]

Deemed apportionment provisions apply where one or more of the Participating Companies is liable to a tax-related penalty under paragraph 18 of Schedule 18 to the Finance Act 1998. In this case payments will be deemed to be apportioned (to the extent that they have not been repaid or apportioned to a company that has left the group) to the Participating Companies in the following order:

(i) to those which have not incurred a late-filing penalty, or have only incurred a fixed-rate penalty;

(ii) to those which have incurred a tax-related penalty at the lower rate of 10 per cent; and

(iii) to those which have incurred a tax-related penalty at the higher rate of 20 per cent, either by failing to file a return or by filing it more than two years after the end of the period for which it is required.[14]

---

[8] See Guidance Notes on clause 19.
[9] Clause 8.
[10] Clause 9.
[11] Clause 10.
[12] Guidance Notes on clause 10.
[13] Clause 11.
[14] Clause 12.

The purpose of this provision is to ensure that a company which has filed its return late and which is therefore liable to a tax-related penalty cannot have the amount of the penalty reduced as a result of the Nominated Member's apportionment.

## V. Self Assessment

### Duty to keep and preserve records

The Inland Revenue issued guidance on the records which a company will be **4–43** required to keep under self-assessment in *Tax Bulletin*, October 1998.[15] Under section 221 of the Companies Act 1985, companies are required to keep and preserve specific accounting records. Where a company's accounting records satisfy the requirements of the Companies Act the Inland Revenue will accept that the requirements of Schedule 18, paragraphs 21 to 23 to the Finance Act 1998 are also satisfied. This is subject to the proviso that additional evidence will be required to justify arm's length pricing in the case of cross-border transactions with connected parties (see paragraph 8-16 of this Supplement).

For Companies Act purposes a company is only required to retain its accounting records for three years. For tax purposes a company will be required to retain its accounting records for six years, or, if later, until an Inland Revenue enquiry into the return for that year has been completed, or until the deadline for such an enquiry has expired in a case where no enquiry is initiated by the Inland Revenue. These records can be preserved on microfiche or in electronic form. Standard information such as contractual terms and conditions printed on each invoice does not need to be reproduced as part of the record of each transaction. Original records still have to be retained in certain cases[16] and these include vouchers for tax withheld from income or in support of double tax relief claims.

### Revenue enquiries

The Inland Revenue Published Code of Practice 14 *Enquiries into company tax* **4–44** *returns* in July 1999. This booklet describes the basis on which the Inland Revenue carries out its enquiries into company tax returns under the self-assessment regime. It does not cover enquiries which are handled by Special Compliance Office.

---

[15] pp. 587–588.
[16] See FA 1998, Sched. 18, para. 22(3).

VI. Penalties

**Penalties for record keeping**

**4–46A**     Under Schedule 18, paragraph 23 to the Finance Act 1998 a company can be liable for a maximum penalty of up to £3,000 for an accounting period if it fails to keep the accounting records for that period which are specified in Finance Act 1998, Schedule 18, paragraph 21. In an article in *Tax Bulletin*, October 1998[17] the Inland Revenue stated that a penalty will only be sought in the more serious cases, for example, where records have been destroyed deliberately to obstruct an enquiry or where there has been a history of serious record keeping failures. The Inland Revenue also stated that a penalty would only be sought following approval from its Compliance Division.

---

[17] pp. 587–588.

# CHAPTER 5

# CAPITAL ALLOWANCES FOR PLANT AND MACHINERY

## II. Scheme of Allowances

### First year allowances for small and medium-sized companies

Finance Act 2000, section 70 makes 40 per cent first year allowances for small or medium sized companies indefinite.   **5–10**

Section 71 gives 100 per cent first year allowances to small companies (but not medium sized companies) for expenditure on information and communications technology incurred between April 1, 2000 and March 31, 2003. The detail is contained in new sub-sections (3E)–(3H) of CAA section 22. For the purposes of the 100 per cent allowance, "small company" is defined in a new section 22AA by reference to the Companies Act. To be "small" a company must meet at least two of the following criteria in the period in which the expenditure is incurred:

1. turnover not more than £2.8m
2. assets not more than £1.4m
3. not more than 50 employees

or have been small for the previous period. If a company is a member of a group, the group must also be small when the expenditure is incurred. If a company is part of a foreign group, the whole group must satisfy the Companies Act criteria.

**Claims**

5–16    Claims under self-assessment are governed by FA 1998, Sched. 18, paras 78–83.

**Notification**

5–17    For accounting periods ending on or after April 1, 1998 the notification requirement is repealed.[1]

### III. Long- Life Assets

**Components with a shorter life than the entirety**

5–25    In *Tax Bulletin*, June 1999, the Revenue explains the agreement reached with BATA on the application of the long life asset rules to jet aircraft.

### IV. Writing Down Allowances

**Writing down allowances: main conditions**

5–27    *"has belonged to"*: allowances are not given unless claimed. It is therefore possible to incur expenditure, but for that expenditure not to be included in a person's qualifying expenditure within the meaning of CAA section 25. Where expenditure has not previously been the subject of a claim, it may not be claimed for an accounting period beginning after the plant has ceased to belong to the company.[2]

**Section 60 of the CAA and fixtures: section 60A**

5–28A    Section 60 is treated as never having been applicable to expenditure on fixtures.[3] Section 60A provides that where an asset is treated as belonging to a person under a contract to which section 60 applies, and the asset subsequently becomes a fixture, it is treated as ceasing to belong to that person unless under the fixtures code it is then treated as belonging to him.[4]

---

[1] FA 2000 s.73.

[2] FA 1994 s.118(6).

[3] CAA 1990 s.60A(1), deemed always to have had effect by FA 2000 s.80(3)(b).

[4] *ibid*. s.60A(2). This rule applies from the Royal Assent to FA 2000: s.80(3)(b).

## Sale and leaseback of nearly new plant

It sometimes happens that the purchaser of plant wishes to re-finance the purchase **5–29A**
by sale and leaseback while the plant is new or nearly new. This commonly arises
where plant is under construction and by virtue of section 60, the prospective owner
is treated as the owner from the commencement of the construction contract: see
para. 5–28 of the main text. Such transactions are caught by section 75(1)(b) or the
corresponding provisions of subsection (2) or (3), and this brings into play the restrictions on allowances for the purchaser contained in sections 76 and 76A. By section
76B, these restrictions are modified where certain conditions are met and if the parties
so elect.[5] Correspondingly, the vendor's expenditure is disregarded for capital allowances purposes.[6] The chief conditions are that:

(a) the plant was new[7] when acquired by the seller;
(b) the sale is effected not more than four months after the plant first being
    brought into use by any person for any purposes.[8]

The modifications to the restrictions on the purchaser's allowances are that under
section 76, the market value of the plant is not relevant so that allowances are given
on the lesser of cost to the vendor (or a connected person) and cost to the purchaser.
Where the leaseback is a finance lease, the notional written down value rule in section
76A(5) is disapplied.[9]

## Allowances for non-resident companies

For accounting periods ending on or after March 21, 2000 a non-resident company **5–31A**
trading through a branch or agency in the United Kingdom is brought within the
notional trade provisions discussed in para. 5–31 of the main text. This is achieved
by an amendment to the definition of "trade" so as to exclude activities insofar as
they are not within the charge to tax.[10] The result is that where plant is used both for
the purposes of a U.K. branch and non-U.K. activites, allowances are given by reference to the proportion of U.K. use. Further, transfers between the branch and overseas
operations are treated as cessations or commencements of trade use as the case may
be. Where the proportion of trade use is reduced and at the end of the chargeable

---

[5] CAA 1990 s.76B(1) The election must be made within two years of the sale and is irrevocable: *ibid.* subs. (4)(5). Sections 76 and 76A are modified accordingly: s.76B(3)(c)(d).
[6] *ibid.* s.76B(3)(a)(b).
[7] Defined by *ibid.* s.83(1) as "unused and not second hand".
[8] *ibid.* subs. (2)(b)(d). Plant is not regarded as "brought into use" if it has been used only for
testing or training: see Treasury Notes to clause 76 of the Finance Bill 2000. See subs. (2)
for the remaining conditions. "Seller" is adapted to fit with s.75(2) and (3): *ibid.* S.76B(6)(7).
[9] *ibid.* s.76B(3)(c)(d).
[10] CAA 1990 s.83(2A).

period the market value of the asset exceeds the qualifying expenditure by more than £1m, a balancing adjustment is made.[11]

## V. Expenditure

### Appropriations

5–37    Replace existing text with: For accounting periods ending on or after March 21, 2000 allowances are given on the lower of cost or market value.[12] Where the cost is incurred under a sale and leaseback transaction, cost is adjusted under the provisions applicable to such transactions.[13]

## VII. Equipment Leasing

### Use by "foreign lessees": section 42

5–54    The practice noted in the text of having regard only to the status of the end lessee, has been ended, and the Revenue now applies section 42 where any lessee in a chain meets the tests in section 42(1). This change of practice does not apply to leases entered into before the date of the announcement (April 19, 1999), nor to leases entered into within three months after that date pursuant to a written agreement of main terms agreed before that date and not materially altered since.[14]

---

[11] *ibid.* s.79A.
[12] *ibid.* s.81(2AA).
[13] *ibid.* s.81 (2AB).
[14] Inland Revenue, *Tax Bulletin*, April 1999, at p. 654.

CHAPTER 6

# FIXTURES

II. OWNERSHIP OF FIXTURES

## Fixtures

Section 52(2A) provides that "fixture" includes any boiler or water-filled radiator, **6–15**
and is deemed always to have had effect.[1]

## Equipment lessors: sections 53 and 58

For accounting periods ending on or after March 21, 2000 section 53(1)(bb) (which **6–24**
required the lessee to be within the charge to tax) is repealed.

---

[1] FA 2000, s.78(6).

CHAPTER 8

# TRANSFER PRICING

I. Transfer Pricing Under Domestic Law

## The scope of Schedule 28AA: provisions made by transactions

8–03    It is Inland Revenue practice not to apply the new transfer pricing rules in Schedule 28AA to the Taxes Act 1988 so as to impute rental income to a non-resident company controlled by a United Kingdom resident where the company owns a house in the United Kingdom which is occupied by that United Kingdom resident rent-free.[1] It is understood that a similar practice will apply where the controlling individual is non-United Kingdom resident and that it does not matter whether the controlling individual owns the shares in the non-United Kingdom resident company directly. The Inland Revenue have also confirmed that in a straightforward case where an individual controls a non-United Kingdom resident company and it provides an asset such as a yacht to him rent-free, Schedule 28AA will not be applied.

## The OECD guidelines: a question of context

8–06    The Inland Revenue have confirmed that separately contracted transactions between associated companies can only be evaluated together to determine whether a tax advantage arises where the transactions are between the same associates and form part of the same overall provision.[2]

---

[1] Article by Jonathan Schwarz, *Taxation*, May 13, 1999.
[2] Inland Revenue *Tax Bulletin*, October 1998, p. 581.

## The adjustment: recharacterising the transaction

The Inland Revenue consider that the transfer pricing rules are in point where a foreign associate provides a guarantee to a bank which then, on the strength of the guarantee, makes a loan to a United Kingdom company. If, however, the United Kingdom company is not thinly capitalised and the only effect of the guarantee is to reduce the interest charged, the legislation will not apply since there will be no United Kingdom tax advantage.[3]

8–07

## Transfer pricing and loan relationships

The Inland Revenue have confirmed that their approach in determining for the purpose of the distribution legislation whether a company is thinly capitalised will also apply for the purpose of the transfer pricing legislation in cases where there is common control but not a 75 per cent relationship.[4]

8–08

The Inland Revenue accept that where an interest-free loan is made to a foreign associate that could not have borrowed money at arm's length, no transfer pricing adjustment should be made because no interest would have arisen at arm's length.

In their FICO Newsletter,[5] the Inland Revenue have drawn attention to the implications of Schedule 28AA where a non-resident company borrows from a connected person to purchase a property for letting. The company can only deduct for tax purposes the amount of interest that would have been payable if loans had been obtained from lenders acting entirely "at arm's length" and having regard only to the assets of the company. If the only assets are the let property, the Revenue comment that a third party lender is only likely to lend a percentage of the purchase cost, typically 65–80 per cent, depending on the situation of the property and market conditions.

For an article on the approach of the Inland Revenue to the application of the transfer pricing rules to non-resident landlords, see Inland Revenue *Tax Bulletin*, April 2000. The Revenue reaffirm that the transfer pricing rules apply where there is a third party bank loan obtained by means of a guarantee, back to back deposit or letter of comfort from an associate. If the amount of interest paid to the bank exceeds the amount which would have been paid without the guarantee, etc., the amount claimed should be recalculated as if no guarantee, etc., had been given.

The same article makes the point that it is the circumstances at the time the loan is made that must be considered in determining whether the interest payable would have arisn at arm's length. Subsequent changes in value of the property owned by the landlord are not relevant.

Finally, the article confirms that it is not Inland Revenue practice to impute a charge to tax under the transfer pricing rules on a non-resident landlord providing rent-free

---

[3] Inland Revenue *Tax Bulletin*, October 1998, p. 581.
[4] *ibid.*
[5] Issue No. 4, July 1999.

residential accommodation within the United Kingdom to a United Kingdom individual who is a participant in the landlord.

## Exclusion for transactions wholly within the charge to United Kingdom tax

**8–12** In principle, loans between charities and their trading subsidiaries are within the transfer pricing legislation because the charity is exempt from tax on interest.[6] However, when the charity is following the advice and guidelines of the Charity Commission in relation to their investments in their subsidiaries the transfer pricing rules will not normally be applied.[7]

## Tonnage Tax Companies

**8–13A** Where there is a transaction or series of transactions entered into by a tonnage tax company in the course of or with respect to its tonnage tax trade with another company otherwise than in the course of or with respect to a tonnage tax trade of that other company the normal exclusion from the transfer pricing rules for United Kingdom to United Kingdom transactions does not apply. The rules for compensating adjustments discussed in paragraph 8–13 of the main work also do not apply.[8]

The transfer pricing rules apply to provision made or imposed between a company's tonnage tax trade and its other activities as if the provision were made between two persons under common control. The normal exclusion for United Kingdom to United Kingdom transactions and the rules for compensating adjustments do not apply.[9]

The special rules for tonnage tax companies do not affect the computation of a company's tonnage tax profits.[10]

## Arm's length price: the OECD guidelines

### Financial global trading

**8–15** The Inland Revenue's current approach to financial global trading is discussed in the Inland Revenue's *Tax Bulletin*, December 1998.[11]

---

[6] ICTA 1988, Sched. 28AA, para. 5(3)(b) and s.505(1)(c)(ii).
[7] Inland Revenue *Tax Bulletin*, October 1998, p. 582.
[8] FA 2000, Sched. 22, para. 58.
[9] *ibid*. para. 59.
[10] *ibid*. paras. 58(3), 59(4).
[11] At p. 617.

## Compliance

### Documentation

Under self-assessment, companies must keep and preserve such records as may be **8–16** needed to enable them to deliver correct and complete company tax returns.[12] The Inland Revenue have published guidance concerning the records they expect to be kept for transfer pricing purposes.[13] For full details, the reader should refer to the *Tax Bulletin* article. Briefly, the Inland Revenue expects taxpayers to prepare and retain such documentation as is reasonable given the complexity of the relevant transaction and which identifies:

(i) relevant commercial or financial relations which fall within the transfer pricing legislation;

(ii) the nature and terms (including prices) of relevant transactions (including transactions which form a series, and any relevant off-setting transactions);

(iii) the method by which the nature and terms of relevant transactions were arrived at, including any study of comparables and any functional analysis undertaken;

(iv) how that method has resulted in arm's length terms, or, where it has not, the computational adjustments required and how they have been calculated. The Inland Revenue comment that this will usually include an analysis of market data or other information on third party comparables; and

(v) the terms of relevant commercial arrangements with both third party and affiliated customers, including commercial agreements and any budgets, forecasts or other papers containing information relied on.

This documentation needs to exist at the latest by the time the company tax return is filed, although if the company is claiming that its existing arrangements are on arm's length terms it is clearly preferable that the documents should exist when the arrangements are entered into.

### Penalties

Where a company fraudulently or negligently delivers a company tax return which is incorrect it can be liable to a penalty not exceeding the tax understated.[14] The Inland Revenue have published their practice on the imposition of penalties under the new transfer pricing rules in the *Tax Bulletin*.[15] They stress that their approach will be consistent with the approach of Chapter IV of the 1995 *Transfer Pricing Guidelines for Multinational Enterprises and Tax Administrations*, published by the OECD. Even

---

[12] FA 1998, Sched. 18, para. 21.
[13] Inland Revenue *Tax Bulletin*, October 1998, p. 579.
[14] FA 1998, Sched. 18, para. 20.
[15] Inland Revenue *Tax Bulletin*, December 1998, p. 603.

where the Inland Revenue adjust a company's tax return under the transfer pricing rules, no penalty will be imposed if the company has made an honest and reasonable attempt to comply with the legislation. The Inland Revenue consider that companies must do what a reasonable person would to ensure that their tax returns are made in accordance with the arm's length principle. This involves

(i) using their commercial knowledge and judgment to make arrangements and set prices which conform to the arm's length standard (or to make computational adjustments in their returns where they do not);

(ii) being able to show that they made an honest and reasonable attempt to comply with the arm's length standard and with the legislation; and

(iii) seeking professional help where they know they need it.

Documenting their arrangements in accordance with the guidelines set out in the *Tax Bulletin*, October 1998 article will help demonstrate that companies have made an honest and reasonable attempt to arrive at appropriate transfer prices.

In deciding how far to abate a penalty, the Inland Revenue will have regard to both the absolute size of any transfer pricing adjustment and size relative to the turnover and profitability of the business and volume and value of related party transactions.

### Advance pricing agreements

**8–16A**    Provisions have been introduced in the Finance Act 1999[16] to permit a taxpayer to enter into an advance pricing agreement (APA) with the Inland Revenue. These measures took effect from July 27, 1999 and an APA can be made with the Inland Revenue for accounting periods ending on or after that date. The Inland Revenue has since issued a statement of practice (SP3/99) which gives further guidance on the APA process.

There are five circumstances in which a company can enter into an APA with the Inland Revenue:

(1) To agree the attribution of income to a branch or agency of the taxpayer in the United Kingdom. The application can be made either in respect of an existing branch or agency or an intended branch or agency.[17] From the Explanatory notes which accompanied the 1999 Finance Bill and SP3/99[18] it appears that this provision is intended only to cover cases where there is no double tax treaty between the United Kingdom and the territory in which the taxpayer is resident.

(2) To determine the attribution of income to any permanent establishment of

---

[16] FA 1999, ss.85–87.
[17] FA 1999, s.85(2)(a).
[18] See SP3/99 paragraph 5.

the taxpayer, whether in the United Kingdom or overseas, through which it is or is proposing to carrying on business.[19] This particular provision will apply to a United Kingdom company which has an overseas branch or to an overseas company which has a branch in the United Kingdom. From the Explanatory Notes which accompanied the 1999 Finance Bill and SP3/99,[20] it seems that this measure is aimed at cases where there is a double tax treaty between the United Kingdom and the overseas territory in question.

(3) To determine the extent to which income which has arisen or which may arise to the taxpayer is to be taken for any purpose to be income arising in a country or territory outside the United Kingdom.[21] From the Explanatory Notes on the 1999 Finance Bill and SP3/99[22] it appears that this provision is intended to deal with cases where there is no double taxation agreement between the United Kingdom and the overseas territory in question and where credit relief is available for tax suffered on the overseas income.

(4) To agree the treatment for tax purposes of any provision made or imposed as between the taxpayer and any associate of his.[23]

(5) To determine the treatment for tax purposes of any provision made or imposed as between a ring fence trade carried on by the taxpayer and any other activities carried on by him.[24]

In the case of (1), (2) and (3) above for all periods in respect of which an APA is in force the tax treatment of the relevant transactions will be determined by reference to the agreement and not the legislative provisions which would otherwise apply.[25] In the case of a matter falling within (4) and (5) and which does not relate to matters

---

[19] FA 1999, s.85(2)(b).

[20] See SP3/99 paragraph 5. Whilst the APA provisions contain no mechanism for determining whether an overseas associate of a taxpayer has a permanent establishment in the U.K. in relation to matters covered by the APA, an applicant can raise the issue in the APA request with a view to a nil attribution being agreed in respect of that permanent establishment; see *ibid.* para. 6.

[21] *ibid.* s.85(2)(c).

[22] See SP3/99 paragraph 5.

[23] FA 1999, s.85(2)(d). For these purposes two persons are associates in relation to the provision imposed as between them if, within the meaning of ICTA 1988, Schedule 28AA:
  (a) one of them is directly or indirectly participating in the management, control or capital of the other; or
  (b) the same person or persons is or are directly or indirectly participating in the management, control or capital of each of the two persons.
In the case of provision made or imposed by or in relation to the terms of any sale of oil (as defined in ICTA 1988, Schedule 28AA paragraph 9), two persons are also treated as associates where the two persons would be treated as being under the control of the same person by the provisions of Schedule 28AA paragraph 9(2): FA 1999, s.85(6).

[24] FA 1999, s.85(2)(e). Ring fence is defined by reference to ICTA 1988 s.492(1): FA 1999 s.85(7).

[25] *ibid.* s.85(3).

falling within (1) to (3) only the application of Schedule 28AA to the Taxes Act will be excluded by the advance pricing agreement.[1]

Should a taxpayer wish to enter into an APA with the Inland Revenue he is required to submit a formal written application to the Inland Revenue which must set out his understanding of what would be the effect, in the absence of any agreement, of the relevant legislation, including the effect of any double tax treaty, in relation to which clarification is sought, the respects in which it appears to the taxpayer that clarification is required in relation to those provisions and how the taxpayer proposes that matters should be clarified.[2] The taxpayer's proposal should set out a description of the method by which it is proposed to determine the relevant transfer pricing issues in accordance with the arm's length principle as well as an analysis which demonstrates how the proposed method satisfies the requirements of United Kingdom legislation and of the OECD Transfer Pricing Guidelines for Multinational Enterprises and Tax Administrations (OECD Transfer Pricing Guidelines).[3] An APA will normally be entered into for an initial period of three to five years.[4] A taxpayer will be required to deliver an annual report to the Inland Revenue to demonstrate adherence to the terms of the agreement.[5] The information submitted in connection with an APA application can be used by the Inland Revenue in connection with its review of the taxpayer's affairs, including the reopening of prior period computations. In view of this the Inland Revenue is prepared for an initial request to be made on an anonymised basis where a business is uncertain whether the Inland Revenue would be prepared to consider its request for an APA.[6]

In SP3/99 the Inland Revenue states that an APA is designed to offer assistance in resolving complex transfer pricing issues and that it is unlikely to agree to a request for an APA where reliable market comparables can be established that enable transfer pricing methods to be accurately employed in accordance with OECD Transfer Pricing Guidelines. The request may also be turned down where the affected transactions are thought to be of a hypothetical nature or it appears to be an inefficient use of resources to pursue an advance pricing agreement, for example because the relevant transactions are of a very limited nature or they are of limited value relative to the value of the taxpayer's transactions, or because the determination of the method by which the arm's length standard can reliably be applied is not materially in doubt.[7]

It is possible for the terms of an APA to be back dated but not beyond an accounting period ending before July 27, 1999. Where an APA is back dated, the terms of the

---

[1] *ibid*. s.85(4).
[2] FA 1999 s.85(5).
[3] SP3/99 paras. 34 to 39. Further details of the information which should accompany a formal request for an APA are set out in *ibid* paras 35 to 39.
[4] SP3/99 para. 23.
[5] FA 1999, s.86(4) & SP 2/99 paras 45 & 46.
[6] SP3/99 para. 27.
[7] SP3/99 paras 19 & 52.

agreement will be applied to the accounting period or periods in question in order to determine the company's taxable profits.[8]

An APA will cease to have effect from:

(i) a time as from which an officer of the Board has revoked the agreement in accordance with its terms;

(ii) a time after or in relation to which there has been a failure by a party to the agreement to comply with any provision of the agreement where compliance with this provision is a condition of the agreement; or

(iii) a time at which any other conditions, which under the terms of the agreement are conditions of it having effect, cease to be satisfied.[9]

An APA will be deemed never to have been entered into if a person fraudulently or negligently provided the Board with information which was false or misleading in connection with the advance pricing agreement application.[10]

Where an APA deals with cross border issues and there is a mutual agreement procedure in the double tax agreement between the United Kingdom and the overseas territory in question, the Inland Revenue will generally invite the tax authorities of that territory to participate under the mutual agreement procedure (and any domestic arrangements governing APAs in that territory) in order to endeavour to resolve difficulties or doubts as to the interpretation or application of the double tax agreement by mutual agreement. The Inland Revenue will, however, be prepared to consider a unilateral agreement if, for whatever reason, it proves not to be possible to reach an agreement with the relevant overseas tax authority or if the treaty partner does not respond within a specified period.[11] The Inland Revenue will also be prepared to consider a request by the taxpayer for a unilateral APA where the taxpayer considers that the extension to a bilateral APA would unnecessarily complicate or delay the process. The mutual agreement provisions of a double tax treaty take precedence over an APA in any event and so a taxpayer should not lose out if it negotiates a unilateral APA and the overseas treaty partner subsequently takes action which would give rise to double taxation in respect of the transfer pricing issues addressed in the APA.[12]

The Inland Revenue will also be willing to agree to requests for multilateral APAs where a taxpayer operates in several territories although, in practice, as there is no mechanism for reaching such agreements these will take the form of two or more bilateral agreements.[13]

In an article in their October 1999 Tax Bulletin the Inland Revenue stated that during the term of an APA which agrees how matters within Schedule 28AA of the

---

[8] FA 1999, s.85(8) & s.86(1) & (7).

[9] *ibid.* s.86(2).

[10] *ibid.* s.86(5).

[11] SP3/99 paras 7 to 10.

[12] FA 1999 s.86(3). See also SP 2/99 para. 10.

[13] SP 2/99 paras 11 to 14.

Taxes Act 1988 are to be determined in relation to specified arrangements, it would not invoke other rules on arm's length pricing to argue for a different interpretation of the arm's length principle as regards the arrangements to which the APA applies. The other rules cited in the article are the special relationship provisions of a Double Tax Treaty and the case law principles deriving from *Sharkey v. Wernher*[14] and *Petrotim Securities v. Ayres*.[15]

*Penalties*

The taxpayer will be liable to a penalty of up to £10,000 if he fraudulently or negligently makes a false or misleading statement to the Inland Revenue for or in connection with an APA application, or otherwise in connection with the preparation of such an agreement.[16] At the same time, if an APA is deemed never to have been entered into as a result of fraud or neglect by the taxpayer in connection with the application, the taxpayer may have filed incorrect returns for prior periods (assuming that such returns were prepared in accordance with the APA) and, in this case the taxpayer may also be liable to tax geared penalties in respect of those periods.[17]

A taxpayer may also be liable to penalties where an APA has been validly made and a return is submitted on a basis other than that set out in the APA if the taxpayer acted fraudulently or negligently in submitting the return.[18]

*Effect on other parties within the charge to United Kingdom corporation tax*

Where an APA is in force and it covers transactions with associated persons, for the purposes of Schedule 28AA paragraphs 6 and 7 to the Taxes Act (relief from double counting), the provisions of the APA will be applied to determine:

(a) whether the taxpayer is a person on whom a potential advantage in relation to United Kingdom tax is conferred by the actual provisions; and

(b) what constitutes the arm's length provision in relation to the actual provision.[19]

**Practical experience**

**8–16B**  The October 1999 Tax Bulletin contains an article giving guidance about the procedures relating to bilateral advance pricing agreements which draws upon the experi-

---

[14] 36 T.C. 275.

[15] 41 T.C. 389.

[16] FA 1999, s.86(8).

[17] In SP3/99 at para. 56 the Inland Revenue states that where a tax geared penalty is imposed on a taxpayer as a result of the nullification of an APA it will not seek to impose a penalty under s.86(8).

[18] FA 1999 s.85(3) and FA 1998, Sched. 18 para. 20. See also SP3/99 para 55.

[19] *ibid.* s.87.

ences and observations of the Inland Revenue in concluding APAs with its treaty partners under the authority of the Mutual Agreement procedure of Double Tax Treaties. The Inland Revenue do not envisage that the new statutory basis for such agreements introduced by the Finance Act 1999 will affect such procedures.

The article notes that there are five key principles to the negotiation of an APA:

1. Simultaneous procedures. The application should be submitted to the relevant tax administrations at approximately the same time. It is the applicant's responsibility to ensure that all information is provided promptly to the relevant tax administrations and where meetings are held with one tax administration, to make notes which can be forwarded to the other tax administration as soon as practicable and ideally within four weeks of the meeting.
2. Co-ordinated approaches. The relevant tax administrations should seek to co-ordinate their respective approaches as much as practicable to improve efficiency.
3. Timetable. The relevant tax administrations should agree to a joint target timetable for dealing with the various stages of the application and will, depending on the applicant's ability to provide information timeously, aim to complete the APA within eighteen months of formal applications.
4. Continuous contact. The relevant tax administrations should keep each other informed of progress through regular exchanges in correspondence, by telephone and video case conferences, and in face to face meetings.
5. Competent Authority Role. Negotiations to conclude the APA are conducted by the Competent Authorities of the relevant tax administrations. The exchange of information between the tax administrations is also conducted under the authority of the Competent Authority. APA information is confidential and subject to the safeguards against disclosure provided by the terms of the Exchange of Information Article of the Double Tax Treaty. The relevant tax administrations should begin Competent Authority negotiations as soon as practicable and develop provisional agreements which can be adapted as additional facts are obtained.

The remainder of the article discusses the arrangements for pre-filing meetings and the timetable for a formal application.

III. TREATY PROVISIONS

## E.C. Arbitration Convention

Originally, the Arbitration Convention was due to expire on December 31, 1999. **8–29** E.U. Finance Ministers, however, agreed on May 19, 1998 its extension for at least a further five years from the end of 1999.[20] A protocol amending the convention to give effect to this extension has now been published in the Official Journal of the European Communities.[21] This protocol provides for automatic extensions of the Convention for further periods of five years at a time unless a Member State objects at least six months before the expiry of a five-year period. The protocol must be ratified by the Member States.

---

[20] Inland Revenue *Tax Bulletin*, August 1998, p. 575.
[21] [1999] S.T.I. 1326.

# THE RAMSAY DOCTRINE

## II. EXPLORING THE LIMITS OF RAMSAY

**Purposive construction**

Where any conclusion is said to rest on purposive construction it is well to remember that as recently as 1996 in *ICI v. Colmer*, the House of Lords affirmed the authority of *IRC v. Mangin* where it was said:

> "... the object of the construction of a statute being to ascertain the will of the legislature it may be presumed that neither injustice nor absurdity was intended. If therefore a literal interpretation would produce such a result, *and the language admits of an interpretation which would avoid it*, then such an interpretation may be adopted."

**10–11**

The words in italics are often a fatal objection. A recent example of this difficulty is *R. v. I.R.C. ex p. Newfields Developments Ltd* discussed in para. 2–29 of this Supplement. In that case both parties submitted that in applying the control tests of section 416 of the Taxes Act for the purposes of section 13 (small companies rate: associated companies), the closing words of section 416(6) fell to be disregarded as inapplicable to the section 13 issue. It was held that to disregard words in this way was not permissible.

But in *Bibby v. Prudential Assurance plc*[1] the High Court has struck out in a completely new direction. The question in that case was whether a proprietary life assurance company that was in fact taxed on the I-E basis, was "dealer" for the purposes

---

[1] [2000] S.T.C. 459.

of section 95 of the Taxes Act. The Revenue contended that on a plain reading of the section, it applied to the taxpayer company. As to this the Court held:

> "*WT Ramsay Ltd v. I.R.C.* makes clear that a literal construction of a taxing Act is not necessarily the correct one. The House of Lords in *Ramsay* was considering artificial tax avoidance schemes designed to make use of taxing provisions for purposes never intended by Parliament. The case signalled an end to some of the excesses that a literal approach to construction had appeared to invite. The warning against a literal construction that would permit the use of a taxing provision for a purpose never intended or contemplated by Parliament was directed at taxpayers, or their tax advisers, but must, in my judgement, be heeded also by the Revenue. The assessments in the present case have represented, in my view, *an attempt to use s.95 for a purpose never intended or contemplated by Parliament. Such an attempt is no more acceptable from the Revenue than it would be from a taxpayer.*"

The authors consider that this is out of line with all previous authority both in the field of taxation and elsewhere. Whilst it is open to the House of Lords to sanction new approaches to the interpretation of statutes (*cf. Pepper v. Hart*), the High Court has no such prerogative. Pending review by the higher courts, this decision should not be regarded as authoritative.

### Tax avoidance: tax mitigation

**10–12**    In *Willoughby*,[2] Lord Nolan referred to taking advantage of a fiscally attractive option afforded by the tax legislation as the "hallmark of tax mitigation". The limit to which this observation holds true was explored in *Carvill v. I.R.C.*[3] in the context of section 741(b), where on the facts the Special Commissioners found that the taxpayer was not attempting to avoid tax when by transferring assets abroad he became eligible for reliefs attaching to income earned abroad.

The taxpayer, a non-domiciled resident, owned a U.K. company (H) which carried on business as a reinsurance broker, placing risk from U.S. insurance companies with Lloyds of London. Its clients were U.S. brokers who acted as intermediaries between the insurance companies and brokers such as H. As part of a strategy to compete with these U.S. brokers and deal directly with the insurance companies, the taxpayer transferred shares in H to a Bermudan holding company ("IH"). The existence of IH conferred various benefits in terms of tax, in particular entitlement to assessment on the remittance basis for employment income for non-United Kingdom duties and to foreign emoluments deduction on employment income for United Kingdom duties.

---

[2] *I.R.C. v. Willoughby* [1997] S.T.C. 995 at 1003.
[3] [2000] S.T.C. (S.C.D.) 167.

He was also thereby entitled to be assessed on the remittance basis for dividends from H paid through IH. It was admitted that this was a transfer of assets, by virtue of which income had become payable to a non-domiciled person which the taxpayer had power to enjoy. The Revenue claimed that this brought the taxpayer within the provisions of section 739, which applies in such circumstances to deem income so paid as income of the individual for the purpose of the Taxes Acts. The taxpayer argued that he was entitled to rely on section 741(b). This provides that section 739 does not apply where the transfer was a bona fide commercial transaction and was not designed for the purpose of avoiding liability to tax. The Special Commissioner found that the transfer was a bona fide commercial transaction. He found that only if the main purpose of the transfer was to avoid tax was it caught by section 739.

The Special Commissioner then considered the meaning of "avoidance" in relation to the taxpayer's claim to the various reliefs provided for overseas income. At the heart of the Special Commissioner's decision is the recognition that a taxpayer's entitlement to take advantage of a fiscally attractive option is not absolute. The mere existence of the circumstances in which the statute grants relief is not sufficient to enable the taxpayer to claim that relief[4]: he may still be avoiding rather than mitigating. The facts giving rise to the claim to relief must be evaluated having regard to Lord Nolan's comment in *Willoughby*[5] that tax avoidance for the purpose of section 741(a) is ". . . a course of action designed to conflict with or defeat the evident intention of Parliament". Thus in *Furniss* the taxpayer used a relieving provision but was still avoiding tax because he was trying to use the provision in circumstances for which it was not intended. The Special Commissioners expressed it thus:

> "It is not enough to say that if you find a relieving provision then it is the evident intention of Parliament that the taxpayer should be entitled to us it whatever the circumstances . . . The taxpayer must do more than point to the existence of a relieving provision; he must be using, rather than misusing, the relieving provision in a way consistent with Parliament's evident intention." (p. 167).

He held on the facts that there was no tax avoidance purpose, nor did tax considerations form any of the taxpayer's purposes in designing the transaction. The use of a Bermudan company was necessitated by the business strategy the taxpayer was trying to implement. The decision to use IH was made to enable the taxpayer to make contacts in the USA to build up the necessary client base to compete with the U.S. reinsurance brokers, whilst maintaining its supply of work from them; and then to provide a neutral place from which to direct the strategy of the group, where neither U.S. nor U.K. directors dominated. The entitlement to use the relieving provisions was merely a consequence of having the company, not a purpose.

---

[4] The contention on behalf of the taxpayer that the tax mitigation is not limited to cases where there are specific relieving provisions is noted without direct comment.
[5] *I.R.C. v. Willoughby* [1997] S.T.C. 995 at 1004.

159

### Circular payments

**10–13**     The decision of the High Court in *MacNiven v. Westmoreland Investments Ltd* has been reversed by the Court of Appeal.[6] Peter Gibson L.J. begins by recording that: "the blatant circularity of the payments made with the obvious purpose of achieving a tax advantage",[7] had made him think initially that the case was one where recharacterisation might be in point. The chief points that led him to the contrary conclusion were as follows:

> (i) the loans were genuine and the accruals of interest were genuine: the circular payments had simply enabled the parties to crystallise a genuine tax loss;
>
> (ii) because the loans and the interest accruals were genuine, it could not be disputed that as a matter of general law, the interest obligations had been discharged by means of the circular payments, yet the Crown asserted that for tax purposes, the interest was unpaid and could be paid by non-circular means in the future: "Such strange consequences make me doubt the correctness of the contention giving rise to them";
>
> (iii) the case was one of "mitigation" not "avoidance" (see paragraph 10–12 of the main work).[8]

### The limits of re-characterisation

**10–15**     In *Citibank Investments Ltd v. Griffin*,[9] the Special Commissioners considered a scheme designed to create within a group both a capital gain (to match an existing loss) and corresponding Case I deduction. The scheme was known as the "equity box" strategy under which a group member taxed as a financial trader entered into two options with another group member, the second group member having capital losses. The options were linked to the FTSE 100 and were structured so that however the market performed, the exercise of both options gave a guaranteed return over the option period. Thus, the options cost in aggregate £150m and would yield in total £161m.

It was contended on behalf of the Inspector that on *Ramsay* principles the two options should be treated as a single composite transaction. Somewhat surprisingly, the Commissioners rejected this contention:

> "The fact that the two options were intended to have effect together does not make them a single composite transaction within the meaning given to that phrase in *Ramsay*. The description of the sort of scheme to which the principles in

---

[6] [1998] S.T.C. 1131.
[7] All 1142c.
[8] At 1144, citing in particular *I.R.C. v. Willoughby* [1997] S.T.C. 995 at 1003.
[9] [2000] S.T.C. (S.C.D.) 92.

*Ramsay* was intended to apply is very far removed from the transactions between the taxpayer company and International. There was no rapid timetable relating to the options; indeed there was an interval of 16 months between their purchase and their exercise. There was no appearance of short-lived assets which cancelled each other out and then disappeared; the options were long lived; they were real; and they did not disappear. At the end of the operation the taxpayer company's financial position was not precisely the same as it was the beginning; it had changed as it became entitled to the sums payable on the exercise of the options, which represented not only the purchase price but also an additional sum. And the taxpayer company did have to put its corporate hand into its corporate pocket to find the considerable sums for the purchase of the options. In short, the taxpayer company took advantage of a fiscally attractive option afforded to it by the tax legislation and genuinely suffered the economic consequences of entering into the agreement[10]"

The Commissioners went on to hold that even if there was a single transaction, it was not (as contended on behalf of the Inspector) one of loan. They said:

"[W]e proceed on the basis, for the purpose of this issue, that each option was intended to have effect as a composite transaction or part of a series of transactions. However, that composite transaction or series of transactions was the two options taken together. The legal analysis of the transactions reveals that they were options and not loans. It follows that the legal nature of the transaction to which it is sought to attach a tax consequence is still an option and not a loan. To recharacterise the two options as a loan would be to disregard the legal form and nature of the transactions and to go behind them to some supposed underlying substance[11]."

### Any re-characterisation must be applied consistently

The principles embodied in *Fitzwilliam v. I.R.C.* were applied in *DTE Financial Services Ltd v. Wilson.*[12] That case concerned a scheme designed to avoid NI contributions and PAYE on bonuses to employees. It involved a series of steps which on behalf of the taxpayer were accepted as pre-ordained and which resulted in money reaching the hands of the employee (it was accepted that the employee was liable to tax under Schedule E by direct assessment). PAYE determinations were made on the basis that on *Ramsay* principles there had been a "payment" by the employer to the employee. However, it was held that it was not possible both to ignore a step and to recharacterise it:  **10–17**

---

[10] *ibid.* at p.102*j.*
[11] *ibid.* at p.103*j.*
[12] [1999] S.T.C. 1061.

"*IRC v. McGuckian* does not license the recharacterisation of a transaction which is accepted as genuine as something which it is not. It may allow that transaction to be ignored altogether but it does not permit the Crown to pick out one element from it, rechristen it and then ignore everything else[13]."

Reversing the decision of the Special Commissioners on this point, the Court held that there had been no "payment" by the employee. However, the Court held that by ignoring the inserted steps, the assessment could be supported on an alternative basis, namely, a payment by an "intermediary".

---

[13] At p.1075*b*.

# DISTRIBUTIONS AND STOCK-DIVIDEND OPTIONS

III. DISTRIBUTIONS IN RESPECT OF SECURITIES

**Returns inversely related to results**

As respects payments made on or after March 21, 2000 the consideration given by the company for the use of the principal secured is not treated as being to any extent dependent on the results of the company's business or any part of it by reason only of the fact that the terms of the security provide— **11–36A**

(a) for the consideration to be reduced in the event of the results improving, or

(b) for the consideration to be increased in the event of the results deteriorating.[1]

V. STOCK DIVIDEND OPTIONS

**Income tax**

*Individuals*

Whilst the Revenue appears to accept that the effective rate for higher rate taxpayers is an amount equal to 25 per cent of the appropriate amount in cash,[2] the legislation **11–47A**

---

[1] ICTA 1988, s.209(3B).

[2] That is to say, the upper Schedule F rate of 32.5 per cent reduced by the 10 per cent tax credit on the appropriate amount in cash grossed up at 10 per cent: *e.g.* the appropriate amount in cash is 90 which is grossed up to 100. The tax is 22.5 which is equal to 25 per cent of 90.

does not achieve this result. Section 249 was amended by Finance (No. 2) Act 1997, Schedule 4, paragraph 10 so as to read:

(4) Subject to the following provisions of this section, where a company issues any share capital in a case in which an individual is beneficially entitled to that share capital, that individual shall be treated as having received on the due date of issue income of an amount which, if reduced by an amount equal to income tax on that income at the Schedule F ordinary rate for the year of assessment in which that date fell, would be equal to the appropriate amount in cash, and—

(a) the individual shall be treated as having paid income tax at the Schedule F ordinary rate on that income or, if his total income is reduced by any deductions, on so much of it as is part of his total income as so reduced;

(b) no repayment shall be made of income tax treated by virtue of paragraph (a) above as having been paid; and

(c) that income shall be treated (without prejudice to paragraph (a) above), as if it were income to which section 1A applies as it applies to income chargeable under Schedule F, but shall be treated for the purposes of sections 348 and 349(1) as not brought into charge to income tax.

Subsection (4)(a) is intended to give a credit of 10 per cent and subsection (4)(c) makes the Schedule F ordinary rate the only rate applicable to non-higher rate tax-payers, but it does not bring section 1B into play for higher rate taxpayers. That is the only provision under which the Schedule F upper rate could be applicable, and as a stock dividend is not Schedule F income, section 1B does not apply in the absence of any express extension. Thus, in strictness, the higher rate of 40 per cent applies.

In Issue 3 of *The Personal Tax Planning Review* for the year 2000 at p. 193, it is contended that as a matter of interpretation, words would be read into section 249 as amended to make the Schedule F upper rate applicable. This view is not supported by the authorities on statutory interpretation and we do not agree with the conclusion reached.[3] However, the *Tax Computation Guide* issued for self-assessment purposes confirms the practice of applying Schedule F upper rate.

*Discretionary trustees*

**11–47B**     As respects the rate of tax applicable to trustees of a discretionary trust, Finance (No. 2) Act 1997 amends section 686 to apply "the Schedule F trust rate" of 25 per cent to Schedule F income and "Schedule F type" income. This last category includes stock dividends.[4] Accordingly, when read with section 249(6) as amended, the result is that trustees bear an effective rate of tax of 16.66 per cent on the appropriate amount in cash. That is to say, under section 249(6)(a), the appropriate amount in cash is

---

[3] For a fuller discussion see *Taxation*, August 2000 (RB).

[4] ICTA 1988, s.686(5A)(e).

grossed up by 10 per cent, but the result is treated as having borne tax at 10 per cent (subsection (6)(b)). So, if the appropriate amount in cash is 90, tax of 15 is paid which equals 16.66 per cent.

It is sometimes suggested that a stock dividend received by trustees of a discretionary trust falls outside the charge to income tax if under the terms of the settlement, the stock dividend is capital. In such cases it is argued that the charge under section 686 cannot apply because the stock dividend is not:

> "income which is to be accumulated or which is payable at the discretion of the trustees or any other person (whether or not the trustees have power to accumulate it)."[5]

However, this overlooks the point that section 249(6) applies section 686 by reference to hypothetical income:

> "Where a company issues any share capital to trustees in respect of any shares in the company held by them (or by them and one or more other persons) *in a case in which a dividend in cash* paid to the trustees in respect of those shares *would have been to any extent income to which section 686 applies*, then—
>
> (a) there shall be ascertained the amount of income which, if the case had been one in which an individual was beneficially entitled to that share capital, that individual would have been treated under subsection (4) above as having received; and
>
> (b) *income of that amount shall be treated as having arisen to the trustees* on the due date of issue and as if it had been chargeable to income tax at the Schedule F ordinary rate".

Accordingly, whether or not the stock dividend is income for the purposes of the settlement is immaterial.

In the same Issue of the *PTPR* as is referred to above, a second article (at p.233) discusses the above passage on the taxation of discretionary trustees. The article criticises the conclusions reached on the ground that the reference in section 249(6) to section 686 is "merely to define the precondition of section 249(6) applying". The authors do not understand how this is to be squared with section 249(6)(b) "income of that amount shall be treated as having arisen to the trustees. . . .", nor do they see what scope there is for the application of section 249(6) if the article is correct.

---

[5] *ibid.* s.686(2)(a).

CHAPTER 12

# TAXATION OF DISTRIBUTIONS

## I. Transition from the Imputation System

### The April 1999 changes

*Fixed dividend preference shares*

**12–04A**    Without provision to the contrary, the change in 1973 to the imputation system of corporation tax would have represented a considerable bonus for persons holding fixed dividend shares. In 1972–73, a person entitled to a fixed dividend of £10 would have received cash of £6.125 after deduction of tax at the rate of 38.75 per cent. Without provision to the contrary, in 1973–74 the same person would have received £10 in cash and would have paid no tax at the basic rate on the sum received. To prevent anomalies of this kind, it was provided[1] that in the case of fixed dividend shares[2] held on April 6, 1973, the dividend to which the holder was entitled after that date was to be such an amount as, when there was added to it such proportion thereof as corresponded to the rate of ACT in force on that date,[3] equalled the stipulated dividend.

This transitional rule ceased to apply on April 6, 1999 when ACT was abolished.[4]

---

[1] By what became ICTA 1988, s.255.

[2] "Fixed dividend" referred to a dividend at a gross rate or of a gross amount or partly at a gross rate or of a gross amount: *ibid.*

[3] The rate in force on that date was 3/7.

[4] FA 1998, Sched. 3, para. 23.

As a result, the holder of a fixed rate preference share entitling him to a dividend of £10 before 1973 will once again receive a dividend of £10, even though between 1973 and 1999 he was only entitled to a dividend of £7. The result of this change is to give the holder an unmerited windfall, since the holder continues to be entitled to a tax credit which satisfies any liability to income tax at the Schedule F ordinary rate. The Revenue have confirmed that the change is intentional.[5]

### III. RESIDENT SHAREHOLDERS

#### Payments of tax credits

The Individual Savings Account (Insurance Companies) (Amendment) Regulations 2000[6] have corrected a technical defect in the legislation designed to give insurance companies refunds of tax credits in respect of dividends referable to individual savings account business. Entitlement to refunds of tax credits is only available until April 5, 2004.

**12–16**

#### Discretionary trusts

Section 686 is amended from April 1999 by the Finance (No. 2) Act 1997. By reason of these amendments, trustees of settlements to which section 686 applies pay tax at the "trust rate" of 25 per cent on Schedule F income and "Schedule F type income" (discussed at paragraph 11-47B of this Supplement in relation to stock dividends). The trust rate applies to the amount of the distribution plus the tax credit of one-ninth: the effective rate of tax on the amount of the dividend is therefore 16.66 per cent: a distribution of 90 is treated as income of 100: tax on 100 less the credit is 15, which is 16.66 per cent of 90. The implications of the post-April 1999 system for payments from trusts to which section 687 applies, are discussed in detail in *Tax Bulletin*.[7]

**12–19A**

#### Share Dealers

Two cases[8] before the Special Commissioners have raised the question whether the taxpayer was a dealer in relation to a distribution which he received. Both concerned

**12–21**

---

[5] Taxline, November 1998.
[6] S.I. 2000 No. 2075.
[7] Inland Revenue *Tax Bulletin*, February 1999, p. 631.
[8] *The Equitable Life Assurance Society v. Oakes* [1999] S.T.C. (S.C.D.) 147 and *The Prudential Assurance Co. Ltd v. Bibby (No. 2)* [1999] S.T.C. (S.C.D.) 153, affirmed by the High Court [2000] S.T.C. 459.

life insurance companies. It was held in those cases that the term "dealer" covered any taxable person, where the proceeds of sale of shares by him would come into charge as Schedule D, Case I receipts, irrespective of whether the person was a dealer in the normal sense of the term. The term was not confined to taxpayers who kept shares as stock in trade of a business which consisted in buying and selling shares. It covered all taxpayers for whom the making and holding of investments was an integral part of their trade, whether that trade was pure share dealing or banking or another financial trade.

It was further held that the function of section 95 was to reconcile the competing demands of the systems for taxing trading profits and for taxing distributions by giving priority to the former. It only applied where the proceeds of an assumed sale of the shares on which the distribution was made would actually be subjected to tax under Schedule D, Case I or II.

The actual decisions in those cases are now of historical interest only since it is specifically provided in section 95 of the Taxes Act 1988 as it now stands that it does not apply to insurance business or any category of insurance business.[9] The general comments about dealers and section 95 nevertheless remain relevant.

The main work points out that it is not clear whether the special rules for dealers apply to interest treated as a qualifying distribution, but concludes that the more likely interpretation is that they do. It is considered that a court would reach this conclusion not by holding that the reference to "stock" in section 95(2) includes loan or debenture stock, but on the basis that section 95(2) is not an exhaustive definition of a "dealer".

## IV. NON RESIDENT SHAREHOLDERS

### Compatibility of United Kingdom tax with Parent-Subsidiary Directive

**12–27**    In *Oce Van Der Grinten NV v. I.R.C.*[10] the Special Commissioners have referred to the European Court the questions whether the tax deducted from a payment of a tax credit to a foreign parent company is a withholding tax, whether article 7(2) of the Parent-Subsidiary Directive[11] preserves the right to make the deduction and whether article 7(2) is valid.

---

[9] ICTA 1988, s.95(2A).

[10] [2000] S.T.C. (S.C.D.) 127. The Revenue's subsequent appeal to the High Court against the holding that the tax deducted from a payment of a tax credit is a tax as a matter of U.K. law has been dismissed. The High Court held that the concept of withholding tax was a global question of European law. Whether a particular national law characterised a particular consequence of national fiscal legislation as a "tax" or not was immaterial.

[11] E.C. Directive 90/435/EEC.

CHAPTER 12A

# SHADOW ACT

## I. INTRODUCTION

Since April 6, 1999 companies have no longer been required to account for ACT **12A–01** when they make distributions. However, it remains possible for ACT paid before that date which has not already been utilised, to be set against corporation tax in respect of profits earned after that date. The professed aim of the shadow ACT rules is to maintain the legitimate expectations of companies concerning the use of ACT. Broadly, the function of shadow ACT is to limit the amount of ACT that can be set against corporation tax to approximately the amount that would have been set off under the old ACT rules.

A company which incurs shadow ACT does not have to make an actual payment of shadow ACT. It is only a notional figure. When shadow ACT is set against corporation tax, it does not reduce the amount of corporation tax which has to be paid. The only impact is to reduce the amount of surplus ACT that can be offset against that corporation tax.

ACT paid in respect of distributions made before April 6, 1999 can be carried forward and offset against corporation tax up to a limit of 20 per cent of a company's taxable profits, to the extent that this limit has not already been used to offset shadow ACT. A lower limit may apply where a company has income or gains that have borne foreign tax. Shadow ACT arises at the rate of 25 per cent on both qualifying and non qualifying distributions made on or after April 6, 1999. The amount of shadow ACT

169

may be reduced by franked investment income and intra group distributions only give rise to shadow ACT in limited circumstances.

**12A–02**    Shadow ACT is offset against corporation tax in the following order:

  (i) corporation tax on the profits of the distributing company for the accounting period in which the distribution is made;
 (ii) corporation tax on the profits of the distributing company for accounting periods beginning in the previous six years but after April 5, 1999[1];
(iii) corporation tax on the profits of other group members for accounting periods falling in whole or in part within the accounting period in which the distribution is made, or the previous period; and
 (iv) corporation tax on the profits of the distributing company for future accounting periods.

## II. Application of Shadow Act Regulations

**12A–03**    The shadow ACT regulations apply to companies or groups which had surplus ACT at April 5, 1999. Where a company's accounting period spans April 6, 1999 it is deemed for the purpose of the shadow ACT regulations only to be composed of two accounting periods, one ending on April 5, 1999 and another beginning on April 6, 1999.[2] The regulations apply for accounting periods from the deemed accounting period beginning on April 6, 1999 to the end of the company or group's "final accounting period".[3]

### Accounting period spanning April 6, 1999

**12A–04**    Where an accounting period spans April 6, 1999, it is treated for the purposes of the regulations as being split into two accounting periods, the first ending on April 5, 1999, and the profits of the actual accounting period are time apportioned to the two component accounting periods.[4]

---

[1] For this purpose, an accounting period which straddles April 6, 1999 is deemed to end on April 5, 1999 and a new one is deemed to begin on April 6, 1999: see below, para. 12A–03.
[2] Corporation Tax (Treatment of Unrelieved Surplus Advance Corporation Tax) Regulations 1999, reg. 3(4).
[3] *ibid.* reg. 2(1).
[4] *ibid.*, reg. 3(4).

### Final accounting period

*Companies not belonging to a group*

Where a company is not a member of a group, its final accounting period is the last **12A–05** accounting period to begin in the period of 12 months after the end of the accounting period in which the company uses up its surplus ACT.[5] Normally, a company's final accounting period would be the accounting period which immediately follows the accounting period in which it uses up all its surplus ACT. If, however, the next accounting period is less than 12 months in length a later accounting period will become the company's final accounting period.

EXAMPLE

A Ltd's accounting periods end on December 31, 1999, September 30, 2000 and September 30, 2001. It uses up all its surplus ACT in the accounting period ended December 31, 1999. Its final accounting period is the period ending on September 30, 2001.

The reason A Ltd's final accounting period is later than the period in which it uses up its surplus ACT is that surplus shadow ACT can be carried back and displace surplus ACT offset in the previous 12 months. The rules aim to prevent companies from offsetting surplus ACT by deferring dividends for a short period to maximise capacity to offset surplus ACT.

A Ltd could opt out of the regulations by notifying the Inland Revenue at any time **12A–06** in its first accounting period to begin on or after April 6, 1999 that it will not seek recovery of surplus ACT.[6] If it decides not to opt out in its first accounting period to begin on or after April 6, 1999, it can nevertheless opt out in a later period. In that case, its final accounting period is the period in which it opts out, unless there is surplus shadow ACT that can be carried back to that period from the latest accounting period to begin in the 12 months after that period. The latest period then becomes the final accounting period.[7]

---

[5] Corporation Tax (Treatment of Unrelieved Surplus Advance Corporation Tax) Regulations 1999, reg. 4(1)(2).

[6] *ibid.* reg. 4(3).

[7] *ibid.* reg. 4(4), (5).

EXAMPLE

> A Ltd opts out in its accounting period ended December 31, 2000. It has no surplus shadow ACT for the accounting period ended September 30, 2001 but has surplus shadow ACT for the period ended September 30, 2002 that can be carried back to the period ended December 31, 2000. Its final accounting period is the period ended September 30, 2002.

Curiously, the rules only look at the last accounting period to begin in the 12 months after the period of opt out. If, in the above example, A Ltd had had surplus shadow ACT for the period ended September 30, 2001 but none for the period ended September 30, 2002, the final accounting period would have been the period of opt out. It might be possible to exploit this weakness in the rules by incurring surplus shadow ACT in a short accounting period after the period of opt out.

By opting out of the rules, a company saves itself the compliance cost of doing the calculations required by the rules, but at the cost of forfeiting any possibility of recovering its surplus ACT.

*Group members*

**12A–07**   Where a company is a member of a group at any time in the accounting period in which the group uses up its surplus ACT, the final accounting period is the last accounting period to begin in the 12 months following that period.[8]

The group can opt out of the shadow ACT regime. In order to do so, its parent company must during its first accounting period to begin on or after April 6, 1999 notify the Inland Revenue that the group will not seek to recover surplus ACT. This notification binds all companies which were members of the group on April 6, 1999.[9]

It is possible for a group to opt out of the shadow ACT regime after the end of its first accounting period to begin on or after April 6, 1999. If the group parent company notifies the Inland Revenue in a subsequent accounting period that the group will not seek recovery of surplus ACT remaining at the end of that accounting period, that accounting period is the group's final accounting period.[10] The notification binds all companies which are members of the group when it is made, as well as any companies which join the group before the end of the parent's final accounting period.[11] If a subsidiary within the group has an accounting period which does not coincide with

---

[8] Corporation Tax (Treatment of Unrelieved Surplus Advance Corporation Tax) Regulations 1999, reg. 5(1), (2).

[9] *ibid.* reg. 5(3), (4).

[10] *ibid.* reg. 5(5).

[11] *ibid.* reg. 5(6).

the parent's final accounting period, the subsidiary's accounting period is split into two, and the part ending with the end of the parent's final accounting period is treated as the subsidiary's final accounting period.[12]

EXAMPLE

A Ltd has two subsidiaries, B Ltd and C Ltd. A Ltd and C Ltd have March 31 year ends, but B Ltd has a December 31 year end. A Ltd notifies the Inland Revenue on February 20, 2001 that the group will cease to recover surplus ACT. B Ltd's accounting period ending December 31, 2001 is split into two and its deemed accounting period ending on March 31, 2001 is its final accounting period.

If in an accounting period beginning in the 12 months after the accounting period **12A–08** in which the parent notifies the Inland Revenue in accordance with the rule just mentioned that the group will cease to recover surplus ACT, a member of the group has surplus shadow ACT that falls to be carried back to a period before that 12-month period, the final accounting period is not the accounting period of notification but the latest accounting period beginning in that 12-month period from which surplus shadow ACT falls to be carried back.[13]

EXAMPLE

A Ltd has two subsidiaries, B Ltd and C Ltd. All have March 31 year ends. A Ltd notifies the Inland Revenue on February 20, 2001 that the group will cease to recover surplus ACT. In its accounting period ended March 31, 2002, B Ltd has surplus shadow ACT that falls to be carried back. The final accounting period is the accounting period ending March 31, 2002.

If a parent notifies the Inland Revenue in its first accounting period to begin on or after April 6, 1999 that the group will not seek recovery of surplus ACT, and a company with surplus ACT subsequently joins the group, the shadow ACT rules apply to the group from the accounting period in which the company joins the group. However, the original group members cannot recover their surplus

---

[12] Corporation Tax (Treatment of Unrelieved Surplus Advance Corporation Tax) Regulations 1999, reg. 5(7).
[13] *ibid.* reg. 5(8).

ACT.[14] The regulation only expressly states that the shadow ACT rules apply to the accounting period in which the company with surplus ACT joins the group, but it is considered that the effect of stating that the rules apply in relation to this accounting period "as if no notification had been made" is to apply the rules for future accounting periods as well until the group's final accounting period is once again reached. It is considered that shadow ACT could not be carried back to an accounting period prior to the period in which the company with surplus ACT joined the group.

Similarly, if after the group's final accounting period a company with surplus ACT joins the group, the shadow ACT rules apply to the group from the accounting period in which the company joins the group until the group's final accounting period is once again determined. This does not, however, enable other members of the group with surplus ACT to recover their surplus ACT.[15] Although the shadow ACT rules are only expressly applied to the accounting period in which the company joins the group, it is considered that they will also apply for later periods. It is also considered that surplus shadow ACT could not be carried back before the accounting period in which the company joined the group.

If a company is a member of more than one group, and the final accounting period of at least one of them has been determined because the parent of that group has opted out of the shadow ACT regime after its first accounting period within the rules, the shadow ACT rules apply as if all the company's surplus ACT had been used up.[16]

## III. Shadow ACT Groups

### Significance of groups

**12A–09**     There are two main reasons why the composition of a shadow ACT group is significant. First, distributions made within a group do not generally generate shadow ACT and are not treated as franked investment income of the recipient. Secondly, surplus shadow ACT of one group member must be allocated to other members of the group.

---

[14] Corporation Tax (Treatment of Unrelieved Surplus Advance Corporation Tax) Regulations 1999, reg. 5(9).

[15] *ibid*. reg. 5(10).

[16] *ibid*. reg. 5(11).

## Definition of group

EXAMPLE

A Inc

| 100%

B Ltd

| 100%

C Ltd

| 100%

D Ltd

A United Kingdom resident company and its 51 per cent United Kingdom resident **12A–10** subsidiaries form a group for shadow ACT purposes.[17] In the above example, A Inc cannot be a member of the group because it is not resident in the United Kingdom. B Ltd, C Ltd and D Ltd, however, form a group. A company cannot be the parent of a group if it has no 51 per cent subsidiaries and it is itself a 51 per cent subsidiary of another company. Thus, in the above example, D Ltd cannot be the parent of a group. Similarly, a company cannot be the parent of a group if it and its 51 per cent subsidiaries are all members of another group.[18] So, C Ltd also cannot be the parent of a group.

It is possible for a company to be a member of more than one group at the same time.

EXAMPLE

A Ltd

| 51%

B Ltd

| 51%

C Ltd

---

[17] Corporation Tax (Treatment of Unrelieved Surplus Advance Corporation Tax) Regulations 1999, reg. 6(1), (2)(a). ICTA 1988, s.838 applies to determine whether a company is a 51 per cent subsidiary.
[18] *ibid.* reg. 6(2)(b).

A Ltd and B Ltd comprise one group. C Ltd is not a member of that group because it is not a 51 per cent subsidiary of A Ltd, A Ltd only owning indirectly 26.01 per cent of its ordinary share capital. B Ltd and C Ltd comprise a second group with the result that B Ltd is a member of two groups at the same time.

**12A–11**  A company is a 51 per cent subsidiary of another company if that other company beneficially owns directly or indirectly more than 50 per cent of its ordinary share capital. For this purpose, however, shares held in non-resident companies and shares held as trading stock are ignored.[19]

EXAMPLE

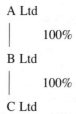

A Ltd

| 100%

B Ltd

| 100%

C Ltd

If either A Ltd held B Ltd's shares as trading stock or B Ltd held C Ltd's shares as trading stock A Ltd and C Ltd would not be members of the same group. A Ltd and C Ltd would also not be grouped if B Ltd were non-United Kingdom resident.

**E.U. law**

**12A–12**  It is doubtful whether the rule requiring shares in non-resident companies to be disregarded in determining group membership, complies with E.U. law requirements relating to freedom of establishment. If, in the above example, B Ltd were non-United Kingdom resident, C Ltd would incur shadow ACT on its dividends to B Ltd, and A Ltd would incur further shadow ACT when dividends deriving from C Ltd were distributed outside the group.

It is also arguable that a United Kingdom subsidiary of an E.U. resident parent company ought to be able to pay dividends to its parent without shadow ACT. In the *Hoechst* case the European Court has been asked to consider whether a United King-

---

[19] Corporation Tax (Treatment of Unrelieved Surplus Advance Corporation Tax) Regulations 1999, reg. 6(2)(c).

dom subsidiary of a German company should be able to pay dividends to its parent under the old ACT regime under a group income election. The eventual result in that case will have a direct bearing on whether shadow ACT should arise on a dividend paid by a United Kingdom subsidiary to its E.U. parent.

It follows from the decision of the European Court in *Compagnie de Saint-Gobain, Zweigniederlassung Deutschland v. Finanzamt Aachen-Innenstadt*[20] that no shadow ACT should arise when a U.K. subsidiary makes a distribution to the U.K. branch of an E.U. group company if there would have been no shadow ACT had the E.U. group company been a U.K. resident group company. In that case, the German government's attempt to justify the different treatment of German companies and German branches on the basis that no German tax could be levied when the company with the German branch paid a dividend failed. Similarly, any attempt to justify the U.K. provisions on the basis that shadow ACT arises when a U.K. group member pays a dividend outside the group but does not arise when an E.U. company with a U.K. branch pays a dividend outside the group is likely to fail.

**Anti-avoidance rules**

The basic test of group membership is supplemented by a number of anti-avoidance **12A–13** rules.

1. Where persons enjoy extraordinary rights or powers under the constitutional documents of the company and for that reason ownership of ordinary share capital is not an appropriate test of whether a company is a 51 per cent subsidiary, then in determining whether one company is a 51 per cent subsidiary of another, holdings of all kinds of share capital or of any particular category of share capital or voting power or other kinds of share capital can be taken into account instead of ordinary share capital.[21]

EXAMPLE

A Ltd owns 250 £1 ordinary shares in B Ltd. A friendly merchant bank owns 750 £1 participating preference shares entitling it to a 5 per cent dividend and to a 0.1 per cent share of any profits above £1m per share. The participating preference shares are ordinary share capital because of their 0.1 per cent participation but, because they carry extraordinary rights (the 0.1 per cent participation), the 51 per cent subsidiary test can be applied by reference to the ordinary shares alone so that B Ltd is a 51 per cent subsidiary of A Ltd.

---

[20] [2000] S.T.C. 854 discussed at para. 25–04 of this Supplement.
[21] Corporation Tax (Treatment of Unrelieved Surplus Advance Corporation Tax) Regulations 1999, reg. 6(3).

The aim of this rule is to prevent the artificial manipulation of the group test either to include a company or to exclude it artificially from a group. Its effectiveness in preventing the artificial exclusion of a company from a group is limited by the next rule.

**12A–14**  2. A 51 per cent subsidiary is not treated as a 51 per cent subsidiary unless its parent is beneficially entitled to more than 50 per cent of any profits available for distribution to its equity holders and would be entitled to more than 50 per cent of the assets that would be available for distribution to equity holders on a winding up, applying the familiar group relief rules in the Taxes Act 1988, Schedule 18.[22] Subject to the possible application of the *Furniss v. Dawson* doctrine the application of these rules makes it possible to exclude a company from group membership by capping either the dividend or the liquidation rights of the parent company's shares.[23]

**12A–15**  3. A 51 per cent subsidiary is not treated as a 51 per cent subsidiary if there are arrangements in existence by virtue of which any person has or could obtain, or any persons together have or could obtain, control[24] of the subsidiary but not of the parent.[25] For this purpose, "arrangements" means arrangements of any kind, whether or not in writing, other than arrangements whose main purpose is to reduce the surplus shadow ACT available to be utilised by a company other than the subsidiary.[1] The reason for this exclusion from the meaning of "arrangements" is obscure. Statutory powers empowering the Government to direct statutory bodies or their subsidiaries to dispose of assets are not regarded as arrangements within this rule.[2] If, however, the powers are exercised, arrangements may come into being. Apart from the exclusion for arrangements whose main purpose is to reduce surplus shadow ACT, this is the familiar arrangements test which used to apply for the purpose of the surrender of ACT. The Inland Revenue have confirmed to the authors that regard will be had to Inland Revenue Statement of Practice SP 3/93 and Extra Statutory Concession C10 in determining whether arrangements are in existence. The decision of the Special Commissioners in the group relief case, *Scottish and Universal Newspapers Ltd v. Fisher*,[3] will also be relevant in applying this rule.

### Immediate parent company

**12A–16**  A company is the immediate parent company of another company if it is the direct parent of that company.[4]

---

[22] Corporation Tax (Treatment of Unrelieved Surplus Advance Corporation Tax) Regulations 1999, reg. 6(4)(b), (7).

[23] Relying on ICTA 1988, Sched. 18, para. 4 to treat the capped rights as having been waived.

[24] "Control" has its ICTA 1988, s.840 meaning: the Corporation Tax (Treatment of Unrelieved Surplus Advance Corporation Tax) Regulations 1999, reg. 6(5).

[25] *ibid.* reg. 6(4)(a).

[1] *ibid.* reg. 6(5).

[2] *ibid.* reg. 6(6).

[3] [1996] S.T.C. (S.C.D.) 311, discussed in para. 22–64 of the main work.

[4] Corporation Tax (Treatment of Unrelieved Surplus Advance Corporation Tax) Regulations 1999, reg. 6(8).

## IV. Computing Shadow ACT

### When shadow ACT arises

Shadow ACT is treated as having been paid whenever a United Kingdom resident **12A–17** company makes a distribution on or after April 6, 1999, other than a manufactured dividend paid under a contract or arrangement for the transfer of shares in a United Kingdom resident company or (unless an election is made) an intra group distribution.[5] The rate of shadow ACT is 25 per cent of the amount or value of the distribution.[6]

EXAMPLE

A PLC pays a dividend of £1,000,000 on September 30, 1999. The shadow ACT is £250,000.

Shadow ACT arises on both qualifying and non-qualifying distributions. Shadow ACT will therefore arise on a bonus issue of loan notes even though no ACT would have arisen before April 6, 1999 on the issue.

### Group Distributions

Distributions within a group will not generally give rise to shadow ACT. This **12A–18** treatment is automatic: there is no need to make a group income election to avoid shadow ACT on an intra group distribution.[7]

Exceptionally, a company may elect to bring an intra group distribution within the shadow ACT rules to the extent that it has franked investment income. This enables franked investment income received by a subsidiary within a group to be passed on up the group in a form which franks the parent's dividend payments. The election must be made in the distributing company's tax return or an amendment to the return within two years of the end of the accounting period in which the distribution is made and is irrevocable. The recipient of the distribution must be notified of the election and the amount of the distribution affected by it. For this purpose, franked investment income has to be grossed up by 9/8 to relect the differential between the rate of tax credit (1/9) and the rate of shadow ACT (1/4).[8]

---

[5] Corporation Tax (Treatment of Unrelieved Surplus Advance Corporation Tax) Regulations 1999, regs 11(1), (2) and 3(1).

[6] *ibid.* reg. 11(9).

[7] *ibid.* reg. 11(2)(b).

[8] *ibid.* reg. 11(3), (4).

EXAMPLE

> A Ltd receives franked investment income in the form of a dividend of £90. This carries a tax credit of £10. A Ltd pays a dividend of £90 to its parent company and elects for the dividend to be paid within the shadow ACT rules. The dividend is a franked distribution of £112.50. When the franked investment income of £100 is grossed up by 9/8, it is equal to the amount of the franked distribution and no shadow ACT is treated as having been paid on the intra group distribution.

### Dividends paid outside accounting periods

**12A–19**    If a company makes a distribution outside an accounting period, it is treated as falling within an accounting period beginning on the later of the beginning of the company's immediate parent company's accounting period in which the distribution falls and the end of the distributing company's previous accounting period and ending on the earlier of the end of the accounting period of the company's immediate parent company in which the distribution falls and the beginning of the distributing company's next accounting period.[9]

EXAMPLE

> A Ltd has an accounting period that runs from January 1, 2000 to December 31, 2000. Its subsidiary B Ltd's last accounting period ends on March 31, 2000. B Ltd pays a dividend on April 30, 2000. This dividend is treated as having been paid in an accounting period running from April 1, 2000 to December 31, 2000.

If A Ltd had no accounting period at the time the distribution was made, it would be necessary to look further up the corporate chain to A Ltd's immediate parent company and so on until an accounting period was determined.[10] The regulations do not deal with the situation where there is no direct or indirect parent company with an accounting period current when the distribution is made.

---

[9] Corporation Tax (Treatment of Unrelieved Surplus Advance Corporation Tax) Regulations 1999, reg. 11(5).
[10] *ibid.* reg. 11(6).

### Company leaving group

Where a company leaves a group, shadow ACT is computed as if an accounting **12A–20** period had ended when the company left the group.[11]

EXAMPLE

> A Ltd and its subsidiary, B Ltd, have calendar year accounting periods. A Ltd agrees subject to contract to sell B Ltd on April 1, 2000. A contract is signed on May 1, 2000. The contract becomes unconditional on June 1, 2000, and is completed on June 10, 2000. B Ltd leaves the group on April 1, 2000 when arrangements for the sale come into existence.[12] B Ltd's accounting periods are deemed to run from January 1, 2000 to March 31, 2000 and from April 1, 2000 to December 31, 2000.

### Change of ownership

An accounting period is also deemed to end for the purpose of computing shadow **12A–21** ACT when there is a change of ownership to which the provisions discussed in paragraphs 12A–45 to 12A–47 restricting the carry forward of surplus ACT in certain cases apply, even though this is not the occasion of the company leaving a group.[13]

### V. FRANKED INVESTMENT INCOME

### Franking

Franked investment income reduces the shadow ACT a company is treated as **12A–22** having paid on its distributions. Franked investment income carries a tax credit of 1/9. A dividend of £90 gives rise to franked investment income of £100. The rate of shadow ACT is, however, 25 per cent of the amount or value of the distribution in question. So a dividend of £90 is treated as a franked distribution of £112.50. For the purpose of franking distributions, franked investment income is grossed up by 9/8 so that a dividend of £90 (franked investment income of £100) is treated as income of

---

[11] Corporation Tax (Treatment of Unrelieved Surplus Advance Corporation Tax) Regulations 1999, reg. 11(7).
[12] *ibid.* reg. 6(4)(a).
[13] *ibid.* reg. 11(8).

£112.50 for the purpose of franking. The practical effect is that the receipt of a franked dividend of £90 will frank the shadow ACT on a dividend of £90.

Where a company receives franked investment income, it is only treated as having paid shadow ACT to the extent that the franked distributions made by it in the accounting period exceed the aggregate of 9/8 of the franked investment income received by it in the period and the franked investment income carried forward to the period.[14]

EXAMPLE

A Ltd pays dividends of £800 which are treated as franked distributions of £1,000. It receives franked investment income of £500 in the same accounting period and has franked investment income of £100 carried forward to the period. Its franked investment income for the period has to be grossed up by 9/8 to £562.50. It is then added to the carried forward franked investment income of £100, giving total franked investment income of £662.50 (the carried forward franked investment income is not grossed up because grossing up will already have been taken into account in computing the surplus franked investment income to be carried forward; see below). Shadow ACT is treated as having been paid in respect of franked distributions of £1,000 − £662.50 = £337.50. Shadow ACT is therefore taken to be £67.50.

**12A–23**  When a company has surplus franked investment income, the surplus is carried forward to the next accounting period.[15] For this purpose, the surplus is the excess of 9/8 of the franked investment income received in the accounting period and the franked investment income carried forward to the period over the franked distributions made in the period.[16]

EXAMPLE

A Ltd pays dividends of £480 (franked distributions of £600) in its accounting period ended December 31, 2000. It receives dividends of £540 in the same period and has no franked investment income carried forward to the period. The dividends received by A Ltd are treated as franked investment income of £600,

---

[14] Corporation Tax (Treatment of Unrelieved Surplus Advance Corporation Tax) Regulations 1999, reg. 11(10), (11).
[15] *ibid*. reg. 11(12).
[16] *ibid*. reg. 11(13).

which is then grossed up by 9/8 o £675. A Ltd has a surplus of franked investment income of £75.

Where an accounting period ends on April 5, 1999 and a new one begins on April 6, 1999 or an accounting period spans April 5, 1999, any surplus franked investment income for the accounting period ending or deemed to end on April 5, 1999 is carried forward to the accounting period beginning or deemed to begin on April 6, 1999.[17]

**Intra group dividends**

Shadow ACT does not arise on an intra group distribution unless the company **12A–24** making the distribution has received franked investment income and elects to make the distribution as a franked distribution.[18] The corollary is that an intra group distribution will only be treated as franked investment income to the extent that the election is made. In the normal case, an intra group distribution will be disregarded in computing the shadow ACT treated as paid by the recipient.[19]

The rule that intra group distributions are generally not treated as franked investment income is supplemented by two further provisions designed to counter attempts to avoid the rules by temporary degrouping:

1. A distribution is not treated as franked investment income where it is made by a company outside the recipient's group but there are arrangements giving rise to a reasonable expectation that the company will join or rejoin that group.[20] The authors consider that the mere presence of pre-emption rights in a joint venture company's articles of association would not be enough to trigger the application of this rule.

2. A distribution will not be treated as franked investment income if it is made by reference to shareholdings at a time when the distributing company and the recipient were grouped.[21] This rule is designed to cover the case where a group sells a subsidiary ex dividend to another group with either no surplus ACT or the capacity to absorb shadow ACT. It would not apply where a parent company sold its only subsidiary ex dividend to a group with no surplus ACT because the rule only applies where the parent is a member of a group when the dividend is received.

---

[17] Corporation Tax (Treatment of Unrelieved Surplus Advance Corporation Tax) Regulations 1999, reg. 11(14).
[18] *ibid.* reg. 11(2), (3).
[19] *ibid.* reg. 10(1), (4).
[20] *ibid.* reg. 10(2).
[21] *ibid.* reg. 10(3).

### Franked investment income—anti-avoidance

**12A–25**    There are a number of circumstances outside the group context in which distribu-tions from United Kingdom resident companies are not treated as franked investment income.

*Replacement of interest with distributions*

**12A–26**    A distribution is not treated as franked investment income where a company has taken action the effect of which is to replace interest income with distributions and the main purpose of that action is to reduce the shadow ACT the company is treated as having paid.[22]

EXAMPLE

> A Ltd invests its surplus cash in preference shares issued by a bank in order to generate franked investment income to reduce the shadow ACT on its own distributions. The dividends on the preference shares are not treated as franked investment income.

This rule only applies where the shadow ACT which would be avoided is that of the company taking the action in question. The rule may therefore not apply if the action is taken by a subsidiary within the group.

EXAMPLE

> A Ltd has a subsidiary, B Ltd, with surplus cash. B Ltd invests the surplus cash in preference shares issued by a bank. B Ltd receives dividends on the preference shares and elects to pass them on to A Ltd as franked investment income.[23] A Ltd's shadow ACT on its own dividends is therefore reduced. Provided that A Ltd cannot be said to have taken any action the rule does not apply since B Ltd has not reduced its shadow ACT: B Ltd could never have incurred shadow ACT on its dividends to A Ltd since they are intra group. In practice, any participation by A Ltd in the transaction is likely to be regarded as action causing the rule to apply.

---

[22] Corporation Tax (Treatment of Unrelieved Surplus Advance Corporation Tax) Regulations 1999, reg. 7.
[23] Pursuant to an election made under *ibid.* reg. 11(3).

*Arrangements to pass on franked investment income*

Where:                                                                              **12A–27**

(a) a company (A Ltd) is entitled to franked investment income;
(b) arrangements subsist under which another person (B) directly or indirectly obtains a payment representing any of the value of that franked investment income and exceeding the payment which would have been made between companies dealing at arm's length neither of whom were or had been group members or carrying forward surplus ACT;
(c) A Ltd's purposes in being a party to the arrangements include reducing the shadow ACT treated as paid by A Ltd or any other member of its group; and
(d) neither A Ltd's nor B's final accounting period under the shadow ACT regime has been determined

the franked investment income is not treated as franked investment income.[24]

For this purpose, "arrangements" includes arrangements of any kind, whether in writing or oral, and includes a series of arrangements, whether or not between the same persons.[25]

For the purpose of (c), it does not matter that the arrangements are not made directly between A Ltd and B and it is assumed that A Ltd uses its other franked investment income before that deriving from the arrangement in question.[1]

This rule does not apply where another anti-avoidance rule would counter the tax advantage obtained. So, for example, section 703 of the Taxes Act 1988 would prevail over this rule.[2]

EXAMPLE

In order to reduce its shadow ACT in respect of its own dividends, A Ltd subscribes for preference shares issued by B Ltd, the subscription price reflecting the value to A Ltd of the tax credit attaching to dividends on the shares and exceeding the price that would have applied if A Ltd had not had surplus ACT. The dividends on the preference shares are not treated as franked investment income.

---

[24] Corporation Tax (Treatment of Unrelieved Surplus Advance Corporation Tax) Regulations 1999, reg. 8(1), (2), (4)–(6).
[25] *ibid.* reg. 8(8).
[1] *ibid.* reg. 8(1)(c), (7).
[2] *ibid.* reg. 8(3).

It is unclear why it is a requirement of the rule that B's final accounting period should not have been determined under the shadow ACT rules.

*Share dealers*

**12A–28**　Where a dealer receives either a distribution from a United Kingdom resident company or a payment representative of such a distribution and in either case it is taken into account in computing its Schedule D, Case I or II profits, the distribution or payment is not treated as franked investment income.[3] A company is a dealer for this purpose if a profit on the sale of the shares or stock on which the distribution is paid would be taxable under Schedule D, Case I or II.[4]

*Section 703 of the Taxes Act 1988*

**12A–29**　Section 703 of the Taxes Act 1988 is potentially applicable where, in connection with the distribution of profits of a company or in connection with a purchase or sale of securities followed by a sale or purchase of securities, a person receives an abnormal amount by way of dividend which is taken into account as franked investment income under the shadow ACT rules.[5]

VI. Setting Off Shadow ACT

**General**

**12A–30**　Shadow ACT has to be offset against corporation tax liabilities in the following order:

　　(i)　corporation tax liabilities of the distributing company for the year of distribution;

　　(ii)　corporation tax liabilities of the distributing company for the previous six years (but not before April 6, 1999);

　　(iii)　corporation tax liabilities of other group members;

　　(iv)　future corporation tax liabilities of the distributing company.

---

[3] Corporation Tax (Treatment of Unrelieved Surplus Advance Corporation Tax) Regulations 1999, reg. 9(1).

[4] *ibid.* reg. 9(2) and ICTA 1988, s.95(2). When determining whether a person is a dealer, reference should be made to the decisions in *The Equitable Life Assurance Society v. Oakes* [2000] S.T.C. 459 and *The Prudential Assurance Co. Ltd v. Bibby (No. 2)* [2000] S.T.C. 459 and the discussion in para. 12–21 of the main work and of this supplement.

[5] ICTA 1988, s.704A(da), as inserted by the Corporation Tax (Treatment of Unrelieved Surplus Advance Corporation Tax) Regulations 1999, reg. 23.

## Corporation tax liabilities of the distributing company for the year of distribution

In the first instance, shadow ACT is set against the distributing company's liability **12A–31** to corporation tax on its profits charged to corporation tax for the accounting period in which the distribution is made.[6] "Profits charged to corporation tax" are the profits of the company on which corporation tax falls finally to be borne.[7] For this purpose, these profits include any profits on which the company is taxed under the controlled foreign companies legislation.[8]

Shadow ACT must be set against corporation tax before unrelieved surplus ACT but, unlike unrelieved surplus ACT, does not reduce the company's liability to pay corporation tax.[9]

The amount of shadow ACT that can be set against the company's corporation tax for any accounting period (the company's ACT capacity) cannot exceed the amount of shadow ACT which would have been treated as paid (ignoring franked investment income) in respect of a distribution made at the end of the accounting period of an amount which, together with the shadow ACT in respect of it, equalled the company's profits charged to corporation tax.[10] In other words, the maximum amount of shadow ACT that can be offset is an amount equal to 20 per cent of the company's profits for the accounting period.

EXAMPLE

A Ltd pays a dividend of £5,000,000 on June 1, 2000, on which the shadow ACT is £1,250,000. Its profits for the year to December 31, 2000 are £6,000,000 and the corporation tax due is £1,800,000. The maximum amount of shadow ACT that can be offset is £1,200,000, leaving £50,000 of surplus shadow ACT.

Where the carry forward of unrelieved surplus ACT is restricted on a charge of ownership, the accounting period in which the change occurs is split into two accounting periods, the first ending with the change of ownership.[11]

Shadow ACT cannot be set against corporation tax on a company's tonnage tax profits. Tonnage tax profits are also ignored in computing a company's profits charged

---

[6] Corporation Tax (Treatment of Unrelieved Surplus Advance Corporation Tax) Regulations 1999, reg. 12(1).

[7] *ibid.* reg. 3(2).

[8] *ibid.* reg. 3(3).

[9] *ibid.* reg. 12(1), (2).

[10] *ibid.* reg. 12(3)(a).

[11] *ibid.* reg. 12(3)(b).

to corporation tax for the purpose of determining the maximum amount of shadow ACT that can be set off in any accounting period.[12] Thus, for a tonnage tax company, the maximum amount of shadow ACT that can be set off is 20 per cent of the company's non tonnage tax profits for the accounting period.

*Foreign income*

**12A–32**    The limit on the set off of shadow ACT is computed separately for foreign income. The company's corporation tax liability is taken to be reduced by double tax relief and the maximum amount of shadow ACT that can be set off is the lower of:

(i) 20 per cent of the foreign income or gain, after deducting any deductions allocated to it under section 797(3) of the Taxes Act 1988; and

(ii) the corporation tax on the foreign income or gain after deducting double tax relief.[13]

EXAMPLE

A Ltd receives a foreign dividend of £100, on which it suffers withholding tax of £15. Its net receipt is £85 and its corporation tax liability after double tax relief is £15. The maximum amount of shadow ACT that can be set off against corporation tax on the foreign dividend is the lower of £20 and £15.

**Carry back of shadow ACT**

**12A–33**    Any surplus shadow ACT is then carried back to accounting periods beginning on or after April 6, 1999[14] up to a maximum of six years. The shadow ACT is set off against corporation tax on a LIFO basis, and the same limit on the amount which can be set off for any accounting period applies as for current year set off. When shadow ACT is carried back, it is only set off against corporation tax liabilities of the distributing company, not against those of other group members.[15]

Where surplus shadow ACT is carried back, it can displace unrelieved surplus ACT set against corporation tax in the period from the date two years before the end of the period from which it is carried back to the beginning of that period. If the date two years before the end of the period from which the surplus shadow ACT is carried

---

[12] FA 2000, Sched. 22, para. 57(5).

[13] Corporation Tax (Treatment of Unrelieved Surplus Advance Corporation Tax) Regulations 1999, reg. 12(4)–(6).

[14] Including deemed accounting periods where the carry forward of unrelieved surplus ACT is restricted on a change of ownership: *ibid.* reg. 12(8)(a).

[15] *ibid.* reg. 12(7).

back is not the beginning of an accounting period, the amount of unrelieved surplus ACT displaced is appropriately reduced.[16]

EXAMPLE

A Ltd has calendar year accounting periods. It has surplus shadow ACT of £200,000 for the year 2001. In the year 2000 it had capacity to offset shadow ACT and surplus ACT up to a maximum of £200,000. No shadow ACT was actually incurred in that period but £200,000 of surplus ACT was offset against corporation tax. The surplus shadow ACT arising in 2001 is carried back and displaces the surplus ACT set off in the year 2000.

There are a number of obscurities in the drafting of the regulations. In particular, it **12A–34** is not as clear as it might have been that where surplus shadow ACT is carried back to a period in which surplus ACT has been set off, the surplus shadow ACT is offset against the same slice of the corporation tax liability of the company against which surplus ACT is set, *i.e.* that the maximum set off of shadow ACT and surplus ACT in any period is 20 per cent of profits. It is believed that the following example is correct, and that this interpretation is implicit in regulation 14(4) and 12(7)(d).

EXAMPLE

A Ltd has calendar year accounting periods. It pays no dividends in 2000 or 2001 but pays a dividend in 2002 in respect of which it incurs surplus shadow ACT of £1,000,000. It has profits of £3,000,000 for 2000 and £2,000,000 for 2001, giving capacity to absorb shadow ACT of, respectively, £600,000 and £400,000. Unrelieved surplus ACT of £600,000 has been set off in 2000 and a further £200,000 has been set off in 2001. £400,000 of surplus shadow ACT is carried back from 2002 to 2001, displacing the surplus ACT offset in that period and causing A Ltd to have to pay further corporation tax of £200,000. No surplus shadow ACT can be carried back to 2000 because unrelieved surplus ACT has fully utilised the available capacity.

---

[16] *ibid.* reg. 12(7)(d), (8)(b).

### Carry forward of surplus shadow ACT

**12A–35**     Any surplus shadow ACT that cannot be carried back or allocated to other group members under the rules to be discussed in the next section is carried forward to the next accounting period.[17]

It is not clear whether surplus shadow ACT that has to be carried forward to a later period must, if it exceeds the distributing company's capacity to offset it in that period, be allocated to other group members. The carry forward is expressed to be for the purpose of regulation 12 rather than regulations 12 and 13. However, the absence of any counterpart to regulation 12(7)(c) suggests that carried forward shadow ACT can be allocated to other group members. It is understood that the Inland Revenue consider that regulation 13 does apply to carried forward shadow ACT.

### Allocation to other group members

**12A–36**     Where a company is a member of a group at any time in an accounting period, it must allocate any surplus shadow ACT that cannot be carried back to other group members.[18] The shadow ACT allocated to another group member is then set against the corporation tax liability of that group member after that group member's own shadow ACT and any shadow ACT reallocated to it when another company leaves the group,[19] subject to the normal limit on the amount of shadow ACT that can be offset in any period.[20]

The shadow ACT regulations provide that a member of a group cannot set any unrelieved surplus ACT against its corporation tax liability for an accounting period until all its surplus shadow ACT for that period has been allocated to other members of its group.[21] It is difficult to see the point of this rule, since a company with surplus shadow ACT for a period will not have any capacity to offset unrelieved surplus ACT.

If a group's total capacity to use surplus shadow ACT exceeds the surplus shadow ACT available, the group's parent company must allocate the surplus shadow ACT among the members of the group.[22] If it does not do so, the Inland Revenue can allocate the surplus shadow ACT.[23] Any subsequent allocation by the parent company will, however, prevail over the Inland Revenue's allocation.[24]

---

[17] Corporation Tax (Treatment of Unrelieved Surplus Advance Corporation Tax) Regulations 1999, reg. 12(9).

[18] Corporation Tax (Treatment of Unrelieved Surplus Advance Corporation Tax) Regulations 1999, reg. 13(1).

[19] See para. 12A–38 below.

[20] Corporation Tax (Treatment of Unrelieved Surplus Advance Corporation Tax) Regulations 1999, reg. 13(2).

[21] *ibid.* reg. 13(3).

[22] *ibid.* reg. 13(4).

[23] *ibid.* reg. 13(15).

[24] *ibid.* reg. 13(15)(b).

EXAMPLE

A Ltd has two subsidiaries, B Ltd and C Ltd. A Ltd has surplus shadow ACT of £1,000,000. B Ltd has ACT capacity of £750,000 and C Ltd has capacity of £500,000. A Ltd can allocate up to £750,000 shadow ACT to B Ltd and up to £500,000 shadow ACT to C Ltd. It could therefore choose to allocate £500,000 to each subsidiary or to allocate £750,000 to B Ltd and £250,000 to C Ltd.

A parent company can at any time reallocate surplus shadow ACT among its group **12A–37** members, except that it cannot reduce the amount allocated to any particular company below its capacity to use shadow ACT after the time limit for amending that company's company tax return has expired.[25]

Where a group's total capacity to use surplus shadow ACT is less than the surplus shadow ACT available, the group parent must allocate to each group member the maximum amount that it can use, and the balance is carried forward by the company whose distributions gave rise to the shadow ACT in question.[1]

EXAMPLE

A Ltd has two subsidiaries, B Ltd and C Ltd. A Ltd has surplus shadow ACT of £2,000,000. B Ltd has ACT capacity of £750,000 and C Ltd has capacity of £350,000. A Ltd must allocate £750,000 to B Ltd and £350,000 to C Ltd. A Ltd carries £900,000 forward to its next accounting period.

*Artificial degrouping*

In order to prevent the artificial degrouping of subsidiaries with surplus shadow **12A–38** ACT, the regulations provide that where a group member leaves a group otherwise than because of a transaction or arrangements between the company or a parent of that company and an unconnected person, its surplus shadow ACT is treated as belonging to the nearest company further up the corporate chain which remains in the group.[2]

---

[25] Corporation Tax (Treatment of Unrelieved Surplus Advance Corporation Tax) Regulations 1999, reg. 13(7).

[1] *ibid.* reg. 13(5).

[2] *ibid.* reg. 13(6). The test of "connection" is that contained in ICTA 1988, s.839.

EXAMPLE

A U.S. resident company, A Inc, owns the whole of B Ltd, which in turn owns C Ltd, with C Ltd owning D Ltd. D Ltd has surplus shadow ACT. In order to degroup it from the B Ltd group, D Ltd issues shares to A Inc. D Ltd's surplus shadow ACT is treated as belonging to C Ltd.

Strictly, it appears that this rule could apply where the parent of a group has surplus shadow ACT and is taken over by another United Kingdom resident company, with the result that the parent's surplus shadow ACT passes to the acquiror. This is because on the takeover the parent's group would cease to exist.[3]

*Accounting periods of group members to which surplus shadow ACT is allocated*

**12A–39**  Surplus shadow ACT can only be allocated to an accounting period of a group member if at some point during that accounting period both the group member and the company whose surplus shadow ACT is being allocated ("the surrendering company") are members of the same group.[4] Subject to that, surplus shadow ACT allocated to a group member is allocated to accounting periods in the following order of priority:

    (i)  an accounting period coinciding with or contained within the surrendering company's accounting period;

   (ii)  an accounting period beginning before but ending in the surrendering company's accounting period;

  (iii)  an accounting period beginning in but ending after the surrendering company's accounting period; and

  (iv)  the period beginning 24 months before the end of the surrendering company's accounting period.[5] If this 24-month period includes part of an accounting period beginning before that period, the ACT capacity of the group member for the accounting period in question is apportioned between the parts of the accounting period within and outside that period on a time basis.[6]

---

[3] Corporation Tax (Treatment of Unrelieved Surplus Advance Corporation Tax) Regulations 1999, reg. 6(2)(b)(ii).

[4] *ibid*. reg. 13(8), (9).

[5] *ibid*. reg. 13(8).

[6] *ibid*. reg. 13(10).

EXAMPLE

A Ltd has surplus shadow ACT for its accounting period January 1–December 31, 2002 of £5,000,000 which it does not have the capacity to carry back. It has one subsidiary, B Ltd, with the following accounting periods and ACT capacity:

| Accounting period | ACT Capacity |
|---|---|
| April 1, 2000–March 31, 2001 | £1,000,000 |
| April 1, 2001–March 31, 2002 | £2,000,000 |
| April 1, 2002–March 31, 2003 | £1,500,000 |

A Ltd's surplus shadow ACT is allocated as follows:

(1) April 1, 2001–March 31, 2002: £2,000,000 (reg. 13(8)(b));
(2) April 1, 2002–March 31, 2003: £1,500,000 (reg. 13(8)(c));
(3) January 1, 2001–March 31,2001: £250,000 (reg. 13(8)(d) and (10)).

If more than one company with surplus shadow ACT allocates shadow ACT to the **12A–40** same group member for the same accounting period, the group parent must determine the order of priority, and that order applies on any subsequent reallocation.[7]

Where a company is a member of more than one group and companies from more than one group allocate surplus shadow ACT to the company the surplus shadow ACT is allocated to accounting periods in the order in which the allocations are made.[8]

*Companies joining or leaving group*

Where a company joins or leaves a group in an accounting period to which surplus **12A–41** shadow ACT of another company is allocated, the company's ACT capacity is reduced to reflect the part of the accounting period for which it was a member of the group and any other attributions of surplus shadow ACT to that period and the surplus shadow ACT is deemed to be attributed to a separate accounting period throughout which both the company and the surrendering company were members of the same group.[9]

---

[7] Corporation Tax (Treatment of Unrelieved Surplus Advance Corporation Tax) Regulations 1999, reg. 13(11).
[8] *ibid*. reg. 13(12).
[9] *ibid*. reg. 13(13).

EXAMPLE

> A Ltd buys B Ltd on June 30, 2000. A Ltd and B Ltd both have calendar year accounting periods. A Ltd has surplus shadow ACT for 2000 of £2,000,000 and B Ltd has ACT capacity for the same period of £1,000,000. Only £500,000 of A Ltd's surplus shadow ACT can be allocated to B Ltd.

It should be noted that there is no restriction on shadow ACT arising on a distribution made by A Ltd before it acquired B Ltd being allocated to B Ltd. It should also be noted that while the ACT capacity of a subsidiary leaving the group is reduced for the accounting period in which it leaves the group, its parent's surplus shadow ACT of that period may fall to be allocated without any reduction to the previous accounting period of the subsidiary under the 24-month carry back rule discussed in the previous section.

EXAMPLE

> A Ltd and its subsidiary, B Ltd, have calendar year accounting periods. A Ltd has surplus shadow ACT of £1,000,000 for 2001. A Ltd has no capacity to carry back shadow ACT and has no other subsidiaries. B Ltd has profits of £3,000,000 for 2000 and £5,000,000 for 2001, giving ACT capacity for those periods of, respectively, £600,000 and £1,000,000. A Ltd sells B Ltd on June 30, 2001. £500,000 of the surplus shadow ACT is allocated to B Ltd for the year 2001 and the balance is allocated to B Ltd for the previous period.

*Displacement of surplus ACT*

**12A–42**    Where surplus shadow ACT is allocated to an accounting period beginning before the surrendering company's accounting period (whether or not it ends during that accounting period), it can displace unrelieved surplus ACT set against corporation tax for that period but does not displace other shadow ACT already set off.[10]

EXAMPLE

> A Ltd has a subsidiary, B Ltd. Both have calendar year accounting periods. A Ltd has surplus shadow ACT of £3,000,000 for 2001. B Ltd has ACT capacity

---

[10] Corporation Tax (Treatment of Unrelieved Surplus Advance Corporation Tax) Regulations 1999, reg. 13(14).

for 2000 of £1,000,000 and 2001 of £2,000,000, but has offset surplus ACT of £750,000 against its corporation tax liability for 2000. A Ltd's surplus shadow ACT must be allocated to B Ltd's 2000 and 2001 accounting periods and displaces the unrelieved surplus ACT set off in 2000.

## VII. Setting Off Unrelieved Surplus ACT

### Basic rule

ACT which has not been set against corporation tax for an accounting period ending **12A–43** before April 6, 1999 is set against corporation tax for an accounting period ending on or after that date and, unlike shadow ACT, discharges the corporation tax to the extent of the set off.[11] Unrelieved surplus ACT is set against corporation tax of an earlier period before corporation tax of a later period.[12] Where the anti-avoidance provisions of section 116 of the Taxes Act 1988[13] apply to a corporate member of a partnership, unrelieved surplus ACT cannot be set against corporation tax on its share of the partnership profits for any accounting period of the partnership in which the arrangements to which that section applies exist or to which they apply.[14]

The maximum amount of unrelieved surplus ACT that can be set off in any period is equal to the maximum amount of shadow ACT that could be set off, less any shadow ACT in fact set off. Assuming no foreign income or gains, this will be equal to 20 per cent of the company's profits, less any shadow ACT set off against corporation tax on those profits.[15]

Example

A Ltd has profits of £2,000,000 for 2000, those profits including no foreign income or gains. Its corporation tax liability for 2000 is therefore £600,000. It pays a dividend on June 1, 2000 of £500,000, giving rise to shadow ACT of £125,000. It has unrelieved surplus ACT carried forward to 2000 of £400,000. Its ACT capacity for 2000 is 20 per cent of £2,000,000 or £400,000. Shadow ACT is offset first reducing the capacity for unrelieved surplus ACT to £275,000.

---

[11] Corporation Tax (Treatment of Unrelieved Surplus Advance Corporation Tax) Regulations 1999, reg. 14(1).

[12] *ibid.* reg. 14(2).

[13] See para. 19–09 of the main work.

[14] Corporation Tax (Treatment of Unrelieved Surplus Advance Corporation Tax) Regulations 1999, reg. 14(3), (5).

[15] *ibid.* reg. 14(4).

ACT of £275,000 is set off, leaving the company to pay £325,000 corporation tax. The balance of the ACT of £125,000 is carried forward to 2001.

Unrelieved surplus ACT cannot be set-off against corporation tax on a company's tonnage tax profits or against tax on the tonnage profits of a controlled foreign company apportioned to the company.[16]

### Surrendered ACT

**12A–44**   Surrendered ACT is set against corporation tax before ACT arising in respect of a company's own distributions.[17] Surrendered ACT can, however, only be set against corporation tax for an accounting period if throughout the accounting period the company with the surrendered ACT is a subsidiary of the surrendering company or both companies are subsidiaries of a third company.[18] For this purpose, "subsidiary" means a 51 per cent subsidiary under the old ACT surrender rules.[19]

### Anti-avoidance—changes in ownership

**12A–45**   If it were not for the provision now under consideration, a traffic would no doubt arise in companies whose principal asset is unrelieved surplus ACT: that is to say, companies that once had a substantial business during the heyday of which the surplus arose, but by reason of a decline in the business have been unable to use the surplus. Such companies would be bought with the object of injecting into them a new, profitable activity and setting off against the mainstream corporation tax liability arising in respect of it the unrelieved surplus ACT brought forward from accounting periods before the revival of prosperity. Such transactions are frustrated by it being provided that where:

> (i) within any period of three years there is both a "change in the ownership" of a company and (either earlier or later in that period, or at the same time) a major change in the nature or conduct of a trade or business carried on by the company; or
> (ii) at any time after the scale of the activities in a trade or business carried on by a company has become small or negligible, and before any considerable

---

[16] FA 2000, Sched. 22, para. 57.
[17] Corporation Tax (Treatment of Unrelieved Surplus Advance Corporation Tax) Regulations 1999, reg. 15(1).
[18] *ibid.* reg. 15(2).
[19] *ibid.* reg. 15(3).

revival of the trade or business, there is "a change in the ownership" of the company

no unrelieved surplus ACT (including surrendered ACT) can be set against corporation tax for an accounting period ending after the change in ownership.[20]

For this purpose, the accounting period in which the change of ownership takes place is treated as two accounting periods, the first ending with the change, the second beginning with it. Profits arising in the accounting period in which the change takes place are apportioned to the two parts on a time basis, or such other basis as is just and reasonable where a time basis is unjust and unreasonable.[21] Where it is necessary to wait and see what happens after a change of ownership before it is known whether these rules apply, an assessment to give effect to these rules is not out of time if made within six years from the last relevant event to occur within three years after the change of ownership.[22]

A "major change in the nature or conduct of a trade or business" includes:[23]   **12A–46**

  (i) a major change in the type of property dealt in, or services or facilities provided in the trade or business; or

  (ii) a major change in customers, outlets or markets of the trade or business; or

  (iii) a change whereby the company ceases to be a trading company[24] and becomes an investment company[25] or vice versa; or

  (iv) where the company is an investment company, a major change in the nature of the investments held by the company.

The rule applies even if the major change is a gradual process beginning outside the three-year period.[1] It seems likely that the Revenue will interpret the rule in line with SP10/91 but the authors are not aware of any official statement to this effect.

The rules for ascertaining whether there has been a change of ownership are pre-

---

[20] *ibid.* reg. 16(1), (3), (4).

[21] Corporation Tax (Treatment of Unrelieved Surplus Advance Corporation Tax) Regulations 1999, regs 16(2) and 3(6).

[22] *ibid.* reg. 16(5), applying ICTA 1988, s.768(8).

[23] Corporation Tax (Treatment of Unrelieved Surplus Advance Corporation Tax) Regulations 1999, reg. 16(6).

[24] A "trading company" is a company whose business consists wholly or mainly of the carrying on of a trade or trades: *ibid.* reg. 16(7).

[25] An "investment company" is a company, other than a "holding company", whose business consists wholly or mainly in the making of investments and the principal part of whose income is derived therefrom; and a "holding company" is a company whose business consists wholly or mainly in the holding of shares or securities of companies which are its 90% subsidiaries and which are trading companies: *ibid.* reg. 16(7). For the meaning of the expression "90% subsidiary" see Chap. 21 of the main work.

[1] *ibid.* reg. 16(6).

cisely the same as those considered in Chapter 7 of the main work.[2] It is to be noticed that for the purpose of determining whether or not a change of ownership has taken place, the registered owner of shares, stock or securities may be required to state who is their beneficial owner.[3]

### Change in ownership—surrendered ACT

**12A–47**    There is deemed to be a change of ownership of a company if its parent company changes ownership.[4] Accordingly, if a parent which has surrendered ACT to a subsidiary is sold, the subsidiary will not from the date of sale be able to use the surrendered ACT if it undergoes a major change in the nature or conduct of its trade or business— the major change in its trade, along with the notional change of ownership of the subsidiary when the parent is sold, mean that regulation 16 applies to the subsidiary.

Correspondingly, a similar restriction also applies to the subsidiary if its parent is sold, and it is the parent, and not the subsidiary, that suffers the major change in its trade, with the consequence that the subsidiary cannot use the surrendered ACT after the date of the sale of its parent, even though the subsidiary has not itself suffered either a change in its ownership or a change in its trade.[5] Where the change in ownership occurs during an accounting period, the part ending with the change and the part afterwards are treated as different accounting periods.[6]

The definitions of "change of ownership" and "major change in the nature or conduct of a trade or business" are as for the rule discussed in the previous section. Similarly, the rules about time-limits for assessments and nominee shareholders being required to give information about beneficial ownership also apply.[7]

### Channelling assets through recently acquired companies

**12A–48**    But for the provision now to be considered, it would be possible to acquire a company with unrelieved surplus ACT and channel the sale of assets through that company, setting the ACT off against the charge to corporation tax on the disposal. However, the use of such a company's ACT in respect of that disposal is restricted in the following circumstances:

---

[2] *ibid.* reg. 16(5).
[3] *ibid.* reg. 16(5) and ICTA 1988, s.769(9).
[4] ICTA 1988, s.769(6).
[5] Corporation Tax (Treatment of Unrelieved Surplus Advance Corporation Tax) Regulations 1999, reg. 17(1), (2).
[6] *ibid.* reg. 17(2).
[7] *ibid.* reg. 17(3).

(i) there is a change of ownership[8] of the company;
(ii) after the change the company acquires an asset from another company in the same group so that section 171 of the Taxation of Chargeable Gains Act 1992 deems the disposal to have been made on a "no gain, no loss" basis for the purposes of corporation tax on chargeable gains; and
(iii) a capital gain accrues to the company on a disposal of the asset within a period of three years beginning with the change of ownership.[9]

In these circumstances, the unrelieved surplus ACT cannot be set off against the corporation tax payable in respect of the disposal of the asset. The maximum amount of unrelieved surplus ACT that can be set against corporation tax for the accounting period in which the chargeable gain arises is reduced by 20 per cent of the gain.[10]

EXAMPLE

A Ltd acquires B Ltd which has unrelieved surplus ACT of £50,000. A Ltd then transfers a building to B Ltd on a "no gain, no loss" basis under section 171 of the 1992 Act which B Ltd sells within one year, realising a chargeable gain of £100,000. The corporation tax on the gain is £30,000. The gain is the only profit made by B Ltd in the period. The maximum unrelieved surplus ACT that could be set off against corporation tax for the period under normal circumstances would be £20,000 but this is reduced to zero by the rule under consideration, since £20,000 is 20 per cent of the chargeable gain.

This provision also applies if the asset in question is subsumed into another asset, for example where a lease becomes a freehold by virtue of the lessee acquiring the reversion. Both assets are regarded as one and the same for this purpose.[11]

The restriction applies even where the asset acquired intra group is acquired from a company which joined the group together with the company with the unrelieved surplus ACT.

---

[8] The change in ownership rules contained in ICTA 1988, s.769 apply for this purpose: Corporation Tax (Treatment of Unrelieved Surplus Advance Corporation Tax) Regulations 1999, reg. 18(4).
[9] *ibid.* reg. 18(1).
[10] *ibid.* reg. 18(3).
[11] *ibid.* reg. 18(2).

### Recovery of ACT wrongly set off

**12A–49**  If the Revenue discover that any set off of unrelieved surplus ACT ought not to have been made or has become excessive they can make any assessments required to recover any tax that ought to have been paid and to ensure that the resulting tax liabilities (including interest on unpaid tax) are what they should have been.[12]

### Secondary liability where shadow ACT carried back

**12A–50**  Where shadow ACT is set against corporation tax of an accounting period beginning before the accounting period in which it is treated as being paid it may in certain circumstances displace unrelieved surplus ACT set off in that period. The consequence of this is that further corporation tax is due. If this corporation tax is not paid within six months of the later of the date the corporation tax becomes due and payable (under the instalment payment rules if applicable) and the date the company's self-assessment is amended the corporation tax can at any time within six years be recovered from any other company which is a member of the same group in the relevant accounting period. Any company from which the corporation tax is recovered has a statutory right to recover it and any interest paid on it from the company that should have paid it.[13]

Where a group sells a subsidiary which has offset unrelieved surplus ACT, it should take an indemnity from the purchaser to cover any possible liability arising to members of the vendor group under this provision.

### VIII. Controlled Foreign Companies

**12A–51**  Where a company is assessed to tax under the controlled foreign companies legislation and the company has surplus shadow ACT calculated in accordance with regulations 12 and 13 of the shadow ACT regulations, the surplus shadow ACT is set against the company's tax liability under the controlled foreign companies legislation.[14] The maximum amount of surplus shadow ACT that can be set off is given by the formula:

$$20\% \ (E - F) - D$$

where

E = the profits charged under the controlled foreign companies legislation;

F = any tax reliefs available under paragraph 1 of Schedule 26 to the Taxes Act

---

[12] *ibid*. reg. 19.

[13] Corporation Tax (Treatment of Unrelieved Surplus Advance Corporation Tax) Regulations 1999, reg. 21.

[14] *ibid*. reg. 20(1).

1988 to reduce tax charged under the controlled foreign companies legislation; and

D = the creditable tax apportioned to the company.[15]

Where a company still has surplus shadow ACT after applying the normal set off rules and setting it against its own tax liability under the controlled foreign companies legislation, the remaining surplus shadow ACT can be allocated by the group parent to other group members liable to tax under the controlled foreign companies legislation.[16] The maximum amount that can be set off against any group member's tax liability under the controlled foreign companies legislation is as described above.

Unrelieved surplus ACT can be set off against tax under the controlled foreign companies legislation up to a maximum amount equal to the difference between the maximum amount of surplus shadow ACT that could be set off under the foregoing rules and the amount of shadow ACT in fact set off.[17]

## IX. Planning

The key to optimising the use of unrelieved surplus ACT lies in two formulae:     **12A–52**

(i) $SACT = 20\%P - S$

where

SACT = unrelieved surplus ACT set against corporation tax;
P = profits charged to corporation tax; and
S = shadow ACT set against corporation tax

(ii) $S = 25\%D - F$

where

S = shadow ACT;
D = distributions made by company; and
F = franked investment income

It follows from these formulae that strategies to optimise the use of unrelieved surplus ACT will involve increasing taxable profits, reducing or deferring distributions or increasing franked investment income.

---

[15] *ibid.* reg. 20(4)(c), (5).
[16] *ibid.* reg. 20(3).
[17] Corporation Tax (Treatment of Unrelieved Surplus Advance Corporation Tax) Regulations 1999, reg. 20(2), (4)(b).

### Increasing taxable profits

**12A–53**  Possible methods of increasing taxable profits include:

    (i) buying or commencing new United Kingdom trades or buying profitable United Kingdom companies;

    (ii) entering into sales and leasebacks;

    (iii) adjusting transfer pricing, to the extent that transfer pricing legislation allows latitude;

    (iv) not claiming or withdrawing claims for capital allowances; and

    (v) carrying trading losses or non-trading loan relationship deficits forward rather than setting them against other income or surrendering them as group relief.

### Reducing or deferring distributions

**12A–54**  Possible strategies include:

    (i) deferring dividends until unrelieved surplus ACT is fully utilised. It needs to be remembered when adopting this strategy that surplus shadow ACT of a later period can be carried back and displace unrelieved surplus ACT set off in the previous 12 months. It is easier for a foreign multinational to defer distributions from a United Kingdom subgroup until unrelieved surplus ACT is fully utilised than it is for a quoted United Kingdom group;

    (ii) paying enhanced scrip rather than cash dividends;

    (iii) returning cash to shareholders in the course of putting a new holding company on top of an existing parent company;

    (iv) reorganising capital or doing a bonus issue paid up out of share premium account and then repurchasing or redeeming the newly created shares; or

    (v) (where the unrelieved surplus ACT is in a subsidiary) degrouping the subsidiary from the remainder of the group so that surplus shadow ACT arising on the parent's dividends is not allocated to the subsidiary.

### Increasing franked investment income

**12A–55**  This is in practice the most difficult of the strategies to adopt since there are a number of anti-avoidance rules which seek to prevent the artificial acquisition of franked investment income.

Rather surprisingly, there are no specific rules countering the buying of companies with surplus franked investment income, although section 703 of the Taxes Act 1988 must be carefully considered when such companies pay franked dividends to their parents in order to frank their parents' own dividends.

# CHAPTER 14

# CLOSE COMPANIES

Contents      *Para.*      Contents      *Para.*

## II. Close Companies: Section 419 Loans

**Relevant borrowers**

In *Deanby Investment Co. Ltd v. Brennan*,[1] a Special Commissioner reached a **14–28**
decision on the "loans in the ordinary course of the business" exception in which he
distinguished *Steen v. Law* referred to in the main text. The case concerned an investment company which had been in business since 1926. Up to 1978 the taxpayer
company's investments consisted substantially of properties for letting. Between 1983
and 1990 the taxpayer company made six loans to Mr M who at all material times
was the associate of a participator. During the 10 years from 1984–85 to 1993–94 the
interest paid by Mr M to the taxpayer company, contributed 58.7 per cent of its
turnover. Those loans were repaid in 1994 and the taxpayer company used the funds
to purchase shares. On February 1, 1994 the taxpayer company made a loan of £5,000
to a third party company, (of which Mr M was chairman). That loan was repaid in
July 1998. In September 1997 the taxpayer company made a further loan of £30,000
to Mr M, and it is that loan that formed the basis of the assessment under appeal.
   The terms of the exception are:

> "... where a close company, *otherwise than in the ordinary course of a business
> carried on by it which includes the lending of money, makes any loan* ... to an
> individual who is ... an associate of a participator."

---

[1] [2000] S.T.C. (S.C.D.) 172.

It was accepted by the Inspector that the exception did not require that the company should be carrying on a trade of money lending. The Special Commissioner found as a fact that all of the loans to Mr M were made as investments. Was the loan in question made in the "ordinary course" of the investment business? As to this the Special Commissioner held:

> "Clearly the management of its investments is an essential part of an investment company's business; and if it considers that a loan would be a better investment than a particular asset currently in its portfolio, the switch will be made 'in the ordinary course of its business'. In my opinion that, quite simply, is how the 1997 loan should be viewed. To my mind, it does not matter who the purchaser of the unwanted asset is, or to whom the loan is made. And, after all, s.418 envisages excluded loans being made to participators or their close relations."

In distinguishing *Steen v. Law* (a company law case) the Special Commissioner referred to the passage set out in the main text and said that investment companies were not in mind, the facts were different and that in any case it arose out of a legislative context which had different policy objectives. The Special Commissioner went on to explain what he considered to be the purpose of section 419(1) (namely, to tax loans out of distributable reserves) and observed:

> "It is no part of the object of the section to treat a company's capital as distributable income. Yet that would be the effect of upholding the assessment under appeal."

It is respectfully considered that this appeal to policy considerations is misguided and may have distracted attention from the statutory issue, which is whether the loan to the partcipator or associate is made in the ordinary course of a business which includes the lending of money. When Lord Radcliffe in *Steen v. Law*[2] spoke of: " 'lending of money,' to be part of the ordinary business of a company, must be what may be called a lending of money in general," he was indicating that the context required a comparison to be made between the loan in question (falling within the target category), and loans not falling within the target category made by the company in the ordinary course of its business. In the opinion of the author the conclusion that target loans can of themselves define the ordinary course of a business that includes the lending of money is open to doubt.

## Meaning of "loan"

**14–29**  The anonymised decision of the Special Commissioners in *Gold v. HMIT* referred to in note 2 has been taken to the High Court under the name *Grant v. Watton*.[3] That

---

[2] [1964] A.C. at p.302.
[3] [1999] S.T.C. 330.

case concerned services provided to a participator by a service compny. The participator ran an estate agency business and the staff together with all the usual services were supplied by the company. The charge for the sevices were claculated annually by reference to aggregate direct and indirect costs (including depreciation) to which was added a mark-up.

For the taxpayer it was contended that no "debt was incurred" for the purposes of section 419(2) until the liability was ascertained after the end of each year. It was held that the debt was incurred as the services were provided day by day albeit that the amount could not then be ascertained. The Court rejected an argument that on the facts, a precondition to liability was that a full year's services should be provided, but indicated that if those had been the facts, no debt would have been incurred until the completion of performance.[4]

On the facts the decision is difficult to accept. The Special Commissioner had held that debts were incurred as from the dates on which the company paid its own suppliers. The Court rejected this approach in favour of the notion that credit was given on a daily basis as the services were supplied. But as the parties never envisaged a daily breakdown it is hard to see how it can be said that the debt was incurred day by day. If payment is on a piecework basis then of course the debt is incurred as the piece is completed. On the facts here, the better view is that the debts were incurred annually at the end of each accounting period (but before the amount had been claculated).

### Release of loan

On the release of a loan on or after April 5, 1999, the debtor is treated as having received income of an amount equal to the sum released net of income tax at the Schedule F ordinary rate.[5] Such income is treated as taxable under Schedule F so that the Schedule F upper rate applies.[6]   **14–35**

As mentioned in paragraph 14–34 of the main work, for the company the release is treated in the same way as repayment so that the company is entitled to recover the tax paid by it on the making of the loan.

---

[4] *ibid.* p.348*j*.
[5] ICTA 1988, s.421(1)(a).
[6] *ibid.* s.412(1)(c), s.1A(2)(b) and s.1B.

CHAPTER 15

# NON-RESIDENT COMPANIES, MIGRATION OF COMPANIES AND DUAL RESIDENT COMPANIES

Contents | *Para.*

## I. INTRODUCTION

### Company or partnership?

**15–1A**     The Taxes Acts provide that references to a "company" include bodies corporate but not partnerships.[1] The leading case on the classification of foreign business organisations is *Dreyfus v. IRC*[2] which concerned the tax treatment of a French *Société en Nom Collectif*. There were two members of the SNC, and assessments were made upon them on the basis that profits from trading in the United Kingdom were their profits from a trade carried on by them in partnership. They appealed on the ground

---

[1] ICTA 1988, s.832(1), TCGA 1992, s.288(1).
[2] 14 T.C. 460.

206

that the profits belonged to the SNC. The decision against partnership is summarised in the following passage from the judgment of Lawrence L.J.:

> "Without going through all the findings in the case, I would point out one or two which to my mind really decide this case, the first being this, that on complying with certain formalities, which, as I understand it, consisted of depositing a document with the Registrar of the Commercial and Civil Court and publishing a notice in the paper, an entity, to use a neutral term, springs into existence, and that entity is one which owns the property of the Society, and which incurs the liability in respect of the debts of the concern, and which has the sole right to receive the earnings of the concern, and has the control of the distribution of the profits. Added to that, it is plain on the findings that a member of that entity is not an agent for the others in carrying on the business of the concern. Without going into the other findings in the case, those facts alone seem to me to be wholly inconsistent with the notion of a partnership as existing in this country.[3]"

In paragraph 1673 of the International Tax Manual, the Revenue states that it does not follow *Dreyfus* on the grounds that the facts were wrongly appreciated by the Commissioners! This question of classification has been highlighted by the judicial review application in *R. v. IRC, ex p. Bishop*.[4] That case involved a proposal by an English firm of accountants to seek registration in Jersey as a "LLP". Under Jersey law, a limited liability partnership is a separate legal person distinct from its members, and debts contracted by the LLP are not liabilities of members provided that the LLP maintains a bond of at least £5m. The English firm sought confirmation from the Revenue that if did register as a LLP, it would remain taxable in the United Kingdom as a partnership. The Revenue's response was that the firm would fall to be taxed as a company.

In the judicial review proceedings, the firm sought a declaration that the Revenue's view was wrong. The court declined jurisdiction so that the point was left unresolved, but in reviewing the issues the court said[5]:

> "The applicants make the point that, since the Tax Acts apply alike in England and Scotland, the issue is whether the entity is one which English or Scots law would characterise as a partnership. There are significant differences between English and Scots partnership law. In particular, in Scots law, a firm is a legal person distinct from the partners of which it is composed. It is an important part of the applicant's case that a Jersey LLP would be characterised as a partnership in Scots law, and they have produced a number of expert opinions in support of that proposition. But the Revenue have obtained an expert opinion from Mr Keen Q.C. that the essential requirements of a partnership in Scots law are not to be

---

[3] At 578.
[4] [1999] S.T.C. 531.
[5] *ibid.* at 545.

found in a Jersey LLP. The issues between the experts include the question whether it is essential to the existence of a partnership in Scots law that there should be more than one principal carrying on a business, and whether in Scots law, the partners are to be regarded as both principals and mutual agents."

It will be appreciated from this passage that the question of whether a body is or is not a partnership for the purposes of United Kingdom law is complicated by the fact that under that law, both English and Scottish partnerships are "partnerships" even though in the case of a Scottish partnership, it is a body distinct from its members. Hence the enquiry into the "essential nature" of a Scottish partnership for it is not enough that the overseas body has points in common with either an English or Scottish partnership: if it would not be a partnership if established under either of those laws, then it cannot be a partnership for tax purposes. In this regard, reference should be made to the analysis of the essentials of both English and Scottish partnerships by the Court of Appeal in *Memec plc v. IRC*.[6] The issue there was the treatment under a double tax treaty of dividends received by a "silent partnership" of which the silent partner was a United Kingdom resident company, and the argument was that the silent partner should be regarded in the same light as a member of an English or Scottish partnership. Thus, the context is not the same as the present, but the analysis is of universal application. In consequence of *Memec*, the Revenue has published a *Tax Bulletin* article on "Entity Classification".[7]

### III. Trading in the United Kingdom through a Branch or Agency

**15–24**   The provisions of section 25 of the Taxation of Chargeable Gains Act 1992 that are discussed in the first full paragraph on page 429 of the main text have been amended by Finance Act 2000. A disposal will not be deemed to take place where a non-resident company ceases to trade in the United Kingdom through a branch or agency and the trade is transferred to another company provided that the provisions of section 139 or 171 of the Taxation of Chargeable Gains Act 1992 apply to the assets that are transferred.[8] The amendments that have been made to the provisions of section 139 and 171 by the Finance Act 2000 are considered respectively at paragraph 23–05 and 28–02 of this supplement.

Section 172 of the Taxation of Chargeable Gains Act 1992 (which is referred to in the final paragraph on page 429 of the main text) was repealed by Finance Act 2000 in relation to disposals on or after April 1, 2000.[9] The reason for this is that, following the amendments to the definition of a capital gains group of companies (see 23–05 of this supplement), the provisions of section 172 are no longer required. Now where a

---

[6] [1998] S.T.C. 754 at 764, 766.
[7] Inland Revenue, *Tax Bulletin*, February 1999, p. 631.
[8] TCGA 1992, s.25(3A), as inserted by FA 2000, Sched. 29 para. 6(2).
[9] FA 2000, Sched. 29 para. 3.

United Kingdom branch of a non-resident company transfers its trade and assets to a United Kingdom resident company that is a member of the same worldwide group, the provisions of section 171 of the Taxation of Chargeable Gains Act 1992 will apply to the transfer.

## V. OTHER PROFITS CHARGEABLE

### Gains of non-resident company imputed to shareholders: non-resident groups

TCGA 1992, section 79B removes treaty protection for Trustees as respects gains arising on or after March 21, 2000.  **15–38**

## VI. STRUCTURING BUSINESS ACTIVITIES OF NON-RESIDENT COMPANIES IN THE UNITED KINGDOM: PRACTICAL CONSIDERATIONS

### Transfer pricing—United Kingdom legislation

As noted in paragraph 3-04 of the main work it is considered that the transfer pricing provisions contained in Schedule 28AA to the Taxes Act 1988 can apply to interest payable on loan relationships. Where a loan to a resident United Kingdom company is advanced on the undertaking of support from an overseas parent or fellow overseas-resident subsidiary company the Inland Revenue would be able to restrict relief for the interest payable on the loan, to the extent that the amount of the loan exceeded the amount which would have been lent but for the provision of such support.[10] In an article the Inland Revenue's *Tax Bulletin*, June 1995, it was stated that it was the Inland Revenue's experience that a third party lender would look to the debt to equity ratio of a United Kingdom sub-group as a whole (including any overseas companies which are owned by that sub-group) in determining whether to advance a loan to a member of that group.[11] In an article in *Tax Bulletin*, October 1998 the Inland Revenue confirmed that it would apply the same focus on the United Kingdom grouping for the purposes of Schedule 28AA to the Taxes Act 1988 in determining how much a third party lender would have been prepared to lend in the absence of a guarantee or other undertaking of support from a company outside that sub-group.[12] The June 1995 article stated that in general the Inland Revenue would not consider a company or group to be thinly capitalised where the debt to equity ratio of the United Kingdom sub-group was less than 1:1 and its interest cover (profit before interest and  **15–45**

---

[10] ICTA 1988, Sched. 28AA, paras 1 and 5.
[11] See pp. 218–220.
[12] See pp. 580–582.

taxes) was at least three times the interest payable on the loan. The Inland Revenue is prepared to agree to a higher debt to equity ratio in appropriate cases and in the article in its October 1998 *Tax Bulletin* it stated that International Division will be prepared to give advance rulings on proposed funding structures.[13]

## VII. INVESTMENT IN UNITED KINGDOM PROPERTY

### Relief for interest

**15–51**    Under Schedule 28AA to the Taxes Act 1988 the Inland Revenue is able to restrict tax relief for the interest payable where a non-resident company borrows money from a connected person and the amount of the loan or the interest payable exceeds the amount which would have been lent in the absence of such connection. Interest relief can also be restricted where the company borrows money from an unconnected lender with a guarantee or other undertaking of support from a connected person, and the amount borrowed exceeds the amount which would have been lent in the absence of such arrangements. In both these cases this is because the transfer pricing provisions of Schedule 28AA also apply for income tax purpose from April 6, 1999 onwards.[14]

Where a non-U.K. resident  company's only asset is a property which is let, the Inland Revenue consider that a third party lender would only be likely to lend a percentage of the purchase price of the property, typically 65–80 per cent, depending on the situation of the property and market conditions.[15]

## XI. DUAL RESIDENT INVESTMENT COMPANIES

### Collection of tax on company migration

**15–66**    Footnote 13: Replace the existing text with the following in cases where the migrating company ceases to be resident in the United Kingdom on or after April 1, 2000:

> "Group" has the same meaning as in TCGA 1992, s.170 substituting 51 per cent subsidiaries for 75 per cent subsidiaries: FA 1988, s.132(6), as amended by FA 2000, Sched. 29 para. 15(1). Whether a company was a member of a group of companies in the 12 months before the migrating company ceased to be resident in the United Kingdom is to be determined by reference to the revised definition: FA 2000, Sched. 29 para. 15(3).

---

[13] See p. 582.
[14] FA 1998, s.108(5), (6).
[15] *FICO Newsletter* (1990) 4, July.

## XII. Appendix 1 to Chapter 15—The Treasury General Consents

The definitions of **overseas group resident group** and of **territorial group** have been amended with effect for transactions carried out on or after July 28, 2000.[16] The revised definitions are as follows and replace the definitions currently set out in paragraph 2:

"**overseas group**" means two or more companies, including the non-resident company, which are not resident in the United Kingdom and which:

(a) are liable to tax in the same territory outside the United Kingdom by reason of domicile, residence or place of management, and
(b) would be deemed to be members of a group of companies for the purposes of Chapter IV of Part X of the Income and Corporation Taxes Act 1988;

"**resident group**" means those companies, including the resident company, which are resident in the United Kingdom, and which are deemed to be members of a group of companies for the purposes of Chapter IV of Part X of the Income and Corporation Taxes Act 1988:

"**territorial group**" means two or more companies which are not resident in the United Kingdom and which

(a) are liable to tax in the same territory outside the United Kingdom by reason of domicile, residence or place of management, and
(b) would be deemed to be members of a group of companies for the purposes of Chapter IV of Part X of the Income and Corporation Taxes Act 1988;

The wording of **paragraph 2(3)** has also been amended and the reference to section 413 of the Taxes Act 1988 should be read as a reference to Chapter IV of Part X of the Income and Corporation Taxes Act 1988.

These amendments have been made to ensure that the Treasury General Consents continue to operate as intended following the amendments that have been made to the definition of a group relief group in Finance Act 2000.

---

[16] Inland Revenue press release IR 128/00 issued on July 28, 2000.

CHAPTER 16

# CONTROLLED FOREIGN COMPANIES

## I. Overview

**(The following replaces paragraph 16–04 of the main work.)**

**16–04**  *(b) Control by United Kingdom Residents*

There are now two ways in which a non-resident company can be treated as a CFC:

(i) where the company is controlled by United Kingdom residents [1]; or

(ii) where a company would not otherwise be treated as a CFC, if there are two persons who, taken together, control the company and

   (a) one of those persons is resident in the United Kingdom and has a 40 per cent interest in the CFC[2]; and

   (b) the other is a person who is not resident in the United Kingdom and who has not less than a 40 per cent and not more than a 55 per cent interest in the CFC.[3]

---

[1] ICTA 1988, s.747(1) and s.755D.

[2] *ibid.* s.747(1A)(b) as inserted by Finance Act 2000, Sched. 31 para. 2. For these purposes a person has a 40 per cent interest in a CFC where he has interests, rights and powers representing at least 40 per cent of the holdings, rights and powers in respect of which the two persons fall to be taken as controlling the company: *ibid.* s. 755D(3), as inserted by FA 2000, Sched. 31 para. 4.

[3] *ibid.* s.747(1A)(c) as inserted by FA 2000, Sched. 31 para. 2. A person will satisfy this test if he has interests rights and powers representing at least 40 per cent but not more than 55 per cent of the holdings, rights and powers in respect of which the two persons fall to be taken as controlling the company: *ibid.* s. 755D(3A), as inserted by FA 2000, Sched. 31 para. 4.

*Change to the control definition* The control definition has changed from section 416 of the Taxes Act 1988 to a new definition which it is based on the wording used in section 840 of the Taxes Act 1988, albeit that the definition is included as part of the CFC legislation itself.[4]

Under the revised definition a person is deemed to control the CFC where he has the power to secure that the affairs of the CFC are conducted in accordance with his wishes:

(i) by means of the holding of shares or the possession of voting power in or in relation to the CFC or any other company, or

(ii) by virtue of any powers conferred by the articles of association or other document regulating the CFC or any other company.[5]

Where two or more persons, taken together, have such power, they will be taken to control the company.[6]

In determining whether a company is controlled by a United Kingdom resident person or by two or more such persons, or whether the applicable 40 per cent test is met, the following rights and powers are to be attributed to that person (the first person) to the extent that they are not already taken into account[7]:

(a) the rights and powers which the first person is entitled to acquire at a future date or which he will, at a future date, become entitled to acquire.[8] This definition catches cases where a person will become entitled to exercise the rights and powers in question after the passage of time. It would not cover a case where a person's rights and powers are contingent upon the occurrence of some future event, until that future event has happened;

(b) rights and powers which another person is required or may be required to exercise on behalf of the first person, under the direction of the first person, or for the benefit of the first person.[9] The rights and powers that are taken into account also include any rights and powers which the other person is entitled to acquire at a future date, or will at a future date become entitled to acquire[10];

(c) if the first person is resident in the United Kingdom, the rights and powers

---

[4] *ibid.* s.755D as inserted by FA 2000, Sched. 31, para. 4.

[5] *ibid.* s.755D(1) as inserted by FA 2000, Sched. 31, para. 4.

[6] *ibid.* s.755D(2) as inserted by FA 2000, Sched. 31 para. 4.

[7] *ibid.* s.755D(4) as inserted by FA 2000, Sched. 31 para. 4.

[8] *ibid.* s.755D(6)(a) as inserted by FA 2000, Sched. 31 para. 4.

[9] *ibid.* s. 755D(6), (7)(a) as inserted by FA 2000, Sched. 31 para. 4(1). Where the first person has made a loan to the other person or that other person has made a loan to the CFC, any rights and powers that are attributable to that loan are only taken into account to the extent that they are not confined to rights and powers conferred in relation to the property of the borrower by the terms of any security relating to the loan: *ibid.* s.755D(7)(b).

[10] *ibid.* s.755D(8) as inserted by FA 2000, Sched. 31 para. 4(1).

of any person who is resident in the United Kingdom and connected[11] with the first person.[12] The rights and powers that are taken into account include the rights and powers to which that other person is entitled to acquire at a future date or will at a future date become entitled to acquire[13]; and

(d) if the first person is resident in the United Kingdom, the rights and powers of another United Kingdom resident person (other person) who is connected[14] with the first person which would be attributed to the first person if the other person were the first person.[15] Again this definition is extended to cover the rights and powers which that other person is entitled to acquire at a future date, or will at a future date become entitled to acquire. The rights and powers that are so attributed to the other person include the rights and powers of a person who is connected with that other person or a person who is connected with that person and so on through any number of persons, so long as each person in the chain is resident in the United Kingdom and is connected with at least one of the others.[16]

In the above cases, the references to rights and powers of a person, or to rights and powers which a person is, or will become, entitled to acquire, include references to rights and powers which are exercisable by that person or (when acquired by the person) will be exercisable, only jointly with one or more persons.[17]

This revised definition applies for the purpose of determining whether at any time on after March 31, 2000 a company resident outside the United Kingdom is to be regarded as controlled by persons in the United Kingdom for the purposes of the CFC legislation and for any accounting period of a company resident outside the United Kingdom which begins on or after March 21, 2000.[18]

---

[11] Whether the other person is connected with the first person is to be determined by reference to the provisions of section 839 of the Taxes Act 1988, except that the provisions of subsection (7) of that section are disapplied (*i.e.* a person will not be treated as connected with another person for the purposes of the above tests merely because the two of them are acting together to secure or exercise control of a company): ibid. s.755D(10), as inserted by FA 2000, Sched. 31 para. 4(1).

[12] *ibid.* s755D(6)(c), as inserted by FA 2000, Sched. 31 para 4(1).

[13] *ibid.* s.755D(8), as inserted by FA 2000, Sched. 31, para. 4(1).

[14] Whether a person is connected with another person is to be determined by reference to the provisions of section 839 of the Taxes Act 1988, except that the provisions of subsection (7) of that section are disapplied (*i.e.* a person will not be treated as connected with another person for the above purposes merely because the two of them are acting together to secure or exercise control of a company): *ibid.* s.755D(10), as inserted by FA 2000, Sched. 31 para. 4(1).

[15] *ibid.* s.755D(6)(d), as inserted by FA 2000, Sched. 31, para 4(1).

[16] *ibid.* s.755D(9), as inserted by FA 2000, Sched. 31, para. 4(1).

[17] *ibid.* s.755D(11), as inserted by FA 2000, Sched. 31, para. 4(1).

[18] FA 2000, Sched. 31 para. 9(3).

*(c) lower level of taxation*

### Designer rate provisions

Certain overseas territories contain provisions which enable a company resident in **16–05A** that territory to specify the rate of tax which it pays in that territory. These provisions have been used in the past by companies as a means of satisfying the CFC test through ensuring that the tax that they paid in the territory was at least equal to 75 per cent of the company's U.K. equivalent profits.

Finance Act 2000 has introduced a new section 750A of the Taxes Act 1988 which enables the Board of Inland Revenue to specify, by regulation, provisions in an overseas territory which in its view appear to be designed to enable companies to exercise significant control over the amount of tax which they pay. Such regulations may make different provision for different cases or with respect to different territories and may contain such supplementary, incidental, consequential or transitional provisions as the Board may think fit.[19]

The effect of such measures is that where a company is resident in an overseas territory and its local tax is at least equal to 75 per cent of the U.K. corporation tax which would be payable were the company resident in the United Kingdom, but its local tax is payable under designer rate provisions, the company will be treated as being subject to a lower level of taxation in that territory for the accounting period in question.[20] The company may still escape being treated as a CFC for that accounting period if it satisfies one of the other exemptions which are discussed in the main text.

The above provisions were announced in an Inland Revenue press release issued on October 6, 1999. This press release stated that the provisions would apply to CFC accounting periods beginning on or after October 6, 1999 and this is provided for in the provisions of section 750A of the Taxes Act 1988 which permits the first regulations introduced under the provisions of this section to have effect in relation to accounting periods beginning not more than 15 months before the date on which the regulations are made.[21]

In the Press Release, the Inland Revenue stated that the regulations will initially apply to the following regimes:

1. Guernsey: bodies with international tax status;
2. Jersey: international business companies;
3. Isle of Man: international companies;
4. Gibraltar: income tax qualifying companies; and

---

[19] ICTA 1988, s.750A(1), (2), (3), as inserted by FA 2000, Sched. 31 para. 3.
[20] *ibid.*, s.750A(1), as inserted by FA 2000, Sched. 31 para. 3.
[21] ICTA 1988, s.750A(4), as inserted by FA 2000 Sched. 31 para. 3.

5. Ireland: companies taxed in accordance with section 448(7) of the Irish Taxes Consolidation Act 1997.

## II. DEFENCES

### Acceptable distribution policy

**16–08**     The Finance Act 1999 introduced an amendment to the provisions of the acceptable distribution test which applies to dividends paid on or after March 9, 1999 in respect of a CFC's accounting period ending on or after that date. The amendment is designed to block a scheme whereby a United Kingdom group could minimise the tax paid on a CFC's profits by arranging for the CFC to receive dividends from a United Kingdom company; typically the CFC would invest in preference shares of a United Kingdom resident company within the group. These dividends would be left out of account in determining the CFC's chargeable profits but could be taken into account in computing the underlying tax paid for the purpose of determining the double tax credit relief which was available to the United Kingdom recipient of the dividend. As a result of the amendment a CFC will not be regarded as satisfying the acceptable distribution test to the extent that any dividends which it pays are attributable to dividends which are received from a United Kingdom resident company.[22]

The amendment does not deal with dividends received indirectly by a CFC from a United Kingdom resident company (*e.g.* via another CFC). This is because the exemption in section 208 of the Taxes Act 1988 would not apply in such cases for the purpose of calculating the CFC's chargeable profits and such dividends would thus have to be included for the purposes of determining whether it satisfied the acceptable distribution test.[23]

### General insurance companies

**16–10A**     United Kingdom companies which are carrying on general insurance business generally operate on a three-year funded basis. That is a profit or loss for an accounting period is only finalised three years after the end of the period so that a reasonable estimate can be made for any unsettled liabilities. Section 755B of the Taxes Act 1988 and the Non-Resident Companies (General Insurance Business) Regulations (S.I. 1999 No. 1408) broadly allow CFCs which are carrying on general insurance business to

---

[22] FA 1999, s.88.
[23] Dividends received by one CFC (first CFC) from another CFC (second CFC) are only excluded in computing the chargeable profits of the first CFC to the extent that the first CFC elects to pay a dividend out of the dividend received from the second CFC: ICTA 1988, Sched. 25, para. 3(5).

follow this basis for the purposes of the acceptable distribution test and this basis can also be followed in order to determine the profits which should be apportioned to United Kingdom companies which have a relevant interest in such a CFC if it fails to satisfy the acceptable distribution test. For further information the reader is referred to the above regulations and to section 8.2 of the Inland Revenue CFC Guidance Notes.

**Replace last paragraph with the following:**

In addition, the CFC must not have been mainly engaged in wholesale, distributive, financial or service business where 50 per cent or more of its gross trading receipts[24] from that business are derived directly or indirectly from:      **16–12**

1. persons who are connected or associated with company;
2. persons who have a 25 per cent assessable interest in the company in the case of the accounting period in question; and
3. if the company is a CFC for that accounting period because it is controlled by two persons, each of whom has a 40 per cent interest in the CFC, persons who are connected or associated with either or both of those two persons.[25]

Wholesale distributive and financial business is defined as including the following:

1. dealing in any description of goods wholesale rather than retail[1];
2. the business of shipping or air transport[2];
3. banking, deposit-taking, money-lending or debt-factoring, or any business similar to banking, deposit-taking, money-lending or debt-factoring[3];
4. the administration of trusts[4];
5. dealing in services in the capacity of a broker[5];
6. dealing in the commodity or financial futures[6]; and
7. general or long-term insurance business as defined in section 1 of the Insurance Companies Act 1982[7].

---

[24] Where the gross trading receipts of a company include the proceeds of sale of any description of property or rights, the costs of the property or rights is deducted in calculating the company's gross trading receipts: ICTA 1988, Sched. 25 para 11(2).

[25] ICTA 1988, Sched. 25 para. 6(2)(b), (2A), (4C).

[1] *ibid.* Sched. 25 para. 11(1)(a).

[2] *ibid.* Sched. 25 para. 11(1)(b). The business of shipping and air transport is defined as the business carried on by an owner of ships or the business carried on by the owner of aircraft ("owner" including for this purpose any charterer): *ibid.* para. 11(1)(b).

[3] *ibid.* Sched. 25 para. 11(1)(c).

[4] *ibid.* Sched. 25 para. 11(1)(d).

[5] *ibid.* Sched. 25 para. 11(1)(e). "Broker" includes any person offering to sell securities to, or to purchase securities from, members of the public generally: *ibid.* para 9(2).

[6] *ibid.* Sched. 25 para. 11(1)(f).

[7]*ibid.* Sched. 25 para. 11(1)(g).

Service business is defined as the provision of any services that that do not fall within any of the categories described in 1 to 7 above.[8]

## Exempt activities

## Holding companies

**16–15**  The conditions that have to be satisfied in order for a holding company to qualify as a local holding company, holding company, superior holding company or "Bulletin" holding company have been amended as a result of changes announced in Budget 2000. The changes are designed to counter arrangements that certain international groups had been using in order to mitigate their worldwide tax liability. These arrangements involved additional share capital being injected into a non-resident company that satisfied one of the CFC holding company exemptions and then that company lending this money at interest to other companies in the overseas group. Typically, the arrangements would be structured so that the holding company paid little or no tax on its interest income in the territory in which it was resident, and so long as the holding company exemption was satisfied, the interest income received by the holding company was not apportionable to United Kingdom companies that held an interest in that company. The borrower on the other hand was able to obtain tax relief for the interest payable on the loan in the territory in which it was resident. Such arrangements enabled a United Kingdom based group to mitigate its worldwide tax liability.

The amendments to the various holding company tests are described below. They have effect for an accounting period of a holding company that begins on or after March 21, 2000.[9]

*Local holding company*

The tests remain as described in the main text except that there is now an additional requirement that in order for the 90 per cent of gross income test to be met, this income must be received by it in the territory in which it is resident.[10]

---

[8] *ibid.* Sched. 25 para. 11(1)(h).
[9] FA 2000, Sched. 31 para. 9(4).
[10] ICTA 1988, Sched. 25 para. 6(3), as amended by FA 2000, Sched. 31 para 6.

*Holding company*

In order for a holding company to meet the 90 per cent of income test for an accounting period beginning on or after March 21, 2000, in addition to the conditions discussed in the main text:

1. the company from which it directly derives the income must be resident in the same territory as it throughout the whole of the accounting period in question and further this income must be received by it in that territory; or
2. the income must consist of qualifying dividends. These are defined as any dividend other than one for which the company paying the dividend is entitled to a deduction against its profits for tax purposes under the law of the territory in which is resident.[11]

**The following replaces the existing wording of para. 16–15, footnote 21 on p. 500 of the main work:**

References to a company which a holding company controls include:

(i) a trading company in which the holding company holds the maximum amount of the ordinary share capital which is permitted under the law of the territory in which the trading company is resident and from whose laws the trading company derives its status as a company; and
(ii) a trading company which is treated as a CFC by virtue of the provisions of ICTA 1988, s. 747(1A) (see para. 16–04 above) where the United Kingdom resident who is treated as controlling that company also controls the holding company.

The provisions within (ii) have effect to an accounting period of a CFC that begins on or after March 21, 2000: ICTA 1988, Sched. 25 para. 6(5), (5ZA), (5ZB) and FA 2000, Sched. 31 para 7(8), (9), para. 9(4).

*Superior holding company*

In order for a superior holding company to meet the 90 per cent of income test for an accounting period beginning on or after March 21, 2000, in addition to the conditions that are discussed in the main text:

---

[11] ICTA 1988, Sched. 25 para. 6(4ZA), (5B), as inserted by FA 2000, Sched. 31 para. 7.

1. the company from which it directly derives the income must be resident in the same territory as it throughout the whole of the accounting period in question and the income must be received by it in that territory; or
2. the income must consist of qualifying dividends.[12]

These conditions also apply where a superior holding company is itself a subsidiary of another superior holding company.[13]

**The following replaces the existing wording of 16–15 footnote 4 on p. 501 of the mainwork:**

References to a company which a superior holding company controls include:

(i) a trading company where the superior holding company holds the maximum amount of the ordinary share capital which is permitted under the law of the territory in which the trading company is resident and from whose laws the trading company derives its status as a company; and
(ii) a trading company which is treated as a CFC by virtue of the provisions of ICTA 1988, s. 747(1A) (see 16–04 above) where the United Kingdom resident who is treated as controlling that company also controls the superior holding company.

The provisions within (ii) have effect to an accounting period of a CFC which begins on or after March 21, 2000: ICTA 1988 Sched. 25 para. 6(5), (5ZA) (5ZB) and FA 2000, Sched. 31 para. 7(8),(9), para. 9(4).

*"Bulletin" holding company*

In the guidance notes that accompanied the Budget Day press release which announced changes to the CFC regime[14], the Inland Revenue stated that a change would be made to its concessional practice which was originally announced in its October 1995 Tax Bulletin (and which was at March 21, 2000 summarised in 3.6.34 of the CFC Guidance Notes). For accounting periods beginning on or after March 21, 2000, the Inland Revenue is no longer prepared automatically to apply the motive test exemption where a holding company which does not satisfy any of the above statutory exemptions acts as a mere staging post in the course of the process of reinvestment

---

[12] A qualifying dividend is defined as any dividend other than a dividend for which the company paying the dividend is entitled to a tax deduction in the territory in which it is resident: ICTA 1988, Sched 25 para. 6(5B), as inserted by FA 2000, Sched. 31 para 7(10).

[13] *ibid*. Sched. 25 para. 6(4B)(b)(iii), (4BB), as inserted by FA 2000, Sched. 31 para. 7(6), (7).

[14] BN2K.

of the profits of its overseas trading subsidiaries. For CFC accounting periods begin-ning on or after March 21, 2000 this concession will only apply where 90 per cent of the holding company's gross income is

1. income from companies that it directly controls which are resident in the same territory as it throughout the whole of its accounting period in question, provided that such income is received by it in that territory; or
2. consists of qualifying dividends (as described above in the case of a holding company).

The accompanying notes to the press release stated that the Inland Revenue would still be prepared to consider whether a holding company which did not meet this revised test might otherwise satisfy the motive test.

## Clearance procedure

The Inland Revenue has amended the clearance procedures for CFCs following the **16–18A** introduction of corporation tax self-assessment. Previously the Inland Revenue was prepared to give advance clearances on whether a CFC satisfied the exempt activities or motive test. It is now prepared to give advance rulings on all aspects of the CFC legislation, other than the calculation of the CFC's chargeable profits.[15]

The Inland Revenue aims to work to a 28-day turnaround from the receipt of an application, assuming all relevant information is included.[16] The Inland Revenue's CFC Guidance Notes gives examples of the information which it may be relevant to include in a clearance application.[17] Where clearance is being sought that a CFC satisfies one of the exempt activities tests, or the motive test, sufficient information should be given to enable the Inland Revenue to form a view on whether the appropri-ate conditions have been satisfied. The clearance application can be submitted by a company which has an interest in a CFC and where more than one United Kingdom company has an interest in the CFC, one company can submit a clearance application on behalf of the other companies.[18]

A clearance will state the terms on which it is given and will normally apply indefinitely, so long as the relevant facts and the legislation remain unchanged.[19] The United Kingdom company's local inspector will periodically review the continued application of the clearance to ensure that the facts and circumstances remain unchanged. Under self-assessment the onus is now on the United Kingdom company

---

[15] Inland Revenue Controlled Foreign Company Guidance Notes (as published in July 1999) at 2.6.10.
[16] *ibid.* 2.6.6.
[17] *ibid.* 2.6.13–2.6.17.
[18] *ibid.* 2.6.9.
[19] *ibid.* 2.6.7.

to notify its inspector if there have been any material changes to the facts or projections in the original clearance application and failure to do so could result in it becoming liable for interest and penalties if a return is submitted which relies on a clearance application that is no longer appropriate because of significant changes in the underlying facts.[20]

If a clearance application is refused the Inland Revenue will state its reasons. If a United Kingdom company disagrees with the Inland Revenue's view it can make its self-assessment on its understanding of the law and appeal against any amendment to its self-assessment return which the Inland Revenue may make.[21]

## III. EXCLUDED COUNTRIES

**16–19**    [The following replaces paragraph 16–19 of the main work]

No apportionment falls to be made if a CFC satisfies such conditions as may be specified by regulations.[22] The controlled Foreign Companies (Excluded Country) Regulations[23] were issued on December 9, 1998 and came into force on December 31, 1998. The intention behind these regulations is to incorporate in legislation the Excluded Countries List which was first introduced as a press release in 1984 and was last issued on October 5, 1993. The tests imposed under the regulations are more stringent than those applied under the press release; *inter alia*, the regulations provide for a more restrictive definition as to what constitutes local source income.

The regulations apply for the purpose of calculating the taxable profits of a United Kingdom resident company which has a relevant interest[24] in a non-resident company (CFC) for an accounting period ending on or after July 1, 1999.[25] In order for a United Kingdom company to claim relief from an apportionment under the Excluded Countries Regulations:

  (i) the CFC must be resident[1] in a territory specified in Schedule 1 or 2[2] throughout the whole of its accounting period in question[3]; and

---

[20] *ibid.* 2.6.8.

[21] *ibid.* 2.6.7.

[22] ICTA 1988, s.748(1)(e).

[23] S.I. 1998 No. 3081.

[24] As defined in ICTA 1988, s.752A.

[25] S.I. 1998 No. 3081, reg. 1(2).

[1] For the purposes of the regulations a company is resident in a territory:
  (i) if it is liable to tax in that territory by reason of domicile, residence or place of management or;
  (ii) where (i) does not apply, if the company is incorporated in that territory: *ibid.* reg. 2(2).

[2] Sched. 1 applies to an accounting period of a CFC which began before July 9, 1998 and Sched. 2 applies for accounting periods commencing on or after that date: *ibid.* reg. 3.

[3] *ibid.* regs 2(3) and 4.

(ii) the CFC's non-local source income and gains for that accounting period must not exceed the greater of:

    (a) £50,000 (this limit is proportionally reduced where the CFC's accounting period is less than 12 months in length); or

    (b) an amount equal to 10 per cent of its commercially quantified income arising in that accounting period.[4]

For the purpose of determining whether the CFC's non-local source income exceeds the £50,000 limit, computations should be done in the currency in which the CFC prepares its accounts and the £50,000 limit should then be converted into that currency at the accounting date.[5]

Where a CFC is resident in a territory specified in Part II of Schedule 1 or 2 there is an additional requirement that it is not entitled to any tax exemption, reduction or other benefit and further that it does not fall within any condition specified for that territory.[6] A CFC's commercially quantified income is defined as its profits before tax, as determined in accordance with generally accepted accounting standards (other than an equity basis of accounting), but disregarding capital profits and losses.[7] Capital profits or losses are defined as profits or losses arising in relation to chargeable assets.[8]

A CFC's non-local source income[9] arising in an accounting period is the aggregate of:

1. gross distributions[10] recognised as income in computing the CFC's commercially quantified income for that period (other than income attributable to an overseas branch or agency of the CFC) from companies not resident in that territory;[11]

---

[4] *ibid.* reg. 5(1).

[5] Inland Revenue Controlled Foreign Company Guidance Notes at 3.1.6.

[6] Part II contains a list of countries which have favourable tax regimes for certain types of companies or which offer particular reliefs from tax.

[7] S.I. 1998 No. 3081, reg. 5(2). Where a company prepares its accounts on an equity basis of accounting (*i.e.* profits and losses of subsidiaries are included in the profit and loss account of the parent company whether or not such profits have been distributed) it will be required to compute its commercial profits using another method of accounting which is generally acceptable in that territory: Inland Revenue Controlled Foreign Company Guidance Notes at 3.1.7 and 3.1.8.

[8] These are assets which, on disposal and assuming that the CFC were U.K. resident, would be included in calculating the company's chargeable gains and would not be included in computing the CFC's income profits: *ibid.* reg. 7(1), (7).

[9] The Inland Revenue Controlled Foreign Company Guidance Notes at 3.1.10 state that income which is taken straight to reserves and income which is treated as pre-payment can be excluded in computing a company's non-local source income.

[10] Such distributions before deduction of expenses or reserves: *ibid.* reg. 7(3)(a).

[11] *ibid.* reg. 5(3)(a).

2. gross income and gains[12] recognised as income in computing the commercially quantified income of the CFC for that period from loans to or deposits with persons not resident in the same territory as the CFC or from overseas branches or agencies of companies resident in that territory.[13] Any income and gains attributable to an overseas branch or agency of the CFC are excluded from these calculations,

3. gross income and gains[14] recognised as income in computing the commercially quantified income of the CFC for that period in relation to royalties payable by persons not resident in the same territory as the CFC or from overseas branches or agencies of companies resident in the same territory.[15] Any income and gains attributable to an overseas branch or agency of the CFC are excluded;

4. gross income and gains[16] recognised as income in computing the commercially quantified income of the CFC in relation to premiums and rents payable in respect of property situated outside the territory in which the CFC is resident by persons not resident in that territory or by branches situated outside that territory of companies resident in that territory.[17] Any income and gains attributable to an overseas branch or agency of the CFC are excluded;

5. the amount of any branch of agency income and gains recognised as income in computing the commercially quantified income of the CFC for that period calculated in accordance with the conditions described below (see non-local source branch or agency income)[18];

6. gross income[19] not falling within 1 to 5 above that is recognised as income in computing the commercially quantified income of the CFC for the period that is within the charge to tax in the territory in which the CFC is resident and which either:

---

[12] Such income and gains found after:
    (i) excluding any gain or loss arising on any loan or deposit which is offset by a loss or a gain on a currency or interest rate contract ancillary to that loan or deposit which would be a qualifying contract for the purposes of FA 1993, s.126(1) or FA 1994, s.147(1) were the company within the charge to corporation tax (*i.e.* where the CFC entered into the contract to hedge its currency or interest rate exposure on the loan or deposit); and
    (ii) deducting any exchange losses attributable to the loans or deposits if such exchange losses have not been excluded under (i) above; but before deducting any other expenses or reserves: *ibid.* reg. 7(3)(b).

[13] *ibid.* reg. 5(3)(c).

[14] Such income and gains after deducting any exchange losses attributable to the royalties but before deducting other expenses or reserves: *ibid.* reg. 7(3)(c).

[15] S.I. 1998 No. 3081, reg. 5(3)(c).

[16] Such income and gains after deducting any exchange losses attributable to the premiums and rents but before deducting other expenses or reserves: *ibid.* reg. 7(3)(c).

[17] *ibid.* reg. 5(3)(d).

[18] *ibid.* reg. 5(3)(e).

[19] Such income before deduction of expenses or reserves: *ibid.* reg. 7(3)(a).

(i) is not treated under the laws of that territory as accruing, arising or derived from that territory; or

(ii) where there is no concept of local source income, as, for example, is the case in the Netherlands, would not be treated as accruing, in arising in, or derived from that territory if it were to be assumed that the source of the CFC's income was determined using United Kingdom principles.[20]

For the purpose of 1 to 6 above, income and gains derived from a company resident in another territory are treated as local source income to the extent that these are derived from contracts made with a branch or agency of that company which is situated in the same territory as that in which the CFC is resident.[21]

Where the CFC is carrying on the business of banking or of an assurance company, and income falling with 1 to 4 above:

(i) is an integral part of income arising or accruing to the CFC from its trade of banking[22] or insurance[23] and would be regarded as forming part of its trading income for corporation tax purposes were the company United Kingdom resident; and

(ii) is within the charge to the tax in the territory in which the CFC is resident;

the aggregate amount of that income is disregarded in computing the company's non-local source income.[24] The Inland Revenue states in its Controlled Foreign Company Guidance Notes that it considers that these special rules also apply where such business is carried on through a branch.[25] This interpretation is not readily apparent from the Regulations as branch or agency income is specifically excluded for the purposes of 1 to 4 above.

### Non-local source branch or agency income

Where the conditions in (a)–(d) below are satisfied, the non-local source income of the branch will be the amount in (c) below.[1] In other cases the non-local source income of the branch will be taken as the higher of:

(i) the net income and gains[2] of the branch or agency; or

---

[20] *ibid.* reg. 5(3)(f).

[21] *ibid.* reg. 7(4).

[22] The regulations do not define what constitutes a trade of banking.

[23] An insurance company is defined as a company carrying on "long-term business" or "general business" within the meaning of Insurance Companies Act 1982, s.1: reg. 2(1).

[24] S.I. 1998 No. 3081, reg. 5(4).

[25] At 3.1.15.

[1] *ibid.* reg. 6(1)(a), (2).

[2] The income gains of the branch, after deducting expenses but before tax, as determined in accordance with a generally accepted method of accounting for profits of branches or agencies of companies: *ibid.* reg. 7(6).

(ii) an amount equal to the gross amount[3] of the branch or agency income and gains for the accounting which would be included within 1 to 4 above, but for the exclusion for income and gains of branches and agencies.[4]

The conditions referred to above are that:

(a) the branch or agency is situated in a territory specified in Schedule 1 or 2. Where the branch or agency is situated in a territory specified in Part II of either Schedule, at no time during the accounting period is it entitled to any tax exemption, tax reduction, or other benefit and nor does it fall within any condition specified for that territory[5];

(b) the profits of the branch or agency are within charge to tax in that territory[6] and are determined on an arm's length and independent basis[7];

(c) assuming that the branch or agency were itself a CFC, not more than 10 per cent of the net amount[8] of the profits of the branch or agency would be attributable to gross income and gains falling within 1 to 4 above and arising outside the territory in which the branch or agency is situated[9];

(d) any deductions in respect of payments made by the branch to the CFC or in respect of expenses incurred by the CFC on behalf of the branch are either liable to tax in the territory in which the CFC is resident or are disallowed as an expense or, where the CFC is liable to tax on its profits wherever arising, are excluded in computing its taxable profits except where paid to a third party.[10]

IV. APPORTIONMENT

## Calculation of chargeable profits

**16–21   Add after the end of the first sentence of 4.**

Where any losses or other amounts are in fact surrendered as group relief by the CFC,

---

[3] The gross amount is the amount of the income or gains before deduction of expenses or reserves: *ibid.* reg. 7(5).

[4] *ibid.* reg. 6(1)(b), (3).

[5] *ibid.* reg. 6(2)(a).

[6] *ibid.* reg. 6(2)(b).

[7] *ibid.* reg. 6(2)(c).

[8] Profits after deductions of expenses but before tax as determined in accordance with a generally accepted method of accounting for profits of branches or agencies of companies: *ibid.* reg. 7(6).

[9] *ibid.* reg. 6(2)(d).

[10] *ibid.* reg. 6(2)(e).

its chargeable profits are required to be increased by the amount of the losses or reliefs that were so surrendered.[11]

## Foreign currency

The foreign exchange legislation applies to CFCs for the purpose of calculating **16–21A** their chargeable profits, broadly in the same way in which it applies to companies within the charge to corporation tax. There are, however, some variations.

## Local currency

As noted in paragraph 16–21A of the main work, a CFC's local currency is the currency in which its accounts are prepared for its first accounting period beginning on or after March 23, 1995, or on or after November 28, 1995 in the case of a trading company, for which a direction was made or for which it avoided a direction by pursuing an acceptable distribution policy.[12] Once a CFC's local currency has been determined, there is no provision for this to be changed even if the CFC changes the currency in which it prepares its accounts except where its local currency is replaced by the euro. In this case the company can use that currency or the euro so long as the currency continues to exist as a legal sub-unit of the euro. Once the currency ceases to exist the CFC's local currency will become the euro.[13] The amendment introduced in the Finance Act 2000 that broadly enables a company's reporting currency to be taken as its local currency does not apply to CFCs.

## Matching

Where a CFC owns an eligible asset and satisfies the conditions for matching (including that any exchange gains or losses on the eligible asset and the matching loan or currency contract are taken to reserves[14]), it is possible for a matching election to be made on behalf of the CFC by a United Kingdom resident company which has, or jointly by United Kingdom resident companies which have, a majority interest in the CFC.[15]

---

[11] ICTA 1988, Sched. 24 para. 5(2), as inserted by FA 2000, Sched. 27 para. 10. This amendment applies to accounting periods ending on or after 1 April 2000: FA 2000, Sched. 27 para. 12(1).

[12] ICTA 1988, s.747A. There are various consequential amendments in ICTA 1988, Sched. 24, paras 13–19.

[13] S.I. 1998 No. 3177, reg. 40.

[14] Except where the eligible asset is a ship or an aircraft: S.I. 1994 No. 3227, reg. 10(4).

[15] S.I. 1994 No. 3227, reg. 6. The provisions of ICTA 1988, Sched. 24, para. 4(3) and (4) are applied to determine whether a U.K. company or companies has or have a majority interest in a CFC: *ibid.* reg. 6(2).

It appears that the matching election will take effect from the date on which it is made unless it is made within 92 days of the date on which the eligible asset was acquired in which case the election can be backdated to that date.[16] If, however, an apportionment falls to be made for an accounting period beginning on or after March 23, 1995, no direction has been given for an earlier period and the company has not avoided an apportionment for an earlier period by pursuing an acceptable distribution policy, a matching election can be backdated to the start of that accounting period provided that it is made within 92 days of the date of the direction.[17] As a direction is no longer required it is not clear how this provision will be applied under the self-assessment regime.

## Deferral

Deferral relief will apply automatically where it would be in the CFC's interest to claim such relief.[18] For these purposes the CFC will not be deemed to be a member of a group of companies.[19]

## Transitional rules

The transitional rules for debts of a fixed amount, fluctuating debts and trading assets and liabilities (where exchange gains and losses would have been taxed on a realisation basis under the pre-foreign exchange regime) apply to a CFC where a direction was given for its accounting period which ended on or which "straddled" March 22, 1995, or where a direction was avoided for that period as a result of the CFC pursuing an acceptable distribution policy.[20] In the case of fluctuating debts it would have been possible for the United Kingdom company, or United Kingdom companies, which held the majority interest in the CFC to have elected to bring such debts within the foreign exchange legislation, as applied for the purposes of Schedule 24 to the Taxes Act 1988. The time-limit for this election was 20 months after the end of the CFC's first accounting period that ended on or after March 23, 1995.[21]

United Kingdom companies that hold relevant interests in a CFC will need to bear

---

[16] These are the normal rules which apply in the case of a matching election: *ibid.* regs 10(1)(b) and 11(2). It is not considered that a matching election can be treated as a relief covered by ICTA 1988, Sched. 24, para. 4 since exchange losses as well as gains will be treated as matched.

[17] S.I. 1994 No. 3227, reg. 11(5).

[18] It is considered that deferral relief will fall within ICTA 1988, Sched. 24, para. 4. See Chap. 3A of this supplement for an outline description of deferral relief.

[19] ICTA 1988, Sched. 24, para. 5.

[20] S.I.1994 No. 3226, reg. 1(5).

[21] *ibid.* reg. 1(5) and ICTA 1988, Sched. 24, para. 4(2).

in mind the impact of the above provisions when calculating the chargeable profits of a CFC.

## Anti-avoidance provisions

The anti-avoidance provisions of sections 135–137 of the Finance Act 1993 apply to a CFC in the same way as they apply to a company within the charge to corporation tax. Particular care should be taken in the case of sections 136, 136A and 137 as these provisions can apply where the loan or contract in question would not have been entered into on the same terms had the parties been dealing at arm's length. For example, the provisions of section 136 or 136A could catch an interest-free loan made to a CFC. If, however, a CFC makes an interest-free, or a low-interest, loan to a United Kingdom connected company and an adjustment is made to impute interest on the loan under the provisions of Schedule 28AA to the Taxes Act 1988 for the purpose of calculating the CFC's chargeable profits.[22] it is considered that the exemption within section 136(7) or (9) or section 136A(5) to (7) of the Finance Act 1993, as appropriate, would apply.

## Financial instruments legislation

The financial instruments legislation broadly applies to a CFC in the same way in **16–21B** which it applies to a company within the charge to corporation tax. Particular attention should be given to the anti-avoidance provisions of section 168 of the Finance Act 1994 (qualifying contracts with non-residents) which apply automatically where the counterparty is not resident in a territory which has an interest article in its double tax treaty with the United Kingdom. Where this provision applies, the CFC would be denied relief for any net loss on the contract in question whilst any net gain would remain taxable. If the counterparty were another CFC, that company would still have to include the corresponding profit in computing its chargeable profits since a CFC is only considered to be United Kingdom resident for the purpose of calculating its chargeable profits.[23]

The effect of the transitional provisions for interest rate contracts and options will also need to be considered where a direction was made for an accounting period (earlier accounting period) which ended before the company's first accounting period which began on or after March 23, 1995, or where a direction was avoided for an earlier accounting period as a result of the CFC pursuing an ADP.[24] Unless an election

---

[22] ICTA 1988, Sched. 28AA, para. 5(2) is disapplied in such cases by ICTA 1988, Sched. 24, para. 20(1).

[23] ICTA 1988, Sched. 24 only applies for the purpose of calculating the CFC's chargeable profits: see ICTA 1988, s.747(6)(a).

[24] In such cases the CFC would be deemed to have become U.K. resident for the purpose of ICTA 1988, Sched. 24 from the start of that accounting period and would continue to be treated as deemed U.K. resident for those purposes for so long as it is controlled by U.K. residents: ICTA 1988, Sched. 24, para. 2.

was made by the United Kingdom company, or companies, which held the majority interest in the CFC within 20 months of the end of the CFC's first accounting period which began on or after March 23, 1995, contracts or options to which the CFC was a party at the start of that period will remain outside the financial instruments regime for the next six years for the purpose of calculating its chargeable profits.[25]

### Loan relationships legislation

**16–21C**    The loan relationships legislation will apply to a CFC in the same way as it applies to United Kingdom resident companies. The loan relationship transitional provisions will apply to a CFC where it was considered to be United Kingdom resident for the purposes of Schedule 24 to the Taxes Act 1988 at April 1, 1996. The exception to this is that the transitional provisions dealing with chargeable assets will not apply as chargeable gains are excluded in computing a CFC's chargeable profits.[1] Where a CFC is only deemed to come within the scope of Schedule 24 some time after it was incorporated, for example, where it previously fell within one of the exemptions other than the ADP test, the provisions of the Finance Act 1996, Schedule 9, paragraph 10 will restrict relief for losses on loan relationships to which it was a party at the date it became deemed United Kingdom resident, to the extent that these accrued before that date.

An important point to note in this context is that a CFC is deemed not to be a close company[2] and thus it will be able to obtain tax relief for interest payable to participators on an accruals basis whether or not the interest is ever paid, so long as the CFC is not connected with such participators within the meaning of section 87(3)(a) or (b) of the Finance Act 1996 (see paragraph 3-64 of the main work). In this latter case the provisions of Schedule 9, paragraph 2 to the Finance Act 1996 will not apply where the recipient is within the charge to United Kingdom corporation tax on the interest or where the interest is paid within 12 months of the end of the accounting period in which it accrued. As a CFC is not treated as a close company this means that the provisions of Schedule 9, paragraph 18 to the Finance Act 1996 (relevant discounted securities issued by a close company) will also not apply where such securities are issued to shareholders or loan creditors which do not control the CFC. The provisions of Schedule 9 paragraph 17 (relevant discounted securities issued by a non-close company) could still apply where the CFC is connected with the holder within the meaning of that paragraph unless the holder is liable to corporation tax on the full amount of the discount which accrues on the security.[3]

---

[25] FA 1994, s.148 and ICTA 1988, Sched. 24, paras 2(1), 4.

[1] ICTA 1988, s.747(6)(b).

[2] *ibid.* Sched. 24, para. 3.

[3] See paras 3–73 to 3–74 of the main work and para 3–45 of this Supplement which considers the amendments to the definition of a relevant discounted security which were introduced by FA 1996.

**Companies carrying on life assurance business**

Special rules apply where profits of a CFC are apportioned to a company carrying **16–23A** on life assurance business. These are beyond the scope of this book. For further information the reader is referred to sections 8.1.1 to 8.1.5 of the Inland Revenue CFC Guidance Notes.

CHAPTER 17

# DOUBLE TAX RELIEF AND E.U. LAW

I. INTRODUCTION

**Duty to minimise overseas tax suffered**

**17–01**    The amount of double tax credit relief that a taxpayer may claim for United Kingdom tax purposes may not exceed the credit which would have been allowed had all reasonable steps been taken under the law of the territory concerned and under the terms of any Double Tax Treaty between the United Kingdom and that territory to minimise the amount of tax payable in that territory. The steps in question include:

1. claiming or otherwise securing the benefit of reliefs, deductions, reductions or allowances; and
2. making elections for tax purposes.

What constitutes "all reasonable steps" is to be determined on the basis of what the taxpayer might reasonably be expected to have done in the absence of credit relief in the United Kingdom for the overseas tax in question.[1] The scope of "all reasonable steps: is not limited to actions which are open to the taxpayer to take. This measure has effect in relation to claims for credit made on or after March 21, 2000.[2]

---

[1] ICTA 1988, s.795A, as inserted by FA 2000, Sched. 30 para. 6. While s.795A refers to cases where relief is claimed under the terms of a double tax treaty, the provisions of the section are extended to unilateral relief by ICTA 1988, s.790.

[2] FA 2000, Sched. 30 para. 6(2).

232

In a Guidance Note[3] issued on October 3, 2000, the Inland Revenue stated that examples of cases in which this provision would apply were:

    (i) the acceptance of an estimated tax assessment in the other country which is likely to prove excessive;

    (ii) not claiming an allowance or relief (*e.g.*, capital allowances or losses) which is generally known to be available; and

    (iii) if the other country's domestic law or the relevant double tax treaty provides for alternative bases of taxation, not choosing the basis which would produce the lowest bill.

The Guidance Note, however, confirmed that, as the Paymaster General had stated during the Committee Stage Debate, the measure would not apply in the following cases:

    (a) not claiming a relief, the availability of which is uncertain, when disproportionate expenditure would have to be incurred in researching the other country's tax laws in order to pursue the claim;

    (b) claiming that a loss incurred in the other territory should be carried forwards rather than backwards or vice versa; and

    (c) in the case of underlying tax paid by an overseas subsidiary company, where the United Kingdom company that claims underlying tax credit relief is not in a position to influence the amount of tax paid.

### Relief for foreign tax obtained by deduction

Where a taxpayer elects against credit and the amount of the foreign tax suffered is subsequently reduced, the taxpayer is required to notify the Inland Revenue within one year of the date that the adjustment takes place. The normal six year time limit for an adjustment to a taxpayer's tax computation will not apply in such cases. (This measure does not apply in the case of corporate members of Lloyds where the adjustment is dealt with by regulations made under section 229 of the Finance Act 1994.) This provision applies in respect of adjustments to foreign tax made on or after March 21, 2000.[4] If a corporate taxpayer fails to notify the Inland Revenue of such an adjustment, it will be liable to a penalty equal to the increase in the corporation tax liability for that period which is due to the reduction in the foreign tax payable.[5]

---

[3] Double Taxation Relief—Guidance on non-mixer aspects of FA 2000 provisions.
[4] FA 2000, Sched. 30 para. 27(3).
[5] ICTA 1988, s.811(4)-(10) as inserted by FA 2000, Sched. 30 para. 27.

### Mutual agreement procedure

**17–01A**    Most double tax treaties contain provisions for a taxpayer who considers that the actions of one or both of the tax authorities of the two territories result, or will result, in taxation that is not in accordance with the terms of the double tax treaty to present his case to the competent authorities of either contracting state. A new section 815AA of the Taxes Act 1988 has been inserted by the Finance Act 2000[6] to provide a statutory basis for adjustments made following a case brought by a taxpayer under the mutual agreement procedure of a double tax treaty. The section applies where a case is made to the Board of Inland Revenue, or to an authority in the other territory, by a United Kingdom resident or a person resident in the other territory and the Board arrives at a solution to the case or makes a mutual agreement with an authority in the other territory for the resolution of the case.[7]

This section permits the Board to give effect to the solution or mutual agreement, notwithstanding anything in any enactment and it may make such adjustment as is appropriate, whether the adjustment takes the form of discharge or repayment of tax, the allowance of credit against tax payable in the United Kingdom, or the making of an assessment or otherwise. A claim for relief under any provision of the Tax Acts may be made in pursuance of the solution or mutual agreement at any time before the end of 12 months from the date on which the solution or mutual agreement is notified to the person, even if the statutory time limit for such a claim has otherwise expired.[8] The above measures apply where the solution or mutual agreement is reached or made on or after July 28, 2000.[9]

Where the terms of a double tax treaty permit a person to present a case to the Board of Inland Revenue concerning his being taxed otherwise than in accordance with the provisions of that treaty, any such case does not constitute a claim for relief under the Tax Acts and must be presented before the end of:

1. the period of six years following the end of the accounting period or year of assessment to which the case relates; or
2. such longer period as may be specified in the terms of the double tax treaty.[10]

This provision applies to a case which is presented for the first time on or after July 28, 2000.[11]

### Interaction between treaty relief and unilateral relief

**17–02A**    Provisions have been included in the Finance Act 2000 regarding the interaction of treaty relief and unilateral relief.

---

[6] FA 2000, Sched. 30 para. 28(1).
[7] ICTA 1988, s.815AA(1).
[8] *ibid.* s.815AA(2), (3).
[9] FA 2000, Sched. 30 para. 28(2).
[10] ICTA 1988, s.815AA(4), (5), (6).
[11] FA 2000, Sched. 30 para. 28 (3).

Where relief for an amount of overseas tax may be claimed under the terms of a Double Tax Treaty, or under the law of an overseas territory by virtue of provisions in a Double Tax Treaty, the taxpayer is not able to claim double tax credit relief for the tax in question, whether or not relief has been claimed for the tax.[12]

Where credit may be allowed in respect of an amount of overseas tax under the terms of a Double Tax Treaty, a taxpayer may not claim credit by way of unilateral relief in respect of that tax.[13] The effect of this provision is that where only a limited credit is available under the terms of a particular Double Tax Treaty for overseas tax suffered, a taxpayer is prevented from obtaining greater relief by claiming relief for that tax under the unilateral provisions set out in the Taxes Act 1988.

Both the above measures take effect for claims made for credit relief on or after March 21, 2000.[14]

Where the terms of a Double Tax Treaty contain express provision that credit relief is not to be given in cases or circumstances specified or described in the Treaty, for example, express restrictions on dual residents, a taxpayer is not able to claim unilateral tax credit relief for the tax in the cases or circumstances so specified.[15] This measure has effect in relation to Double Tax Treaties concluded on or after March 21, 2000.[16]

**Chargeable gains**

**Footnote 22 page 525—add to end of existing wording:**                    **17–03**

Where a taxpayer claims relief for foreign tax by deduction and the amount of the foreign tax suffered is subsequently reduced, the taxpayer is required to notify the Inland Revenue of this reduction within one year of the date on which the overseas tax was adjusted. If a corporate taxpayer fails to notify the Inland Revenue within this time period it will be liable to a penalty equal to the increase in the corporation tax for the period in question as a result of the reduction of the foreign tax liability. The normal six year time limit for an amendment to an assessment does not apply in such case: TCGA 1992, s.278(2), as inserted by FA 2000, Sched. 30 para. 30. This provision applies in relation to adjustments to foreign tax made on or after March 21, 2000: FA 2000, Sched. 30 para. 30(4).

---

[12] ICTA 1988, s.793A(1), as inserted by FA 2000, Sched. 30 para. 5(1).
[13] *ibid*. s.793A(2), as inserted FA 2000, Sched. 30 para. 5(1).
[14] FA 2000, Sched. 30 para. 5(2).
[15] ICTA 1988, s.793A(3), as inserted by FA 2000, Sched. 30 para. 5(1).
[16] FA 2000, Sched. 30 para. 5(3).

## II. Relief for Underlying Tax on Dividends

### Computation of underlying tax

*Change to the definition of relevant profits*

**17–04**    Where a dividend is paid to a United Kingdom resident company by an overseas resident related company on or after March 31, 2001, relevant profits will be defined as follows:

1. where the dividend is paid for a specified period, the profits of that period;
2. if the dividend is not paid for a specified period, the profits of the last period for which the accounts of the body corporate were made up which ended before the dividend became payable.[17]

Rules 1. and 2. will, however, be qualified where the profits for the period are insufficient to pay a dividend of the amount in question. In that event, any excess is treated as having come out of profits of preceding periods which are available for distribution, taking later periods before earlier periods. Profits previously treated as having been distributed are ignored.[18]

*Definition of profits*

For the purposes of 1 and 2 above, profits are defined as the profits available for distribution as shown in the accounts of the company, provided that such accounts:

(a) are drawn up in accordance with the law of the company's home State; and
(b) contain no provision for reserves, bad debts or contingencies other than such as is required to be made under that law.[19]

The company's home State is the country or territory under whose law the company is incorporated or formed.[20]

This revised definition applies in relation to any claim for credit whether under the

---

[17] ICTA 1988, s.799(3), as amended by FA 2000, Sched. 30 para. 8(4).
[18] *ibid.* s.799(4).
[19] *ibid.* s.799(5),(6), as inserted by FA 2000, Sched. 30 para. 9(2).
[20] *ibid.* s.799(7), as inserted by FA 2000, Sched. 30 para. 9(2).

terms of a Double Tax Treaty or by way of unilateral relief in relation to a dividend paid on or after March 21, 2000 by a non-resident company to a United Kingdom resident company.[21]

The restriction discussed in (b) above could cause difficulties where the company law of an overseas state does not require accounts to be drawn up on a "true and fair" basis, or even does not require accounts to be prepared. In such cases, were the provisions in (b) to be applied strictly, any provisions for reserves, bad debts or contingencies made in the accounts of the overseas company in question would have to be added back for the purpose of determining the underlying tax credit relief to which a United Kingdom resident company is entitled. The result would be that the company's profits would be increased and thus the tax credit attributable to the dividend would be reduced. The authors understand, however, that the Inland Revenue has indicated to representative bodies that it only intends to apply this provision in respect of general provisions and that it will not require an adjustment to be made in respect of specific provisions. The above measures will also apply to a United Kingdom branch of a non-resident company as unilateral relief applies in the same way as if double tax arrangements applied.[22]

### Underlying tax credit relief—taxation of overseas group on a consolidated basis

A new section 803A of the Taxes Act 1988 has been introduced by Finance Act **17–04A** 2000.[23] This section applies where tax is paid on a consolidated basis under the law of an overseas territory by one company (responsible company) resident in that territory in respect of the aggregate profits, or the aggregate profits and aggregate gains, of that company and one or more other companies that are so resident (consolidated group).[24] The provisions of the section apply to determine the underlying tax credit

---

[21] FA 2000, Sched. 30 para. 9(3). For claims made in respect of a dividend paid by a non-resident company to a United Kingdom resident company before March 31, 2001, the definition of profits applies to the provisions of ICTA 1988, s. 799(3)(a), (c) and not to s. 799(3)(b) (dividends paid out of specified profits) which has been repealed by FA 2000, Sched. 30 para. 8(4) in respect of dividends paid to a United Kingdom resident company on or after March 31, 2001.

[22] ICTA 1988, s.790(3), (6A).

[23] FA 2000, Sched. 30 para. 15(1).

[24] ICTA 1988, s.803A(1). In a guidance note issued on October 3, 2000 (Double Taxation Relief—Guidance on non-mixer aspects of FA 2000 provisions), the Inland Revenue confirmed that a company which is not resident in that territory could not be treated as a member of the consolidated group for these purposes but stated that a dual resident member could be treated as a member of the non-resident group where it was treated as resident in that territory for tax purposes.

that is attributable to a dividend paid by any company that is a member of the consolidated group to a company that is related to that member.[25]

In such cases the underlying tax credit that is attributable to the dividend that is paid by the member of the consolidated group is determined on the basis that:

1. the non-resident companies, taken together, were a single company;
2. the relevant profits[1] for the purposes of section 799(1) of the Taxes Act 1988 were a single figure;
3. the tax that is paid by the responsible company is treated as foreign tax paid by that single company;
4. the dividend was paid by that single company; and
5. the single company was related to the recipient (provided that the recipient of the dividend is related to the company that actually paid the dividend).[2]

This measure applies to any claim that is made for underlying tax credit relief in relation to a dividend paid to a United Kingdom resident company by a non-resident company on or after March 21, 2000.[3] In a Guidance Note that was issued on October 3, 2000, the Inland Revenue stated that it was possible that in certain cases a consolidated group may have no relevant profits but could still be subject to foreign tax and as a result where a company within the group pays a dividend to a United Kingdom resident company, the recipient could be disadvantaged under the new rules. In such cases the Inland Revenue stated that it would, by concession, be prepared to continue with its pre-Finance Act 2000 practice for dividends that were paid to the United Kingdom, before March 31, 2001.[4]

### Extension of relief for underlying tax

**17–05**     **Paragraph 1 page 528**—Section 800 of the Taxes Act 1988 was repealed by the Finance Act 2000 in relation to dividends paid on or after April 1, 2000.[5]

---

[25] *ibid.* s.803A(2). A company (first company) is related to another company (second company) if the first company controls directly or indirectly not less than 10 per cent of the voting power in the second company or is a subsidiary of a company that controls directly or indirectly not less than 10 per cent of the voting power in the second company: *ibid.* s.803A(3).

[1] In a Guidance Note (Double Taxation Relief—Guidance on non-mixer aspects of FA 2000 provisions) issued on October 3, the Inland Revenue stated that if a new company joins the group and brings accumulated profits with it, these profits should be include within the aggregate figure of relevant profits for the group where the parent can access the accumulated profits and pay a dividend out of them. It stated that the converse applies where a company leaves the group.

[2] *ibid.* s.803A(2).

[3] FA 2000, Sched. 30 para. 15(2).

[4] Double Taxation Relief—Guidance on non-mixer aspects of FA 2000 provisions.

[5] *ibid.* Sched. 30 para. 10.

### Finance Act 2000 limitations on underlying tax credit relief

Provisions have been included in the Finance Act 2000 to restrict the underlying tax credit that may be claimed where dividends are paid by a non-resident company to a United Kingdom resident company, or to a United Kingdom branch or agency of a non-resident company. The double tax credit relief that may be claimed in respect of underlying tax is restricted to an amount equal to:

$$\frac{D \times M}{(100\text{-}M)}$$

Where D is the amount of the dividend and M is the rate of corporation tax in force at the time at which the dividend was paid.[6]

In a press release issued following the Green Budget on November 8, 2000 the Inland Revenue stated that this formula would be changed and that the revised formula would be;

$$(D + U) \times M$$

D is the amount of the dividend and U is the actual underlying tax paid in relation to that dividend and M is the rate of corporation tax in force at the time at which the dividend was paid. It is assumed throughout the remainder of this chapter that this amendment will be introduced and that it will take effect from April 1, 2001.

The effect of the amendment proposed in the Green Budget would be to limit the relief for underlying tax to an amount (creditable underlying tax) equal, at the current corporation tax rate, to 30 per cent of the dividend and underlying tax. The restriction reflected the position pre- Finance Act 2000 so far as a United Kingdom resident company is concerned, in that under section 797 of the Taxes Act 1988 double tax credit relief is restricted to the corporation tax payable on the income in question. What is new, however, is that this restriction is applied where a non-resident company that is not within the charge to corporation tax receives a dividend from another non-resident company, to which it is related, for the purpose of determining the under-lying tax credit relief that is available to the ultimate United Kingdom recipient. The creditable underlying tax in relation to such dividends is limited to the underlying credit relief that a United Kingdom resident company would be able to claim in respect of that dividend (*i.e.* the above restriction is applied).[7] The effect of the provision is to prevent the mixing of dividends paid by companies that are resident in high and low tax jurisdictions. This is considered further at 17–21 below and mixing is discussed at 17–21 of the main text.

These restrictions only apply, however, in the case of dividends paid between overseas resident related companies, where the two companies are resident in different overseas territories or in certain other cases specified in regulations where

---

[6] ICTA 1988, s.799(1)(b), (1A), as inserted by FA 2000, Sched. 30 para. 8(2), (3).
[7] *ibid.* s.801(2).

the two companies are resident in the same territory.[8] The scope of such regulations is to be decided following consultation by the Inland Revenue with interested parties.

The above measures apply to any claim for credit relief on or after March 31, 2001 in respect of dividends paid by a non-resident company to a United Kingdom resident company, unless the dividend was paid to the United Kingdom resident company before that date. Where a dividend is paid to a United Kingdom resident company on or after March 31, 2001 and the dividend is in whole or part derived from dividends paid by one or more related companies[9], the restrictions discussed above are deemed to have applied at the time at which each non-resident related company paid its dividend, even if that dividend was paid before March 31, 2001.[10]

### Double tax relief for United Kingdom branches of non-residents

**17–05A** Following amendments introduced by Finance Act 2000, a United Kingdom branch of a non-resident company is able to claim double tax credit relief in respect of dividends received from overseas companies where the dividends form part of the profits of that branch or agency. It is possible for the branch or agency to claim relief for the underlying tax attributable to the dividend, subject to the new restrictions that are discussed at 17–05 and 17–21 of this supplement, provided that the non-resident company controls directly or indirectly, or it is a subsidiary of a company that controls directly or indirectly, at least 10 per cent of the voting power in the non-resident company that paid the dividend.[11]

The provisions of section 801 of the Taxes Act 1988, which permit underlying tax credit relief to be traced through a chain of non-resident companies where each of the companies in the chain controls directly or indirectly, or is a subsidiary of a company that controls directly or indirectly, at least 10% of the voting power in the company

---

[8] *ibid.* s.801(2A), as inserted by FA 2000, Sched. 30 para. 11(2).

[9] A company (first company) is related to another company if that other company is able to control directly or indirectly, or is a subsidiary of a company that is able to control directly or indirectly, not less than 10 per cent of the voting power in the first company: ICTA 1988 s.790(6). A company is a subsidiary of another company for these purposes if the other company is able to control not less than 50% of the voting power in the company: ICTA 1988, s.792(2). In certain cases where a company or its parent controls directly or indirectly less than 10 per cent of the voting power in the first company unilateral relief is available for underlying tax under the provisions of ICTA 1988, s.790(6)(b), (7). These cases are considered at section 17–04 p. 527 of the main text.

[10] FA 2000, Sched. 30 para. 8(5), (6).

[11] ICTA 1988, s.790(6A), as inserted by FA 2000 Sched. 30, para. 4(3), (14) for accounting periods ending on or after March 21, 2000.

from which it receives the dividend, have also been extended to a United Kingdom branch of a non-resident company.[12]

Example

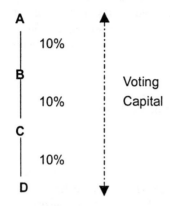

A is a United Kingdom branch of a non-resident company. B, C and D are all non-resident. A holds 10 per cent of the voting power of B, B holds 10 per cent of the voting power of C and C holds 10 per cent of the voting power of D.

Were D to pay a dividend and the dividend from D were to be paid on as a dividend by each of the other companies in the chain, A would be able to claim underlying tax credit relief in respect of the tax paid by D on the profits out of which its dividend was paid, subject to the new restrictions on dividend mixing.

The anti-avoidance provisions of section 801A (buying in foreign tax credits) which are considered at 17–22 of the main text, have also been extended to United Kingdom branches of non-United Kingdom resident companies.[13]

A non-resident company is also able to claim unilateral relief for tax paid under the law of any territory outside the United Kingdom in respect of the income or chargeable gains of a branch or agency in the United Kingdom provided that:

1. the territory under whose law the tax was paid is not one in which the non-resident is liable to tax by reason of domicile, residence or place of management; and

---

[12] ibid., s.801(1A), as inserted by FA 2000 Sched. 30, para. 4(9), (14) for accounting periods ending on or after March 21, 2000.

[13] *ibid.* s.801A(1)(a), (2), (7), (11), as amended by FA 2000, Sched. 30 para. 4(10), (11), (12), (14) for accounting periods ending on or after March 21, 2000.

2. the amount of relief claimed does not exceed (or is by the claim expressly limited to) that which would have been available if the branch or agency had been a person resident in the United Kingdom and the income or gains in question had been income or gains of that person.[14]

The provisions that permitted United Kingdom branches of non-resident banks to claim double tax credit relief in respect of withholding tax suffered on interest income[15] have been repealed[16] in relation to accounting periods ending on or after March 21, 2000 as this relief has been superseded by the extension of double tax relief to United Kingdom branches and agencies of non-residents.

### Double tax relief for United Kingdom branches of EU/EEA residents

**17–05B**    In a Budget 2000 press release[17] the Inland Revenue stated that following the decision of the European Court of Justice in *Compagnie de Saint-Gobain v. Finanzamt Aachen-Innenstadt*[18] it would permit E.U. and EEA residents to claim double tax credit relief in respect of income and gains of their United Kingdom branches for previous periods, subject to the normal six year time limit. The press release also stated that underlying tax credit relief would be available where the conditions that applied in the case of a United Kingdom resident company before the Finance Act 2000 amendments took effect were satisfied.

As noted above, the provisions dealing with double tax credit relief have been amended to permit any non-resident to claim double tax credit relief in respect of income and gains of its United Kingdom branch or agency for accounting periods ending on or after March 21, 2000.

### Transfers of profit

**17–05B**    Finance Act 2000 has introduced a new section 801B of the Taxes Act 1988 which permits the benefit of underlying tax credit relief to be preserved where one non-resident company (company A) has paid tax in respect of any of its profits under the law of an overseas territory and it transfers some or all of those profits to another non-resident company (company B) and company B subsequently pays a dividend out of the profits transferred to it by company A. This provision applies where some or all of company A's profits in question, in respect of which it has paid tax, are trans-

---

[14] *ibid*. s.794(2)(bb), as inserted by FA 2000, Sched. 30 para. 4(4), (5) for accounting periods ending on or after March 21, 2000.

[15] *ibid*. s.794(2)(c).

[16] FA 2000, Sched. 30 para. 4(6), (14).

[17] REV 14

[18] Case C—307/97 [2000] S.T.C. 854.

ferred to company B otherwise than by the payment of a dividend (for example, where company A's activities are amalgamated with those of company B).[19]

Section 801B determines the underlying tax that is attributable to any dividend that is paid by a non-resident company to a United Kingdom resident company (whether or not the dividend is paid directly to the United Kingdom resident company by company B) out of the profits so transferred by company A to company B. The underlying tax that is attributable to the dividend paid out of such profits is determined on the assumption that the overseas tax paid by company A on those profits had in fact been paid by company B. The tax credit that is attributable to a company resident in the United Kingdom, however, is limited to the underlying tax credit that would have been available had company B received a dividend from company A, instead of the profits having been transferred otherwise than by the payment of a dividend.[20] The limitation on the underlying tax credit relief that is available where a dividend is paid by one non-resident company to another non-resident company, which in turn pays on the dividend to the United Kingdom, is considered in 17–05 of this supplement.

Section 801B applies to claims for underlying tax credit made on or after March 21, 2000.[21]

### E.U. Law

In *Staatssecretaris van Financien v. Verkooijen*[22] the European Court ruled that it **17–09A** was contrary to European Law for the Netherlands to restrict an exemption from Dutch income tax for dividends (up to a certain limit) to dividends from a Dutch company. This case has potentially very significant ramifications for the tax treatment in the United Kingdom of foreign dividends since it is arguable that the exemption from corporation tax for dividends from United Kingdom companies conferred by section 208 of the Taxes Act 1988 should be extended to cover dividends from E.U. subsidiaries.

Dutch law exempted from Dutch income tax up to a certain limit dividends on which Dutch withholding tax had been levied. The taxpayer received dividends from a Belgian company and claimed the exemption even though no Dutch withholding tax had been levied. The claim was based on the free movement of capital provisions before their amendment by the Treaty of Amsterdam although the reasoning of the court suggests that the same result would have followed under current rules. It was

---

[19] ICTA 1988, s.801B(1), as inserted by FA 2000, Sched. 30 para. 12(1).
[20] *ibid.* s.801B(2),(3), as inserted by FA 2000, Sched. 30 para. 12(1). This wording would appear to apply the provisions of ICTA 1988, s.801(2A) (see 17–05 above) where A and B are resident in the same territory such that the provisions of ICTA 1988, s.799(1)(b) would not apply in such cases to restrict the amount of underlying tax that is deemed to be transferred to company B.
[21] FA 2000, Sched. 30 para. 12(2).
[22] Case C–35/98.

held that to limit the exemption to dividends from Dutch companies was a restriction on capital movements. This was because it was an obstacle to Belgian companies raising capital in the Netherlands since dividends from Belgian companies were taxed less favourably than dividends from Dutch companies.

The Dutch government sought to justify the Dutch law by the need to preserve the cohesion of the Dutch tax system. They argued that the exemption of dividends was intended to mitigate the effects of double taxation in the Netherlands and that where dividends were received from a Belgian company there was no double taxation in the Netherlands. It was also argued that the exemption was justified by the intention to promote the Dutch economy and the desire to avoid loss of tax. It was held that neither aims of an economic nature nor loss of revenue could justify a restriction on a fundamental freedom. As regards the cohesion argument, the court stated

> "In *Bachmann and Commission v. Belgium*, a direct link existed, in the case of one and the same taxpayer, between the grant of a tax advantage and the offsetting of that tax advantage by a fiscal levy, both of which related to the same tax. In this case, there was a link between the deductibility of contributions and the taxation of sums payable by insurers under old-age insurance and life assurance policies, which it was necessary to preserve in order to safeguard the cohesion of the tax system at issue.
>
> No such direct link exists in this case between the grant to shareholders residing in the Netherlands of income tax exemption in respect of dividends received and taxation of the profits of companies with their seat in another Member State. They are two separate taxes levied on different taxpayers."

### Loan relationships

**17–15**   The provisions of section 797A of the Taxes Act 1988 that previously only applied where withholding tax was suffered on interest income have been extended to any case where withholding tax is suffered on any item that is brought into account for any accounting period for the purposes of the loan relationship legislation. This amendment applies for accounting periods ending on or after March 21, 2000.[23]

III. Manner of Giving Relief by Credit

### Time limit for claims for credit relief

**17–16A**   The time limit for claims for credit relief in the case of any income or chargeable gain which falls to be charged to corporation tax for an accounting period is now the later of:

---

[23] FA 2000, Sched. 30 para. 20(3).

1. six years after the end of that accounting period; or
2. one year after the end of the accounting period in which the foreign tax is paid.[24]

This revised time limit applies to claims for credit made on after March 21, 2000.[25]

IV. Tax Planning

**Other tax reliefs**

Section 810 of the Taxes Act 1988 that is considered in 17–20 of the main work **17–20** was repealed by the Finance Act 2000 with effect for claims made on or after April 1, 2000.[1] Section 810 only applied to claims made in respect of expenditure incurred before October 26, 1970 and therefore its repeal should be of little consequence. It is still permissible for a company to disclaim capital allowances under the provisions of the Capital Allowances Act 1990 in order to maximise the amount of a double tax credit relief claim.

**"Averaging" or "mixer" companies**

Provisions have been included in the Finance Act 2000 to counter the use of "aver- **17–21** aging" or "mixer" companies. These provisions take two forms:

1. the restriction of underlying tax credit relief that is available to a United Kingdom resident company or to a United Kingdom branch or agency of a non-resident company in respect of a dividend paid by a non-resident company where that dividend is funded in whole or in part out of dividends received directly or indirectly by the non-resident company from other non-resident related companies. These restrictions are discussed at 17–05 of this supplement and are referred to in the legislation as the "mixer cap".
2. a restriction on "blending" dividends that are paid by CFCs to meet the acceptable distribution policy test with other dividends.

*Mixer cap*

The provisions referred to in 1. above will prevent the blending of dividends from high and low tax companies via the use of an offshore "mixer" company in the case of dividends paid to a United Kingdom resident company or a United Kingdom branch or

---

[24] ICTA 1988, s.797A(1), as amended by FA 2000, Sched. 30 para. 7.
[25] ICTA 1988, s.806(1), as amended by FA 2000, Sched. 30 para. 20(2).
[1] FA 2000, Sched. 30 para. 26.

agency of a non-resident company on or after March 31, 2001. The provisions as revised by the proposals set out in the Inland Revenue press release of November 8, 2000, however, only cap underlying credit relief at 30 per cent of the dividend and underlying tax and do not prevent dividends from low tax countries being blended with profits of a corporate shareholder (second company) that is resident in a higher tax jurisdiction for the purpose of determining the ultimate underlying tax credit relief to which a United Kingdom resident company or United Kingdom branch or agency of a non-resident company is entitled in respect of a dividend paid by the second company.

Example

Company A is resident in the United Kingdom. Company B is resident in the Netherlands and company C is resident in Ruritania.

Company C pays tax on its profits at an effective rate of 25.6 per cent. Company B pays tax in the Netherlands on its profits at an effective rate of 35 per cent. The benefit of the participation exemption is available in respect of the dividends received from company C. Company B's profits (excluding the dividend received from company C) are 65, after taking account of tax paid on those profits of 35 and company C's profits are 87, after taking account of tax paid on those profits of 30. Company C pays a dividend of 87 to company B. Were company B then to pay a dividend equal to its own profits after tax (including the dividend received by company C), the net result would be that company A would be deemed to have received a net dividend of 152 (65 + 87) and the maximum double tax credit relief which could be claimed in respect of that dividend, 65, would be equal to the full amount of the eligible underlying tax (30 + 35).

*Controlled foreign companies*

It was presumably for the above reason that the measures referred to in 2. above were introduced. These provisions operate by requiring a dividend that is paid by a CFC in order to satisfy the ADP test (ADP exempt CFC) to be separately identified where such dividend flows to a United Kingdom resident company through a chain of one or more non-resident intermediate companies.[2] In such cases, to the extent that an intermediate company pays a dividend that represents the dividend received from the ADP exempt CFC, for the purpose of determining the double tax relief to which a United Kingdom resident company is entitled, the subsequent dividend is deemed to be comprised of two elements: the element that represents the dividend received from the ADP exempt CFC and the balance. The dividend received from the ADP exempt CFC and any underlying tax or withholding tax that is attributable to that dividend is excluded for the purpose of determining any underlying tax credit relief

---

[2] ICTA 1988, s.801C(1), (2), as inserted by FA 2000, Sched. 30 para. 13(1).

that is attributable to the balance of the dividend paid by the intermediate company. The same treatment applies where an intermediate company pays a dividend to another non-resident intermediate company and that company in turn pays a dividend that to any extent represents the dividend received from the ADP exempt CFC.[3]

This streaming also applies where an ADP exempt CFC receives a dividend that is paid by one of its subsidiaries to satisfy the ADP test. In such case the dividend that is received from the subsidiary is treated as a separate dividend all the way up the overseas group for the purposes of determining double tax credit relief to which a United Kingdom resident company is entitled.[4]

Example

Company A

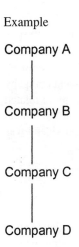

Company B

Company C

Company D

Company A is United Kingdom resident, company B is resident in the Netherlands and satisfies the requirements of the excluded countries regulations (see 16–19 of this Supplement). Companies C and D are both ADP exempt CFCs. Company D pays a dividend to company C of 100 in order to satisfy the ADP test and company C then pays on this dividend together with a further dividend of 80 which is required in order for company C to meet the ADP test in respect of its own taxable profits for that period. Company B's own profits for the period after tax are 60 and its tax charge for the year was 30 (the dividend received from company C is excluded from tax under the participation exemption). Company B pays a dividend for the period of 200. This dividend will be deemed to be comprised of three elements:

(a) a dividend of 100 paid by company D;

---

[3] *ibid.* s.801C(3), (4), (5), (6),(7), (8), (9) as inserted by FA 2000, Sched. 30 para. 13(1).
[4] *ibid.* s.801C(14), as inserted by FA 2000, Sched. 30 para. 13(1).

(b) a dividend of 80 paid by company C; and

(c) a dividend of 20 paid by company B.

The underlying tax credit relief available in respect of the dividend that is deemed to have been paid by company B out of its own profits (*i.e.* ignoring the ADP dividends that it received) will be determined by reference to:

$^{20}/_{60} \times 30 = 10$ (to determine the underlying tax attributable to the dividend) subject to the tax credit not exceeding the maximum amount determined in accordance with the formula set out in section 799(1A) of the Taxes Act 1988 (see 17–05 above). In this example the maximum underlying tax credit permitted by the revised formula would be 9.

These measures apply to any claim for credit relief on or after March 31, 2001 in respect of a dividend paid by a non-resident company to a United Kingdom resident company, unless the dividend was paid to the United Kingdom resident company before this date.[5] Where a dividend that is paid to a United Kingdom resident company after this date is in whole or part derived from dividends paid by one or more related companies, the restrictions discussed above are deemed to have applied at the time at which each non-resident related company paid its dividend, even if that dividend was paid before March 31, 2001.[6]

**Onshore pooling**

**17–23A**    In response to representations made by taxpayers and their advisers following the introduction of the mixer cap, the Government introduced provisions to permit excess tax credit relief on certain dividends to be relieved against certain other overseas dividends. These measures have been termed 'onshore pooling' and are set out in sections 806A to 806J of the Taxes Act 1988.[7] They apply to dividends arising on or after March 31, 2001 and foreign tax in respect of such dividends.[8]

The dividends in respect of which excess tax credit relief may be taken into account are any dividends chargeable under Case V of Schedule D other than:

1. any dividend which is trading income for the purposes of section 393 of the Taxes Act 1988;
2. any dividend which would be eligible to be treated as trading income for the purposes of the relief of brought forward Schedule D Case I trading losses under the provisions of section 393(8) of the Taxes Act 1988;
3. dividends to which the provisions of section 801A of the Taxes Act 1988

---

[5] FA 2000, Sched. 30 para. 13(2).

[6] *ibid*. Sched. 30 para. 13(3).

[7] As inserted by FA 2000, Sched. 30 para. 21(1).

[8] FA 2000, Sched. 30 para. 21(2).

(purchase of foreign tax credits) apply to restrict relief for underlying tax, see section 17–22 of the main text for an explanation of these provisions;

4. any dividends to which section 803(1)(b) of the Taxes Act 1988 applies. This provision applies in a case where a bank, or a company connected with a bank, makes a claim for underlying tax credit relief and the dividend from the overseas company is directly or indirectly funded out of interest or dividends to which the provisions of section 798 of the Taxes Act 1988 would have applied, had the income in question been received directly by the bank or a United Kingdom resident company with which it is connected. This provision is discussed further at section 17–26 of the main text; and

5. any dividend in respect of which double tax relief has been claimed by deduction under the provisions of section 811 of the Taxes Act 1988 (see 17–01 of the main text—final paragraph on page 521).[9]

### Determination of eligible unrelieved foreign tax

The onshore pooling provisions apply separately to determine the amount of the excess underlying and withholding tax credits that arise in respect of a dividend which can be taken into account for the purposes of onshore pooling. For the purposes of the following discussion these amounts are referred to as eligible unrelieved underlying tax and eligible unrelieved withholding tax. The eligible unrelieved underlying and withholding tax is determined by what in the legislation is referred to as Case A and Case B.[10]

*Case A*

Case A applies where the eligible foreign tax credits attributable to a dividend exceed the corporation tax payable on the gross dividend (*i.e.*, inclusive of any underlying and withholding tax credits).[11] For these purposes where the mixer cap has applied to restrict the underlying tax attributable to the dividend, the underlying tax is taken as 30 per cent of the gross dividend (*i.e.* inclusive of underlying tax). As the underlying tax that is attributable to a dividend is deemed to be relieved in precedence to withholding tax,[12] generally Case A will apply to determine the eligible unrelieved withholding tax attributable to that dividend. This will not always be the case and Case A may also determine an amount of eligible unrelieved underlying tax, where the effect-

---

[9] ICTA 1988, s.806A(2), as inserted by FA 2000, Sched. 30 para. 21(1).

[10] *ibid.* s.806A(4), (5), as inserted by FA 2000, Sched. 30 para. 21(1).

[11] Under ICTA 1988, s.795(2) the corporation tax due on a dividend is calculated by reference to the gross amount of the dividend and under the provisions of ICTA 1988, s.797, double tax credit relief is restricted to an amount equal to the corporation tax payable on the gross dividend.

[12] ICTA 1988, s.806F(1)(a), (b), as inserted by FA 2000, Sched. 30 para. 21(1).

249

ive rate of corporation tax on the dividend is less than 30 per cent, for example, as the result of the offset of losses or other reliefs.

Where double tax credit relief is restricted by the provisions of section 797 of the Taxes Act 1988, the unrelieved withholding tax is eligible to be taken into account for "onshore pooling" purposes, subject to this not exceeding the lower of:

(i) the underlying[13] and withholding tax which would be creditable, but for the restriction imposed by section 797; and

(ii) an amount equal to 45% of the gross dividend.[14]

## Case B

Case B applies to determine the amount of eligible unrelieved underlying tax that arises in respect of a dividend to which the mixer cap has applied. In such cases the amount of the eligible unrelieved underlying tax that may be taken into account for the purposes of onshore pooling depends on the level at which the mixer cap has applied.

(a) *Mixer cap applies to a dividend paid to a United Kingdom resident company*
If the mixer cap applies to a dividend that is received by a United Kingdom resident company from a non-resident company, the eligible unrelieved tax that can be taken into account is the difference between the capped amount and the overseas tax that was actually paid, or is treated as having been paid by the non-resident company. Under the measures introduced in the Finance Act 2000, the non-resident company (first company) received a dividend from another non-resident company (second company) and the mixer cap applied to that dividend, the tax that the first company is deemed to have paid in respect of the dividend would be restricted to the capped amount. The full amount of any withholding tax suffered on the dividend received from the second company could, however, be treated as tax paid by the first company and could be included in computing the first company's eligible unrelieved underlying tax. Any withholding tax that was suffered on dividends paid to the second company from another non-resident company, however, would be treated as part of the underlying tax paid by the second company and thus would be subject to the mixer cap in the usual way.

In a case where the mixer cap applies to a dividend that is paid to a United Kingdom resident company by a non-resident company, the eligible unrelieved underlying tax is the lower of:

(i) the amount by which the underlying tax that is attributable to the dividend paid by the non-resident company exceeds the mixer cap; and

---

[13] Where the mixer cap applies the underlying tax attributable to the dividend is limited to the capped amount.

[14] ICTA 1988, s.806A(4), s.806B(2), as inserted by FA 2000, Sched. 30 para. 21(1).

      (ii) the amount which would be relievable were 45 per cent substituted in the mixer cap formula as discussed at 17–05 above (*i.e.*, forty-five per cent of the gross dividend, *i.e.* inclusive of underlying tax).[15]

(b) *Mixer cap does not apply to a dividend paid to a United Kingdom resident company*

Where the mixer cap does not apply to a dividend that is paid to a United Kingdom resident company, regard may be had to the underlying tax that is attributable to the highest overseas dividend in a chain of related company dividends to which the mixer cap has applied.

Example

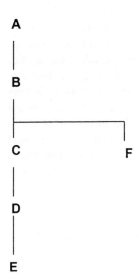

A is resident in the United Kingdom B, C, D and E are all non-resident and are resident in different overseas territories. All the companies are related.

If E paid a dividend to D and this dividend was ultimately received by A as a result of a dividend paid by B, in determining the unrelieved underlying tax that is attributable to the dividend that is paid by B to A regard can be had to the highest level dividend in the chain to which the mixer cap applies (subject to the point discussed below in the case of a dividend paid by F).

---

[15] *ibid.* s.806A(5), s.806B(3), as inserted by FA 2000, Sched. 30 para. 21(1).

If the mixer cap applies to the dividend paid by E to D, but no higher, the unrelieved underlying tax within E could be taken into account. If however, the mixer cap also applies to a dividend paid by D to C, but no higher, the unrelieved tax within D could be taken into account. In this case the underlying tax that D is deemed to have paid on the dividend that it received from E would be restricted to three-sevenths of that dividend.

Suppose, however, that F also paid a dividend in that accounting period and the mixer cap applied to that dividend. Even though F is not in the overseas chain, the Inland Revenue has suggested[16] that this would mean that it would not be possible to have regard to the unrelieved underlying tax in C or D. The authors have some difficulty in reconciling this statement to the legislation. Section 806B(4) clearly refers to a dividend that is paid up a chain of overseas companies and a higher level dividend is defined as a dividend that to any extent represents that dividend. In this case the higher level dividend would be paid by B and so long as the mixer cap does not apply to that dividend then the provisions of section 806B(5) would permit regard to be had to the highest lower level dividend in the chain to which the mixer cap applied. The fact that the mixer cap applies to a dividend paid by a sister subsidiary that is not in the chain (i.e., F in the above example) would not appear to prevent a look through to unrelieved underlying tax in C or D (depending at what level in the chain the mixer cap applied) as the test is applied looking up the chain. (Under the original version of the dividend cap formula, where dividends from two companies were "blended" and were paid on as a single dividend the mixer cap would not automatically have applied. At the time of writing it is unclear whether this will remain the case assuming that the amendment to the formula, as announced in the November 2000 Green Budget is introduced).

The unrelieved underlying tax that can be taken into account for the purposes of onshore pooling is limited to the lower of:

(i) the amount by which the underlying tax that is attributable to the dividend paid by the non-resident company exceeds the mixer cap; and

(ii) the underlying tax that would be eligible to be taken into account were 45 per cent substituted in the mixer cap formula as discussed at 17–05 above (i.e., forty-five per cent of the gross dividend).[17]

This is subject to the proration discussed in the following paragraph.

Where a lower level company pays a dividend and this dividend passes through a chain of non-resident related companies (higher level companies) before it reaches the

---

[16] Inland Revenue Guidance Note: Double Taxation Changes in FA 2000: The mixer cap, onshore pooling and eligible unrelieved foreign tax, which was issued on October 3, 2000.

[17] *ibid*. ss.806A(5), 806B(4), (5), as inserted by FA 2000, Sched. 30 para. 21(1).

ultimate United Kingdom recipient, the excess eligible unrelieved underlying tax is restricted at each level by reference to the following fraction:

$$\frac{\text{dividend paid by the higher level company}}{\text{relevant profits of that company out of which the dividend was paid}^{18}}$$

The effect of this is that if each higher level company does not distribute in full the amount of its relevant profits out of which it paid the dividend, there will be a corresponding restriction to the amount of excess unrelieved underlying tax. There appear to be no provisions for an adjustment to be made to this restriction if a higher level company only partially distributes the relevant profits and later makes a further distribution out of those profits.

Example

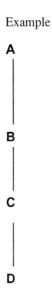

**A**

**B**

**C**

**D**

    A is resident in the United Kingdom and B, C and D are all non-resident and are not resident in the same territory.

    D has net profits after tax of £650,000 and its tax charge for the year is £350,000.

    If D pays a dividend to C of £650,000, A will only be able to obtain the maximum benefit for the unrelieved underlying tax of £50,000 if C and B make a full distribution of their relevant profits for the accounting period.

For the purpose of determining whether the mixer cap applies to any dividends that are payable by each higher level company (companies C and B in the above example),

---

[18] *ibid.* s.806B(6), (7), as inserted by FA 2000, Sched. 30 para. 21(1).

any withholding tax that has been deducted from the lower level dividend (i.e. dividend paid by D and later by C in the above example) is treated as tax paid by the recipient. Before the amendment announced in the Inland Revenue press release of November 8, 2000 (see 17–05 above) the result of this would have been that where withholding tax was deducted from a dividend (lower dividend) and the mixer cap applied to the lower dividend, the mixer cap would also have applied to a dividend paid by the recipient unless the recipient's effective tax rate (after reflecting such withholding tax) did not exceed the United Kingdom mainstream rate of corporation tax such that the mixer cap would not apply to any higher level dividends. As the revised formula looks to the underlying tax attributable to a dividend, this problem should be resolved, assuming that the amendment is made.

Under the original provisions introduced in the Finance Act 2000, problems could arise where there are expenses within a higher level company that are not offset by other income within that company. If the expenses have to be relieved against a dividend to which the mixer cap has applied the result is that the company's distributable profits for that accounting period would be less than the dividend that it received and thus the mixer cap would apply to the dividend paid by that company. At the time of writing it was unclear whether this problem would be resolved by the change to the formula or as a result of other amendments to the legislation that the Inland Revenue stated that it was considering.

### Method of giving relief for eligible unrelieved foreign tax

*Qualifying dividends*

Surplus foreign tax can be relieved against dividends received from overseas resident companies by United Kingdom resident companies and United Kingdom branches or agencies of non-residents which are themselves dividends in respect of which eligible unrelieved foreign tax can arise (*i.e.*, excluding the dividends considered at 1. to 5. at page 248 above), subject to the following exceptions:

1. dividends that are paid by a CFC to meet the acceptable distribution test;
2. a dividend paid by a non-resident company to the extent that the dividend represents a dividend paid by a CFC to meet the acceptable distribution test[19]; and
3. a dividend on which an amount of eligible unrelieved foreign tax has arisen.[20]

---

[19] In a Guidance Note Double Taxation changes:The mixer cap, onshore pooling and eligible unrelieved foreign tax, issued on October 3, 2000, the Inland Revenue confirmed that where a non-resident company pays a dividend which in part represents an ADP received from a CFC and in part a distribution of its own profits, that part of the dividend that represents its own profits could be included for onshore pooling purposes, subject to that part of the dividend satisfying the other conditions for inclusion within the eligible pool of dividends.

[20] *ibid.* s.806C(1), as inserted by FA 2000, Sched. 30 para. 21(1).

The provisions of 3. above mean that a dividend paid by an offshore mixer company may not qualify for onshore pooling treatment, even if the effective rate of underlying tax attributable to that dividend were less than 30 per cent.

Example

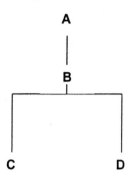

A is resident in the United Kingdom. B, C and D are all non-resident and are resident in different territories. C pays a dividend to B of £60 and the tax attributable to that dividend is £40. D pays a dividend to B of £80 and the tax attributable to the dividend is £20.

The mixer cap will apply to restrict the underlying tax credit that is attributable to the dividend paid by C to £30. The mixer cap will not apply to the dividend paid by D.

B has no other profits for the period and pays a dividend of £140 (£60 + £80) to A. The underlying tax attributable to that dividend is £30+ £20 = £50 or an effective rate of 26.32 per cent.

Whilst the dividend will not be treated as a qualifying dividend, it will carry eligible underlying foreign tax credits which can be relieved against qualifying dividends.

As the restriction within 3. would apply in any event where the mixer cap applied to a dividend received by a United Kingdom resident company, it can only be assumed that this restriction is aimed at offshore mixer companies.

Dividends that qualify for onshore pooling (qualifying dividends) are then grouped into two classes, being qualifying dividends received from related companies and qualifying dividends received from unrelated companies and are treated respectively as a single related and as a single unrelated qualifying dividend arising in that accounting period.[21] For the purposes of the onshore pooling provisions, a company is deemed to be related to another company if that other company controls directly or indirectly,

---

[21] *ibid.* s.806C(2), (3), ( 4) as inserted by FA 2000, Sched. 30 para. 21(1).

or is a subsidiary of a company that controls directly or indirectly, at least 10 per cent of the voting rights of the first company.[22] Dividends paid up a chain of companies are treated as related party dividends where each company in the chain is related to the company from which it received the dividend.[23]

Example

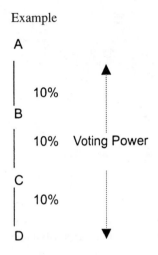

A

| 10%

B

| 10%    Voting Power

C

| 10%

D

A is a United Kingdom resident company and B, C and D are all non-resident. A dividend paid by D to C and then paid on by C to B and finally on to A would be treated as a related dividend in A's hands.

A company will also be treated as related to an overseas company where the United Kingdom resident company has a less than 10% holding in the voting power of the non-resident company, provided that the circumstances specified in section 790(6)(b) of the Taxes Act 1988 are satisfied[24] (see 17–04 at page 527 of the main text for an explanation of these circumstances).

The eligible unrelieved foreign tax is then split between underlying tax (eligible underlying tax) and withholding tax (eligible withholding tax). Eligible underlying tax can only be relieved against the deemed single related dividend whilst eligible withholding tax may be set against both the deemed single related dividend and the deemed single unrelated dividend.[25]

---

[22] *ibid.* s.806J(3), (6) as inserted by FA 2000, Sched. 30 para. 21(1).
[23] *ibid.* s.806J(4), (6), as inserted by FA 2000, Sched. 30 para. 21(1).
[24] ibid., s.806(J)(5), as inserted by FA 2000, Sched. 30 para. 21(1).
[25] *ibid.* s.806C(3)(c), (d), (4)(c), (d) as inserted by FA 2000, Sched. 30 para. 21(1).

### Order of set off—related dividends

Under the onshore pooling rules, relief is given first for underlying tax and then for withholding tax that is attributable to each individual dividend that forms part of the deemed single related dividend. Once such tax has been relieved, then eligible underlying tax and eligible withholding tax may be relieved. Eligible underlying tax is deemed to be relieved in precedence to eligible withholding tax.[1]

### Relief for excess eligible underlying tax

Where the deemed single related dividend in an accounting period is insufficient to absorb the eligible underlying tax arising in that period, there are two ways in which the company can obtain relief for such tax:

1. the company may elect to carry forward the unrelieved eligible underlying tax to the next accounting period where it is treated as if it were eligible underlying tax arising in that next accounting period, even if no dividends are received from related companies in that period. To the extend that any such tax remains unrelieved at the end of that next accounting period, the company can elect to carry forward the tax to the following accounting period (and so on).[2]
2. the company can elect to carry back such tax against eligible dividends received from related companies in the preceding three years on a later year first basis (or if later after March 30, 2001[3]). A company may only carry back unrelieved eligible underlying tax to an earlier period provided that this does not result in unrelieved foreign tax (whether withholding or underlying tax) arising in that accounting period. Further, where eligible unrelieved tax is brought forward to an accounting period from a preceding period, such eligible tax takes precedence over tax which is carried back to that accounting period from a later accounting period.[4]

Example

Company A's eligible underlying tax position is as follows:
In year one it has unrelieved eligible underlying tax of £10,000.

---

[1] *ibid*. s.806F(1)(c), as inserted by FA 2000, Sched. 30 para. 21(1).
[2] *ibid*. s.806D(4)(b), s. 806G as inserted by FA 2000, Sched. 30 para. 21(1).
[3] FA 2000, Sched. 30 para. 21(2).
[4] ICTA 1988, s.806D(4)(c), s. 806E, as inserted by FA 2000, Sched. 30 para. 21(1).

In year two it has capacity to absorb £20,000 of eligible unrelieved foreign tax.

In year three it has unrelieved eligible underlying tax of £20,000.

Under the set off rules, the £10,000 surplus arising in year 1 would be set off against the capacity in year 2, in preference to the surplus arising in year 3. Thus only £10,000 of the £20,000 surplus in year 3 could be carried back to year 2.

There are no express rules to prevent eligible unrelieved underlying tax credits which are carried forward to a later period from being included in calculating the unrelieved underlying tax that may be carried back to an earlier period. This restriction is achieved, however, by the provision which requires unrelieved eligible foreign tax credits which are brought forward to an accounting period to be relieved in advance of unrelieved eligible foreign tax credits that are carried back to that period from a later period.[5]

Equally there is nothing in the legislation that requires unrelieved eligible underlying tax to first be relieved against qualifying dividends received in the current accounting period before a carry back claim is made. This point is addressed, however, by the rules governing interest on tax repayments that are considered below. The effect is that a company is not in a better position if it makes a carry back claim.

It is unclear, however, whether, if a company is eligible to make a carry back claim for a particular period, but does not do so, whether the company would be restricted in the amount of the eligible underlying tax that it can carry back from a later period.

Example

Company A's eligible underlying tax position is as follows:

In year one it has capacity to absorb £20,000 of eligible unrelieved underlying tax.

In year two it has unrelieved eligible underlying tax of £10,000.

In year three it has capacity to absorb £15,000 of eligible unrelieved underlying tax.

In year four it has unrelieved eligible underlying tax of £25,000.

The company does not elect to carry back the unrelieved eligible underlying tax that arises in year two and such tax is thus relieved in year three. The question is whether the failure of Company A to make the carry back election would prejudice its ability to carry back eligible unrelieved underlying tax arising in year four to year one.

It is unclear from the wording of section 806E(4)(a) of the Taxes Act 1988 whether

---

[5] *ibid.* s.806E(4)(b),as inserted by FA 2000, Sched. 30 para. 21(1).

this would prevent eligible unrelieved tax that arises in year 4 in the above example from being carried back to year 1 where eligible unrelieved underlying tax arose in year 2 but no carry back claim was made. This is because the condition in section 806E(4)(b) is that where a carry back claim is made, relief should be given for eligible unrelieved underlying tax arising in **any** accounting period before that in which the eligible unrelieved underlying tax in question arises. The obvious meaning to the words to subsection (4)(b) is that eligible unrelieved underlying tax that is carried forward to an accounting period from an earlier period should be relieved before eligible underlying tax that is carried back to that period from a later period. It is unclear whether subsection (4)(b) is intended to have the effect discussed above. Given that the intention is that a company should be free to determine how eligible unrelieved underlying tax should be relieved it would be strange were this intended but this interpretation of the legislation cannot be ruled out. In practice this question in unlikely to arise as in most cases where eligible unrelieved underlying tax arises in an accounting period and there is scope to carry the underlying tax back to an earlier period, a company would generally make a carry back claim.

### Relief for eligible withholding tax

Unrelieved eligible withholding tax can be set against the deemed single dividend from related companies as well as the deemed single dividend from unrelated companies. As noted above, excess eligible underlying tax credit relief has to be set against dividends received from related companies in preference to excess unrelieved withholding tax.[6]

Where a company is not able to relieve all the eligible withholding tax that arises in an accounting period, a company may:

1. elect to carry forward the unrelieved eligible withholding tax to the next accounting period. In such cases the unrelieved eligible withholding tax will be deemed to arise in that next accounting period, whether or not any dividends are received from overseas resident companies in that accounting period. To the extent that the brought forward unrelieved eligible withholding tax remains unrelieved at the end of that next accounting period, the company may elect to carry it forward to the following accounting period (and so on).[7]
2. elect to carry back the unrelieved eligible withholding tax against eligible dividends received from related and unrelated companies in the preceding three years on a later year first basis (or if later, after March 30, 2001[8]). As in the case of unrelieved eligible underlying tax, unrelieved eligible with-

---

[6] *ibid.* s.806C(3)(d), (4)(d), s. 806D(3)(b), (5), s.806F, as inserted by FA 2000, Sched. 30 para. 21(1).

[7] *ibid.* s.806D(5)(b), s.806G, as inserted by FA 2000, Sched. 30 para. 21(1).

[8] FA 2000, Sched. 30 para. 21(2).

holding tax may not be carried back to an earlier accounting period to the extent that this would result in unrelieved foreign tax (whether underlying or withholding tax) arising in that earlier accounting period. Further, where eligible withholding tax is brought forward to an accounting period from a preceding period, such tax is to be set off in precedence to tax carried back to that accounting period from a later accounting period.[9] As in the case of eligible underlying tax it is uncertain whether, if a company is able to carry back eligible withholding tax in accounting period two to accounting period one, but fails to do so, whether this would restrict the amount of eligible withholding tax that a company is able to carry back to period one from (say) period four.[10] The reader is referred to the discussion on this point under relief for eligible underlying tax above.

As in the case of eligible underlying tax, there is no requirement that unrelieved eligible withholding tax should first be relieved against qualifying dividends received in the current accounting period before a carry back claim is made.

### Interest on repayment of tax

Where unrelieved eligible underlying tax or unrelieved eligible withholding tax arising in an accounting period (later period) is carried back to an earlier period by virtue of a claim under the provisions of section 806G of the Taxes Act 1988 and a repayment of tax arises for that earlier period, interest will only start to accrue on the tax repayment after nine months and one day after the end of the later period.[11]

If unrelieved eligible tax arises in an earlier accounting period as a result of a carry back of a trading loss to that period under the provisions of section 393A(1) of the Taxes Act 1988 and the eligible unrelieved tax is carried back to an earlier period as a result of a claim under section 806G of the Taxes Act 1988, interest will only start to accrue on the tax refund obtained as a result of the section 806G claim from 9 months and 1 day after the end of the accounting period in which the trading loss arose.[12]

### Claims

A company is required to make a claim to relieve an amount of eligible underlying tax or eligible withholding tax in the current accounting period or to carry forward or

---

[9] ICTA 1988, ss.806D(5)(c), 806E, 806G, as inserted by FA 2000, Sched. 30 para. 21(1).

[10] The provisions of ICTA 1988, s. 806E(4)(b) also apply to determine the amount of unrelieved eligible withholding tax that may be carried back to an earlier period.

[11] *ibid.* s.826(7BB), (7D), as inserted or amended by FA 2000, Sched. 30 para. 29.

[12] *ibid.* s.826(7A), (7BC), (7D), as inserted or amended by FA 2000, Sched. 30 para. 29.

carry back such tax. The claim must specify the amount of the tax in question which the company wishes to relieve in the current accounting period, or to carry forward or to carry back. A claim must be made before the later of:

1. six years after the end of the accounting period in which the unrelieved eligible underlying tax or unrelieved eligible withholding tax arose; or
2. if later, one year after the end of the accounting period in which the foreign tax in question is paid.[13]

## Surrender of eligible unrelieved foreign tax by one company in a group to another

The onshore pooling measures permit the Board to make provision, by regulation, to enable a company which is a member of a group to surrender all or any part of the amount of the excess eligible underlying tax and excess eligible withholding tax arising in an accounting period to a company which is a member of that group at that time, or throughout the period, prescribed by the regulations. These regulations may:

1. prescribe the conditions which must be satisfied if a surrender is to be made;
2. determine the amount of relievable tax which may be surrendered in any accounting period;
3. prescribe the conditions which must be satisfied if a claim to surrender is to be made;
4. prescribe the consequences for tax purposes if a claim to surrender is made; and
5. allow a claim to be withdrawn and prescribe the effects of such a withdrawal.

The regulations may make different provision for different cases and may contain such supplementary, incidental, consequential, or transitional provisions as the Board may think fit. A company will be treated as a member of a group for these purposes if the conditions prescribed in such regulations are satisfied.[14]

At the time of writing, the draft form of the regulations had yet to be published.

## Planning

Under the pre-Finance Act 2000 regime the advantages of holding non-resident companies via a non-resident holding company were:

---

[13] *ibid.* s.806G, as inserted by FA 2000, Sched. 30 para. 21(1).
[14] *ibid.* s.806H, as inserted by FA 2000, Sched. 30 para. 21(1).

1. it permitted mixing of dividends (see 17–21 of the main text); and
2. it enabled groups to defer paying tax on the proceeds realised from the sale of shares in a non-resident company until such proceeds were remitted to the United Kingdom.

Even after the Finance Act 2000 changes have come into force the advantage in 2. above will still remain. In order to maximise double tax credit relief, however, a group may want either to hold its investments direct (thus losing the tax deferral advantage if the shares in a subsidiary are sold unless the proposed capital gains roll-over relief for a substantial holding in shares in a trading company or in a trading group is introduced); or it will need to ensure that the mixer cap does not apply to any higher level dividends.

Groups with a traditional mixer company may need to re-organise the investments held by such companies in order to ensure that, to the extent that the effective rate of underlying tax attributable to a dividend is less than 30 per cent, the dividend can be treated as a qualifying dividend for onshore pooling purposes (see example at pp. 254–255 above.

For example shares in companies which have an effective tax rate of less than 30 per cent (and are not ADP CFCs) could be held via a separate holding company so that eligible underlying tax and eligible withholding tax may be relieved against such dividends. In practice things will not be straightforward as an overseas company could be subject to a tax rate which is equal to or greater than that of the United Kingdom, but it could have an effective tax rate of less than 30 per cent for an accounting period as a result of, say, accelerated tax depreciation being given on assets, or relief being given for revenue expenditure, which relates to a number of periods, when such expenditure is incurred (and not when it is recognised in the company's accounts).

It should be noted that it may still be possible to achieve a measure of offshore pooling if shares in companies that have an effective tax rate of less than 30 per cent (and which are not CFCs) are held by a company with a high effective tax rate. This is considered further at 17–21 above.

### Onshore pooling for UK branches of non-residents

**17–23B**    The rules discussed at 17–23A above apply in the same way to United Kingdom branches of non-resident companies subject to the following modifications:

1. the reference to an accounting period is taken as a reference to a chargeable period, which is defined in section 832(1) of the Taxes Act 1988 as an accounting period (in the case of corporation tax) or a year of assessment (in the case of income tax);
2. any reference to corporation tax is taken as including a reference to income tax;

3. any reference to section 797 of the Taxes Act 1988 is also taken as a reference to section 796 of that Act (limits on credit: income tax);

4. in the case of income tax, the excess foreign tax is the difference between the overseas tax that qualifies for relief under section 796 of the Taxes Act 1988 and the lower of:

    (a) the amount of the underlying and withholding tax that would be creditable but for the restriction imposed by section 796; and

    (b) the amount that would be relievable were income tax charged on the gross dividend at a rate of 45 per cent.[15]

The provisions apply to dividends arising on or after 31 March 2001 and foreign tax in respect of such dividends.[16]

### Relief for excess foreign tax credit of an overseas branch of a UK resident company

Provisions have been included in the Finance Act 2000 to enable a company to **17–25A** elect to carry forward or to carry back foreign tax that arises in respect of qualifying income from an overseas branch or agency[17] where such tax exceeds the corporation tax payable on that income.[18] Qualifying income is defined as income chargeable under Schedule D Case I, or that is included in the profits of life reinsurance business or overseas life assurance business which is chargeable under Schedule D Case VI by virtue of Section 439B or 441 of the Taxes Act 1988.[19] The excess foreign tax may only be relieved against corporation tax payable on the qualifying income arising from the same branch.[20] These provisions apply to unrelieved foreign tax arising in an accounting period ending on or after April 1, 2000.[21]

Where a company operates via two or more branches in an overseas territory and under the law of that overseas territory, the branches are taxed as a single entity, the branches will be treated as a single entity for these purposes. If a company ceases to trade in an overseas territory via a branch and at a later date, whether in the same accounting period or in a later period, it again begins to trade in that territory via a branch, any unrelieved foreign tax arising in respect of the first branch cannot be

---

[15] *ibid.* s.806K, as inserted by FA 2000, Sched. 30 para. 22(1).

[16] FA 2000, Sched. 30 para. 22(2).

[17] An overseas branch or agency is defined as a branch or agency through which a company carries on a trade in an overseas territory: ICTA 1988, s. 806L(7), as inserted by FA 2000, Sched. 30 para. 23(1).

[18] ICTA 1988, s.806L(1), (4), as inserted by FA 2000, Sched. 30 para. 23(1).

[19] *ibid.* s.806L(5), as inserted by FA 2000, Sched. 30 para. 23(1).

[20] *ibid.* s.806L(2), as inserted by FA 2000, Sched. 30 para. 23(1).

[21] FA 2000, Sched. 30 para. 23(2).

relieved against corporation tax payable on the qualifying income of the second branch.[22]

If a company elects to carry forward excess foreign tax, such tax is treated as if it were foreign tax paid on the qualifying income of the branch in the next accounting period (whether or not the company has any such income). To the extent that such excess tax remains unrelieved at the end of that next accounting period the company can elect to carry it forward to the following accounting period (and so on).[23]

A company may only carry back excess foreign tax to an accounting period which ends on or after April 1, 2000.[24] Where a company elects to carry back excess foreign tax to earlier accounting periods, such tax must first be set off against corporation tax payable on qualifying income of a later period before an earlier period. Further, excess foreign tax which is brought forward to an accounting period takes precedence over excess foreign tax carried back to that accounting period from a later accounting period.[25]

Example

A plc has a branch in Ruritania. For the year ended March 31, 2001 the branch has excess foreign tax of £50,000. In the year to March 31, 2002 there is capacity to absorb £100,000 of excess foreign tax against the corporation tax charge on the profits of the branch. In the year to March 31, 2003, the branch has excess foreign tax of £100,000.

As it is not possible to carry back excess foreign tax to an accounting period ending before April 1, 2000, A plc can only obtain relief for the excess foreign tax arising in the year to March 31, 2001 by electing to carry forward such tax to the year ending March 31, 2002. The excess foreign tax that is brought forward from the year ended March 31, 2001 will set off in precedence to any excess foreign tax which is carried back from the year ended March 31, 2003. Thus it will only be possible for A plc to carry back £50,000 of the £100,000 excess foreign tax that arises in the year to March 31, 2003. The balance of £50,000 arising in that year can only be relieved by the company electing to carry forward such tax for relief against future corporation tax payable on the qualifying income of that branch.

## Time limit for claims

The time limit for a company to make a claim to carry forward or to carry back excess foreign tax arising in respect of an overseas branch is:

---

[22] ICTA 1988, s.806M(2), (3), as inserted by FA 2000, Sched. 30 para. 23(1).
[23] *ibid.* s.806L(1), (2)(a), as inserted by FA 2000, Sched. 30 para. 23(1).
[24] FA 2000, Sched. 30 para. 23(3).
[25] ICTA 1988, s. 806L(2)(b), (3), (6), as inserted by FA 2000, Sched. 30 para. 23(1).

(a) Six years after the end of the accounting period in which the excess foreign tax arose; or

(b) if later, one year after the end of the accounting period in which the foreign tax in question is paid.

A claim must specify the amount (if any) of the unrelieved foreign tax which is to be carried forward to the next accounting period and which is to be carried back to earlier periods.[1]


## Planning

As discussed above, it is not possible to set off unrelieved foreign tax of one branch against another branch. It would be possible for such pooling to be achieved, however, were the activities of the overseas branch to be transferred to a non-resident company. In this case excess tax credit relief attributable to any dividends paid by that non-resident company could be taken into account for onshore pooling purposes (see 17–23A above). Clearly, it would be necessary to consider the wider United Kingdom and foreign tax consequences of a transfer of the branch's activities to a non-resident company before effecting such a reorganisation.


V. Banks and Overseas Lending

*Restrictions on tax credit*

**Page 550 of the seventh edition**     **17–26**

The Double Taxation Relief (Taxes on Income) (Foreign Loan Interest) Regulations (S.I. 1988 No.88) have now been replaced by the Double Taxation Relief (Taxes on Income) (Foreign Interest and Dividends) Regulations S.I. 1999 No. 3330. These are regulations that prescribe the amount that is to be taken into account for the purposes of section 798B(3) of the Taxes Act 1988 as being just and reasonable to attribute to the earning of the foreign interest or foreign dividends and took effect on January 3, 2000. The reader is referred to the Regulations for further information.


**Relief for United Kingdom branches for foreign banks**

The provisions of section 794(2)(c) of the Taxes Act 1988 that are considered at    **17–28**
17–28 of the main text have been repealed by Finance Act 2000 in relation to account-

---

[1] ibid., s.806M(5), (6), (7), as inserted by FA 2000, Sched. 30 para. 23(1).

ing periods ending on or after 21 March 2000.[2] This is because the provision has been superseded following the extension of double tax credit relief to UK branches and agencies of non-residents (see 17–05A above).

## VI. E.U. Law

### Freedom of establishment

**17–33**   Article 59 provides for the abolition of restrictions on the provision of services. In *Safir v. SDL*[3] it was held that a Swedish tax on life premiums paid to non-Swedish companies infringed this Article and was not objectively justifiable.

### Discrimination contrary to Article 6

**17–36**   *Add to footnote 8*: in *Gilly v. DSF* [1998] S.T.C. 1014 it was held that Art. 220 was not of direct effect.

---

[2] FA 2000, Sched. 30 para. 4(6), (14).
[3] [1998] S.T.C. 1043.

CHAPTER 18

# INVESTMENT COMPANIES

## II. Investment Companies

### Definition

*Add to footnote 4*: The Inland Revenue did not appeal the High Court decision    **18–03**
that Westmoreland Investments Limited had not ceased to be an investment company
following the decline in its investment activity when the case was taken to the Court
of Appeal [1998] S.T.C. 1131.

### Expenses of appraising take-over target: *Hibernian Insurance*

The Revenue is citing a recent decision of the Supreme Court of Ireland[1] as author-   **18–10A**
ity for disallowing the expenses of appraising a possible take-over target. The Irish
legislation is in all material respects the same, and the decision was reached after an
examination of the United Kingdom authorities on management expenses. In such
circumstances the decision is of persuasive authority, but is not binding on any United
Kingdom body of Commissioners.

The Supreme Court consists of three Justices. Reasoned decisions were given by
only two members of the Court: Barron and Murphy J. J.

The facts of the case were that Hibernian Group plc was the holding company of
group of insurance companies. In the periods in question Group explored the possibility of acquiring by purchase three further subsidiaries. In the course of evaluating the

---

[1] *Hibernian Insurance Co. Ltd v. Macuimis (HMIT)*. Judgment was given on January 20, 2000.
The case is not yet reported.

possible purchases, Group incurred costs in obtaining advice from accountants, lawyers and investment bankers. In events, none of the three companies was purchased.

The issue was whether the costs were incurred as "expenses of management". In the Courts below it had been held that the costs were not allowable on the ground that they represented capital expenditure. Barron J. held that the distinction between capital and revenue expenditure was not relevant in the case a taxpayer who was not taxed as trader. Murphy J. held that under the Irish legislation corresponding to section 9 of the Taxes Act, income for the purposes of Irish corporation tax fell to be computed in accordance with "income tax principles", and that those principles precluded the deduction of capital expenditure. It is submitted that this is fallacous: income tax principles are not universal: they vary according to the class of income under consideration. Management expenses have no counterpart in income tax law and there are no relevant income tax principles to apply. It is considered that Barron J. is correct on this point.

Both members of the Court agreed that the costs in question were not expenses of management because they were analogous to the stamp duty and brokerage in *Sun Life, i.e.* were part of the cost of the investment. Murphy J. said:

> Unquestionably the Respondent is correct in saying that different judges, and in particular Lord Reid in the Sun Life Assurance Case, had referred to the severability of certain items from the cost of the purchase. Other judges spoke of "*divorcing*" particular sums from the price paid or the amount received when changes took place in the investments of a taxpayer company. There is no doubt that such distinctions can be made. In fact it must be possible to identify a variety of phases between the stage when one company considers the desirability acquiring all of or a substantial share holding in another company and the ultimate completion of such an acqusition. The question arises, however, as to why one should classify differently work of the same character but carried on in different phases or stages such an acqusition. Undoubtedly, the Group is entitled to pray in aid the observations of Lord Reid both as to the severability and deductibility of the costs incurred in relation to such activities. The other judges in the Sun Life Assurance Case placed a different emphasis on the relationship between expenditure and acquisition. Their views might be summarised by saying that a particular expenditure could not consitute an expense of management if it formed an "*integral part*" of the acquisition of an asset. Whilst taxes and duties imposed on transactions are inescapably associated with such transaction and professional advice in relation thereto are, in theory at any rate, optional, it would be impossible in practice to suggest that the legal costs of, say, investigating the title to land the subject matter of a contract for sale or professional advice in relation to a "*due diligence*" investigation for a take over could be dispensed with. Indeed the Appelants would not suggest otherwise. The argument on their behalf is that such costs and expenses are deductible when incurred before the decision to purchase but not if incurred after it. In my view such a decision cannot change the nature of the service provided. If a purchase were completed I do not doubt

that it would be universally accepted that all of the costs incurred in relation to the exploration, evaluation and investigation of the company to be acquired, would be *"cost of the purchase"*.

It is submitted that here the learned Justice has lost sight of the statutory issue. It is surely plain the costs incurred in enabling the management to reach *a decision of management* viz. whether to make an investment, is an expense of management. The fact that the costs may also be classed as an incidental cost of the purchase (if the purchase is made) is neither here nor there. The point about the stamp duty in *Sun Life* was that it was not a "matter of management" (in Lord Reid's phrase), whereas consideration of due diligence report is a "matter of management". In the respectful view of the authors, the Supreme Court's decision is wrong.

# CHAPTER 19

# COMPANIES IN PARTNERSHIP

## II. COMPANY PARTNERSHIPS

### Company partners

**19–08**     The practice as to the taxation of loan relationships set out in paragraph 19-08 is restated in SP 4/98. That Statement also confirms that:

(a) group treatment cannot apply where a loan is transferred between a partnership and a member;

(b) a change in profit sharing ratios does not give rise to a "related transaction";

(c) a corporate partnership is not a "company" for the purposes of the connected persons rules.

CHAPTER 20

# INVESTMENT TRUSTS, VENTURE CAPITAL TRUSTS, UNIT TRUSTS AND OPEN-ENDED INVESTMENT COMPANIES

III. VENTURE CAPITAL TRUSTS

## Tax reliefs

*Add to footnote 6*: Tax credits ceased to be recoverable from April 6, 1999: S.I. 1999 No. 819 which amended S.I. 1995 No. 1979.  **20–07**

*Add to footnote 8*: The Inland Revenue has issued a revised Statement of Practice (SP 6/98) which replaces SP 3/94. The revised Statement contains no significant changes.

## Venture capital trust: definition

An amendment has been made to the definition of eligible shares in the Finance  **20–10**
Act 1999. This amendment permits shares which are received under a share for share exchange to be treated as eligible shares provided certain conditions are satisfied, including that the reorganisation was effected for bona fide commercial purposes.[1] The provisions of Schedule 28B to the Taxes Act 1988 have also been amended to permit shares issued to a VCT as a result of the exercise by it of conversion rights attached to shares or securities which it held to be treated as eligible shares provided certain conditions are satisfied.[2]

---

[1] See ICTA 1988, Sched. 28B, para. 10C (as inserted by FA 1999, s.69) for details of the relevant conditions.

[2] *ibid.* para. 10D (as inserted by FA 1999, s.69) for details of the relevant conditions.

*Add to footnote 23*: SP 2/94 has been replaced by SP 7/98 with effect from April 5, 1998. The wording of the new Statement of Practice is very similar to that which it replaces.

**20–11**    *Add to footnote 8*: The Inland Revenue has issued a revised Statement of Practice (SP5/98). The content of the revised statement is broadly similar to the earlier statement and it contains no significant changes.

CHAPTER 21

# GROUPS, SUBSIDIARIES AND CONSORTIA: AN OVERVIEW

## I. INTRODUCTION

Schedule 2 to the Finance Act 1999 has altered the tests for membership of a VAT   **21–03**
group so that bodies corporate are now eligible to be treated as members of a VAT
group if they are:

(i) each established or have fixed establishments in the United Kingdom; and

(ii) one of them controls each of the others or a person or partnership of individuals controls each of them.

For this purpose, a body corporate controls another body corporate if it is empowered by statute to control that body's activities or it is that body's holding company for company law purposes. An individual or partnership controls a body corporate if it would be that body's holding company if he or they were a company.[1]

**21–04 Replace Table on Pages 623–624 of the seventh edition with the following**

|   |   | *Description* | *Basic Test for Entitlement* | *Statutory Reference* | *Text* |
|---|---|---|---|---|---|
| 1. | Group Income | (i) before April 6 1999, enabled dividends to be paid without ACT; (ii) now enables charges on income and interest to be paid without deducting income tax | 51% of ordinary share capital, profits available for distribution and surplus assets on a winding-up; paying company, recipient company and parent must all be U.K. resident; shares held in non-resident companies and shares held as trading stock disregarded. | ss.247, 248 ICTA 1988 | Chapter 25 |

---

[1] VATA 1994, s.43A, as substituted by FA 1999, Sched. 2, para. 2.

273

| | | Description | Basic Test for Entitlement | Statutory Reference | Text |
|---|---|---|---|---|---|
| 2. | Distributions | (i) enables assets to be transferred between a subsidiary and another shareholder member of the group at other than market value without a distribution occurring. (ii) extended meaning of distribution "in respect of shares" for 90% groups | (i) 51% of ordinary share capital; subsidiary, shareholder and common parent must all be U.K. resident; shares held in non-resident companies and shares held as trading stock disregarded. | s.209(5), (7), s.254(2), (3), ICTA 1988 | Chapter 11 |
| 3. | Reconstruction without change of ownership | enables (i) successor to trade to take over predecessor's capital allowance position (ii) successor to trade to utilise predecessor's surplus trading losses | 75% common ownership; successor, predecessor and common owners need not be U.K. resident; common owners need not be bodies corporate | ss.343, 344 ICTA 1988 | Chapter 29 |
| 4. | Group relief | enables trading losses and certain other reliefs of one group member to be surrendered to another group member | 75% of ordinary share capital, profits available for distribution and surplus assets on a winding-up; shares held as trading stock disregarded; for accounting periods ending before April 1, 2000 (subject to E.U. law arguments), the parent company, surrendering company and claimant company had to be U.K. resident and group relationship could not be traced through non-resident companies; for accounting periods ending after March 31, 2000 claimant company and surrendering company must be within the charge to U.K. corporation tax. | ss.402–413; Scheds 17, 18 ICTA 1988, Sched. 18 FA 1998. | Chapter 22 |
| 5. | Surrender of ACT (accounting periods beginning before April 6, 1999) | enables a parent company to surrender advance corporation tax to its subsidiaries | 51% of ordinary share capital, profits available for distribution and surplus assets on a winding-up; both parent and subsidiary must be U.K. resident; shares held as trading stock disregarded. | s.240; Sched. 18 ICTA 1988 | — |
| 6. | Shadow ACT Group | applies for the purpose of determining the ability of a company with surplus ACT to recover that ACT | 51% of ordinary share capital, profits available for distribution and surplus assets on a winding-up; both parent and subsidiary must be U.K. resident; shareholdings via overseas companies are disregarded. | S.I. 1999 No. 358 reg. 6 | Chapter 12A (see supplement) |

| | | Description | Basic Test for Entitlement | Statutory Reference | Text |
|---|---|---|---|---|---|
| 7. | Chargeable Gains Group | enables<br>(i) one group member to transfer assets to another group member on a tax-free basis<br>(ii) one group member to roll over a gain on a disposal of an asset into expenditure by another group member | 75% of ordinary share capital and 51% of profits available for distribution and surplus assets on a winding-up.<br>For transfers pre-April 1, 2000, both group members and parent had to be U.K. resident; group relationship could be traced through non-resident companies.<br><br>For transfers on or after April 1, 2000, requirement for the holding company, the transferor and the transferee company to be U.K. resident removed and only requirement is that the asset remains a chargeable asset following the transfer. | ss.170, 171, 175 TCGA 1992. | Chapter 23 |
| 8. | Loan Relationships | enables asset and liability loan relationships to be transferred without giving rise to debits or credits | As for chargeable gains groups. The revised definition of a chargeable gains group applies for transfers on or after April 1, 2000. | Para. 12, Sched. 9 FA 1996 | Chapter 3 |
| 9. | VAT Group | enables supplies of goods and services to be made free of VAT within the group | Common control; each company satisfies one of the following conditions:<br>(i) it is established in the UK; or<br>(ii) it has a fixed establishment in the U.K.<br>(This change took effect from July 27, 1999 following an amendment in FA 1999.) | ss.43–43C VATA 1994 | — |
| 10. | Stamp Duty | enables<br>(i) an asset to be transferred between group members free of stamp duty<br>(ii) a lease to be granted between group members free of stamp duty | 75% of ordinary share capital, profits available for distribution and surplus assets on a winding-up; none of relevant companies need be U.K. resident. | s.42 FA 1930, s.27 FA 1967; s.151 FA 1995 | Chapter 30 |

| | | Description | Basic Test for Entitlement | Statutory Reference | Text |
|---|---|---|---|---|---|
| 11. | Surrender of company tax refund | enables a tax refund owing to one group member to be set against tax owing for the same period by another group member | 75% ordinary share capital, profits available for distribution and surplus assets on a winding-up. For accounting periods ending before April 1, 2000, both parties to surrender and common parent had to be U.K. resident and shares held in non-resident companies and shares held as trading stock were disregarded.<br><br>For accounting periods ending on or after April 1, 2000 requirement that the common parent company and the transferor and transferee company must be U.K. resident has been removed and group can be traced through non-resident companies. Shares held as trading stock are still disregarded. | s.102 FA 1989 | Chapter 4 |

## II. Subsidiaries

### Ordinary share capital

*Non-cumulative preference shares*

**21–06**     Ordinary share capital comprises all the issued share capital of a company, other than capital the holders of which have a right to a dividend at a fixed rate but have no other right to share in the profits of the company.[2] Fixed rate preference shares will not, therefore, generally be ordinary share capital. The Inland Revenue, however, are understood to consider that non-cumulative fixed rate preference shares do not carry a *right* to a dividend at a fixed rate and are therefore ordinary share capital.

The Revenue argue that the dividend on a non-cumulative preference share is effectively variable because if there are insufficient distributable profits in any accounting period it will never be paid. In contrast, if there are insufficient distributable profits in any accounting period to pay the dividend on a cumulative preference share the

---

[2] ICTA 1988, s.832(1).

dividend is paid as soon as later profits allow, suggesting that the dividend is merely deferred. The authors do not find this line of argument entirely convincing. The dividend on a cumulative preference share will only ever be paid if there are eventually sufficient distributable profits. The argument confuses the right of the shareholder with the question of whether the right can be satisfied. It is considered that in testing the rights of a shareholder it has to be assumed that the company has sufficient distributable profits to satisfy them.

In *South Shore Mutual Insurance Co Ltd v. Blair*[3] it was held that a company limited by guarantee had no "issued share capital" and hence no "ordinary share capital". Accordingly, it could not be a member of a group for the purposes of group relief.

---

[3] [1999] S.T.C. (S.C.D.) 296.

CHAPTER 22

# GROUP RELIEF

II. GROUP CLAIMS

### Residence

**22–04**     The restrictions on residence that are discussed in 22–04 of the main work ceased to apply from the start of an accounting period ending on or after 1 April 2000.[1] As a result of these amendments it is possible for companies to be treated as being in a group relief group where there is no common UK resident holding company, so long as each company is a 75 percent subsidiary of a common parent company (wherever that company is resident), and it is also possible to trace a group through non-resident companies. Further, it is now possible for group relief to be claimed from and surrendered to a United Kingdom branch of a non-resident company, subject to certain restrictions in the case of the surrender of losses by the branch (see section 22–04A below). Finally, the definition of a company for the purposes of group relief has been changed to include any body corporate. Where a company is treated as being in a group relief group as a result of the Finance Act 2000 reforms, and its first accounting period ending after 31 March 2000 'straddles' 1 April 2000, it can only claim or

---

[1] FA 2000, Sched.27 paras 2, 6(4).

surrender group relief in respect of that part of its accounting period which falls after 1 April 2000.[2]

Example 1

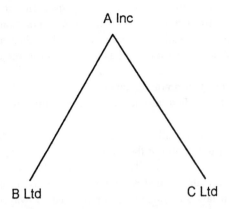

A Inc is a US resident company and B Ltd and C Ltd are both UK resident companies. The group has a calendar year end. Claims for group relief may be made between B Ltd and C Ltd from the accounting period which ended on 31 December 2000 and subsequent accounting periods. Neither company, however, could claim or surrender group relief in respect of the period to 31 March 2000 since, as discussed above, the changes to the definition of a group relief group only took effect from 1 April 2000.

## United Kingdom branches of non-resident companies

Following amendments introduced in the Finance Act 2000, it is now possible for **22–04A** group relief claims and surrenders to be made between a UK branch of a non-resident company and a United Kingdom resident company in the same worldwide group.[3] This amendment applies for accounting periods ending on or after 1 April 2000.[4] Where an accounting period of a non-resident company 'straddles' 1 April 2000, it may only make claims for or surrenders of group relief in respect of its United Kingdom branch for the portion of the branch's accounting period that falls on or after 1 April 2000.[5]

---

[2] FA 2000, Sched. 27 para. 6(1) which provides that the Finance Act 2000 amendments do not apply for the purpose of determining whether the qualifying conditions of ICTA 1988, s. 403A(9) were met at any time before 1 April 2000.

[3] ICTA 1988, s.402(3A), (3B), as inserted by FA 2000, Sched. 27 para.1.

[4] FA 2000, Sched. 27 para. 6(4).

[5] FA 2000, Sched. 27 para. 6(1).

It is only possible for group relief to be claimed from a United Kingdom branch of a non-resident company to the extent that the losses, or other amounts eligible to be surrendered as group relief, relate to activities in respect of which the company is within the charge to corporation tax for the accounting period in question and are not attributable to activities from which it is exempt from corporation tax for that accounting period by virtue of any double tax arrangements.[6] It is then only possible for such losses or other amounts to be surrendered as group relief to the extent that:

1. such losses or other amounts; and/or
2. amounts that are taken into account in computing such losses or amounts,

are not deductible or otherwise allowable in computing the taxable profits (other than UK branch profits) for any period of the company or any other person for any foreign tax purposes.[7] Where the deductibility of the loss under foreign law depends on whether it is deductible under United Kingdom law, the loss is assumed to be deductible under the foreign law and cannot be surrendered by way of group relief.[8] The restriction on the surrender of the branch's losses by way of group relief only applies to the extent that the profits against which such losses or other amounts are deductible, or are otherwise allowable, are not taken into account in computing the United Kingdom taxable profits of such persons.[9]

Since the legislation refers to such losses being deductible in **any** period, the restriction still applies if the loss is not relieved against the non-United Kingdom profits of the non-resident company or of any other non-resident company in the accounting period in which it is incurred, for example because there are insufficient taxable profits to absorb the loss, so long as the loss is eligible to be carried forward in the overseas territory in question for relief against the future taxable profits of the non-resident company, or of the non-resident group. For example, in the United States the profits of a group are determined on a consolidated basis and carried forward net operating losses can be relieved against the consolidated profits of the companies that are treated as being members of the United States group. The authors have confirmed with the Inland Revenue that this is also its interpretation of this provision.

Foreign tax is defined as tax chargeable under the law of a territory outside the United Kingdom which corresponds to United Kingdom income tax or corporation tax and the definition also includes local taxes, for example United States State and City taxes.[10] A loss will not be treated as deductible or otherwise allowable

---

[6] ICTA 1988, s.403D(1)(a), (b), as inserted by FA 2000, Sched. 27, para. 4. Where the exemption from tax under a double tax treaty is dependent on a claim being made, the requirement for a claim to be made is disregarded for these purposes: ICTA 1988, s.403D(10).

[7] ICTA 1988, s.403D(1)(c), as inserted by FA 2000, Sched. 27 para. 4. See Inland Revenue Tax Bulletin Issue 49 (October 2000) for examples of the application of this rule.

[8] *ibid.* s.403D(6), as inserted by FA 2000, Sched. 27 para. 4.

[9] *ibid.*, s.403D (3), as inserted by FA 2000, Sched. 27, para. 4.

[10] ICTA 1988, s.403D(9), as inserted by FA 2000, Sched. 27, para 4.

against non-United Kingdom profits if the profits of the United Kingdom branch are excluded in computing the taxable profits of the non-United Kingdom resident company.[11] Some territories, for example, France do not generally tax the profits of overseas branches.

The effect of the above limitations is that a non-resident company will only be able to surrender losses as group relief where the losses of its United Kingdom branch are excluded in computing the taxable profits of the company or of the overseas group in the territory in which it is resident for tax purposes. Not all EU territories exclude profits of an overseas branch from tax and in such cases United Kingdom branches of companies that are resident in such territories will not be able to surrender losses as group relief to other United Kingdom branches of non-resident companies in the same worldwide group, or to United Kingdom resident subsidiaries of the common parent company, unless it is clear at the time of the group relief claim that the loss can never be used against non-U.K. profits. It is not sufficient that relief available overseas is not in fact claimed.[11a] It is understood that where the carry forward of a loss expires in a foreign jurisdiction without there being any profits against which the loss could have been set, group relief will be available in the United Kingdom. Where a United Kingdom branch loss forms part of a non-resident company's loss and some part of the non-resident company's loss is used against non-U.K. profits, no group relief will be available even if the part off set is less than the loss of the non-resident company's activities outside the United Kingdom.

The provisions of section 403D of the Taxes Act 1988 were introduced following the decision in *Imperial Chemical Industries plc v Colmer*[12] in order to comply with EU law. An EU resident company that is resident in another Member State that does not exempt the profits of an overseas branch from tax in that territory would only be able to claim against the government of the United Kingdom on the basis of the freedom of establishment and non-discrimination principles in Articles 43 (formerly 52) and 48 (formerly 58) of the EU Treaty if it could establish that the tax treatment afforded to it in the United Kingdom was less favourable than that afforded to United Kingdom resident companies. No doubt with such challenges in mind, restrictions were introduced by Finance Act 2000 on the ability of a United Kingdom resident company to surrender losses suffered by an overseas branch, to the extent that such losses could be taken into account in computing the overseas taxable profits of a company that is resident in the same territory in which the branch is operating (see 22–05A below).

Where a UK branch of a non-resident company claims losses and other amounts eligible for surrender as group relief from another company in its group or from a consortium company, in determining its total profits for the purposes of sections 403A and 403C of the Taxes Act 1988, any amounts that are not taken into account in

---

[11] ICTA 1988, s.403D(5), as inserted by FA 2000, Sched. 27, para.4.
[11a] Inland Revenue Tax Bulletin, Issue 49, October 2000.
[12] [1998] S.T.C. 874.

computing the chargeable profits[13] of the branch for corporation tax purposes, or which relate to amounts arising from activities in respect of which the company is exempt from corporation tax for that accounting period by virtue of the provisions of a double tax agreement, are disregarded.[14] Where the exemption from United Kingdom tax is dependent on a claim being made by the non-resident company, the requirement for a claim to be made is disregarded.[15]

*E.U. law*

**22–05**    The Inland Revenue issued a Press Release on February 26, 1999 announcing how they would deal with open corporation tax cases following the European Court's decision in *Imperial Chemicals Industries plc v. Colmer*.[15a]

The Inland Revenue stated that they now accepted that the existence of a group or consortium could be established by reference to a company or companies resident in the E.U. or the European Economic Area. They therefore accepted that group relief could be surrendered between two United Kingdom resident direct subsidiaries of an E.U./EEA parent company.

Similarly, the Revenue accepted that a consortium company could be owned by a combination of United Kingdom resident and E.U./EEA resident companies, and, where this was the case, that consortium relief could be surrendered by the United Kingdom resident members of the consortium to the consortium company and vice versa.

Finally, the Inland Revenue accepted that in the following example consortium relief would be available between the United Kingdom resident companies:

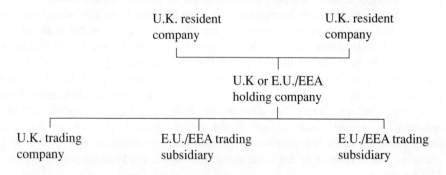

---

[13] "Chargeable profits" are not defined in ICTA 1988, s.403D and therefore the definition in ICTA 1988, s. 11(2) applies. In essence the chargeable profits of a United Kingdom branch of a non-resident company are its income and chargeable gains in respect of which it is chargeable to corporation tax.

[14] ICTA 1988, s.403D(2), as inserted by FA 2000, Sched. 27 para. 4. The ICTA 1988 s.11(2) definition of chargeable profits applies, i.e., the income and gains which are included in computing the company's liability to corporation tax.

[15] ICTA 1988, s.403D(10), as inserted by FA 2000, Sched. 27 para. 4.

[15a] [1998] S.T.C. 874.

The above was given legislative effect as a result of amendments to the group relief legislation that were introduced by the Finance Act 2000. The Inland Revenue also decided to extend group relief to United Kingdom branches of non-resident companies, though the ability of such branches to surrender losses is restricted. These changes are discussed at 22–04, 22–04A, and 22–05A of this supplement.

### Overseas branches of United Kingdom resident companies

As a quid pro quo for permitting United Kingdom branches of non-resident companies **22–05A** to claim and surrender losses and other amounts as group relief, a United Kingdom resident company is not permitted to surrender losses and other amounts available for surrender as group relief to the extent that:

1. such amounts are attributable to a branch or agency through which it carries on a trade in another territory; and
2. under the law of the territory in which the branch or agency is situated, the whole or any part of the loss or other amount is deductible or is otherwise allowable in any period against the non-United Kingdom profits of another person (for example where a loss suffered by the branch is included in computing the consolidated tax liability of an overseas group of companies, as can happen in the United States).[16]

For these purposes the loss or other amount that is attributable to an overseas branch is calculated as if the branch were a stand alone entity and by reference to the principles that are used to determine the equivalent losses, or other amounts eligible for surrender as group relief, of a United Kingdom branch of a non-resident company.[17]

Where the deductibility of any amount for foreign tax purposes is dependent on whether or not the amount, or a corresponding amount, is deductible for United Kingdom purposes, the restriction on the surrender of losses only applies if the United Kingdom resident company is treated as being resident in the overseas territory under the tax law of the relevant overseas territory.[18] The effect of this provision is that in such cases it will be possible for a company to group relieve the losses and other amounts eligible for surrender of an overseas branch without the restriction in section 403E of the Taxes Act 1988 applying, unless the company is a dual resident company.

---

[16] ICTA 1988, s.403E (1)-(3),(6), as inserted by FA 2000, Sched. 27 para. 4. See Inland Revenue Tax Bulletin, Issue 49, October 2000 for examples of the operation of this provision. The question of whether losses are deductible from non-U.K. profits is decided without hypothesising entities and structures that do not exist at the time of the claim.

[17] ICTA 1988, s.403E(4), (5), as inserted by FA 2000, Sched. 27 para. 4.

[18] ICTA 1988, s.403E(8), as inserted by FA 2000, Sched. 27 para. 4.

### III. Consortium Claims

**Insert new paragraph at the end of section 22–19 on page 650.**—In the light of the guidance on the scope of EU law given in the European Court's judgment, the House of Lords concluded that CAHH did not qualify as a holding company as the majority of its trading subsidiaries were not EU resident.[19] As noted at 22–15 above, this decision was reversed with effect for accounting periods ending on or after 1 April 2000 by the Finance Act 2000.[20]

### Definitions

#### *"Trading Company"*

22–24  In an article in the Tax Bulletin[21] the Inland Revenue have set out their view on when consortium companies established to carry out projects under the private finance initiative qualify as trading companies. Commonly, the body commissioning the project grants a lease to the consortium company. That company develops the land, leases it back to the public sector body and contracts to provide fully serviced accommodation for a unitary charge. To the extent that it reflects the provision of land, the unitary charge is taxed under Schedule A and to the extent that it reflects the provision of services it is taxed under Schedule D Case I.

The question which arises is whether the consortium company is a trading company so that it can surrender tax losses to the consortium members. That depends on whether the business of the company consists wholly or mainly in the carrying on of a trade or trades.[22] The Inland Revenue consider that the fact that a significant part of the company's income, or even the majority, is taxed under Schedule A is not fatal to the claim that the company is a trading company. The test is a factual test. Is the main activity of the company trading? It is necessary to look not only at the level of income from each of the company's activities but also to consider how the company's resources (such as management time, capital employed) have been used.

22–25  The amendments to the group relief legislation that are discussed at section 22–04 of this supplement apply equally for the purposes of consortium relief. Whilst the test for a company to be treated as a holding company of a consortium remains that the company's business must consist wholly or mainly in the holding of

---

[19] [1999] S.T.C. 1089.
[20] FA 2000, Sched. 27 paras 1, 2, 6.
[21] October 1999, page 696.
[22] ICTA 1988, s.413(3).

shares or securities of trading companies that are its 90% subsidiaries[23], it is no longer necessary for the holding company, or the majority of its trading subsidiaries, to be UK or even EU resident, or to be trading in the United Kingdom through a branch or agency in the case of a non-resident company.[24] (This change reverses the House of Lords decision in *Imperial Chemicals Industries plc v. Colmer* [1999] S.T.C. 1089—see section 22–20 of this supplement). The amendment applies for accounting periods ending on or after 1 April 2000.[25] Where an accounting period of a non-resident company 'straddles' 1 April 2000, that company will only be able to claim or surrender consortium relief in respect of that portion of its accounting period which falls on or after 1 April 2000.[1]

Example 2

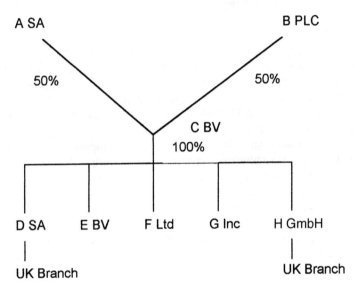

A SA is a French incorporated and resident company and B PLC is a U.K. incorporated and resident company. The two companies each hold a 50% interest in C BV, a Dutch resident holding company of a trading group. C BV does not have any U.K. operations. C BV's subsidiaries are as follows:-

---

[23] ICTA 1988, s.413(3)(b).
[24] The provisions of ICTA 1988, s.413(5) which previously restricted group relief to UK resident companies were repeated by FA 2000 Sched.27, para. 2(2).
[25] FA 2000, Sched.27 para.6(4).
[1] FA 2000, Sched.27 para.6(1) which provides that the FA 2000, will not have effect for the purpose of determining whether the qualifying conditions in ICTA 1988, s.403A(9) were met at any time before 1 April 2000.

D SA, a company that is incorporated and resident in France. This company has a U.K. branch.

E BV, a company that is incorporated and resident in the Netherlands. It is not trading in the U.K. through a branch or agency.

F Ltd, a U.K. resident and incorporated in the U.K.

G Inc, a U.S. resident company which is not trading in the U.K. through a branch or agency.

H GmbH, a German resident and incorporated company which has a U.K. branch.

In this example B PLC could claim or surrender consortium relief to or from any or all of F Ltd and the U.K. branches of D SA and H GmbH.[2]

The amount of any losses that could be surrendered by F Ltd or the UK branches of D SA and H GmbH to B PLC would be restricted by the amount of losses that could be claimed as group relief by the companies within the BV group that are eligible to claim group relief, i.e. F Ltd, and the UK branches of D SA and H GmbH (see 22–78 of the main work for further discussion on this latter restriction).

While the above amendments apply to all companies, wherever resident, from the start of a company's first accounting period that ended on or after 1 April 2000, in the case of EU resident companies the changes took effect for all open cases at 26 February 1999 on the basis of an Inland Revenue Press Release issued on that day following the European Court's decision in *Imperial Chemical Industries plc v. Colmer*.[3] In this Press Release the Inland Revenue stated that it accepted that the existence of a group or consortium can be established by reference to companies resident in the EU or European Economic Area. Under the Pre-Finance Act 2000 practice, however, it was necessary for a company to be UK resident in order to claim or surrender losses as group relief (although this restriction is open to question in the light of the European Court's decision in *Saint Gobain v Finanzamt Aachen-Innenstadt*).[4]

## Link Company

The provisions of section 406 of the Taxes Act 1988 were not amended by Finance Act 2000. This means that in order for a consortium company to be able

---

[2] Both France and Germany exclude the profits of an overseas branch in determining the taxable profits of a resident company. Thus the restriction in ICTA 1988, s.403D(1)(c) will not apply (see 22–04 above).

[3] 1998] S.T.C. 874.

[4] [2000] S.T.C. 854.

to claim or surrender losses and other expenses as group relief from or to companies in the same group as the consortium member, that member (link company)
must either be a United Kingdom resident company or must be carrying on a
trade in the United Kingdom through a branch or agency. This is because a
company that is a member of the same group as the link company can only claim
or surrender group relief from or to a consortium company if the link company
can claim or surrender group relief from or to the consortium company and its
subsidiaries[5] and because, under the revised provisions of section 402, a company
can only claim or surrender group relief where it is resident in the United Kingdom
or is carrying on a trade in the United Kingdom through a branch or agency.[6] It
is doubtful whether this requirement complies with E.U. law.

Example 3

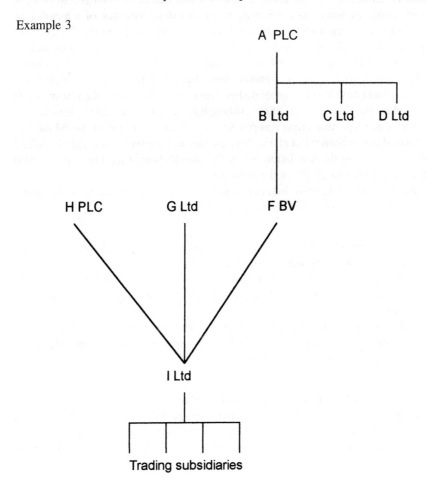

---

[5] ICTA 1988, s.406(2).
[6] ICTA 1988, s.402(3A), (3B), as inserted by FA 2000 Sched. 27 para. 1.

H PLC, G Ltd and F BV are all equal shareholders in I Ltd which is the holding company of a trading group. Unless F BV has a U.K. branch, the companies in the A PLC group that are eligible to claim or surrender group relief will not be able to claim or surrender group relief from or to companies in the I Ltd group. Where the link company is E.U. resident, as in this example, the authors consider that consortium relief should be available under E.U. law.

### Share of a consortium member

**22–27**    The "double restriction" of the amount of losses that can be surrendered to or by a consortium company where its accounting period overlaps with that of a member of the consortium has been addressed by an amendment introduced in the Finance Act 2000 that is deemed always to have had effect. Essentially the provisions of section 413(7) to (9) of the Taxes Act 1988 that set out the restrictions on consortium relief before the Finance (No2) Act 1997 amendments, have now been repealed with retrospective effect and have been incorporated in a revised section 403C, the text of which was inserted by the Finance Act 2000.[7] Although the Finance Act 2000 measures are stated to have retrospective effect[8], in practice few, if any, companies should have to submit revised consortium relief claims because this was the basis on which the Inland Revenue was applying the legislation before the introduction of the Finance Act 2000 amendments as noted in 22–27 of the main work.

A member's share in a consortium in relation to an overlapping period of the surrendering company is the lowest of the following percentages:

1. the percentage of the ordinary share capital of the surrendering or claimant company that is beneficially owned by that member;
2. the percentage to which that member is beneficially entitled of any profits available for distribution to equity holders of the surrendering or claimant company; and
3. the percentage to which that member would be beneficially entitled of any assets of the surrendering or claimant company available for distribution to its equity holders on a winding up.

Where any of these percentages fluctuates during an overlapping period, an average for the whole period is taken. The average taken is a weighted average rather than a flat average, so that a major change in the share of the consortium member towards the end of the overlapping period will not unduly distort the

---

[7] FA 2000, s.100.
[8] *ibid.* s.101(5).

result.[9] Where the surrendering or claimant company is a subsidiary of a holding company owned by the consortium, the percentage rules apply to the interests of the members in the holding company instead of in the surrendering or claimant company.

The result of these rules is that where the members of the consortium each **22–28** have a different percentage share in the ordinary share capital, profits and assets, not all the losses of the consortium company may be surrendered by way of consortium relief. Suppose that A Ltd, B Ltd and C Ltd own D Ltd and their shares are as follows:

|  | A Ltd | B Ltd | C Ltd |
|---|---|---|---|
| Ordinary share capital | 40% | 30% | 30% |
| Profits | $33\frac{1}{3}\%$ | $33\frac{1}{3}\%$ | $33\frac{1}{3}\%$ |
| Assets on a winding up | 25% | 50% | 25% |

Their shares in the consortium would be limited to A Ltd - 25 per cent; B Ltd - 30%; and C Ltd - 25%. If D Ltd had reliefs available to surrender, only 25% could be surrendered to each of A Ltd and C Ltd and 30% to B Ltd. The remaining 20% could not be surrendered by way of consortium relief.

## IV Shedule 18: Equity Entitlement

### Defintions

*"Fixed-rate preference shares"*

The Inland Revenue consider that non-cumulative preference shares cannot be fixed **22–33** rate preference shares because the fact that the non-cumulative dividend will not be paid in any accounting period in which profits are insufficient makes the right to the dividend effectively variable. For the reasons given in paragraph 21-06 of this supplement, it is considered that the Inland Revenue's argument is incorrect.

---

[9] The predecessor provisions of ICTA 1988, s.413(8),(9) operated on a weighted average basis as noted in footnote 6 on page 652 of the main work. The authors have confirmed with the Inland Revenue that the same principles will be applicable to the provision in its revised form.

*"Normal commercial loan"*

**22–34**  **page 656 point 3: Substitute the following for cases where the provisions of paragraph 1(5) of Schedule 18 to the Taxes Act are applied for times after (but not before) 1 April 2000:**

3. in respect of which the loan creditor is entitled, on repayment, to an amount which either does not exceed the new consideration lent or is reasonably comparable with the amount generally repayable under the terms of issue of securities listed on a recognised stock exchange.[9a]

**(b) Interest reducing if business improves**

**22–36**  Despite the rule that a loan is not a normal commercial loan if the amount of interest to which the lender is entitled depends to any extent on the results of the company's business or any part of it, a loan is still a normal commercial loan if its terms provide for the interest to reduce if there is an improvement in the results of the company's business.[10] As noted in the main text, the Inland Revenue used to consider that provisions in such loans for the interest rate to revert to the original rate if there was a subsequent deterioration in the company's business did not prevent paragraph 1(5E) of Schedule 18 to the Taxes Act 1988 applying to treat the loan as a normal commercial loan. The Inland Revenue's practice changed after the publication of the main text and it considered that, if a loan provided for a reduction in the interest rate if business results improve, with a reversion of the interest rate if the business subsequently deteriorates, the loan was not a normal commercial loan for the purposes of paragraph 1(1)(b) of Schedule 18.

This issue has been resolved by an amendment to the provisions of paragraph 1(5) of Schedule 18 to the Taxes Act 1988 which was introduced by the Finance Act 2000. Following this amendment, a loan will not be prevented from being treated as a normal commercial loan if it provides for the rate of interest to be increased in the event of the results of the company's business or any part of it deteriorating, or in the event of the value of any of the company's assets diminishing.[11] This amendment applies for the purposes of determining whether a loan is a normal commercial loan for the purposes of paragraph 1(1)(b) of Schedule 18 at any time on or after 21 March 2000.

*"Quoted parent company"*

**22–43**  Footnote 8 refers to scientific research allowances. These have now been renamed "research and development allowances".[12]

---

[9a] ICTA 1988, Sched. 18 para. 1(5), as amended by FA 2000 Sched. 27 paras 5(2) and 6(3).
[10] ICTA 1988, Sched 18 para. 1(5E).
[11] *ibid.* Sched. 18 para 1(5E), as amended by FA 2000, s.86(2).
[12] FA 2000, Sched. 19, para 6.

## Securities issued in exchange for shares

Where on a take-over securities are issued in exchange for shares, there is no "loan" **22–43A** to the company issuing the securities. However, "loan creditor" is defined by reference to the meaning given to that term in the close companies legislation.[13] Under that legislation, "loan creditor" includes a creditor in respect of a debt incurred for any capital asset acquired by the company. Accordingly, any person holding the securities is treated as a loan creditor for the purposes of Schedule 18, and will be an equity holder if the "loan" is not a normal commercial loan.

## Profits test

Paragraph 22–44 of the main work records the Inland Revenue's view that for the **22–44** purposes of the profits test "profits" means accounting and not tax profits. The basis for this view is not stated in the Revenue Manuals, and the reference to "total profits" in paragraph 2(1)(a) of Schedule 18 to the Taxes Act 1988 could equally refer to the corporation tax profits computed in accordance with section 9(3) of the Taxes Act 1988. However, the closing words of the sub-paragraph "(whether or not any of those profits are in fact distributed)" arguably points to "total profits" meaning distributable profits.

The expression "total profits" is used elsewhere in the group relief legislation. For example, in section 407 ICTA 1988 it is provided that group relief is to be allowed as a deduction against the claimant company's total profits. Here, the reference must be to the section 9(3) profits. It is unlikely that the same term has different meanings in different parts of the group relief legislation. The new paragraph 2(1A) Schedule 18 ICTA 1988 inserted by the Finance Act 2000, which provides that the total profits of a non-resident company are to be determined as if it were UK resident, also only makes sense if "total profits" means the section 9 (3) profits, since distributable profits do not vary with tax residence.

In *Prudential Assurance v Bibby*[14] (a case on the tax treatment of life assurance companies) the meaning of "total profits" in FA 1989 section 88 fell to be considered. For the Revenue it was contended that the expression has no set meaning for the purposes of corporation tax, but it was held that[15]:

> "the expression "total profits" is a term of art, as a result of and for the purposes of sections 9(3) and 338(1) of the 1988 Act, and as used in other contexts, in particular group relief and management expenses."

---

[13] ICTA 1988 section 417(7) applied by *ibid.* Sch. 18 para. 1(4). Section 417(9) (exclusion for banks) does not apply: *ibid.*

[14] [1999] STC 952.

[15] At p. 97 1h.

While the contrary is arguable, this does seem the better view. In practice, it is understand that the Revenue are content for companies to use either accounting profits or tax profits to satisfy the tests for group membership or shares in a consortium.

### Profits test—non-resident companies

**22–44A**   A new subparagraph (1A) has been introduced to paragraph 2 of Schedule 18 by the Finance Act 2000.[16] This provides that for the purposes of the profits test, the total profits of a non-resident company arising in an accounting period shall be determined for the purposes of paragraph 2(1) of Schedule 18 of the Taxes Act 1988 as if that company were UK resident. As noted in section 22–44 of the main work, it is the Inland Revenue's view that the reference to total profits in paragraph 2 is a reference to the company's profits available for distribution for the accounting period and not to the company's taxable profits for that period. Taking this interpretation, it is not clear what purpose the new subparagraph (1A) serves since the residence of a company will have no bearing on the determination of its profits which are available for distribution; rather a company's distributable profits are determined by reference to the company law of the territory in which it is incorporated. If the reference to total profits is read as a reference to the company's taxable profits (which the authors consider to be the correct interpretation of these words in the context of the provisions of Chapter IV of Part X of the Taxes Act 1988), then the wording of subparagraph (1A) would appear to suggest that the company's profits as a whole would have to be computed for United Kingdom tax purposes. The authors have corresponded with the Inland Revenue on this point and have been advised that it has always been prepared to accept that if the tests were passed using either the tax or the commercial profits, then the tests were passed. It intends to permit non-resident companies to use either commercial or United Kingdom taxable profits for the purposes of this test. On this basis a non-resident company's taxable profits would only have to be calculated for United Kingdom tax purposes if the company decided to use taxable profits rather than commercial profits as the measure.

### 22–48A Profits and assets tests: sale of subsidiary

It will be seen from para. 22–83 of the main text that provision is made to restrict group relief where a company leaves a group part way through an accounting period. The apportionment rules that apply for that purpose are not applied to the profits and assets tests and accordingly the issue arises of how those tests are to be applied up to the time of departure given that the profits are measured for the whole of the subsidi-

---

[16] FA 2000, Sched. 27 para. 5(3).

ary's "relevant accounting period", and net assets are determined at the end of that period:

**Example**

A1 is a wholly owned subsidiary of A. The accounting periods of A1 end on December 31. In the year 2000, A1 is sold on July 1. How is A's entitlement to profits and net assets for the accounting period to December 31, 2000 to be established?

This problem is highlighted by the application of these tests for the purposes of the CGT group rules and Stamp Duty associated companies rules where one is necessarily applying the tests in relation to a given transaction.

The two tests are as follows:

*Profits*

". . . the percentage to which one company is beneficially entitled of any profits available for distribution to the equity holders of another company means the percentage to which the first company would be so entitled in the relevant accounting period on a distribution in money to those equity holders of—

(a) an amount of profits equal to the total profits of the other company which arise in that accounting period (whether or not any of those profits are in fact distributed); or

(b) if there are no profits of the other company in that accounting period, profits of £100[16a];

"Relevant accounting period" means the acounting period current at the time in question[16b]. It is considered that the profits test falls to be applied at any given time in the relevant accounting period but in relation to the actual profits ascertained for that period. So, in relation to the Example, if at any time up to July 1 a distribution is postulated of an amount equal to the profits to December 31, A would have been entitled to the whole of that distribution. It is immaterial that such a distribution would be impossible in practice: the test is purely notional. The same approach makes the assets test workable:

*Assets*

". . . the percentage to which one company would be beneficially entitled of any assets of another company available for distribution to its equity holders on a winding-up means the percentage to which the first company would be so entitled if the other company were to be wound up and on that winding-up the value of the assets available

---

[16a] ICTA 1988, Sched 18, para. 2(1).
[16b] *Ibid.* para. 7(1).

for distribution to its equity holders (that is to say, after deducting any liabilities to other persons) were equal to—

(a) the excess, if any, of the total amount of the assets of the company, as shown in the balance sheet relating to its affairs as at the end of the relevant accounting period, over the total amount of those of its liabilities as so shown which are not liabilities to equity holders as such; or

(b) if there is no such excess or if the company's balance sheet is prepared to a date other than the end of the relevant accounting period, £100."

Thus, in the Example, in relation to A, this test can be applied at any time up to July 1 by postulating at that time a distribution of net assets as at December 31.

## Option arrangements

### (a) Contingent rights

22–52    It will be seen from paragraph 22–64 of the main work that in *Scottish and Universal Newspapers Ltd v. Fisher*,[17] the Special Commissioners considered a contingent option in the context of the "arrangements" rules of section 410. Paragraph 5B did not apply in that case as the option was entered into before the commencement date of that paragraph. It will also be seen from paragraph 22–64 that the *ratio* of the decision was that the option did not constitute a relevant arrangement because so long as the option remained contingent, control could not be obtained "by virtue" of the option. The same point arises under paragraph 5B in that so long as an option is contingent, the option arrangements are not such as "by virtue of which" there could be a variation in the percentage entitlement to profits or assets: paragraph 5B(2).

## Additional tests for non-resident companies

22–60A    A new paragraph 5F has been inserted in Schedule 18 by paragraph 5(5) of Schedule 27 of the Finance Act 2000. This paragraph applies for the purpose of determining whether a non-resident company, which is claiming or surrendering group relief, is a 90 percent or a 75 percent subsidiary of another company[18]; and also for the purpose of determining a member's share in a consortium where the surrendering company or the claimant company is a non-resident company owned by the consortium.[19] The provisions of paragraph 5F apply in two cases:

---

[17] [1996] S.T.C. (S.C.D.) 311.
[18] ICTA 1988, Sched 18 para. 5F(1)(a).
[19] ibid. Sched. 18 para. 5F(1)(b).

1. where any of the equity holders to whom a profit distribution is assumed to be made for the purposes of Schedule 18, or who is entitled to participate in the notional winding-up of the non-resident company holds, in his capacity as an equity holder of the company, any shares or securities which carry rights in respect of dividends or interest or assets on a winding up which are in any way linked to the non-resident company's UK trade[20]; or
2. where there are option arrangements within the meaning of paragraph 5B of Schedule 18 (see section 22–51 of the main work) over shares or securities where the rights attaching to such shares or securities are to any extent linked to the company's United Kingdom trade.[21]

Where the circumstances discussed in 1 or 2 above exist, the calculations that are set out in sections 403C and 413(7) and in paragraphs 1 to 5E of Schedule 18 of the Taxes Act 1988, which are applied to determine a person's percentage interest in a company, have to be done with and without making the assumptions that are set out below. In each case the lowest of the percentages produced is to be taken.[22] For the purposes of paragraph 4 of Schedule 18, any limitations by reference to the non-resident company's United Kingdom trade are ignored and are instead dealt with by the paragraph 5F tests.[23]

**Assumptions**

The assumptions are that:

(a) the profit distribution, or the distribution on the notional winding-up, is confined to a distribution of profits or assets that are referable to the non-resident company's United Kingdom trade; and

(b) the amount of the distribution does not exceed whichever is the greater of £100 and,

    (i) in the case of a profit distribution, the amount (if any) of so much of the company's chargeable profits[24] for the relevant accounting period as is referable to its United Kingdom trade; and

---

[20] *ibid.* Sched. 18 para. 5F(2).
[21] *ibid.* Sched. 18 para. 5F(3).
[22] *ibid.* Sched. 18 para. 5F(4 ) to (6).
[23] ICTA 1988, Sched. 18 para.4(5), as inserted by FA 2000, Sched.27 para. 5(4).
[24] The profits on which the branch is chargeable to corporation tax as defined in ICTA 1988, s.11(2).

(ii) in the case of a distribution on a notional winding-up, its net UK assets[25]; and

(c) none of the ordinary equity holders[1] has an entitlement to a proportion of the profits or assets mentioned in (a) above that is any greater than the proportion of the distribution to which he would be entitled if:

(i) the assumptions specified in paragraphs (a) and (b) above were disregarded; but

(ii) it is assumed, where it is less, that the distribution is equal to £100.[2]

## VII. ANCILLARY PROVISIONS

### Total Profits

22–77    Group relief cannot be set against a tonnage tax company's tonnage tax profits.[3]

### Surrender of losses against profits of same period only

#### *Apportionment of losses and profits*

22–84    Another circumstance in which it may be unjust and unreasonable to use time apportionment to apportion losses and profits is illustrated by *Camcrown Ltd v McDonald*[4], a case on an almost identically worded apportionment provision in the transitional rules relating to the shortening of the period for which trading losses can

---

[25] Net UK assets are defined as the amount, if any, of the total amount of the assets of the company that are referable to its UK trade (as shown in its balance sheet for the end of the relevant accounting period) over the total amount of its liabilities that are so referable (and which are not liabilities to the equity holders as such). The legislation, does not address the position where the company has a different accounting period from its UK branch, for example, where the initial accounts of the branch are prepared for (say) an 18 month period. Assets and liabilities are only taken to be referable to the UK trade to the extent that they are attributable to, or are used for, the purposes of activities, the income and gains from which are or, were there any, would be brought into account in computing the company's chargeable profits for any accounting period, and are not attributable to any of the company's activities which are made exempt from corporation tax by any double taxation agreement (eg where part of a non-resident company's activities are not attributable to a permanent establishment and thus fall outside the scope of tax): ICTA 1988, Sched. 18 para 5F (8), (9) (10), as inserted by FA 2000,Sched 27, para 5.

[1] An ordinary equity holder is defined as any equity holder whose rights are not linked to the company's United Kingdom trade: ICTA 1988, Sched. 18 para. 5F(8).

[2] ICTA 1988, Sched. 18 para 5F(7).

[3] FA 2000, Sched. 22, para. 55.

[4] [1999] STC (SCD) 255.

be carried back. It was held in that case that it was unjust and unreasonable to use time apportionment where a loss during an accounting period was almost wholly attributable to capital allowances in respect of capital expenditure incurred during the later part of an accounting period.

## IX. CLAIMS AND ADJUSTMENTS

Section 411A of the Taxes Act 1988 has been repealed by paragraph 1 of Schedule **22–87** 11 to the Finance Act 1999. Under self-assessment, it has been superseded by paragraph 72 of Schedule 18 to the Finance Act 1998. This paragraph is discussed in paragraph 22–88 of the main work.

The Inland Revenue have power to extend time-limits for making or withdrawing claims for group relief.[5] They have announced that they will issue an updated version of SP 11/93 in due course to set out their practice on extending time-limits.[6]

A group relief claim must specify the amount of relief claimed and the identity of **22–88** the surrendering company.[7] The amount specified must be quantified when the claim is made. This means that the claim must be expressed in figures rather than by a formula.[8]

Strictly, where a company withdraws a consent to the surrender of group relief, it must notify the Inland Revenue officer to whom the original notice of consent was given.[9] In practice, where responsibility for the tax affairs of the surrendering company has been transferred from one Inland Revenue office to another, the Revenue require the withdrawal to be notified to the new office.[10]

Under the pre-Finance Act 2000 legislation a group relief claim had to specify the amount of the relief claimed and the name of the surrendering company.[11] The amount of the relief that is so claimed must be quantified at the time at which the claim is made.[12] Following changes introduced by the Finance Act 2000, a claim for relief must now also specify whether the surrendering company was non-resident for its accounting period to which the claim relates or whether the claimant company was non-resident for its corresponding accounting period. The claim must specify whether the claimant company and the surrendering company are eligible to claim group or consortium relief though a common link with a non-resident company.[13]

With effect for accounting periods of claimant companies ending on or after 1 July

---

[5] FA 1998, Sched. 18, para. 74(2).
[6] Inland Revenue Guide to Corporation Tax Self Assessment, para. 8.7.7.
[7] FA 1998, Sched. 18, para. 68(1).
[8] Inland Revenue Guide to Corporation Tax Self Assessment, para. 8.3.1.
[9] *ibid.* Sched. 18, para. 71(3).
[10] Inland Revenue Guide to Corporation Tax Self Assessment, para. 8.6.1.
[11] FA 1998, Sched. 18 para. 68(1).
[12] *ibid.*, Sched. 18 para. 68(2).
[13] *ibid.*, Sched. 18 para. 68(3), (4), as inserted by FA 2000, Sched. 27 para. 11.

1999, the Corporation Tax (Simplified Arrangements for Group Relief) Regulations 1999 permit groups of companies to adopt a simplified procedure for claiming group relief.

The group of companies can authorise a member to act on their behalf in making and withdrawing group relief claims. Where one of its shareholders is a member of the group, a consortium company can be included in the arrangements.[14] A written application to enter into such arrangements must be made to the Inland Revenue and must include:—

   (i)  the names and tax office references of the companies included in the arrangements;

   (ii)  sufficient details of the group structure to demonstrate that the companies are members of the same group or are consortium companies one of whose shareholders is a member of the group;

   (iii)  the written agreement of each of the companies to be covered by the arrangements and to be bound by claims, surrenders and withdrawals under the arrangements;

   (iv)  a copy of the statement which the authorised company intends to use to make and withdraw group relief claims; and

   (v)  where one of the companies is a consortium company, an agreement by all the consortium members and the consortium company consenting to the authorised company acting on their behalf.[15]

The Inland Revenue have three months to consider the application. They can within this period accept it, accept it subject to the exclusion of companies which have not complied with their corporation tax obligations or in relation to which an insolvency practitioner[16] has been appointed or refuse it on the grounds that:—

   (i)  a company is not a member of the group or a consortium company;

   (ii)  a company has not complied with its corporation tax obligations;

   (iii)  the same tax office does not deal with substantially all the companies; or

   (iv)  the statement to be used to make and withdraw group relief claims is inadequate.[17]

If a consortium company is included in the arrangements and there is a change in the members of the consortium, the authorised company can only continue to act on behalf of the consortium company if a new agreement between the members of the consor-

---

[14] Corporation Tax (Simplified Arrangements for Group Relief) Regulations 1999, reg. 5.
[15] *ibid.* reg. 6.
[16] "Insolvency practitioner" includes a liquidator, a provisional liquidator, administrator, administrative receiver or the supervisor of a voluntary arrangement: *ibid.* reg. 3(1).
[17] *ibid.* reg. 7.

tium and the consortium company consenting to the authorised company so acting is sent to the Revenue.[18]

Where arrangements have been entered into, the Revenue may at any time exclude a company from the arrangements on the grounds that the company is not a member of the group or a consortium company one of the shareholders of which is a member of the group, that it has failed to comply with its corporation tax obligations or that an insolvency practitioner has been appointed in respect of the company.[19] Both the Revenue and the authorised company can terminate the arrangements, and the authorised company can by notice exclude a company from the arrangements.[20]

Where arrangements are entered into, they enable the authorised company to provide the Revenue with a statement with the necessary information to allow the company tax returns of the group members and any consortium company included in the arrangements to be amended to reflect any claims and withdrawals of claims for group relief. The normal information must be given. The statement must also show the effect of the claim on each company's self assessment and which company tax returns are being enquired into. If the statement does not give sufficient information to enable the company tax returns of the relevant companies to be amended it is ineffective. Amendments made to the company tax returns in reliance on the statement bind the companies concerned and each company remains liable for an incorrect claim or company tax return made on its behalf.[21]

Where the amount which a company has surrendered by way of group relief has **22–89** become excessive because the total amount available for group relief has been reduced to less than the amount stated in the notices of consent to surrender given by the company, the surrendering company must withdraw notices of consent to surrender and may issue new notices to reduce the amount surrendered to the total amount available for surrender.[22] If the surrendering company fails to do so, the Inland Revenue can direct which notices are ineffective or to be reduced in amount.[23] The consequence of such a withdrawal or direction is that a claimant company may have to pay more corporation tax. If the claimant fails to pay the extra corporation tax within six months of the last day on which it could make or withdraw a group relief claim for the accounting period in question, the extra tax can be recovered from any other company which has obtained group relief from the surrendering company for the same period.[24] The assessment to recover the extra tax must be made within two years of the last day on which the claimant company could make or withdraw a claim for group relief for the accounting period in question.[25] The maximum amount that can

---

[18] *ibid.* reg. 8.
[19] *ibid.* reg. 9.
[20] *ibid.* reg. 11.
[21] *ibid.* reg. 10.
[22] FA 1998, Sched. 18, para. 75(2).
[23] *ibid.* para. 75(4).
[24] FA 1998, para. 75A(1), (2), (6), inserted by FA 1999, s.92(3).
[25] *ibid.* Sched. 18, para. 75A(3).

be recovered from any one other company is the lower of the unpaid tax and the tax saved by that company by claiming group relief for the period in question from the surrendering company.[1] A company assessed under this provision can recover the tax recovered from it and any interest paid on it from the company that should have paid it.[2]

EXAMPLE

A Ltd has surrendered £500,000 to B Ltd and £300,000 to C Ltd. The total amount available for surrender by A Ltd is then reduced to £600,000. A Ltd will have to withdraw consent to surrender losses to B Ltd and/or C Ltd and give new consents. If it reduces the amount surrendered to C Ltd to £100,000 C Ltd will have to pay further tax on £200,000. If C Ltd fails to pay the tax it can be recovered from B Ltd.

When a claimant company receives a copy of the withdrawal of a consent to a surrender of group relief or receives a copy of a direction from the Inland Revenue treating a consent as ineffective or reduced in amount, the claimant company must amend its company tax return for the period in question to reflect the new position.[3] If it fails to do so or cannot do so, the Revenue can make an assessment to recover the tax which ought to be charged within a year of the date on which the surrendering company gives the claimant notice of the withdrawal of consent or, if later, the new consent or the Inland Revenue give the claimant a copy of their direction.[4]

---

[1] *ibid.* para. 75A(4).
[2] *ibid.* para. 75A(5).
[3] *ibid.* para. 75(6).
[4] *ibid.* para. 76(1), (3). Para. 76(3) was inserted by FA 1999, s.92(4).

# CHARGEABLE GAINS AND GROUPS

## I. CGT GROUPS

### Residence of group members

The limitation that a company had to be resident in the United Kingdom in order **23–05** for it to be included in a CGT group was removed in the Finance Act 2000 with effect for transfers of assets on or after 1 April 2000.[1]

The effect of the Finance Act 2000 amendments is that it is now possible for assets that are within the charge to corporation tax on capital gains to be transferred between companies that are members of the same worldwide capital gains group, as defined for the purposes of section 170 of the Taxation of Chargeable Gains Act 1992, so long as the assets remain within the charge to corporation tax on capital gains following the transfer. This means that the transferee company must either be United Kingdom resident or the asset must be acquired for use by or for the purposes of a United Kingdom branch of that company. See sections 23–01 to 23 – 04 of the main text. The effect of the extended definition of a CGT group is that a charge could arise under section 179 of the Taxation of Chargeable Gains Act 1992 where a non-resident company leaves the CGT group (vendor group) where an asset has been transferred to the United Kingdom branch of that company, or to a United Kingdom resident

---

[1] FA 2000, Sched. 29 paras 1, 2(6).

subsidiary of that company, from a group company that is remaining a member of the vendor group.

Example

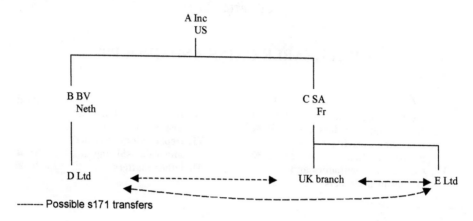

-------- Possible s171 transfers

- All of A Inc, B BV, C SA, D Ltd and E Ltd are within a CGT group.
- Equity issued by B BV/C SA to third party may degroup D Ltd, C SA or E Ltd and cause a charge under section 179 of the Taxation of Chargeable Gains Act 1992.
- Sale of C SA may trigger a s179 charge in its UK branch, or E Ltd, where an asset was acquired by either entity from D Ltd in the last 6 years (and was still held at the date that the company left the group). The same point could arise were the shares in B BV to be sold if D Ltd had received an asset from the United Kingdom branch of C SA or from E Ltd in the last 6 years and again this asset was still held at the date that D Ltd left the group.

Transitional rules apply where a company would have been treated as a member of a CGT group before the Finance Act 2000 changes took effect but the company would not be treated as a member of the new CGT group at 1 April 2000 because it is not an effective 51% subsidiary of the new principal company of the group. In such cases, the company in question will continue to be treated as a member of the CGT group, so long as it remains an effective 51% subsidiary of the company which was the principal company of the group at 31 March 2000.[2] This is illustrated in the example below.

In the example below, A Inc only has a 42.19 percent interest in D Ltd. As D Ltd

---

[2] FA 2000, Sched. 29, para.46(1),(4),(5).

Example

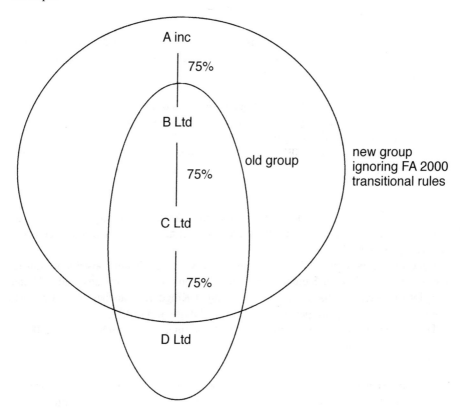

was a member of the B Ltd group at 31 March 2000, it will remain a member of the CGT group so long as it continues to be an effective 51% subsidiary of B Ltd.

## II. Intra-Group transfers

**General Rule**

Section 171 of the Taxation of Chargeable Gains Act 1992 was amended by Finance **23–14** Act 2000 in relation to transfers that take place on or after 1 April 2000. The revised provisions of this section apply where:

1. the transferor is a United Kingdom resident company, or the asset is a chargeable asset in relation to that company; and

2. the transferee is either a United Kingdom resident company or the asset is a chargeable asset in relation to that company.[3]

The definition of a chargeable asset is contained in section 10(2) (as applied and modified by section 10(3)) of the Taxation of Chargeable Gains Act 1992 and an asset is a chargeable asset for these purposes where:

(a) it is situated in the United Kingdom and it is used in, or for the purposes of, a trade carried on by a United Kingdom branch of that company at or before the time at which the gain accrued; or

(b) the asset is situated in the United Kingdom and is used or held for the purposes of the branch or agency at or before the time at which the gain accrued.[4]

As before, for the purposes of section 171 of the Taxation of Chargeable Gains Act 1992, the asset is deemed to be transferred for such an amount as would secure that neither a gain nor a loss would arise.

The effect of the Finance Act 2000 amendments is that it is now possible to transfer assets between a United Kingdom branch of a non-resident company and a United Kingdom resident company and between United Kingdom branches of non-resident companies where they are part of the same worldwide group.

These amendments apply for disposals that take place on or after 1 April 2000.[5]

*Part disposals*

Section 171 has always applied to part disposals within a group.[6] The new wording is less clear in this regard and it seems to require that the asset that is acquired by the transferee should be the same as the asset disposed of by the transferor. This will not be the case where a lease is granted out of a freehold or a head lease or a lease is surrendered to a head lessor or freeholder. The authors have confirmed with the Inland Revenue that section 171, as re-worded, will still apply in such cases.


**Deemed transfers**

**23–14A**     A new section 171A of the Taxation of Chargeable Gains Act 1992 has been introduced by the Finance Act 2000 which permits two group companies, A and B, to elect jointly to treat the whole or any part of an asset disposed of by A to a person outside the capital gains group, as having been disposed of by B. The effect of this provision

---

[3] TCGA 1992, s171(1) and (1A), as inserted by FA 2000, Sched. 29 para. 2.
[4] *ibid.*, s.10(1), (3) as applied by ibid. s.171(1A).
[5] FA 2000, Sched. 29 para. 2(6).
[6] See Inland Revenue Capital Gains Manual at CG45351.

is that it is no longer necessary for an asset to be transferred to a company with capital losses in order for such losses to be set against a gain arising on a disposal of that asset outside the group. At the same time it enables the benefit of an unrealised capital loss to be transferred to another company in the group.

Such an election may only be made when section 171 would have applied to an actual transfer of the asset immediately before the date that it was disposed of outside the group.[7] In the Standing Committee debate on this provision the Paymaster General confirmed that this provision would apply to partial transfers and to transfers of a beneficial interest in an asset.[8] It is debatable, however, whether the parliamentary exchange is sufficiently clear to satisfy *Pepper v Hart* principles in the case of an asset that is by its nature not severable into different parts. The authors have confirmed with the Inland Revenue, however, that it will accept elections for deemed transfers of the beneficial ownership of an asset even where the asset cannot be physically divided.

Equally it is not clear how the election will apply where a company elects to transfer an asset to a United Kingdom branch of a non-resident company. In order for an election to be made the transfer must be capable of falling within section 171. In order for section 171 to apply in such cases, the asset must be a chargeable asset of the branch immediately following the transfer (see 23 – 14 of the supplement). This in turn means that the asset must be held or used for the purposes of the branch's trade. It is not clear how this test is to be judged where no transfer of the asset takes place. The authors have confirmed with the Inland Revenue that it will accept an election under section 171A in the case of a deemed transfer to a United Kingdom branch or agency of a non-resident company on the basis that, had the transfer taken place, the asset could have been brought into use and fallen within the charging provisions of section 10(3) of the Taxation of Chargeable Gains Act 1992.

It would appear that it will not be possible for an election to be made in respect of an asset that is deemed to be disposed of under section 179 of the Taxation of Chargeable Gains Act 1992 as section 171A requires that the asset is disposed of to a person who is not a member of a group, whereas a section 179 disposal is not a disposal *to* anyone.[9]

An election must be made within two years of the end of the accounting period in which A disposes of the asset outside the group.[10]

It is possible for a payment to be made between the two companies in connection with the election and so long as the amount of the payment does not exceed the amount of the chargeable gain or allowable loss that is treated as accruing to B, the payment will not be taken into account in computing the profits or losses of either company and nor will it be treated as a distribution or as a charge on income.[11] The

---

[7] TCGA 1992, s.171A(3), as inserted by FA 2000, s.101.
[8] Hansard, 15 June 2000, column 761.
[9] TCGA 1992, 179(4).
[10] *ibid.*, s.171A(4), as inserted by FA 2000, s.101.
[11] *ibid.*, s.171A(5), as inserted by FA 2000, s.101.

authors understand from the Inland Revenue that it will apply its existing practice for group relief surrenders, as set out in section 46566 of the Inland Revenue Capital Gains Manual. Under this practice, where no payment is made between the parties, or the amount of the payment is less than the tax saving arising as a result of the election, this will not be treated as a depreciatory transaction. If, however, the amount of the payment exceeds the amount of the tax benefit, the Inland Revenue considers that it would be appropriate to make a loss restriction under the provisions of section 176 of the Taxation of Chargeable Gains Act 1992 where there is a disposal of the shares in the company that made the payment.

## Exceptions

**23–25**    Section 23 – 25 of the main text considers a number of exceptions to the provisions of section 171 of the Taxation of Chargeable Gains Act 1992. A number of consequential changes have been made to the wording of this section to reflect the fact that non-resident companies can now be included as members of a CGT group and these changes are considered below.

1. The exclusion for notional disposals that is referred to in (i) of the main text has been moved from section 171(1) to a new subsection (6).[12]
2. The exception referred to in (ii) of the main text has been amended as a result of the changes to the companies that can be included in a CGT group. The exception now applies to a disposal of a debt due from a United Kingdom resident company, or from a United Kingdom branch of a non-resident company, that is effected by the satisfaction of the debt by that other company. This change applies from 1 April 2000. The cases where this provision is likely to be in point will be very limited following the introduction of the Loan Relationships legislation that is discussed in Chapter 3 of the main text. Principally, this provision is likely to apply to held over gains that arose under the transitional provisions included within the Loan Relationships and Forex legislation[13]; and to a convertible security or a security that is linked to the value of chargeable assets which falls outside the loan relationships legislation in the hands of the investor (i.e. the conditions of sections 92 and 93 of the Finance Act 1996 are satisfied – see 3–41 to 3–53 of the main text).

## Subsidiary rules

*(b) Restriction of losses by reference to capital allowances*

**23–27**    Delete the references to section 172 of the Taxation of Chargeable Gains Act 1992

---

[12] FA 2000, Sched. 29 para. 2(5).
[13] See FA 1996 Sched. 15 paras 8 and 9 and FA 1993, Sched. 17 para. 3 and S.I. 1994 No.3226 regs 7, 9 to 14 respectively.

for disposals on or after 1 April 2000.[14] This is because section 172 ceased to apply to disposals on or after this date as a result of the amendments made to the definition of a capital gains group (see 23–89 to 23–94 of this supplement).

### III. Companies Leaving Groups

A change has been made to the scope of section 179 to reflect the fact that it is now possible to include a United Kingdom branch of a non-resident company within a CGT group. The provisions of section 179 now apply where a chargeable asset is acquired by one group company (company A) from another group company (company B) if:

**23–32**

1. company A is either a United Kingdom resident company at that time, or the asset is a chargeable asset immediately following the transfer; and
2. company B is a United Kingdom resident company at the time of the transfer or the asset is a chargeable asset immediately before the transfer.[15]

The revisions discussed above apply to transfers of assets that take place on or after April 1, 2000.[16]

The effect of the changes to the definition of a CGT group is that a section 179 charge can apply if a non-resident company leaves the CGT group (vendor group) where an asset has been transferred to the United Kingdom branch of that company, or to a United Kingdom resident subsidiary of that company, from a group company that is remaining a member of the vendor group.

Page 717 Footnote 6—Section 178 of the Taxation of Chargeable Gains Act 1992 was repealed by the Finance Act 2000 on the grounds that its provisions are spent. Footnote 6 on page 717 mentions that the Inland Revenue considered that the provisions of this section were spent as long ago as February 1994.

**Section 179 disposals of shares**

An interesting question arises where shares are the subject of a disposal under section 179(3). Under that provision, the shares are treated as disposed of and re-acquired immediately after the intra-group acquisition. But that situation is covered by section 105 (share identification). Under section 105 (which takes priority over the other share identification rules[16a]), shares of the same class acquired on the same day are treated as acquired in a single transaction, and are identified with shares disposed of on that

**23–32A**

---

[14] TCGA 1992, s.41(8), as inserted by FA 200, Sched. 29 para. 12.
[15] TCGA 1992, s.179 (1) and (1A), as inserted by FA 2000, Sched. 29 para 4. Chargeable asset is defined in TCGA 1992, s.10 (see section 23 – 14 above for an analysis of this definition).
[16] FA 2000, Sched 29 para. 4(7).
[16a] See TCGA, s.106(9),

day so far as the number of shares acquired does not exceed the number of shares disposed of[16b]. Under section 105, shares acquired intra-group are not disregarded (compare section 106(2)). Thus, if section 105 applies for the purposes of disposals of shares under section 179, then the result is that one-half of the inherent gain is brought into charge:

### Illustration

A1 and A2 are members of the A group. A1 holds 100 shares in B with a CGT base cost of £1m. A1 transfers the B shares to A2 at a time when the 100 shares are worth £2m. One year later, A2 leaves the A group.

As at the date of the intra-group transfer, A2 acquired 100 B shares from A1 (cost £1m.) and is treated as having re-acquired that number of shares at market value (£2m.). Under the single transaction rule, those events are treated as the acquisition of 200 shares for £3m. on the same day, A2 is treated as having disposed of 100 shares for £2m. That is a disposal of half the 200 shares, and accordingly the allowable expenditure is £1.5m. The gain is therefore £0.5m. If section 105 did not apply then the gain would be £1m.

This question of the inter-action between sections 105 and 179 raises in acute form the issue of purposive interpretation discussed in para. 10–11 of the main text and of this Supplement.

### Intra-group roll over

**23–32B** Section 179 does not apply unless there has been an intra-group asset transfer, so that if one member of a group (A1) realises a gain on the disposal of an asset and another member (A2) rolls the gain over into the acquisition of another asset pursuant to section 175, then if A2 were to leave the group, section 179 would not apply. By contrast, if A1 transferred Blackacre to A2 and A2 then realised a gain on the disposal of Blackacre, the gain being rolled-over by A2 into Whiteacre, the departure of A2 from the group within six years from the Blackacre transfer would bring section 179 into play.[16b]

### Subsidiary leaving group

**23–34** *Add to footnote 18*: The Court of Appeal has dismissed Dunlop's appeal in *Dunlop International AG v. Pardoe*,[17] holding that whether a body was a company as defined in

---

[16b] *ibid.* s.105(1).
[16c] *ibid.* s.179(3)(b)(10)(b).
[17] [1999] S.T.C. 909.

section 170 of the Taxation of Chargeable Gains Act 1992 fell to be tested immediately before it ceased to be a member of a group. A company could therefore be a "chargeable company" for the purpose of section 179 even though it left the group on becoming non-resident and ceased at that point to be a company. Following the amendments to the group rules by the Finance Act 2000, this point can no longer arise.

## Associated companies exception

As mentioned above, the Court of Appeal has dismissed Dunlop's appeal in *Dunlop*   **23–39**
*International AG v. Pardoe*, holding that the associated companies exception only applies where the transferor and the transferee are associated both before and after they each leave the group.[18]

The Revenue have confirmed that they consider that section 179(2) of the Taxation of Chargeable Gains Act 1992 only applies where the companies between which the asset was transferred were associated at the time of the asset transfer and remain associated before and after they cease to be members of the group. The authors consider this view to be incorrect and that the law is as stated in Example 16 in the main work.

## Secondary liabilities

The provisions of section 179(11) and (12) that are discussed in section 23–46 of   **23–46**
the main text were repealed by Finance Act 2000 with effect for disposals on or after 1 April 2000. Instead the revised provisions of section 190, which was inserted by Finance Act 2000, will apply to gains accruing on or after this date.[19] The provisions of this section are considered at 23–99 of this supplement.

VI. DEPRECIATING TRANSACTIONS AND VALUE SHIFTING

## Dividend stripping

Delete the reference to section 172 in the second paragraph for disposals that take   **23–70**
place on or after 1 April 2000.[20]
(i) Restriction of losses.
(ii) Adjustment of consideration—section 31 of the TCGA 1992.

---

[18] *ibid.*

[19] *ibid.*, Sched. 29 para 4(5), (7).

[20] *ibid.*, s. 177(2), as amended by FA 2000, Sched. 29 para. 25. TCGA 1992, s.172 ceased to apply for disposals that take place on or after 1 April 2000 as a result of the changes to the definition of a capital gains group: see section 23–14 of this supplement.

## Introduction

**23–75**    It was pointed out in paragraph 23-75 of the main work that section 30 of the Taxation of Chargeable Gains Act 1992 does not apply if the vendor sells a company which has paid a dividend out of artificially generated distributable profits to a foreign 75 per cent subsidiary which in turn disposes of the company to a third party. This weakness led to a scheme for avoiding corporation tax on chargeable gains on the disposal of a subsidiary. The scheme worked as follows:

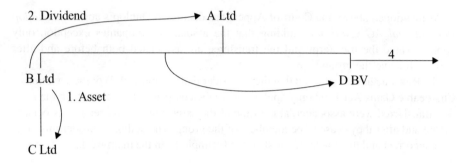

1. B Ltd owns an asset standing at an unrealised gain. It forms a new subsidiary, C Ltd, and transfers the asset intra group to C Ltd at market value. For tax purposes, the transfer is on a no gain no loss basis.[21]
2. The transfer generates distributable reserves which B Ltd uses to pay a dividend to A Ltd.
3. A Ltd sells B Ltd to a non-United Kingdom resident group member, D BV. For tax purposes, this is a market value disposal since the parties are connected. The dividend paid at 2. has, however, reduced the market value of B Ltd so that no gain arises. Section 30 of the 1992 Act does not apply to the disposal to D BV because the condition in section 31(8) is not fulfilled (since the group relationship can be traced through D BV).
4. D BV sells B Ltd. This sale is outside the scope of corporation tax. No section 179 charge arises because B Ltd and C Ltd leave the group as associated companies.

Section 31A of the 1992 Act now renders this scheme ineffective for disposals to non-resident associates on or after March 9, 1999. It does this by deeming A Ltd to realise a chargeable gain equal to the chargeable gain which would have arisen if section 30 had applied to the sale of B Ltd to D BV.

---

[21] TCGA 1992, s.171.

## Section 31A of the 1992 Act

The new rules apply where the distributable profits of a company that has paid a dividend would be chargeable profits for the purposes of section 31 of the 1992 Act but for the fact that immediately after the disposal of that company the asset with enhanced value is owned by the disposing company or a company in the same capital gains group as that company.[22] In other words, it applies where:

(i) the dividend is paid out of distributable profits which arose on an intra group disposal or share exchange or the revaluation of an asset;

(ii) there has been no disposal or deemed disposal under section 179 of the 1992 Act of the asset with enhanced value; and

(iii) following the sale of the company which paid the dividend that asset remains in the same capital gains group.

In the scheme outlined above, these conditions are met because the asset transferred intra group to C Ltd remains in A Ltd's capital gains group following B Ltd's sale to D BV since the group relationship can be traced through D BV.

If, within six years of the disposal of the company which has paid the dividend,

(a) (i) the company owning the asset with enhanced value leaves the disposing company's capital gains group otherwise than because the parent of that group joins another group; or

    (ii) if the company owning the asset with enhanced value leaves that group because the parent of that group joins another group, that company ceases to be a 75 per cent subsidiary or ceases to be an effective 51 per cent subsidiary of a member of that group; and

(b) no section 179 disposal of the asset with enhanced value is treated as having occurred in the period between the disposal of the company paying the dividend and the event mentioned in (a)

the distributable profits generated by the intra group disposal or share exchange or revaluation are treated as chargeable profits.[23]

The condition in (a)(ii) is aimed at the situation where the company owning the asset with enhanced value leaves the group on another group acquiring a majority shareholding in the group parent because it is no longer an effective 51 per cent subsidiary of the ultimate parent of the group.

If these rules stood on their own, their effect would be that the dividend would be treated as paid out of chargeable profits. This would then mean in the example given

---

[22] TCGA 1992, s.31A(1).

[23] TCGA 1992, *ibid.* s.31A(2), (4)–(6).

earlier that the consideration for A Ltd's disposal of B Ltd to D BV could be increased under section 30 of the Taxation of Chargeable Gains Act 1992 to reflect the dividend. The effect of degrouping C Ltd within six years of B Ltd's transfer to D BV would therefore be to require the consideration for A Ltd's disposal of B Ltd to be retrospectively increased for tax purposes. Since this would be practically cumbersome, where the rules apply no adjustment is in fact made under section 30. Instead, a chargeable gain of the "differential amount" is treated as accruing to the company which sold the dividend paying company to the foreign associate immediately before the company owning the asset with enhanced value leaves the group or, as appropriate, ceases to be either a 75 per cent subsidiary or an effective 51 per cent subsidiary of a member of the group. If the company (transferor company) that transferred the dividend paying company to the foreign associate has by this stage left the group, the chargeable gain accrues to the group parent, in a case where the asset holding company ceased to be a member of the group before 1 April 2000. Where the asset holding company ceased to be a member of the group on or after 1 April 2000, and the transferor company has by then left the group, the Inland Revenue is able to collect the tax from any company that was a member of the group immediately before the asset holding company ceased to be a member of the group.[24]

In the above example, A Ltd would be treated as realising a chargeable gain at the time that D BV sells B Ltd.

The "differential amount" is the difference between the loss or gain which would have arisen on the sale to the foreign associate if a value shifting adjustment had arisen and the loss or gain which actually arose on that sale. If the actual gain is bigger or the actual loss is smaller, there is no differential amount.[25]

The deemed chargeable gain is treated as a gain on a disposal between the company selling the dividend paying company and the foreign associate made when they are connected.[1] This enables a loss arising on the actual disposal of the dividend paying company between those companies to be set against the deemed chargeable gain. If, therefore, a loss had arisen on the sale of B Ltd to D BV, the loss could have been set off against the gain arising under section 31A.

A point of some difficulty is whether section 31A can apply where the disposal following the payment of the intra group dividend is a deemed disposal under section 179 of the 1992 Act. When section 179 applies to shares in a company, it deems the shares to be sold at market value and this prevents a value shifting adjustment being made under section 30. Instead, there is special provision[2] for the market value of the asset to be increased to reflect the value shifting adjustment which would have been made on an actual disposal.

Section 31A only brings the differential amount into charge "where section 30 has effect by virtue of this section". Whether it applies where the disposal in question

---

[24] *ibid.*, s.31A(7),(9), as amended by FA 2000, Sched. 29 para. 17.
[25] *ibid.* s.31A(8).
[1] *ibid.* s.31A(10).
[2] *ibid.* s.179(9).

arises under section 179 depends on the meaning of these words. If they mean "where an adjustment could be made under section 30" then section 31A does not apply because no adjustment can be made under section 30 to the amount of a section 179 charge. Section 179(9) is a separate charging provision. Section 31A(10) refers to "the parties to the section 30 disposal", which is also a pointer in favour of the view that the section can only apply to actual disposals and not to deemed disposals.

However, there is another possible view. It can be argued that the words "where section 30 has effect" simply mean "where the conditions of section 30(1) are satisfied". While this interpretation is the less natural reading of the legislation, it has the policy advantage of avoiding a loophole in section 31A and might therefore commend itself to a court concerned to interpret the legislation in a purposive way.

### Assets representing the asset with enhanced value

In certain cases, the asset with enhanced value may come to be represented by more than one asset. Assets are treated as representing the asset with enhanced value in the following cases:

(i) Where there is a part disposal of the asset with enhanced value, both the part that remains and the part acquired on the part disposal are treated as the same asset.[3]

(ii) Where assets have been merged or divided or have changed their nature or rights in or over assets have been created or extinguished and the value of an asset is derived from any other asset owned by the same or an associated company, the first asset and the second asset are treated as the same asset.[4]

If (i) or (ii) applies and in the period between the intra group transfer, share exchange or revaluation generating the distributable reserves and the time the company owning the asset with enhanced value leaves the group or, as appropriate, ceases to be a 75 per cent subsidiary or effective 51 per cent subsidiary of a member of the group, that asset is not disposed of outside the group or the subject of a section 179 disposal, references to the asset with enhanced value refer to all the assets treated under (i) or (ii) as the same as that asset.[5]

EXAMPLE

A Ltd transfers a leasehold interest to its wholly owned subsidiary, B Ltd, and then pays a dividend out of the distributable reserves created by the transfer. A

---

[3] TCGA 1992, s.33(5).
[4] *ibid.* s.33(6).
[5] TCGA 1992, s.33(3B).

Ltd's parent transfers A Ltd to a Dutch resident subsidiary. B Ltd then purchases the freehold and the leasehold interest merges into the freehold. The freehold becomes the asset with enhanced value and section 31A will apply if the Dutch company sells A Ltd within six years of its acquisition of A Ltd.

If, in that period, there has been either a part disposal outside the group of the asset with enhanced value or a section 179 disposal of it, references to the asset with enhanced value are to the assets remaining in the group which represent it.[6]

Where under these rules "the asset with enhanced value" has come to refer to more than one asset all of them are taken to be the same asset and a disposal of one of them is treated as a part disposal.[7]

EXAMPLE

A Ltd owns the whole of B Ltd and C BV. B Ltd owns D Ltd and E Ltd. B Ltd transfers a factory to D Ltd and pays a dividend out of the reserves generated on the transfer. A Ltd then transfers B Ltd to C BV and D Ltd leases part of the factory to E Ltd. The asset with enhanced value is represented by both the freehold owned by D Ltd and the leasehold owned by E Ltd. If E Ltd then assigns its lease to a third party, this is treated as a part disposal of the asset with enhanced value. Similarly, if B Ltd sells E Ltd, the section 179 disposal of the leasehold interest is treated as a part disposal of the asset with enhanced value.

Section 31A only applies where there is no deemed disposal under section 179 of the Taxation of Chargeable Gains Act 1992 of the asset with enhanced value in the period between the transfer of the dividend paying company to the foreign associate and the time the company owning the asset with enhanced value leaves the group or, as appropriate, ceases to be a 75 per cent or effective 51 per cent subsidiary of a member of the group.[8]

Where the asset with enhanced value has come to be represented by more than one asset, section 31A is only disapplied if all of them are subject to a section 179 deemed disposal in that period.[9] If, in the previous example, B Ltd sells E Ltd triggering a section 179 disposal of the leasehold interest, section 31A will nevertheless apply if C BV then sells B Ltd.

If there is a section 179 disposal in that period of only one or some of a number of assets which represent the asset with enhanced value, the amount of the reduction in

---

[6] *ibid.* s.33(3C).
[7] *ibid.* s.33(4).
[8] TCGA 1992, s.31A(6).
[9] *ibid.* s.33(2), (4).

value of the dividend paying company attributable to the dividend is reduced to such amount as is just and reasonable.[10] So if C BV does sell B Ltd after that company has sold E Ltd the amount charged under section 31A will be reduced to reflect the deemed disposal of the leasehold interest.

A similar reduction in the amount charged under section 31A is made where part of the asset with enhanced value has been disposed of outside the group before the company owning the remainder of it leaves the group.[11]

EXAMPLE

A Ltd owns the whole of B Ltd and C BV. B Ltd transfers a factory to a new wholly owned subsidiary, D Ltd, and pays a dividend out of the reserves generated on that transfer. A Ltd then sells B Ltd to C BV. D Ltd leases part of the factory to a third party and B Ltd is then sold. Section 31A applies, but the amount charged under section 31A is reduced.

## Share exchanges

Where the dividend paying company is transferred to the foreign associate by way of a share or debenture exchange or a transaction treated as a share exchange by section 136 of the 1992 Act, the share reorganisation rules do not prevent section 31A applying. In such a case the amount charged under section 31A is the difference between the allowable loss or chargeable gain which would have accrued if the share reorganisation rules had not applied and section 30 had applied to the share exchange and the allowable loss or chargeable gain which would have accrued on the exchange if the share reorganisation rules had not applied. For this purpose, allowable losses are treated as chargeable gains of nil.[12]

EXAMPLE

A Ltd has two subsidiaries, B Ltd and C BV. B Ltd transfers a factory to a new wholly owned subsidiary, D Ltd and pays a dividend out of the reserves generated on that transfer. A Ltd transfers B Ltd to C BV in exchange for shares in C BV and C BV then sells B Ltd. Section 31A applies and the amount charged is the difference between the loss or gain which would have accrued if section 30 had

---

[10] *ibid.* s.33(8A).
[11] *ibid.*
[12] *ibid.* s.34(1A)–(2).

applied and the loss or gain which in fact accrued, in each case ignoring the share reorganisation rules.

## VII. OTHER MATTERS

### Trading stock

**23–78 to**
**23–80**
The provisions of section 173 of the Taxation of Chargeable Gains Act 1992, which are considered in the above sections of the main text, have been amended by Finance Act 2000[13] as a consequence of the change to the definition of a capital gains group. As transfers of chargeable assets to and from a United Kingdom branch of a non-resident group company now fall within the provisions of section 171 of the Taxation of Chargeable Gains Act 1992, the provisions of section 173 of that Act have been amended so that they apply where:

1. a United Kingdom resident company, or a United Kingdom branch of a non-resident company, acquires an asset as trading stock from a company, which is a member of the same capital gains group and the asset did not form part of the trading stock of the transferor company[14]; or
2. a United Kingdom resident company or a United Kingdom branch of a non-resident company, disposes of an asset forming part of its trading stock and the asset is acquired otherwise than as part of its trading stock by another United Kingdom resident company, or by a United Kingdom branch of a non-resident company, which is a member of the same capital gains group as the transferor.[15]

The revised provisions of section 173 apply for acquisitions and disposals that take place on or after 1 April 2000.[16]

### Roll-over relief

**23–82**
Section 175 of the Taxation of Chargeable Gains Act has been amended by the Finance Act 1992 to provide that the trades referred to in the section are any trade

---

[13] FA 2000, Sched. 29 para. 11.
[14] TCGA 1992, s.173(1), (3). For these purposes an asset is regarded as forming part of a company's trading stock where it is held for the purpose of any trade carried on by a United Kingdom resident company, or any trade carried on by a United Kingdom branch or agency of a non-resident company: ibid. s.173(3).
[15] *ibid.*,1992, s.173(2), (3).
[16] FA 2000, Sched. 29 para. 11(2).

carried on by a United Kingdom resident company or by a United Kingdom branch of a non resident company that is a member of the CGT group.[17] Where an asset is disposed of by a United Kingdom branch of a non resident company, roll over relief is only available if the asset was a chargeable asset of the branch immediately before the time of the disposal and where an asset is acquired by a United Kingdom branch of a non resident company, roll over relief is only available if the asset was a chargeable asset of the branch immediately after the date of acquisition. An asset is a chargeable asset if any gain or loss on the disposal of that asset would be included in computing the branch's profits for corporation tax purposes under the provisions of section 10(3) of the Taxation of Chargeable Gains Act 1992 (see 23 – 14 of the supplement).[18]

This amendment applies where the disposal or acquisition takes place on or after 1 April 2000, or both the acquisition and disposal take place on or after that date.[19] Where an asset was disposed of by a UK branch of a non-resident company before 1 April 2000, it will be possible to roll over the gain against an asset acquired by another group company on or after 1 April 2000. Equally, where an asset was acquired by a United Kingdom branch before 1 April 2000, it will be possible to roll over a gain realised by another group company on or after 1 April 2000 against that asset.[20]

**Transfer of a United Kingdom branch**

As discussed at 23–05 above, it has been possible to include a United Kingdom **23–89 to** branch of a non-resident company within a CGT group for transfers that take place **23–94** on or after 1 April 2000. Accordingly, the provisions of section 172 (transfer of assets of a United Kingdom branch to a United Kingdom resident company in return for the issue of shares or securities by the transferee company) were no longer required as such transfers would now be covered by the revised provisions of section 171. The section was therefore repealed by Finance Act 2000 in relation to disposals that took place on or after 1 April 2000.[21]

Where a company ceases to carry on a trade through a United Kingdom branch, there is normally a deemed disposal of any chargeable assets that are used by or are held for the purposes of that branch under the provisions of section 25 of the Taxation of Chargeable Gains Act 1992. Following an amendment introduced in Finance Act 2000, the provisions of this section will not apply where the assets are transferred to

---

[17] TGCA 1992, s.175(1A), as inserted by FA 2000, Sched. 29 para. 10(3).

[18] *ibid.* s. 175(2AA), as inserted by FA 2000, Sched. 29 para. 10(5).

[19] FA 2000, Sched. 29 para. 10(7),(8).

[20] *ibid.* Sched. 29 para. 10(7),(8). This paragraph provides that whether a company was a member of a group of companies at the time of the disposal (or acquisition) is to be determined in accordance with the provisions of TCGA 1992, s.170 as amended by Sched. 29 para. 1. This means that where the disposal or acquisition took place before 1 April 2000, the non-resident company would be treated as a member of the CGT group for these purposes.

[21] FA 2000, Sched. 29 para. 3.

another company under the provisions of section 171 of the Taxation of Chargeable Gains Act 1992 or where the assets are transferred as part of a scheme of amalgamation or reconstruction that falls within the provisions of section 139 of that Act. This change applies to transfers that take place on or after 1 April 2000.[22]

Where a company ceases to trade via a United Kingdom branch and the chargeable assets of that company are not transferred to other group companies under the provisions of section 171 of the Taxation of Chargeable Gains Act 1992, the company will be deemed to have disposed of such assets at their market value at the date that it ceases to trade via the branch.[23] If the company had acquired an asset via an intra-group transfer, it had been treated as having disposed of that asset at market value when it ceased to trade via a branch and it subsequently leaves the group whilst still owning the asset, there is nothing to prevent a charge arising under section 179 of the Taxation of Chargeable Gains Act 1992. This in turn would lead to an adjustment of the section 25 charge. The authors understand from correspondence with the Inland Revenue that it would not normally seek a charge under section 179 in such cases.

**Secondary liabilities**

**23–99**   Replace section 23–99 of the main text with the following:

Finance Act 2000 introduced a new section 190 that gives the Inland Revenue powers to recover unpaid corporation tax that relates to chargeable gains owed by one company in the worldwide group (taxpayer company) from certain other persons. The persons from which the tax may be recovered are:

1. Where the taxpayer company was a member of a CGT group at the time at which the gain accrued:

   (a) the company which was the principal company of the group at that time; and

   (b) any other company (other company) which was a member of the group at any time in the 12 months ending with the time at which the gain accrued and which owned the asset, or any part of the asset in respect of which the gain accrued, or where the asset is an interest or right over another asset, owned either asset or any part of either asset.

2. If the taxpayer company is non-resident and the gain arises under the provisions of section 10(3) of the Taxation of Chargeable Gains Act 1992, any person who is or was a controlling director of that company at any time during the period of 12 months ending with the time at which the gain

---

[22] TCGA 1992, s.25(3A) as inserted by FA 2000 Sched. 29 para 6. The time at which this measure takes effect is dealt with in para. 6(4),(5).
[23] *ibid.* s. 25(3).

accrued, or was a controlling director of a company which had control of the taxpayer company at any time during that 12 month period.[24]

The provisions of the new section 190 apply to gains accruing on or after 1 April 2000.[25]

The Inland Revenue is required to serve a notice on the company or individual in question requiring payment of the tax within 30 days of the date of the notice. Such a notice must be served within three years of the date on which the taxpayer company's corporation tax liability for the relevant accounting period is finally determined.[1] Where the accounting period in question is a period for which the taxpayer company is subject to the corporation tax self-assessment regime, the company's tax liability is deemed to be finally determined on the later of:

1. the last date on which a notice of enquiry may be served on the company in relation to the return in question; or
2. if the Inland Revenue enquires into the company's tax return for that period, 30 days after the last enquiry for the period is completed; or
3. if the Inland Revenue amended the taxpayer's return as a result of an enquiry, 30 days after the notice of amendment is issued; or
4. if the taxpayer appeals against an amendment, 30 days after the date that the appeal is finally determined.[2]

When the Inland Revenue determines the tax due by a taxpayer company under the provisions of paragraph 36 or 37 of Schedule 18 to the Finance Act 1998, in a case where the taxpayer company has failed to file a return or has filed an incomplete return, the relevant date is taken as the date on which the determination was made.[3]

Where the unpaid tax arises as a result of a discovery assessment, the date is taken as the later of the date when the tax becomes due and payable (in a case where there is no appeal) or the date on which an appeal is finally determined.[4]

Where tax due by the taxpayer company is assessed on another person, that other person may recover the tax from the taxpayer company.[5] Interestingly, under the provisions of the new section 190, there is no right of recovery against the principal member of the taxpayer's group, as was formerly the case.

Any amount paid under section 190 is not tax deductible.[6]

---

[24] TCGA 1992, s.190(3), as inserted by FA 2000, Sched. 29 para. 9. A controlling director is a director who has control of the company within the meaning of ICTA 1988, s.416. "Director" is defined by reference to ICTA 1988, s.168(8) and s.417(5): TCGA 1992, s. 190(13).

[25] FA 2000, Sched. 29 para 9(3).

[1] *ibid.* s.190(7), as inserted by FA 2000, Sched. 29 para. 9.

[2] *ibid.* s.190(9), as inserted by FA 2000, Sched. 29 para. 9.

[3] *ibid.* s. 190(8), as inserted by FA 2000, Sched. 29 para. 9.

[4] *ibid.* s. 190(10), as inserted by FA 2000, Sched. 29 para. 9.

[5] *ibid.* s.190(11).

[6] *ibid.* s.190(12).

# CHAPTER 24

# PRE-ENTRY LOSSES AND PRE-ENTRY GAINS

## I. INTRODUCTION

**Pre-entry losses and pre-entry gains**

**24–01**    The scope of Schedule 7A of the Taxation of Chargeable Gains Act 1992 was amended by Finance Act 2000 to deal with the inclusion of United Kingdom branches of non-resident companies within a CGT group.

At the same time, where a company became a member of the CGT group as a result of the amendments to section 170 that were introduced by the Finance Act 2000 (see 23–05 above), Schedule 7A will not apply to any losses that accrued before that date, or to any assets that the company held at that date.[1]

At the same time, where a company was a member of a CGT group immediately before the change to the definition of a CGT group took effect, but would not be regarded as a member of the group under the revised definition because it is not an effective 51% subsidiary of the worldwide holding company, the company will continue to be treated as a member of the group so long as it remains an effective 51 per cent subsidiary of the company that was the principal company of the old group (i.e. the ultimate United Kingdom resident holding company).[2] Thus the provisions of Schedule 7A will not apply in such cases.

The opening words of the last paragraph in paragraph 24-01 of the main work should have begun "There are new rules which apply where a group holding an asset . . ."

---

[1] FA 2000, Sched. 29 para. 7(9).
[2] *ibid*. Sched. 29 para 46(2), (4), (5).

## Pre-entry assets

The definition of a pre-entry asset has been amended and the pre-entry asset provisions apply, where a company joins a group of companies, to assets that are held by the company at that time, so long as the company is resident in the United Kingdom at such time or such assets are chargeable assets[3] Thus the amended definition applies to United Kingdom resident companies and United Kingdom branches of non-resident companies.

**24–04**

Where a company is not resident and does not have a United Kingdom branch at the time that it becomes a member of the new group the provisions of Schedule 7A of the Taxation of Chargeable Gains Act 1992 treat assets held by the company at the earlier of the date that it becomes UK resident or an asset becomes a chargeable asset as pre-entry assets.[4] Interestingly, this wording does not require the asset to be held by the non-resident company at the time that it becomes a member of the new group and thus it would be possible for assets that were acquired by the company before the earlier of the above two dates, but after the date the change in ownership took place, to be treated as pre-entry assets.

The above amendments apply to amounts that are included in respect of chargeable gains in a company's total profits for an accounting period ending on or after March 21, 2000.[5]

The pre-Finance Act 2000 definition of a CGT group of companies is applied for the purpose of determining whether a company was a member of a CGT group of companies before March 21, 2000 and the provisions of the Capital Gains Tax Act 1979 apply for the purpose of determining whether a company was a member of a CGT group before April 6, 1992.[6]

IV. PRE-ENTRY GAINS

## Companies joining another group

Insert the following paragraph at the end of this section: The revised definition of a CGT group applies in relation to accounting periods ending on or after March 21, 2000 except that the pre-Finance Act 2000 definition is applied for the purpose of determining whether a company was a member of the new group before March 21, 2000.[7]

**24–42**

---

[3] TCGA 1992, Sched. 7A para 1(3), as amended by FA 2000, Sched. 29 para. 7(2).

[4] *ibid*. Sched. 7A para. 1(3A)(b), as inserted by FA 2000, Sched. 29 para. 7(3).

[5] FA 2000, Sched. 29 para 7(6).

[6] ibid. Sched. 29 para 7(7), (8). Interestingly the pre-TCGA 1992 grouping provisions were contained in ICTA 1970, s. 272 and not in CGTA 1979.

[7] *ibid*. Sched. 29 para. 8.

# CHAPTER 25

# GROUP INCOME

| Contents | Para. | Contents | Para. |
|---|---|---|---|
| I. Introduction | 25–01 | III. The payments | 25–06 |
| II. Qualifying relation-<br>ships | 25–02 ■ | IV. Elections and adjust-<br>ments | 25–13 |

## II. QUALIFYING RELATIONSHIPS

### Article 52 of the Treaty of Rome

25–04    In *Metallgesellschaft Ltd and others v. IRC and another*[1] the High Court has referred to the European Court the question whether it is consistent with E.U. law, and in particular Articles 6, 52, 58 and 73(b) of the E.C. Treaty, for the United Kingdom to permit group income elections only where both subsidiary and parent are resident in the United Kingdom. Also referred is the question whether it is consistent with the E.C. Treaty for the United Kingdom to deny a tax credit to a company resident in another Member State when tax credits are granted to United Kingdom resident companies and to companies resident in some other Member States by virtue of the terms of the United Kingdom's double tax treaties.

In *Compagnie de Saint-Gobain, Zweigniederlassung Deutschland v Finanzamt Aachen-Innenstadt*[2] the European Court held that it was contrary to Article 52 for German legislation to grant exemption from tax or underlying tax credits to German companies in respect of dividends received from foreign companies and exemption from capital tax for shareholdings in foreign companies while German branches of EU companies, which were subject to German tax only on their German branch income, did not enjoy these privileges. The court held that German branches of E.U. companies and German subsidiaries were in an objectively comparable situation as regards the taxation of foreign dividends and shareholdings. More generally, it held

---

[1] [1999] S.T.I. 295.
[2] [2000] S.T.C. 854.

that Articles 52 and 58 "guarantee nationals of Member States of the community who have exercised their freedom of establishment and companies or firms which are assimilated to them the same treatment in the host Member State as that accorded to nationals of that Member State." It follows from this decision that a United Kingdom branch of an E.U. company should be able to make a group income election in the same circumstances as a UK subsidiary.

CHAPTER 27

# DEMERGERS

II. The purpose of the transaction

**Acquisition of control by third parties**

**27–10**     In paragraph 27–11 it is pointed out that in strictness control may be acquired by "two or more persons" even where they are in no sense acting together. In the experience of the authors, this point is taken in relation to the issue of whether the demerger forms part of an arrangement having as "one of its main purposes" the acquisition of control of the company being distributed, by any person or persons other than members of the distributing company. Further, whereas it is a question of fact in each case as to whether the acquisition of such control is a "main object", the approach of the Revenue appears to be that the acquisition of control is necessarily a main object if it flows from an intended share subscription. Where the intention is that the public will be invited to subscribe for say 51 per cent of the enlarged issued share capital then it does follow that the acquisition of control by two or more outside shareholders is a main object (albeit that strategic control remains with the existing shareholders). But where the company being distributed is not a wholly owned subsidiary (say 20 per cent of shares held by non-members of the distributing company), and it is intended that after distribution other persons will subscribe for 31 per cent of the shares, it is considered that the main object test will be failed only if the new subscribers have commercial links with the existing outside shareholders. In such circumstances, the aggregation of the existing shares with the new shares has to be of commercial significance before it becomes a "main object".

# Chapter 28

# DISPOSALS OF ASSETS IN RECONSTRUCTIONS, AMALGAMATIONS AND PARTITIONS

*Requirements of sections 136 and 139*

The provisions of section 139 were amended by the Finance Act 2000 to remove **28–02** the restriction that each of the companies had to be resident in the United Kingdom. Now it is possible for a scheme of reconstruction or amalgamation to fall within the provisions of this section, so long as the assets that are transferred are chargeable assets in the hands of the transferor and remain chargeable assets in the hands of the transferee. This means that both the transferor and the transferee must satisfy one of the following conditions:

1. the company must be a resident in the United Kingdom; or
2. the assets must be chargeable assets in relation to that company. This means that the assets must be used by or held for the purposes of a United Kingdom branch of that company.

This amendment applies to disposals that take place on or after April 1, 2000.[1]

On a literal reading of the revised provisions of section 139(1A) it would appear that relief would only be available in the case of the transfer of assets by a non-resident company where **all** the assets that are transferred are chargeable assets. The authors

---

[1] TCGA 1992, s.139(1)(b) and (1A), as inserted by FA 2000, Sched. 29 para 5.

have had correspondence with the Inland Revenue on this point and have been advised that the Inland Revenue do not intend to adopt a literal interpretation of the revised wording and will allow non-resident companies to claim relief under section 139 where only **some** of the assets that are transferred are chargeable assets.

CHAPTER 30

# STAMP DUTY

## I. INTRODUCTION

**Transfers to connected companies**

From March 28, 2000 the principle that duty is not charged on gifts is abrogated in **30–03A** relation to the transfer of land (or the grant of a lease) to a connected company. The main object of this provision is to deal with gifts of private residences to new companies with a view to the sale of the donee company (thus saving the difference between duty on shares and duty on land sales). It is also applicable on a hold-over transfer to a company and on a transfer to a company in consideration of a share issue. Normally the latter transaction bears duty on the full value of the land because the consideration shares have a value equal to the land, but this is not always so: see paragraph 30–03B below.

For transactions other than transfers for a share issue, the section applies where:

"an estate or interest in land is transferred to or vested in a company ("A") and—

(a) the person transferring or vesting the estate or interest ("B") is connected with A."[1]

---

[1] F.A. 2000 s.119(1)(a) and see s.121 of leases. "Company" means any body corporate (sub. 8) and "connected persons" is defined by reference to section 839 of the Taxes Act (subs. 9). The Commencment date of March 28, 2000 (subs. (11)) is subject to an exception for instruments executed pursuant to certain contracts made before that date: see subs. (12).

However, this is subject to exceptions, the most important of which for present purposes is that applicable to company distributions in specie. Thus, there is no deemed conveyance on sale where the transferor (B) is a company and the transfer is made in the course of a distribution of assets whether in a winding up or otherwise, provided B acquired the estate or interest by an instrument which was duly stamped.[2] Where the transferor and the transferee are members of the same group, the usual intra-group reliefs are applicable.

Subject to the exceptions mentioned above, on a transfer of land to a connected company for no consideration, the instrument is treated as a transfer on sale.[3] In the case of such a gift, duty is payable on an amount equal to the market value of the land.[4] A cash sale at an undervalue has the same result.[5]

### Shares as consideration

**30–04**    From July 29, 2000 section 55 is amended so as to cover also consideration in the form of a right to an issue of shares: see the new s.55(1A) inserted by FA 2000 s.126.

### Shares and securities as consideration: connected companies

**30–04A**    The rule that where consideration takes the form of shares, the amount of the consideration is the market value of the shares is modified in relation to certain transactions with "connected companies". These modifications have effect from March 28, 2000 and apply to transfers of land and to grants of leases.

The device at which the new rules are directed depends upon the principle that where the shares falling to be valued represent only a small proportion of the issued shares capital, the value per share will be much less than if a majority holding fell to be valued. For example, an individual wishes to incorporate a business. The assets include land worth £1m. The other assets are worth £2m. He could form a new com-

---

[2] *ibid.* s.120(8) applicable from July 29 2000: subs (9). Section 120 provides for other exceptions, mainly to do with nominee and trustee situations. For the application of the exceptions to instruments executed between March 22 and July 28, see s.131.

[3] *ibid.* s.119(2). Corresponding provision is made for the grant of a lease by s.121.

[4] *ibid.* s.119(3)(4) and see s.121 for leases. The "market value" of property at any time is the price which that property might reasonably be expected to fetch on a sale at that time in the open market: subs. (7).

[5] On a sale at an undervalue, subs. (3) provides that if the consideration would otherwise be less than the value determined under subs. (4), it is treated as being of that value. Subs. (4) provides that the value is the market value of the land, but "reduced by the value of so much of any actual consideration as does not consist of property". Consideration "not consisting of property" appears to refer to cases such as that where A agrees to sell Blackacre to B, and in return B agrees to erect a building on another site owned by A. It is considered that cash is "property".

pany with say two subscriber shares and then transfer the assets in consideration of an issue of three million £1 shares. Or he could issue say 1,000 £1 shares. In either case, the market value of the shares issued would be £3m. But if the company has an initial share capital of 990 £1 shares, and the shares issued in return for the business are just 10 £1 shares, the market value of the consideration shares is not more than £30,000. To cover this type of case, section 119 considered above also applies where:

"an estate or interest in land is transfered to or vested in a company ("A") and—

    (b) some or all of the consideration for the transfer or vesting consists of the issue or transfer of shares in a company with which [the person transferring or vesting the estate or interest ("B") is connected."[6]

Whereas the transferee (A) and the company issuing the shares may be the same person, the section applies where they are not the same provided the issuer is connected with B. Where these conditions are met then section 119 applies so as to charge duty by reference to the market value of the land (if this yields more duty than otherwise would be payable)[7]. Where the share issue is made in a reconstruction to which FA 1986 section 76 applies, the rate of duty will be 0.5 per cent applied to the market value of the land.

## Rates of duty

The highest rate of duty is now 4 per cent.[8] This is potentially applicable to all **30–08** transfers on sale except of shares (where the duty is 0.5 per cent) and intellectual property (which from March 28, 2000 are free of duty[9]). For this purpose intellectual property means[10]:

    (a) any patent, trade mark, registered design, copyright or design right,
    (b) any plant breeders' rights and rights under section 7 of the Plant Varieties Act 1997,
    (c) any licence or other right in respect of anything within paragraph (a) or (b), and
    (d) any rights under the law of a country or territory outside the United Kingdom that correspond or are similar to those within paragraph (a), (b) or (c).

---

[6] *ibid.* s.119(1)(b) and see s.121 for leases.
[7] *ibid.* s.119(3), (4) and (6). The definitions mentioned in para. 30–30A apply.
[8] FA 1999, Sched. 13, para 4.
[9] FA 2000 s.129(1).
[10] *ibid.* s.129(2).

### Intellectual property: apportionment of consideration

30–08A  Before the abolition of duty on transfers of intellectual property, it was unimportant how consideration was apportioned as between such property and goodwill. It is obviously now a matter of considerable importance and provision is made to clarify the law on apportionments. First, where an instrument of transfer conveys both intellectual property and other property without any apportionment by the parties, the consideration falls to be apportioned on a just and reasonable basis and duty is charged only on the part not apportioned to intellectual property[11]. Secondly, where the parties have made their own apportionment, the application of section 58 of the Stamp Act is modified so as to substitute a just and reasonable apportionment for that made by the parties (if not otherwise just and reasonable). This applies where property is conveyed between the contracting parties in separate parcels (including cases where there are two or more purchasers who are connected with one another)[12]

## II. Intra-Group Transfer Relief

### Associated companies: additional tests

30–13A  As from July 29, 2000 section 42 is amended so as to align the group membership tests with those applicable to group relief. This involves two changes. First, the definition of associated companies now excludes cases in which arrangements are in existence by virtue of which third parties could obtain control over the transferee but not the transferor. Second, the stability tests of group relief are made applicable.[13] Corresponding amendments are made to section 151 of the Finance Act 1996 (grant of lease to associated company)[14].

*Control exclusion*

As amended, section 42(2) now reads:

"(2) This section applies to any instrument as respects which it is shown to the satisfaction of the Commissioners that—

(a) the effect of the instrument is to convey or transfer a beneficial interest

---

[11] *ibid.* Sched. 34 para. 2. intellectual property is disregarded for certificate of value purposes: *ibid.* para. 4.

[12] *ibid.* Sched. 34 para. 3. "Connected person" is defined by reference to section 839 of the Taxes Act: para. 3(4)(b).

[13] FA 2000 s.123. Separate provision is made for Northern Ireland: *ibid.* s.124.

[14] *ibid.* s.125.

in property from one body corporate ("the transferor") to another ("the transferee"), and

(b) the bodies in question are associated at the time the instrument is executed unless at the time the instrument is executed arrangements are in existence by virtue of which at that time or at some later time any person has or could obtain or any persons have or could obtain, control[15] of the transferee but not of the transferor."

For commentary on the corresponding group relief provision see para. 22–62 *et seq.* of the main text. The type of case in which this requirement makes a difference is where a holding company forms a securitisation vehicle which is associated with the holding company but controlled by a charity.

*Stability tests*

For this purpose the test of beneficial entitlement to 75 per cent or more of ordinary share capital is augmented by a requirement of entitlement to at least 75 per cent of profits and assets available for distribution to equity holders. For this purpose Schedule 18 of the Taxes Act is applied[16] Accordingly, reference should be made to para. 22–31 *et seq.* of the main text and to para 22–48A of this Supplement.

### Section 27: arrangements relating to intra-group transfers

The following Statement of Practice gives valuable guidance on the practical limits **30–14** of section 27. Paragraph 30-14A contains commentary on the Statement.

> **"SP 3/98 Stamp duty—group relief (13 October 1998)**
> 1. FA 1930 s.42 gives relief from stamp duty for transfers of property between members of the same group of companies. FA 1995 s.151 similarly gives relief from duty on the grant of a lease between members of the same group. FA 1967 s.27(3) and FA 1995 s.151(3) are designed to prevent the use of group relief to avoid stamp duty when property, or an economic interest in it, passes out of the group.
> 3. This statement sets out the Stamp Office's current general practice in order to assist practitioners in determining whether claims to relief might qualify. The treatment of a particular case will of course depend on the precise facts. This statement is for general guidance only; and the facts of a particular transaction may, exceptionally, place it outside the guidelines. It applies also to the equivalent Northern Ireland legislation.

---

[15] "Control" is defined by reference to section 840 of the Taxes Act: FA 1930 s.247(7).
[16] *ibid.* s.42(5) except that paras. 5(3) and 5B to 5E do not apply: subs. (6).

*General*

4. Broadly, s.27(3) and the corresponding provisions in s.151, provide that relief is not to be given if the transfer was made in pursuance of, or in connection with, an arrangement under which—

   (a) all or part of the consideration for the transfer was to be provided or received, directly or indirectly, by a person outside the group; or

   (b) the interest being transferred was previously transferred by a person outside the group; or

   (c) the transferor and transferee were no longer to be part of the same group.

5. The person claiming the relief when the relevant instrument is adjudicated has the onus of satisfying the Stamp Office that the intra-group transaction is not carried out in pursuance of, or in connection with, an arrangement of a kind which disqualifies the transaction from relief— *Escoigne Properties Ltd v. IRC* [1958] AC 549, 564.

   *"Arrangement"*

6. In this context, arrangement means the plan or scheme in pursuance of which the things identified in ss.27(3), 151(3) have been or are to be done—*Shop and Store Developments Ltd v. IRC* [1967] 1 AC 472, 493, 494. The arrangement need not be based in contract. It is sufficient if the intra-group transaction is made in connection with that plan or scheme. The intra-group transaction may be the first bi-lateral step by which legal rights and obligations are created in pursuance of the arrangement. If there is an expectation that a disqualifying event will happen in accordance with the arrangement and no likelihood in practice that it will not, relief will be refused.

7. The words "in connection with" are very broad. In *Escoigne*, there was a gap of four years between the two steps in issue.

   *Provision or receipt of consideration by a person outside the group— FA 1967 s.27(3)(a); FA 1995 s.151(3)(a), (4)*

8. Section 27(3)(a) denies relief where the instrument was executed in pursuance of or in connection with an arrangement under which any of the consideration is to be provided or received, directly or indirectly, by a person outside the group. It also denies relief if the arrangement is one under which the transferor or transferee (or a member of the same group as either of them) is to be enabled to provide any of the consideration, or is to part with it, in consequence of a transaction involving a payment or other disposition by a person outside the group. Section 151 lays down similar rules for leases.

9. In some cases, the question arises whether loan finance for the purchase or lease will disqualify an intra-group transaction from relief. It is necessary to look at all the facts of the individual case, but the Stamp Office will interpret the provisions in the light of their general purpose of denying relief where the intra-group transaction is a means of saving stamp

duty when the property, or an interest in it, moves out of the group. Accordingly, the Stamp Office are likely to be satisfied that relief is due if the intra-group transaction is not to be followed by a sale of the property transferred, or an underlease, to a person outside the group. If the intra-group transaction is to be followed by a sale or underlease to a person outside the group, but the claimant can demonstrate that stamp duty will be paid in respect of that transaction in approximately the same amount was would have been payable if the intra-group transferor or lessor had itself sold the property or granted the underlease, the Stamp Office are likely to be satisfied that the intra-group transaction and the transfer or lease out are independent for stamp duty purposes and grant the relief sought.

10. A transaction is not disqualified merely because the transferee within the group obtains a specific loan for the purchase of the asset; or the loan is secured on the asset; or arrangements are made to replace or novate an existing charge on the property transferred. It will be necessary to consider the facts as a whole, especially if the loan finance is not straightforward finance on ordinary commercial terms.

11. Intra-group transactions will be very carefully scrutinised, and relief may be refused, where, for example, the intra-group transaction involves or is to be followed by—
    — the creation or transfer of loan stock or equity capital;
    — a capital reorganisation of the transferee;
    — a guarantee by a third party not associated with the group;
    — the creation of a new charge or financial arrangement whereby title to the property is, or may be, vested in the lender otherwise than in satisfaction of all or part of the debt; or
    — the assignment of the freehold reversion or the intra-group lease to a person outside the group.

12. Similarly transactions will be very carefully scrutinised where—
    — all or part of the consideration for the transaction is to remain outstanding or is represented by intra-group debt, (as the aim and effect may be to reduce the value of the transferee company on a possible future sale outside the group); or
    — the existing shareholders of the transferee include shareholders outside the group and the transaction is to be followed by the declaration of a dividend in specie, or by the liquidation of the transferee.

13. Further assurances by way of statutory declaration—the document in which the claim is made to the Stamp Office—will be required in any case in which the property transferred or vested intra-group is the only, or only substantial, asset of the transferee. Information to that effect should be provided in the statutory declaration submitted with the documents.

14. Where group member A has granted a lease to a person outside the group, and subsequently grants an underlease to its fellow group member B, so that the rent already payable by the lessee becomes payable to B rather than A, relief is likely to be given for the intra-group underlease, provided there are no other factors which suggest that relief should be denied.

*Property previously conveyed by a person outside the group—FA 1967 s.27(3)(b)*

15. Section 27(3)(b) was intended to prevent the avoidance of duty on the transfer of property into a group by means of a sub-sale, so as to take advantage of the Stamp Act 1891 s.58(4). For example, suppose the property is sold to a group member by a vendor outside the group, but the sale rests in contract without a transfer of the legal title. The group member then sells the property to another member of its own group, and directs the vendor to transfer the legal title to that other member. In accordance with s.58(4) the transfer completing the sale and the sub-sale is chargeable to duty only in relation to the sub-sale (thus relieving the effect of s.4 of the Stamp Act). However, s.27(3)(b) would deny group relief for that transfer.

16. The Stamp Office will continue to apply s.27(3)(b) to schemes of this type and to any other scheme where an attempt has been made to avoid the duty payable on the acquisition by the group. However, where an outside vendor sells a property to a member of the group, the sale is completed by a transfer and stamp duty is paid on that transfer, the Stamp Office will normally regard any subsequent intra-group transfer as independent, and grant relief for the transfer within the purchaser's group.

*Dissociation or demerger of transferee—FA 1967 s.27(3)(c): FA 1995 s.151(3)(b)*

17. Before the introduction of s.27(3), almost all the avoidance devices encountered in this area involved the transfer of property to a subsidiary, often created solely as a vehicle for that property, followed by the transfer of the shares in the subsidiary out of the group. Compared with a transfer of the property out of the group, a substantial amount of duty could be avoided even where the subsidiary paid for the property from its own resources. If the consideration for the intra-group transaction remained outstanding or was represented by debt, duty could be reduced further by reducing the value of the shares—hence s.27(3)(a).

18. Section 27(3)(c) was introduced to counter this avoidance in relation to conveyances and transfers on sale. Section 151(3)(b) deals with leases on similar lines.

19 In cases of this kind, the Stamp Office will need to be satisfied that the intra-group transfer or lease is not a step in pursuance of an arrangement to demerge the transferee. The existence of such an arrangement may be

apparent from company documents, correspondence and other dealings between members of the group and professional advisers, or from discussions or negotiations with the potential purchasers, underwriters or minority shareholders.

20. In practice, the Stamp Office will apply these provisions so as to preclude group relief if there is evidence of a plan or scheme to dispose of the subsidiary and there is no practical likelihood that the scheme will not be carried through. It will not be regarded as sufficient for the claimant to contend that such an arrangement which is less than contractual may possibly be frustrated by unforeseen events or unlikely occurrences. Even a contract may be frustrated.

21. As the liability of the relevant instrument must, as a matter of general principle, be determined as at the date of the instrument, the question whether an arrangement of the relevant kind exists must also be determined at that time, although the Stamp Office may have regard to what is said and done thereafter to establish the true position (*Wm Cory and Son Ltd v IRC* [1965] A.C. 1088). For the purposes of stamp duty, it is therefore the existence of the scheme or plan to which these provisions direct attention, not the ultimate outcome of steps, which may be taken to implement that scheme. Accordingly, statements of practice in relation to other taxes have no application in this context."

## Commentary on SP 3/98

*"Arrangement"*

The following sentence in the interpretation of "arrangement" (paragraph 6) **30–14A** appears hard to justify at first sight: "If there is an expectation that a disqualifying event will happen in accordance with the arrangement and *no likelihood in practice that it will not*, relief will be refused." See also paragraph 20 where the same expression is used in relation to the specific case of "bridge company" arrangements. The words in italic seem unduly stringent, but when considered in context, this is not so. Section 27(3) refers to an instrument not being:

"executed in pursuance of or in connection with an arrangement whereunder—
    (a) the consideration, or any part of the consideration, for the conveyance or transfer *was to be provided or received*, directly or indirectly, by a person other than [an associated body corporate] . . .
    (c) the transferor and the transferee *were to cease to be associated* . . . and, without prejudice to the generality of paragraph (a) above, an arrangement shall be treated as within that paragraph if it is one where under the transferor or the transferee or a body corporate associated with either

as there mentioned, *was to be enabled to provide* any of the consideration."

The words in italic require that the parties to the arrangement must have a settled
intention as to the outcome at the time of the transfer in question. It would not be
sufficient that the transfer was made in contemplation of a contingent arrangement
reaching fruition. So, suppose that a property is conveyed intra group to a shell company at a time when a non-associated company has indicated that it will buy the
transferee company subject to completing the usual enquiries relating to the property.
As respects subsection (3)(c), all that can be said is that at the time of the transfer
there is an arrangement under which the transferee company "may" cease to be associated with the transferor. (See also paragraph 21 which correctly emphasises that the
issue is to be determined at the time of the transfer). The position on the facts would
be otherwise if at the time of the intra-group transfer the prospective purchaser had
already completed its enquiries.

Notwithstanding the strictness of the "no practical likelihood" test, the warning in
paragraphs 11 and 12 should be noted. Those paragraphs state that transactions will
be "very carefully scrutinised" where the classic signs of stamp duty saving schemes
are exhibited, in particular, the intra-group transfer of property with the purchase price
left outstanding. Paragraph 13 states that in such cases, further assurances may be
sought. But this merely emphasises the factual nature of the enquiry into the "no
practical likelihood" issue: the test remains the same regardless of the number of
indicators that the parties were motivated by stamp duty saving. The position is similar
to that under "the preordained series of transactions" test familiar from the *Ramsay*
authorities.

*Bank finance*

The Statement of Practice relieves a concern that subsection (3)(a) (provision of
outside finance) might apply where the only arrangement is that an asset would be
sold intra-group and that the price would be met by bank borrowings. Paragraphs 9
and 10 make clear that in such circumstances, the relief is given provided at least the
bank borrowing is on ordinary terms.

**Redeemable shares**

**30–25A**   From July 29, 2000 the requirements of sections 75 and 76 that the consideration
must consist of "shares" is limited to non-redeemable shares: see FA 2000 s.127
amending ss.75 and 76.

CHAPTER 31

# SECTION 703: TAX ADVANTAGES FROM TRANSACTIONS IN SECURITIES

### Dividends as "transactions in securities"

In *Laird Group v. I.R.C.*,[1] the Tribunal constituted under section 706 to re-hear cases   **31–08A**
decided by the Special Commissioners has held that a dividend is not a "transaction in
securities" for the purposes of section 703.

---

[1] [2000] S.T.C. (S.C.D.) 75.

## The "bona fide commercial" test: the importance of full disclosure

**31–21A**    In paragraph 31-21, reference is made to the decision of the Special Commissioners in *Marwood Homes*. Pursuant to section 705(2), the Revenue sought a re-hearing before the section 703 Tribunal of *Marwood Homes'* appeal. In giving its decision in favour of the Revenue, the Tribunal recorded[2]:

> "At the start of the present hearing the Revenue sought an order for discovery. Where, as here, the question of liability depends on the intentions of those responsible for implementing the transactions, the advice they acted on is crucial at every stage of the proceedings. We directed Marwood (and EBC Group where appropriate) to disclose for inspection all documents in their possession or power that contained, recorded or otherwise related to advice given by KPMG and to the accounting and tax implications of the specified transactions. The effect of the direction, as noted above, was that we had available to us a great deal of relevant documentary evidence that had not been seen by the Special Commissioners at the earlier hearing."

It was on the basis of this material that the Tribunal reached a conclusion adverse to the taxpayer company. It is to be noted here that the issue of the extent of the power of discovery is beside the point. The onus is on the taxpayer to prove the existence of facts supporting the "bona fide commercial" defence. If the taxpayer fails to respond adequately to a request for "all documents etc." then it will not be accepted that such material as he does adduce discharges the onus.

*Meaning of "commercial reasons"*

To qualify for the bona fide commercial transactions exemption from section 703 adjustments, the transactions in question must satisfy two tests. First the transactions must be carried out for bona fide commercial reasons or in the course of making or managing investments. Secondly obtaining a tax advantage must be neither the main object nor one of the main objects of the transactions. In *Lewis v. I.R.C.*[3] the Special Commissioners considered the application of the tests to the obtaining of a tax credit by trustees of an occupational pension scheme on a purchase of own shares from the scheme.

It was held on the facts that neither the sole nor a main purpose of the transaction was to obtain a tax advantage. It was further held that the trustees sold the shares in the ordinary course of managing investments. The trustees were put into a situation where they were forced to disinvest and in those "special circumstances" their response was appropriate.

Having thus decided in the taxpayer's favour, the Special Commissioners went on

---

[2] [1998] S.T.C. (S.C.D.) 53.
[3] [1999] S.T.C. (S.C.D.) 349.

to make observations regarding the construction of the word "commercial" in the phrase "bona fide commercial reasons".

It was submitted on behalf of the Revenue that transactions can only be "commercial" if they are to protect or enhance the prosperity of a business. Here the trustees were not carrying on any business. Their duties under the scheme were not commercial, nor did the fact that they acted in compliance with the regulations of the Occupational Pensions Board mean they were acting commercially.

The response on behalf of the taxpayer was based on the analysis of occupational pension schemes set out in *Mettoy Pension Trustees Ltd v. Evans*.[4] The rules of such schemes create a contract between employees and employer and in implementing this commercial agreement the trustees were carrying on the business of providing pensions.

The Special Commissioners indicated that they would have rejected the Revenue's submission on a broader ground. Trustees in discharging their duties are required to act in as diligent a manner as a prudent man of business would act in dealing with his own private affairs. In this sense their duty as trustees is to act commercially. In essence, "commercial" refers to the standard of care required when carrying out a transaction rather than to the reasons for the transaction being business reasons: nothing in principle prevented the trustees' reasons for acting from being "bona fide commercial reasons".

### Capital Receipts: counter-action of the tax advantage

For the year 1999-00 and subsequent years, a new subsection (3A) is inserted in **31–26** section 703. This provision aligns the assessment of capital receipts where paragraph D or E of section 704 apply with the taxation of qualifying distributions under Schedule F. The new subsection provides:

> "The amount of income tax which may be specified in an assessment which is made under subsection (3) above to counteract a tax advantage—
> > (a) obtained by a person in circumstances falling within paragraph D or paragraph E of section 704; and
> > (b) consisting of the avoidance of a charge to income tax,
> shall not exceed the amount of income tax for which that person would be liable in respect of the receipt, on the date on which the consideration mentioned in paragraph D or paragraph E of section 704 is received, of a qualifying distribution of an amount equal to the amount or value of that consideration."

In the case of an assessment in respect of a qualifying distribution, the amount assessed would be at the rate provided for by section 1B of the Taxes Act 1988 (32.5

---

[4] [1990] 1 W.L.R. 1587 at 1610.

per cent for higher rate tax payers, less a tax credit of 10 per cent), or section 686 in the case of discretionary trustees (25 per cent less the tax credit). For individuals, the result is therefore an effective rate of 25 per cent of the amount of the consideration, and for trustees 16.66 per cent.

CHAPTER 32

# BREAK-UP BIDS

## III. BID STRUCTURES

### Offshore variants

Following the changes to the CGT group rules in the Finance Act 2000, the offshore **32–07** variant will no longer be effective to avoid a section 179 charge since Newco 1 will become a member of a worldwide group headed by non-resident bidder and will later leave that group. When Newco 1 is sold, a section 179 charge will arise in respect of shares in Non-Core Ltd.

CHAPTER 33

# CROSS-BORDER MERGERS, DIVISIONS AND TRANSFERS OF ASSETS

## Transfer of assets

## (a) Transfer of United Kingdom trade: capital gains

*Outline*

**33–06**    Following its amendment by Finance Act 2000, the no gain no loss rule for reconstructions and amalgamations contained in TCGA 1992, s.139 provides an alternative relief to that contained in TCGA 1992, s. 140A which may be applicable on the transfer of a UK trade.[1]

---

[1] See Chapter 28 and the supplement to Chapter 28 for further details.